Divine Horror

Divine Horror

*Essays on the Cinematic Battle
Between the Sacred and the Diabolical*

Edited by
Cynthia J. Miller
and A. Bowdoin Van Riper

McFarland & Company, Inc., Publishers
Jefferson, North Carolina

LIBRARY OF CONGRESS CATALOGUING-IN-PUBLICATION DATA

Names: Miller, Cynthia J., 1958– editor. | Van Riper, A. Bowdoin, editor.
Title: Divine horror : essays on the cinematic battle between the sacred and the diabolical / edited by Cynthia J. Miller and A. Bowdoin Van Riper.
Description: Jefferson, North Carolina : McFarland & Company, Inc., Publishers, 2017. | Includes bibliographical references and index.
Identifiers: LCCN 2017016898 | ISBN 9781476669922 (softcover : acid free paper) ∞
Subjects: LCSH: Horror films—History and criticism. | Good and evil in motion pictures.
Classification: LCC PN1995.9.H6 D58 2017 | DDC 791.43/6164—dc23
LC record available at https://lccn.loc.gov/2017016898

BRITISH LIBRARY CATALOGUING DATA ARE AVAILABLE

ISBN (print) 978-1-4766-6992-2
ISBN (ebook) 978-1-4766-2984-1

© 2017 Cynthia J. Miller and A. Bowdoin Van Riper. All rights reserved

No part of this book may be reproduced or transmitted in any form or by any means, electronic or mechanical, including photocopying or recording, or by any information storage and retrieval system, without permission in writing from the publisher.

Front cover images © 2017 iStock/Thinkstock

Printed in the United States of America

*McFarland & Company, Inc., Publishers
Box 611, Jefferson, North Carolina 28640
www.mcfarlandpub.com*

For those who fear the hounds of hell,
whose earnest prayers keep evil at bay;
And those who dance beneath the moon,
then vanish at the break of day

Acknowledgments

We are very grateful that this volume has come into being at the hands of so many thoughtful and talented scholars, and we would like to thank each of them for their contribution. Thanks also go to Cynthia's Making Monsters students for their inspired invocations of gods, demons, witches, and even Satan himself as the sources of failed alarms, crashed computers, and erased film footage—causing her to believe that, indeed, supernatural forces are at work in the world.

Table of Contents

Acknowledgments vi

Introduction 1

Part I. The Past, Bleeding into the Present

"What went we out into this wilderness to find": Supernatural Contest in Robert Eggers's *The Witch: A New-England Folktale* (2015) 11
THOMAS PRASCH

Emily Rose Died for Your Sins: Paranormal Piety, Medieval Theology and Ambiguous Cinematic Soteriology 29
KEVIN J. WETMORE, JR.

"Is this my reward for defending God's church?" Monstrous Crimes and Monstrous Punishments in *Witchfinder General* (1968), *The Devils* (1971) and *The Name of the Rose* (1986) 40
JAMES J. WARD

Reckoning the Number of the Beast: Premillennial Dispensationalism, *The Omen* and 1970s America 53
BRAD L. DUREN

The Fall of a Domestic Angel: Horror and Hierophany in *Rosemary's Baby* (1968) 64
SUE MATHESON

"I have seen things that would make the angels weep. And they do weep": The Devil and Scotland's Religious Horrors in *Let Us Prey* 76
ELEANOR BEAL

Part II. The Boundaries of Good and Evil

God's Bloody Hand: The Horrible Ambiguity of Religious Murder in Bill Paxton's *Frailty* 89
MARK HENDERSON

No Religion or Too Many: Problematizing *God Told Me To* 101
FERNANDO GABRIEL PAGNONI BERNS

Demons to Some, Angels to Others: Eldritch Horrors and Hellbound   113
    Religion in the *Hellraiser* Films
    LÚCIO REIS-FILHO

Redeeming the Demon-Child and the Eco-Horror Fairy Tale: Ambivalent   125
    Theosis and Ambiguous Eucatastrophe in Guillermo del Toro's
    Hellboy Films
    DANIEL OTTO JACK PETERSEN

Binary Opposition, Subversion and Liminality in Francis Lawrence's   140
    Constantine
    CATHERINE BECKER

Monsters of God: Negotiating the Sacred in *Stake Land*   150
    RHONDA R. DASS

Part III. Horrors of Knowledge and Faith

"They're not in charge here": The Collision of Religion and Science   163
    in *[Rec]* and *Quarantine*
    BART BISHOP

Prince of Darkness: The Metaphysics and Quantum Physics of Evil   174
    MATTHEW A. KILLMEIER

The Folly of Faithlessness in *Dracula Has Risen from the Grave*   186
    MARTIN F. NORDEN

Unquenchable *Thirst*: Morality, Theology and Vampires in Chan-wook   200
    Park's Horror Romance
    MICHAEL C. REIFF

Of Heresy and Horror: *Stigmata*   213
    CYNTHIA J. MILLER

The Power of Film Compels You! Transgressing Taboos and the War   225
    on Demonic Possession in *The Exorcist*
    STEVE WEBLEY

About the Contributors   239

Index   241

Introduction

CYNTHIA J. MILLER *and* A. BOWDOIN VAN RIPER

"I will send my terror in front of you..."—Exodus 23:27

Terror ... fear ... dread.... All have been cited as primordial elements of the divine-human experience since the beginnings of civilization. It has been suggested, in fact, that religion finds its genesis in fear: "It is this feeling which, emerging in the mind of primeval man, forms the starting point for the entire religious development in history. 'Deamons' and 'gods' alike spring from this root, and all the product of 'mythological apperception' or 'fantasy' are nothing but different modes in which it has been objectified."[1] The Judeo-Christian scriptures are shot through with the notion of holy fear—more than three hundred instances, in fact—of the Lord, His angels, Divine Wrath, and other manifestations of the Almighty. The religious experience is, eminent theologian Rudolf Otto (1869–1937) argued, a *"mysterium tremendum et fascinans"*—a fearful and fascinating mystery—characterized by an inseparable blending of dread and awe, terror and reverence, powerlessness and presence. Its "potent attraction" holds believers in its grasp, yet delivers "an inward shuddering such as not even the most menacing and overpowering created thing can instill [*sic*]."[2] This attraction is so potent, in fact, that its resonance is capable of endowing secular objects, symbols, and narratives with a similar visceral force.

Interwoven with this sacred terror is a fear of supernatural evil. New Testament scriptures warn of "demonic spirits that perform signs"—that deceive, plague, and possess.[3] These manifestations of evil, threatening individual and collective salvation, are cast in opposition to the limitless power of the divine, yet revel in tormenting those on the earthly plane. They are, as the scriptures relate, "legion," and inseparable from our narratives of the nature of humankind and speculations about the hereafter, offering an anguish-filled counterpoint to the peace and grace of heaven. In his oft-cited 1972 speech on "Confronting the Devil's Power," Pope Paul VI acknowledged these forces, as well, cautioning that "we know that this dark and disturbing spirit really exists and that he still acts with treacherous cunning; he is the secret enemy that sows errors and misfortunes in human history. The Question of the Devil, and the influence he can exert ... is a very important chapter of Catholic doctrine which is given little attention today."[4]

Thus, even while we are alive, our traditions tell us, we have much to fear in both the power of the light and the menace of the darkness. From this deeply felt, partially shared, often conflicted religious heritage derive tales of Divine Horror, giving voice to fears and fantasies—both sacred and secular—of the monstrous and marvelous, the seen and the unseen. As Douglas Cowan relates, "what we fear, how we fear, and the ways in which we react to fear are profoundly shaped by the cultures in which we live."[5] The narratives we employ to express these fears change and evolve as well, bearing—sometimes boldly, sometimes subtly—the stamp of the time and place in which they were created.

Motion pictures have added multiple dimensions to these tales, allowing (perhaps compelling?) us to see what we could once only imagine. Likewise, contemporary cinematic horror, with its reliance on visceral reactions and psychological unease, has provided a fruitful home for stories of supernatural dread and menace, along with an audience that shares a common visual lexicon for things fearful.[6] The result has been half a century of speculative fantasies about Heaven and Hell, God and Satan, blessings and possession—films that address the social, political, and existential hopes and fears that have brought these tales into being. A selection of these films, produced in the decades between *Rosemary's Baby* (1968) and the present day, are the subject of this book.

Gods and Monsters

Belief in the presence of divinity and evil in the world is as old as humankind. Myths and lore of ancient civilizations, along with the sacred texts of major world religions, chronicle the acts of gods and demons, in various forms and guises, as vehicles for both inspiration and social control. Whether toying with humans for amusement, manipulating them in the service of greater goals, or testing their devotion and obedience, tales of active supernatural intervention in the human realm abound.

In the Judeo-Christian tradition, early scriptures are shot through with vivid images of a mighty, just, but wrathful God whose angels—deliverers of both destruction and restoration—appear in flames, smite firstborn children, and rescue the pious. Tests and trials abound: Lot's wife disobeys the Lord and is transformed into a pillar of salt; Abraham is commanded to murder his son as a display of devotion. Allusions to an ever-present evil drawn from the old lore of the Canaanites persist, but are put to rest through more analytical readings of the works and will of the Almighty.[7] Few actual references to Satan—Lucifer, the Devil, the Wicked One—in fact, exist in the early scriptures, and are considered by many biblical scholars to be allegorical references to earthly, human evil.[8]

Over time, however, the sacred history of humankind has come to be popularly understood not as a struggle between divine good and human evil, but as a cosmic battle for the souls of humankind, with Satan as the supernatural embodiment of malevolence and sin—the Adversary. Beginning with the notion of Original Sin, in which the Devil is portrayed as a serpentine presence that brings temptation and corruption into the world, human history has been shaped by the belief that both God and Satan have the ability to manifest their power and will on Earth, parting the veil between our reality and the supernatural realms of heaven and hell.

Key to this shift is the New Testament figure of the Christ—the Son of God—whose life on Earth in human form (born to a virgin untainted by original sin, thanks to her "immaculate conception") erases, perhaps forever, the boundaries between the supernatural and the mundane. Christ is credited with routinely performing miracles—restoring sight, healing sickness, bringing the dead back to life—and ultimately, emerging from his tomb to walk among men and ascend into Heaven. With the introduction of the Christ came manifestations of the Devil in scriptures and other sacred texts. The Devil figures prominently in the New Testament, actively working against divine intervention in the affairs of the world and the fate of humankind. Demons, Satan, Beelzebub … all are acknowledged in the synoptic gospels, as are numerous instances of demonic possession, serving as illustrations of the divine power of the Christ when they are cast out of their unwilling hosts and vanquished from the Earth.

The agency of the Christ in the world after his ascension is affirmed and maintained through sign and symbol, as homes, hospitals, and sacred spaces display likenesses of his tortured, bloodied, and crucified body. Likewise, through the Eucharist—the ritual of Holy Communion—during which the substance of the elements are converted into His body and blood. As Cardinal John O'Connor instructed, "To receive Holy Communion in the Catholic Church means that one believes one is receiving, not a symbol of Christ, but Christ Jesus himself."[9] Whether myth, magic, or miracle, this steadfast belief in transubstantiation beckons the divine into the earthly realm, in order for true believers to eagerly consume their God in a communal display of devotion. This reality of the Catholic supernatural, as Robert A. Orsi observes, this doctrine of the literal, physical, embodied presence of God, was "translated into metaphors and symptoms, and into functions of the social and political."[10] Funerary customs, cemetery practices, and tales of souls in purgatory have all been employed to ensure social control in this world and attention toward those that inhabit the next. True believers, in the Catholic sense, Orsi suggests, are not only people of the Church, but also "people of the living dead."[11]

As presence came to be seen as "evidence of superstition, of magical thinking, of the infantile and irrational, the primitive and the savage," in the modern era, however, "the unseeing of gods" was required.[12] Fetishes, such as crucifixes, rosaries, and holy cards—devotional and sacramental objects—became symbols of Old World ignorance, "objects of purported evil" that marked the boundary between self and Other in an increasingly secular world. Science, technology, and medicine provided answers that once were sought from God. And so, the distance between this world and the next grew vast—miracles, signs, visitations, and visions receded from everyday life—and believers were ridiculed. But from apparitions of the Virgin Mary, to the cult of the saints, to reappearances of the dead, the boundary between life and death remains fixed in the Catholic imaginary.[13] Statues of Mary wept blood, stigmata afflicted the righteous, and the countenance of the Christ appeared on walls and in objects as if by magic.

For others, too, these phenomena remain sites of fear and fascination. Their defiance of the impermeable boundary between this world and the next, along with their insistence that life on the material and supernatural realms are inextricably interwoven, fan the flames of existential questions that modern and postmodern, science and technology cannot answer. New Testament warnings of "hell—where the fire never goes out,"[14] "the blazing furnace, where there will be weeping and gnashing of teeth,"[15] and "the fiery lake of burning sulfur"[16] had already left their imprint on the Western cultural imagination. The erasure of the barriers between life and afterlife meant that supernatural Evil, as well as the Divine, might appear, unbidden, to walk among the living in order to achieve its own ends. Fear and speculation about summonings, possessions, unholy alliances, foul births, fugitives from Hell, and the End of Days have all gained currency in postmodern times, their pagan origins long forgotten. The door to the supernatural realm, once opened by the notion of the "real presence" of the divine, must also, as we shall see, grant entrance to the horror.

The World Behind the World

Divine horror emerged as a cinematic subgenre in the late 1960s and early 1970s, as established cultural norms were under challenge throughout the West and the censorship regime that had governed Hollywood for more than 30 years was crumbling.[17] Filmmakers, simultaneously freed and emboldened by the broader cultural changes taking place around them, conceived that stories of human characters' encounters with spiritual beings—both good and evil—could occur anytime and anywhere, bound neither by biblical tradition nor by ancient or modern folklore. *Time* famously asked, on the cover of its April 8, 1966, issue: "Is God Dead?" Over the next decade, the emerging divine-horror subgenre posited that the answer was "No"—that God and Satan, angels and demons, were all very much alive, acting out their will and shaping the world to serve their ends.

Three early entries in the subgenre—*Rosemary's Baby* (1968), *The Exorcist* (1973), and *The Omen* (1976)—established many of its longstanding tropes and, with their mainstream box-office success, set the stage for dozens more films released during the next four decades. All three offered then-unprecedented scenes of visual horror—the hallucinatory scene of Rosemary's rape by Satan in *Rosemary's Baby*, the demon-possessed actions of 12-year-old Regan MacNeil in *The Exorcist*, and the grotesque deaths of those close to young Damien Thorn in *The Omen*—but their terror was rooted less in shock than in psychology. Set in comfortable middle-class homes and centered on seemingly normal families, the films gradually transform their comfortably mundane settings into terrifying Hell-scapes. The desperate human protagonists, confronted by beings they can barely comprehend, let alone defeat, watch their once-familiar worlds dissolve into something unrecognizable. The jump-scares, when they come, merely confirm what the characters already suspect: The boundary between the material and spiritual worlds is far more tenuous, and "archaic" beliefs and symbols far more significant, than they had ever imagined.

Subsequent divine horror films offered audiences an increasingly diverse array of stories, told on broader canvases and—thanks to continual advances in special effects—embellished with more elaborately grotesque imagery. Seemingly innocuous objects—a rehabbed Brooklyn brownstone in *The Sentinel* (1977), or an elaborate Renaissance-era puzzle box in *Hellraiser* (1987)—were revealed as portals to Hell that, when opened, unleash hordes of grotesque demons. *Children of the Corn* (1988) imagined a small town in rural Iowa populated wholly by children who, under the sway of a charismatic teenaged preacher, ensure the fertility of their fields by sacrificing adults to a shadowy figure they call "He Who Walks Behind the Rows." *The Devil's Advocate* (1997) transferred the story of Faust to a Manhattan law firm, surrounding ambitious young attorney Kevin Lomax (Keanu Reeves) and his wife Mary Ann (Charlize Theron) with seemingly "human" associates whose demonic nature is revealed in quick, half-glimpsed flashes of their real faces. Philadelphia police detective John Hobbes (Denzel Washington) faces a similar nightmare in *Fallen* (1998), in which he is stalked by a malevolent fallen angel named Azazel. Faced with an enemy who can possess any living human with a single touch, Hobbes allows Azazel to invade his body, takes his own life, and dies believing that the angel perished with him. A final scene, however, reveals the truth: Azazel lives on in the body of a stray cat, already seeking his next (human) host.

Divine horror films multiplied in the years surrounding the turn of the millennium, their prophecies, unholy births, and the "End of Days" described in the Book of Revelation—recurring themes in subgenre since the days of *Rosemary's Baby*—taking on renewed cultural resonance. *The Seventh Sign* (1988), released at the beginning of the cycle, featured Demi Moore as Abby Quinn, a California housewife and expectant mother who discovers that the lodger renting her garage apartment is, in fact, Jesus Christ, returned to Earth to "judge the living and the dead."[18] The seemingly inexhaustible well of God's grace has run dry, Christ explains, drained by humankind's ceaseless violence and lack of faith; henceforth babies—beginning with her own—will be born without souls. It falls to Abby, revealed to be the reincarnation of a woman who tried to ease Christ's suffering on the cross, to redeem humankind and avert the apocalypse. She does so, at the moment she gives birth, pleading for God to give her own soul to her son, and declaring (in implicit answer to a question posed in the film's flashback scenes of the Crucifixion): "I will die for him." Similar themes—an impending apocalypse, a Creator disgusted with His creation, and the redemptive, world-saving power of self-sacrifice—also played out, at the far end of the millennial cycle, in *Legion* (2010). An amalgam of divine-horror and last-stand tropes, it features Paul Bettany as the fallen archangel Michael, who arms and rallies the patrons of a New Mexico diner, including a young single mother whose baby has the potential to save the world, against forces sent by God to destroy them.

Legion's deft inversion of *Paradise Lost*—the fallen archangel who rebels against God is the savior, rather than the corruptor, of humankind—is part of a long tradition of divine-horror films that do not just appropriate traditional elements of religious belief, but subvert and transform them. *End of Days* (1999), set in the last days of the dying 20th century, is a virtual catalog of such transformations and subversions. Its hero, Jericho Cane (Arnold Schwarzenegger), is an embittered atheist who blames God for the death of his wife and daughter, and who (seemingly) prays to Him in the film's climax for purely tactical reasons. Satan, meanwhile, makes no pretense of preying only on the sinful and faithless, turning stockbrokers, cops, and Cane's own partner (Kevin Pollack) into agents of mayhem and selecting an innocent young woman (Robin Tunney) to bring about the apocalypse by bearing his child, the Antichrist. Agents of the Catholic Church prove—as in *The Sentinel* and *The Seventh Sign*—to be controlled or allied with Satan, more interested in destroying humankind than in saving it.

This simultaneous invocation and subversion of traditional Christian texts, rituals, and images—along with the invention of new ones designed to serve the dramatic needs of the story—enables divine horror films to create, in both their characters and their audiences, a profound sense of disorientation. It highlights the gulf between the modern, secularized world that the characters (and we) take for granted, and the rejected, forgotten reality—a world of signs and portents, angels and demons, rituals and relics—that lay behind it. They thus achieve the feeling of defamiliarization—of entering a world so strange that we cannot fully appreciate the depth of its strangeness—that has, from the beginning, been a defining quality of divine horror films.

Horrors, Divine and Diabolical

Across the globe, tales abound of gods and demons making their presence known in the world, bestowing favor, wreaking havoc, indulging whims. The intersections between religion and horror are many; no book could do justice to all of them at once, and this book is, by design, a study of one subset of them. The 18 essays that comprise it focus on films—made, with one exception, in the English-speaking West—that explore the interplay of horror and Western forms of Christianity. They draw upon a (broadly) shared historical background and cultural context, and—in the diversity of themes, motifs, and theological concerns that they collectively bring to light—suggest the diversity that can exist within a seemingly monolithic cultural tradition.

Our journey into the terrain where the divine and horror meet begins with a part devoted to "The Past, Bleeding into the Present," which opens with Thomas Prasch's "'What went we out in this wilderness to find': Supernatural Contest in Robert Eggers's *The Witch: A New-England Folktale* (2015)." Eggers's story is set in a meticulously recreated colonial New England landscape. The film builds its horror on twin foundations: the characters' deeply Calvinist faith (steeped in hellfire, exhortations about depravity and original sin, and the fatalism inspired by predestination) and the privation and utter isolation of their edge-of-wilderness home. It is precisely this volatile mixture—excesses of holiness, and the stresses of life on the edge of collapse—that, Prasch argues, gives a foothold to the real presence of evil. Kevin J. Wetmore, Jr.'s "Emily Rose Died for Your Sins: Paranormal Piety, Medieval Theology and Ambiguous Cinematic Soteriology" finds similar themes—social isolation, families under stress, and excessive piety—in the 2005 film *The Exorcism of Emily Rose*, loosely based on the true story of a girl who died during an exorcism in 1976 and narrated through the trial of the priest who conducted the exorcism. While marketed as a horror film and frequently compared with *The Exorcist*, *Emily Rose* is deeply rooted in Christian theology, and ultimately celebrates the title character's belief that her death was purposeful, providing evidence of the existence of supernatural evil and, by extension, testimony to the existence of God and Christ.

The essay that follows, James J. Ward's "'Is this my reward for defending God's church?' Monstrous Crimes and Monstrous Punishments in *Witchfinder General* (1968), *The Devils* (1971) and *The Name of the Rose* (1986)," uses the three films to examine themes of sin, blasphemy, and punishment as they played out within the framework of the medieval and early modern Church. Each tale involves monstrous behavior, demonic possession, and witchery, all leading inevitably to torture, sadism, and misogyny. Ward argues that as the supernatural blurs with the temporal, the rational, and the scientific, these films suggest that faith and reason are but frail instruments against the demonic forces that lurk everywhere and within everyone. The breakdown of reason—this time in the modern world—is also apparent in the next essay: "Reckoning the Number of the Beast: Premillennial Dispensationalism, *The Omen* and 1970s America." Brad L. Duren examines the 1976 summer blockbuster in the context of contemporary American culture's growing obsession with the "end times," arguing that what set *The Omen* apart was its seamless weaving of premillennial dispensationalism—a once-obscure interpretation of biblical prophecy, then rising to national popularity—into a coherent narrative that resonated with the imaginings and anxieties of the era. *The Omen* both benefitted from and contributed to the success of Hal Lindsey's book best-selling book of end-times prophecy, *The Late, Great Planet Earth*, transforming (even within American evangelical Christianity itself) popular conceptions of how the Antichrist would rise and the apocalypse would unfold.

Sue Matheson's essay, "The Fall of a Domestic Angel: Horror and Hierophany in *Rosemary's Baby* (1968)," examines the ways in which acclaimed filmmaker Roman Polanski uses Catholic tropes generally associated with heaven and hell to inform the film's horror. In particular, Matheson explores Polanski's use of labyrinths and mazes to symbolize the struggle between good and evil. While labyrinths depict wholeness, mazes involve choices, and offer an alternate cosmos in which the supernatural calls the moral order into question. Both, as Matheson's essay illustrates, locate the figure of the pregnant woman at the divine center, even as the child she carries—the son of Satan, conceived by his rape of her—is profane. Rosemary herself is, therefore, not merely a pawn in the war between ultimate good and evil, but an onscreen manifestation of that war. A very different take on the interplay of good and evil, Eleanor Beal's essay on *Let Us Prey* and British rural horror, rounds out the part. "'I have seen things that would make the angels weep. And they do weep': The Devil and Scotland's Religious Horrors in *Let Us Prey*" examines how the Devil "invades" the remote Scottish town of Inveree, entering the police station and forcing its inhabitants—four police officers, two prisoners, and the town doctor—to confront the sins they believed they had concealed from the world. The supernatural events of the film, which lead to escalating violence that the Devil tacitly encourages, trouble the boundaries of good and evil, law and justice, guilt and innocence. By doing so, Beal argues, the film also troubles conventional understandings of the Devil as a purely evil figure, and draws the spectator into a pleasurable relationship with the theologically perverse.

The volume's next part, "The Boundaries of Good and Evil," draws together essays on films that trouble our notions of the divine and the diabolical. Mark Henderson's essay, "God's Bloody Hand: The Horrible Ambiguity of Religious Murder in Bill Paxton's *Frailty*," examines the complexities of a narrative in which serial murders are, seemingly, sanctioned by God. The film's presentation of the "God's Hand" killer as a county sheriff—an archetype of American heroism—speaks, Henderson argues, to the unsettling ambiguity of American religious identity. The traditional God/Devil dichotomy is, Henderson suggests, too simplistic for such a troubling history and identity; a dark and wrathful God—a modern-day reflection of the Old-Testament Jehovah, whom we both own and fear—might be more aptly "American." The discussion continues in "No Religion or Too Many: Problematizing *God Told Me To*," in which Fernando Gabriel Pagnoni Berns takes on the famous Euthyphro dilemma: Is something moral because God commands it, or does God command it because it is moral? Larry Cohen's *God Told Me To* depicts a series of murders linked by the killers' shared belief that God compelled them to act. Pagnoni Berns uses the film to point out the ways in which morals, ethics and social context intermingle in the dilemma of abhorrent commands, exploring the ways in which the film mirrors the anarchy of an era shaped intense rage against the status quo and an impulse to nihilism.

Lúcio Reis-Filho shifts the focus of the section from human to supernatural monsters in the next essay, "Demons to Some, Angels to Others: Eldritch Horrors and Hellbound Religion in the *Hellraiser* Films," which illustrates how, across the life of the franchise, notions of the divine and the horrific have become increasingly conventional and polarized. The bleak Lovecraftian vision of the original film and its first sequel—a cosmos that reduces humans and their gods to insignificance and irrelevance—gave way, in later installments, to formulaic battles between good and evil, and Doug Bradley's character "Pinhead"—the series' iconic figure—was transformed from a disciplined priest of pain to a familiar slasher-film villain in the mold of Freddy Krueger or Jason Voorhees. Even when not divine in their own right, lapsed–Catholic filmmaker Guillermo del Toro suggests, monsters are inextricably linked to religion: both call upon us to believe in—to "accept in our heart"—the presence of things wondrous, yet unseen. Daniel Otto Jack Petersen's essay "Redeeming the Demon-Child and the Eco-Horror Fairy Tale: Ambivalent Theosis and Ambiguous Eucatastrophe in Guillermo del Toro's *Hellboy* Films" shows, however, that the resonances run far deeper in two of Del Toro's best-known films: *Hellboy* (2004) and *Hellboy II: The Golden Army* (2008). The first film's story of an infant demon raised by a loving human "father" to fight on the side of Good is, Peterson argues, a striking example of the Christian doctrine of *theosis*—he sinner's adoption—while the ecological themes of the sequel mirror J.R.R. Tolkien's idea of *eucatastrophe*, and the Catholic doctrine that divine grace is made manifest in the natural world.

God is as omnipresent in the *Hellboy* universe as He is terrifyingly absent in the *Hellraiser* cosmos. The final two essays in this middle part of the book examine films that occupy a complicated middle ground—one in which God's presence, and intentions, are far from clear. Catherine Becker, in "Binary Opposition, Subversion and Liminality in Francis Lawrence's *Constantine*," traces the ways in which it places humans in a precarious liminal state: caught between God and Satan in their long, twilight struggle for souls. The film's narrative, Becker argues, is structured around series of binary oppositions—material and spiritual, good and evil, everyday life and afterlife—that are threatened by renegade angels and demons, and defended by an embittered hero who God has already condemned to Hell. *Stake Land* (2014), the subject of Rhonda R. Dass's essay "Monsters of God: Negotiating the Sacred in *Stake Land*" depicts a post-apocalyptic America beset both by vampires and a fanatical religious cult whose leader sees them as "children of God," sent to cleanse the Earth of sinners. The film's hero, an itinerant loner known only as "Mister," makes war on vampires and zealots alike, becoming the center of a small band of followers and, perhaps, a new mythology. His conflict with cult leader Jebediah Loven is, Dass argues, a struggle to redefine "sacred" in a world where old definitions have long since ceased to have meaning.

The third and final part of *Divine Horror* addresses "Horrors of Knowledge and Faith"—a theme as old in Western religious culture as the tale of Adam, Eve, and the serpent. It begins with two essays examining the intersection of religion and cutting-edge science. Bart Bishop's "'They're not in charge here': The Collision of Religion and Science in *[Rec]* and *Quarantine*" explores how a 2007 Spanish-made found-footage horror film and its 2008 American remake take a similar premise—scientific experimentation creates a zombie plague in a downtown apartment building—and develop it in radically different directions. The American remake links the zombies to a biological warfare agent unleashed by a religious cultist, while the Spanish original ties them to a scientist-priest's unsanctioned experiments on kidnapped children, designed to create a "vaccine" capable of driving out demons from the bodies of the possessed. The differences between the films, Bishop argues, are not casual, but reflections of the profoundly different roles played by organized religion in Spanish and American culture. The interweaving of science and faith is even more pronounced in *Prince of Darkness* (1987), one of John Carpenter's lesser-known works, and an unusual film on two counts: It depicts scientists and clergy actively working together, and it makes scientists the victims (rather than the creators) of the malevolent entity both are struggling to understand. Matthew A. Killmeier's essay "*Prince of Darkness*: The Metaphysics and Quantum Physics of Evil" teases apart the film's interwoven themes of physics, faith, and the nature of evil, and historically situates its argument for the compatibility of science and religion in the "culture wars" of the 1980s.

Professor Van Helsing, Dracula's nemesis, is a man of faith as well as science, wielding crucifixes, holy water, and other religious objects as formidable weapons. The central question raised by the 1968 Hammer Studios film *Dracula Has Risen from the Grave* is thus especially provocative: "What if Dracula faced an attacker with no belief in God?" The next essay in the section, Martin F. Norden's "The Folly of Faithlessness in *Dracula Has Risen from the Grave*," explores the film's religious themes and motifs in relation to Stoker's novel. It analyzes the ways in which the film—often crude and inconsistent in its execution, and so far removed conventional vampire lore that its star, Christopher Lee, denounced it—can in fact provide a complex set of perspectives on the place of religious symbols, ritual, and faith in the struggle against vampiric evil. The focus remains on vampires in "Unquenchable *Thirst*: Morality, Theology and Vampires in Chan-wook Park's Horror Romance," Michael C. Reiff's exploration of a landmark 2009 South Korean horror film. From the moment that Father Sang-hyun, the film's vampire-priest hero, awakes from an experimental, life-saving operation with an unquenchable thirst for blood, he is agonizingly aware of his condition and its ramifications. Faced with a stark choice—drink blood or perish—he struggles to craft a new ethics for himself that will enable him to manage his condition without becoming a predatory monster. Reiff's essay focuses on Sang-hyun's struggles to be *both* a vampire and a moral being, and to rein in those—including his vampire lover Tae-ju—who are unencumbered by such scruples.

Knowledge of events and objects from the distant past is central to virtually every religion; comprehension of such knowledge is, indeed, often seen as essential to making sense of the present and preparing for the future. Questions about what those events and objects mean can be ferociously contested. The contest at the center of Rupert Wainwright's *Stigmata* (1999) revolves around the Gospel According to Thomas: an (actual) ancient text declared heretical by the Catholic Church but believed by many to represent the earliest rendering of the words of Christ. Cynthia J. Miller's essay "Of Heresy and Horror: *Stigmata*" examines the tension among truth, knowledge, and doctrine in the film, as the divine struggles for expression in the mundane—the wounds suffered by Christ at the Crucifixion appearing on the body of a rebellious young hair stylist—and evil, in both demonic and earthly form, struggles to suppress it. The shadow cast by the ancient world over the modern one is particularly broad and dark in *The Exorcist*, the tale of a 12-year-old girl possessed by the ancient Assyrian demon Pazuzu. Steve Webley's essay "The Power of Film Compels You! Transgressing Taboos and the War on Demonic Possession in *The Exorcist*," which rounds out the part and the book, analyzes how the film's demon imagery taps into ideas that have long shaped humans' understanding of the cosmos and our place within it. The profound and lasting impact of the film, Webley argues, can be traced not only to its resonances with the cultural upheavals of the era, but to its ability to connect viewers to the ancient, yet very real, anxieties that those upheavals brought to the surface. His essay thus brings the collection full circle, suggesting that we are *never* truly free of our primordial fear of our gods.

10 Introduction

NOTES

1. Rudolf Otto, *The Idea of the Holy*, trans. John W. Harvey (Oxford: Oxford University Press, 1950), 14–15.
2. *Ibid.*, 13–14.
3. Revelation 16:14.
4. "Confronting the Devil's Power," Address of Pope Paul VI to a General Audience, November 15, 1972, *Papal Encyclicals Online*, www.papalencyclicals.net/Paul06/p6devil.htm.
5. Douglas Cowan, *Sacred Terror* (Waco: Baylor University Press, 2008), 171.
6. For more on this, and a discussion of horror as a genre, see Noël Carroll, *The Philosophy of Horror* (London: Routledge, 2003).
7. For more on the Old Testament refutation of Canaanite myth, see Neil Forsyth, *Satan and the Combat Myth* (Princeton: Princeton University Press, 1989), chapter 2.
8. See, for example, John Day, *God's Conflict with the Dragon and the Sea* (Cambridge: Cambridge University Press, 1985), 38–39; and Marvin Pope, *Job* (New York: Doubleday 1965), 164–167.
9. Mary Ann Poust, "It Was Wrong," *Catholic New York*, April 9, 1998. http://cny.org/stories/.
10. Robert A. Orsi, *History and Presence* (Cambridge: Harvard University Press, 2016), dustjacket.
11. *Ibid.*, 163.
12. *Ibid.*, dustjacket.
13. *Ibid.*, 171.
14. Mark 9:43.
15. Matthew 13:42.
16. Revelation 21:8.
17. On the cultural upheavals of the era as a global phenomenon, see Mark Kurlansky, *1968: The Year That Rocked the World* (New York: Random House, 2004) and Thomas Borstelmann, *The 1970s: A New Global History from Civil Rights to Economic Inequality* (Princeton: Princeton University Press, 2011); on the decline of external censorship and its impact on American film, see Mark Harris, *Pictures at a Revolution: Five Movies and the Birth of the New Hollywood* (New York: Penguin, 2008) and Leonard J. Leff and Jerold L. Simmons, *The Dame in the Kimono*, 2d ed. (Lexington: University Press of Kentucky, 2001), 272–284.
18. The wording is from the 1975 translation of the Nicene Creed, the statement of Christian faith first adopted by the Council of Nicaea in 325.

BIBLIOGRAPHY

Borstelmann, Thomas. *The 1970s: A New Global History from Civil Rights to Economic Inequality*. Princeton: Princeton University Press, 2011.
Carroll, Noël. *The Philosophy of Horror*. London: Routledge, 2003.
Cowan, Douglas. *Sacred Terror*. Waco: Baylor University Press, 2008.
Day, John. *God's Conflict with the Dragon and the Sea*. Cambridge: Cambridge University Press, 1985.
Forsyth, Neil. *Satan and the Combat Myth*. Princeton: Princeton University Press, 1989.
Harris, Mark. *Pictures at a Revolution: Five Movies and the Birth of the New Hollywood*. New York: Penguin, 2008.
Kurlansky, Mark. *1968: The Year That Rocked the World*. New York: Random House, 2004.
Leff, Leonard J., and Jerold L. Simmons. *The Dame in the Kimono*, 2d ed. Lexington: University Press of Kentucky, 2001.
Orsi, Robert A. *History and Presence*. Cambridge: Harvard University Press, 2016.
Otto, Rudolf. *The Idea of the Holy*. Trans. John W. Harvey. Oxford: Oxford University Press, 1950.
Pope, Marvin. *Job*. New York: Doubleday 1965.
Poust, Mary Ann. "It Was Wrong." *Catholic New York*, April 9, 1998. http://cny.org/stories/.

Part I

The Past, Bleeding into the Present

"What went we out into this wilderness to find"
Supernatural Contest in Robert Eggers's The Witch: A New-England Folktale (2015)

Thomas Prasch

In the opening scene of Robert Eggers's film *The Witch*, paterfamilias William (Ralph Ineson) addresses a bench of judges in a New England meeting house: "What went we out in this wilderness to find, leaving our country, our kindred, our fathers' houses. We traveled"—his broad Yorkshire accent makes the word sound like "travailed," giving it a Puritan work-ethic edge—"across the wide seas. For what? For what?" As he speaks, the camera takes in, one at a time, his children, expressionlessly watching from the first row: first teenaged Tomasin (Anya Taylor-Joy); then his somewhat younger son Caleb (Harvey Scrimshaw); then the young twins Mercy (Ellie Grainger) and Jonas (Lucas Dawson), on either side of their mother Katherine's (Kate Dickie) apron. A voice from the bench interrupts: "We must ask thee to be silent," but William will not be silenced: "Was it not for the pure and faithful dispensation of the Gospels and the Kingdom of God." The court interrupts: "We are your judges, and not you ours." William counters: "I cannot be judged by false Christians, for I have done nothing save preach Christ's true Gospel." The court remonstrates, "Must you continue to dishonor the laws of the Commonwealth and the church with your prideful conceit?" William, more pure in his faith than the Puritans, so godly in his practices that even the godly find him an irritation, insists, "If God commands it."[1] And the court rules: "Then art thou banished" (accent, of course, on the -ed).

In the subsequent set-up scenes, William and his family leave behind the protective wooden walls of the plantation and head out to the bug-thick edge of the wilderness, an open patch of land beside the deep woods. The family prays as they lay claim to their new home, but their godly voices do not quite overcome the haunted note clusters in the string section (something midway between Krzystof Penderecksi's *Threnody for the Victims of Hiroshima* and Bernard Herrmann's score for *Psycho*; Mark Korvin's music adds much to the atmospheric creepiness of the film). We know no good will come of this move, no godly kingdom overcome the dark spirits of the folk-taled dark woods (it is not for nothing, after all, that the film is subtitled "A New-England Folktale"). And it is less what they came to the wilderness to find but what they brought along with them from the Old World that defines the experience for the perilously isolated family.

14   Part I. The Past, Bleeding into the Present

The family joins in prayer as they prepare to make their new home at the edge of the wilderness in *The Witch* (2015). From left to right: Jonas (Lucas Dawson), Mercy (Ellie Grainger), Katherine (Kate Dickey), William (Ralph Ineson), Caleb (Harvey Scrimshaw) and Thomasin (Anya Taylor-Joy).

The opening scene of *The Witch* sets the film's literal and conceptual territory: a man driven out of his New England colonial homestead for being too Puritan—too austere, too holier-than-thou, too much the prophet in the (literal) wilderness—resettles his family at the edge of the forest. Cue rustles in the woods. Eggers built his script, as a closing title card in the film notes, from period sources, the witchcraft tracts and pamphlets that proliferated in the Reformation's wake, drawing on the newfound godliness and heightened intolerance of the era. The ground upon which *The Witch* builds its horror is on the one hand deeply Calvinist faith (with its hellfires, its theology of original-sinned depravity, its predeterminist fatalism, and the rhythms of its spoken word) and on the other hand the edge-of-wilderness setting (the family's privations, the harsh environment, their utter isolation, with coming-of-age tensions and sibling struggles ladled into the mix). Enter into that setting the real presence of evil (or these deeply-faithed people's conviction of its presence, which amounts to the same thing): witches and magic, blood rituals and naked covens, curses and possessions, hauntings and familiars, unholy as well as holy covenants. It is Eggers's deep insight that recognizes that those two forms of covenant are deeply connected, that it is precisely in excesses of holiness that images of its inversion thrive. As Kathryn Rieklis notes in her review of the film: "The fear of witches went hand in hand with the Calvinist God whose inscrutable will predestined some to hell. Outside the boundaries of grace, evil proliferates, and the boundaries of civilization are mirrored by the boundaries of God's predestination."[2] At the same time, the social fabric provides the ground for specific ways in which such drama plays out: in social order, family troubles, and community crisis, accusations of witchcraft provide a cover for other tensions. This is horror located at that ambiguous nexus between folktale witchcraft and psychological family drama—Jamesian horror (either Henry or William, take your pick).

Looking for Witches

Describing to Anton Bitel the basic ground for his film, Robert Egger explains:

> It wasn't something that just lived in the minds of the clergy and the intelligentsia—it was everybody. The lay people had this idea of the fairytale-witch-ogress-anti-mother-really-fucking-scary-thing. To do the research and to see that the fairytale world and the real world in the early modern period were the same thing, and to find the same tropes in folk tales and fairytales and recorded accounts of historical witchcraft and in court records—it's the same witch. But it's real for these people. If your corn doesn't grow, it's a witch. If your child dies, it's a witch. And there is a reality to it. The little old lady who lived down the lane in this period, people really thought she was flying on a broomstick and cutting up children, it wasn't like she's a witch in some vague sense, there was a specific fairytale mythology built around her, and people would be very frightened of her, so if you think that that's how they're actually viewing this woman, you can see how it could lead to this kind of horror.[3]

When something goes wrong, the witch is to blame. Historians, seeking explanations for that same sudden rise in witch accusations, trials, and killings in the wake of the Reformation, have largely looked elsewhere for their answers.

The tone for modern historiography of witchcraft was set in the 1970s by Keith Thomas and Alan Macfarlane, in breakthrough studies that, borrowing heavily from anthropological work on contemporary witch accusations, sought social and cultural explanations, looking to shifts in broad economic patterns to explain the sudden rise in levels of accusation and to social systems and psychological relationships between accused and accusers to account for specific accusations. Thus, Thomas, in *Religion and the Decline of Magic*, starts his analysis of witch accusations at the personal level, first with an insistence that we note the interaction that preceded the charge—the accuser, Thomas points out, was typically "a person already known to her victim," and the witch "was always believed to bear some previous grudge"—before pushing toward a more surprising conclusion: "but close examination ... reveals that the charge was normally only levied when the accuser felt, not merely that the witch bore a grudge against him, but that the grudge was a *justifiable* one."[4] Looking into that question about what makes the grudge justifiable, in turn, leads Thomas to the broader economic shifts and the disruption and discontent that accompanied them: "The great bulk of witchcraft accusations thus reflected an unresolved conflict between the neighbourly conduct required by the ethical code of the old village community, and the increasingly individualistic forms of behavior which accompanied the economic changes of the sixteenth and seventeenth centuries."[5] Thomas thus shifts the investigation away from the witch and toward the accuser and the social milieu.

Macfarlane, in his close examination of Essex witchcraft, looks to the sparks for the accusations: "quarrels over gifts and loans of food and, to a lesser extent, money and implements precipitated the manifestation of the witch attacks."[6] Again this brings his focus to an anthropologically inflected sociological explanation: "Specific people are accused of being witches, other people are named as their victims. These are observed facts and can be analyzed sociologically, unlike the 'ideology of witchcraft,' which can only be interpreted."[7] For that uptick in accusations, Macfarlane like Thomas looks to changing economies: "population growth and changes in land ownership created a group of poorer villages whose ties to their slightly wealthier neighbours became more tenuous," while at the same time "during the period between 1560 and 1650 the informal institutions which had dealt with the old and poor ... were strained."[8] A quarter century after these works appeared, Malcolm Gaskill, even while declaring that "the time is now ripe for a reappraisal of the English experience of witchcraft," still acknowledged the "towering achievements of Keith Thomas and Alan Macfarlane"[9] as a starting point. And even his reappraisal presumes their basic ground: a more complex, but still essentially sociological, interpretation.

One significant element can be added to the interpretive brew in Thomas and Macfarlane's wake: a more systematic focus on the gender dynamics of witchcraft accusations, consistent with both the period dynamics (that the vast majority of witchcraft accusations target women) and recent historiographic trends (the new emphasis on women's history that modern feminism spawned). Thus Carol F. Karlsen, for example, reads episodes of possession through witchcraft (much as others have read accounts of late-19th-century hysteria) in terms of gender dynamics: "Witchcraft possession in early New England, then, was an interpretation placed upon a physical and emotional response to a set of social conditions that had no intrinsic relationship to witches or the devil.... [T]he New England possessed were rebelling against pressures to internalize stifling gender and class hierarchies."[10] Karlsen sees such an interpretation as a supplement to readings such as those advanced by MacFarlane and Thomas; thus, she lays out broad patterns of cultural shift (demographic and economic) as preliminary background to the argument about gender norms.[11] Clarke Garrett advances a similar argument: "In a world in which men make the rules, female sexuality creates a perpetual dilemma. As the vessels of the biological mysteries ... [and] as creatures of sexual passion, women are mistrusted, but as mothers, women are the nurturers and preservers of society.... When a woman failed to maintain her reputation because of inappropriate female behavior, she faced not ostracism ... but distrust, animosity, and even fear."[12] Such readings again look to the social circumstances for non-supernatural explanations.

It is, broadly speaking, this interpretive framework, informed more directly by investigations of social dynamics than by, say, witchcraft pamphlets of the period, that has dominated understandings of both Old World witchcraft and its New World variations during the burning times of the 16th and 17th centuries.[13] Thus, for example, Paul Boyer and Stephen Nissenbaum map out the geographies and chart differences in social status in their quest for the "social origins" of witchcraft accusations in Salem.[14] John Demos brings a parallel sociological framework to his interpretation of the Salem trials, speaking of the "social matrix" of accusations in terms of boundaries and forms of inclusion in village communities: "Witchcraft proceedings declared a moral *and* social opposition. The lines drawn divided not only right from wrong, but also allies from foes, in-group from out-group, 'us' from 'them.'"[15] More recently, also looking at the Salem trials, Emerson Baker outlines the "battle lines"—the range of divisions within Salem, resulting from growing economic inequality, new political forms, struggles to maintain the purity of the church, conflicts with Native Americans, and personal conflicts—before detailing the roles of accused, accusers, and judges.[16]

Historians thus seek a range of rational explanations for the witchcraft accusations of the period. Filmmakers, at least those who seriously engage with witches rather than using them as pop-out-of-the-dark scary beings without bothering to account for them, typically follow a similar pattern, in which the figure of the witch stands in for something else. Most obviously, and most familiarly, in Arthur Miller's *The Crucible* (1953) or any of its screen adaptations (1957, 1996, or television versions in 1967, 1980, and 2014), the analogy of Salem witch trials and McCarthyite "witch hunt" explains away the witches. In Roman Polanski's *Rosemary's Baby* (1968), the witches mark the faltering of traditional American religious verities (signaled by the referencing of *Time* magazine's famous "Is God Dead?" cover). In a host of other variations, like, for example, *The Craft* (1996) or *Practical Magic* (1998), the witch stands in for some form of autonomous female power, Hollywood nodding to contemporary feminism (while simultaneously demonizing it).[17] Neither historians, searching for non-supernatural explanations for witch prosecutions, nor filmmakers, using witches essentially symbolically, approach the issue as Eggers does: by looking for the witch.

For Eggers, the witch is a real presence. "The witch is a witch like a stone is a stone or a tree is a tree," Eggers told NPR's Rachel Martin.[18] We see the witch creeping through the forest after Samuel is kidnapped, and then in her lair disemboweling the infant to prepare the unguent,[19] even when the family does not (and because they do not, can—sort of—convince themselves that a wolf spirited the child away). We do not quite see Satan himself materialize in the place of the goat Black Phillip, because the scene is too dark, but Eggers certainly sees him: "The puppet of a goat hoof ... is replaced by a cavalier's boot. And this costume, this very elaborate costumed covered with gold and jewels and sporting a cockerel feather, this insanely costume-y beaver hat and earrings and all this shit, you don't see any of it."[20] For Eggers, if not quite for in-the-dark us, Satan is real.

Immersion

For Eggers, *The Witch* works because it speaks to us at an archetypal level: "I like archetypal storytelling. And archetypes constantly reconstellate themselves. So therefore it is timeless."[21] At the same time, however "timeless" the archetype might be, Eggers is also convinced of the need to anchor it in a specific history, that of Puritan New England. In interviews, Eggers has underlined the need for accuracy to the era of the film's setting. As Mekado Murphy writes, of an interview with Eggers: "In his early research, Mr. Eggers said he found that for many people in the 17th century, the real world and the fairy-tale world were one and the same: To them, witches were a reality. To show how deep a hold the witch had on settler's imaginations, Mr. Eggers decided to place viewers in the center of the period, as accurately as he could. He wanted his film to feel like 'a Puritan's nightmare,' he said."[22] As he told Jordan Crucchiola: "To understand why the witch archetype was important and interesting and powerful—and how was I going to make that scary and alive again—we had to go back in time to the early modern period when the witch was a reality. And the only way I was going to do that, I decided, was by having it be insanely accurate."[23] Or, as he told Katie Rife, "we have to be in the Puritan world.... Without the detail, [without] the hand-stitched everything, you can't get there. You can't do it. If we just slapped on some cedar fence post from Home Depot instead of hand-driven clapboards," he suggests, we would sense the difference."[24]

The approach requires full immersion, first by Eggers himself (and his cast and crew), as Matt Patches recounts:

> Eggers spent five years researching, developing, and writing the script for *The Witch*. To forge his authentic colonial setting, the writer-director pored over historical documents at Smithsonian's Plimoth Plantation in Plymouth, Massachusetts. According to Taylor-Joy, Eggers absorbed exhaustive tomes and primary source diaries, reaching encyclopedic knowledge levels. Eggers uncovered architectural notes to appropriately construct Ye Olde Cabin in the Woods and taught his crew era-appropriate farming techniques, just in case his characters' farms ever needed to become fully operational.[25]

Then it works for us, as viewers who need to be transported to the Puritan world.

Immersion for Eggers works at two levels: that of the material world, and that of the ideational realm. At the material level, the work begins with tools and materials: "Everything you see on camera is the authentic materials that would have been used at the time, and often we had to use period construction methods and tools to make it look right."[26] It included preparatory work with the actors as well, as Eggers observes: "We also had a week of rehearsals where we were working on the farm—how do you milk goats? How do you use the bill hooks? What's the layout of the farm?"[27] His interviews and director's commentary makes clear how much attention he paid to material details. Eggers notes: "The family's farm was constructed from scratch. The clapboards that sheathe the siding—no one in Canada [where they filmed] knew how to make them correctly, so we had to find a guy in Massachusetts who knew how to hand-drive oak clapboards and we had to ship them up"[28]; "the men and the women are divided in the meeting room, which is correct to the period"[29]; "rush lights" are made by "dipping grass rushes into wax"; the various "clay pots" in the witch's hovel draw on "all the reference material of all the medieval and early modern paintings and engravings … but of course you see none of it because it was so dark"; "you'll notice she's flying on a stick, not a broomstick. Witches weren't flying on broomsticks in England and New England until the eighteenth century"; the family was "eating unleavened bread made from the meal of their corn"; they eat with "knives and spoons" because "they didn't use forks back then"; the herb poultice and bleeding derive from period medical understandings (and possibly, ironically, suggest a sort of herbalist's "white magic"); "the bill hook that they're using is a very common tool in the period" although it fell out of use later.[30]

Even his consciousness of errors in the film—that "the house is too big" but filming required it; that the goat house would not have been thatched because the goats would eat it; that they "gathered the corn into a corn shock like that is not necessarily period-accurate, but it's iconic New England harvest and there are reasons why I think its plausible"; that "the firewood is too much like modern firewood, it's too uniform"; the horse is the "correct breed," but the goats not quite; that "they're burning way too many candles in this film" but the film needed the light[31]—all suggest Eggers's close attention to detail, even when considering what he could, with his limited budget and the demands of filmmaking, get away with.

The immersive approach similarly applies to the realm of ideas, drawing on two overlapping bodies of research: writings about Puritan beliefs, and the extensive body of period pamphlets, engravings, and theological work on witches. On the Puritan side of things, this begins with the Bible, and for the Puritans that means the Geneva Bible (which they preferred over the less-Reformation-minded King James version).[32] Eggers notes: "I had to read the Geneva Bible cover-to-cover and read the gospels quite a bit to get into that world."³³ He adds in another interview that "the Geneva Bible is a beautifully written book, and it's something they were obsessed with,"³⁴ and his own obsession with the text explains the movie's core cadences.

The film's fullest explication of Calvinist predestinarian theology, in the catechism Caleb recites to his father as they tromp through the forest ("Aren't thou then born a sinner?" William asks; "Aye, I was conceived in sin and born in iniquity," Caleb replies; "Then what is thy birth sin?" William interrogates; "Adam's sin imputed to me and a corrupt nature dwelling within me…. My corrupt nature is empty of grace, bent unto sin, only unto sin, and that continually"), is based (appropriately enough) on John Cotton's *Spiritual Milk for Babes, Drawn out of the Breasts of Both Testaments* (1646).³⁵ Eggers got "nearly all the prayers used in the film" from Lewis Bayly's *Practice of Piety* (1611), and, for "the dialogue, he turned to the diaries of John Winthop, a founder of the Massachusetts Bay Colony, and Samuel Sewall, a judge involved in the Salem witch trials, mainly to better understand the Calvinist worldview. 'Those diaries aren't necessarily riddled with witch stuff,' he said, 'but I tried to capture the Puritan mind-set and get the audience to see how this family would think.'"³⁶ When William eats dirt while praying, Eggers is referencing Charles Hambrick-Stowe's work on Puritan devotional practices.³⁷ One prayer passage, the striking speech with the highly sexualized quotation from the Song of Solomon (or Song of Songs, depending on your Bible)—the one that begins "Oh my Lord, my love, how wholly delectable thou art! Let him kiss me with the kisses of his mouth, for his love is sweeter than wine"—uttered by a possessed Caleb just before his death, is taken from John Winthrop.³⁸

A similar immersion in source texts shows in the explicitly witch-related material of the film, starting with the typeface of the title, featuring the double-V variation of a W that was a feature of some of the period's cheap pamphlets (and that, in this case, doubtless comes from the 1643 pamphlet *Most Certain, Strange, and True Discovery of a Witch*).³⁹ In doing his research, Eggers made the important discovery that there was little distinction between folk tales and theological tracts, no clear lines between high and low culture: "'What was really interesting to me was [that] folktales, fairy tales, and reality in the early modern period were all kind of the same thing,' Eggers says. 'So you have folk stories that are being told by laypeople, but they're pretty much the same as Elizabethan witch pamphlets, which were sort of like the tabloid newspaper of the day.'"⁴⁰ The folk-tale origins of witchcraft lore thus figure in the pamphlet literature and the trial testimony as well, conditioning how people of the period understood the phenomenon (and perhaps also how they respond to it). For the characters in the film, much like the girls of Salem, witch possession followed an established script.

For broad witching background, Eggers drew heavily on the works of Cotton Mather, themselves often compilations from pamphlet sources.⁴¹ But he also drew on specific sources for key material. For example, he says that "Thomasin was very much based on Elizabeth Knap, who was a woman in Massachusetts in the seventeenth century who was a teenager who was having all these fits and things and I truly believe that she thought she was possessed by the devil."⁴² When Caleb spits out an apple during his possession, the references both to the source of temptation at the Garden of Eden and to Caleb's lie, earlier in the film, about looking for an apple tree are clear, but Eggers also has in mind a pamphlet source: "There was an Elizabethan witch who was accused of giving children poison apples. This was earlier than any written accounts of Snow White that I'm aware of."⁴³ Much of what William tells Thomasin, as he struggles with the possibility of her being the witch (as Kate firmly believes, as the twins have accused her of being), are, Eggers relates, "an Elizabethan man's words to his wife who he is trying to convince was not actually a witch; she had I think killed their children by burning the house down."[44] Sometimes he drew on a broader range of sourcing; as witch's familiars, both the hare and goat (the film's creepy Black Phillip) draw more on Continental witch sources than on English or American material.[45] The specificity gives extra texture to the witch encounters and possessions of the film.

What immersion does above all else is insistently place us in the physical and conceptual territory of the film's Puritan family. The supernatural contest between good and evil acts on them, measured in terms of their personal salvation, and all around them, in the nature with which they contend for survival. For them, there is no accident: when things go wrong, there must be a witch.

A Family in Crisis, with a Witch Thrown In

In a revealing comment about her efforts to understand her character in the film, Anya Taylor-Joy remarks: "I keep forgetting there's a witch, because I see this as the story of the deterioration of a family."[46] And in a more conventionally plotted or contextualized witch tale, the family breakdown at the heart of the story would provide an alternative explanation for the spooky goings-on. But here, family crisis—real enough on many levels—is complicated by spiritual understandings. "We will conquer this wilderness, it will not consume us," William declares to his son (as they reset once again the traps that have caught nothing). That it is, indeed, consuming them—that they are, finally, failing in that most foundational Puritan mission to set order upon the world—undermines the family. But such family conflict must be read in the terms their faith provides. William, at one point, offers a Job-ish interpretation: "He hath taken us into a very low condition to humble us and to show us more of His grace." But that is not the most obvious reading of the family's plight. Almost setting things up for the film's finale, the predeterministic fatalism of the family's deep Calvinism insists on the grace-dependent evil of the human condition.

Each of the family members carries deep flaws (except perhaps Samuel, but he disappears almost at the outset).[47] Thomasin's first speech in the film, a private prayer, confesses her sins: "I here confess I've lived in sin. I've been idle of my work, disobedient to my parents, neglectful of my prayer. I have, in secret, played upon my Sabbath. And broken every one of thy commandments in thought. Followed the desires of mine own will, and not the Holy Spirit." But it is less her actual sins, and more her sinning potential, as more woman than girl—"Our daughter hath begat the sign of womanhood," Kate reminds her husband, urging him to take her back to the plantation to work in service to some other family—that troubles her place in the family. Her burgeoning sexuality tests the constraints of Puritan values. As Eggers puts it in one interview: "Thomasin isn't a Puritan. She doesn't belong to that world. So it's very interesting to see her struggle to deal with the world she's stuck in."[48] Bad blood between mother and daughter further disturbs the household.

Thomasin's potent sexuality tests her younger brother as well; he peers closely at the bit of cleavage she exposes while sleeping and enjoys rather too sensually her tickling him by the riverside. Caleb also has difficulty with Calvinist theology; while he can repeat his catechism, he is challenged by the notion that they cannot know whether his lost infant brother is saved ("What wickedness has he done," Caleb demands of his father, as if he has not just provided the answer by speaking of being born "in sin"). As for Kate, calamity turns her depressed and shrewish, distrustful, despairing (lamenting that God "hath cursed this family," longing for her English homeland), and angry at Thomasin, too ready to find more to blame her for (her missing candlestick, the witchery). The twins, speaking their twin language, claiming to talk to the goat Black Phillip, crowning him in their creepy folk-tuney song—"Black Phillip is a merry, merry king.... Black Phillip has a mighty, mighty sting/ He'll knock thee to the Earth/ Sing bah, bah"—seem in a world of their own, and perhaps not a holy one. And then there is Black Phillip himself, the unruly goat. "The Adversary oft comes in the shape of a he-goat," Thomasin reminds her father (as she tries to deflect the witch accusation from herself).

Finally there is William. His pride leads to the family's exile, as the Puritan court declared. His traps come up empty; when he tries to shoot a hare, his gun backfires (only, perhaps, because the hare is the witch's familiar); his crops are failing, the corn beset by fungus.[49] His claimed holiness falls into question as he deceives his wife about her lost chalice (traded to the Indians for more traps), while letting his wife blame Thomasin for it, and he does not call out Caleb's lie about finding an apple tree. In his frustration, he chops wood, but that alone cannot sustain a family. As Thomasin tells him, when she is convinced he has turned from her (having overheard their plans to send her into others' service): "You let mother be as thy master. You cannot bring to crops to yield. You cannot hunt. Is that truth enough? You can do nothing save chop wood." William's failures matter because of the light they may shed on the saved status of his soul.

Works reflect salvation: good works and worldly success. The broadly shared Puritan notion develops through a conflation of two aspects of Calvinist doctrine: his position

Black Phillip rears up as the children (Lucas Dawson and Ellie Granger) chant in *The Witch* (2015).

on calling (secularizing the idea to include worldly occupations) and on predestination (the ability to know one's status as a member of the elect). In relation to the dynamic of "calling," as R. Paul Stevens notes: "Calvin recognizes the burgeoning world of commerce as an area of legitimate activity for a Christian." For Calvin, Stevens argues, "calling is closely related to predestination. Your election is confirmed through your vocation." Stevens highlights the role of calling in the "proper ordering of the world," quoting from John Calvin's *Institutes of the Christian Religion* (final version 1559) to secure the point: "The Lord bids each of us in all life's action to look to his calling. For he knows with what great restlessness human nature flames.... Therefore ... he hath appointed duties for every man in his particular way of life."[50] He notes as well that the same understanding carried over to the English Reformation, quoting Joseph Hall: "The homeliest service that we do in an honest calling, though it be but to plow or to dig ... is crowned with ample reward."[51] What matters is the godly practice of the calling, whatever it might be, a significant departure from both Catholic practice and Lutheran doctrine.

In the context of uncertainty over salvation, the question of whether one has been predestined to be saved or damned, how things go with one's calling begins to matter. As Max Weber long ago observed of Calvinist predestinarian precepts, there was finally, for Calvin himself, no way to know God's decision on the matter: "to the question of how the individual can be certain of his own election, he has at bottom only the answer that we should be content with the knowledge that God has chosen." But that meant, paradoxically, for Calvin's followers, a heightened focus on the status of their election: "for them the *certitudo salutis* in the sense of the recognizability of the state of grace necessarily became of absolutely dominant importance. So, wherever the doctrine of predestination was held, the question could not be suppressed whether there were any infallible criteria by which membership in the *electi* could be known."[52] The anxiety over salvation fuels and inflects, for instance, the Puritan obsession with self-examination and self-accounting, so evident a trait in their spiritual biographies.[53]

It followed for Weber that for "the hard Puritan merchants of the heroic age of capitalism," faced with the question of their salvation, "in order to attain that self-confidence intense worldly activity is recommended as the most suitable means. It and it alone disperses religious doubts and gives the certainty of grace."[54] For Weber, with his interest in seeing this certainty feed into an ideology to support the emergence of capitalism, the keys to that "self-confidence" lay above all else in living a "godly" life and in asceticism, which encouraged accumulation of capital (through that godly virtue of self-control). But a simpler formula also came to figure in Puritan calculations. As Samuel Weber notes, "Calvinism could regard success in business and the accumulation of worldly as a sign of election."[55] Robert Michaelsen observes: "Puritans were quick to point out that a life guided by such a concern for the salvation of the soul and for eternal life would also have its this-worldly rewards. If your heart is right and you have the right goals in mind, God will guide you and preserve you and will 'crown your Endeavours with a prosperous Success.'"[56] Keith Thomas, citing a range of English Puritans, similarly points out: "there was thus a strong tendency to assume that obedience to God's commandments would conduce to prosperity and safety.... It is not surprising that Max Weber concluded that no religion did as much as Puritanism to identify economic achievement with spiritual success."[57] If success suggests salvation, failure hints at damnation.

Family crisis thus manifests in witchcraft accusations, the pattern identified by contemporary anthropologists and historians; or, in the Puritan framework of the film itself, family crisis opens the door to Satan and the witch. Early in the film, Mercy asserts it was the "witch of the wood" that stole Samuel; Thomasin taunts her in turn, in words familiar from the pamphlet literature: "I be the witch of the wood.... When I sleep, my spirit slips away from my body and dances naked with the Devil. That's how I signed his book. He bade me bring him an unbaptized babe, so I stole Sam.... And I'll vanish thee, too, if thou displeaseth me." During Caleb's possession, the twins recall the taunts, turning them into accusation; Kate, inclined against her daughter and toward belief in a "cursed" family, proves willing echo; Thomasin in turn recalls the twins' communion with the goats; and all spirals out of control, above all else out of William's control, he no more able to pull his family together than he is to sustain them. Thomasin's final pact—signing the book, shedding her clothes, going into the woods to join the coven—comes almost as fait accompli, already implicit in her opening prayer.

"'A family's a little church, a little commonwealth,' is a saying from the period, and so we were trying to emulate that here," Eggers has commented.[58] In this sense, the family reproduces the plantation they left behind. The film's central tension is between the colonists' desire to impose order upon the world—their shining city on the hill or, in the reduced variant offered here, the clapboard hovel the family calls home, their small acreage of corn—and the world's deep resistance to such endeavors, represented in the uncontained, indeed uncontainable, always dark and mysterious woods, the wild of the wilderness. In this episode in that great contest, the witch wins. But the witch is not really "what we went out into the wilderness to find," as William puts it at the film's outset; it, too, is something the Puritans bring along with them. For those of us still living with the Puritan dream of the city on the hill—there every time a politician speaks of American exceptionalism, for example—the dark portent of the story helps lend the film its eerie edge.

NOTES

1. In the director's commentary on the DVD edition, Eggers frames this conflict in terms of the traditional historiographic division between Separatists and less-separated Puritans: "There are many different kinds of Puritans in this period, and the way we talk about it now, the two most basic types are Puritans who wanted to purify the Church of England and Separatists who wanted to separate entirely from the Church of England. The Plymouth pilgrims, who had the alleged first Thanksgiving, they wanted to separate entirely, but the Massachusetts Bay colony was [non-Separatist] Puritan. And so William is a Separatist who has come to the Massachusetts Bay colony," thus the wrong move from the start. For background on the Separatist issue, see Kenneth L. Campbell, *Windows into Men's Souls: Religious Nonconformity in Tudor and Early Stuart England* (Lanham, MD: Lexington Books, 2012), esp. chs. 4 and 7.

2. Kathryn Reklis, "On Media: Theological Horror," *Christian Century*, 11 May 2016, 58.

3. Anton Bitel, "Voices of the Undead: Robert Eggers on The Witch," *Sight & Sound* (4 July 2016), http://www.bfi.org.uk/news-opinion/sight-sound-magazine/interviews/robert-eggers-witch. Eggers reiterates the point in Katie Rife, "*The Witch* Director Robert Eggers on Fellini, Feminism, and Period-Accurate Candlelight," *A.V. Club*, 23 February 2016, http://www.avclub.com/article/witch-director-robert-eggers-fellini-feminism-and-232450.

4. Keith Thomas, *Religion and the Decline of Magic: Studies in Popular Beliefs in Sixteenth and Seventeenth Century England* (Oxford: Oxford University Press, 1971), 552.

5. *Ibid.*, 561.

6. Alan MacFarlane, *Witchcraft in Tudor and Stuart England: A Regional and Comparative Study*, 2d ed. (1970; London: Routledge, 1999), 176.

7. *Ibid.*, 226.

8. *Ibid.*, 205.

9. Martin Gaskill, "Witchcraft in Early Modern Kent: Stereotype and the Background to Accusations," in *Witchcraft in Early Modern Europe: Studies in Culture and Belief*, ed. Jonathan Barry, Marianne Hester, and Gareth Roberts, 257–287 (Cambridge: Cambridge University Press, 1996), 257.

10. Carol F. Karlsen, *The Devil in the Shape of a Woman: Witchcraft in Colonial New England* (New York: W.W. Norton, 1987), 250–251. For the parallel reading of hysteria, see Elaine Showalter, "Hysteria, Fem-

24   Part I. The Past, Bleeding into the Present

inism, and Gender," Sander L. Gilman, et al., *Hysteria Beyond Freud*, 286–344 (Berkeley: University of California Press, 1993).

11. Karlsen, *Devil in the Shape of a Woman*, chaps. 2–3.

12. Clarke Garrett, "Women and Witches: Patterns of Analysis," *Signs* 3, no. 2 (1977): 466. One weakness of Garrett's argument lies in temporality. Since women's position changes little between late medieval and early modern eras, the explanation provides no mechanism to understand a sudden boom in accusations.

13. John Demos usefully surveys the specific range of recent interpretations in *The Enemy Within: A Short History of Witch-Hunting* (London: Penguin, 2008), 198–212.

14. Paul Boyer and Stephen Nissenbaum, *Salem Possessed: The Social Origins of Witchcraft* (Cambridge: Harvard University Press, 1974). See also their fascinating 40-years-later perspective on the work, "*Salem Possessed* in Retrospect" [*William and Mary Quarterly* 3d series 65, no. 3 (2008): 314–24] in particular for the illuminating retrospective positioning of their own work in relation to the New Left politics and cultural developments that informed their research.

15. John Demos, *Entertaining Satan: Witchcraft and the Culture of Early New England* (Oxford: Oxford University Press, 1982), 305. See also, for an overview of such avenues of investigation in relation to the Salem trials, Robert Detweiler, "Shifting Perspectives on the Salem Witches."

16. Emerson W. Baker, *A Storm of Witches: The Salem Trials and the American Experience* (Oxford: Oxford University Press, 2015), 69–98.

17. This rather differs from the argument Eggers puts forward, in a number of interviews, that *The Witch* is a "feminist" film. The difference is two-fold: first, that *The Witch* focuses less on witchery as a mode of female power and far more, simply, on the oppressed position of women within Puritan culture; and second, that the film's feminist edge seemed to have caught even Eggers by surprise. As he told Rachel Martin on NPR: "And in making this film about Thomasin, I didn't set out to make a feminist film. But feminism or female empowerment just rises to the top." See Rachel Martin, "'The Witch' Achieves Puritan American Horror Without The Gore," 6 March 2016, http://www.npr.org/2016/03/06/469383396/-the-witch-achieves-puritan-american-horror-without-the-gore. Others, however, have taken feminism as more central to the film. For example, David Sims argues: "The film's exploration of patriarchal power was the key to unlocking Thomasin's story. As a woman in the 17th century, she's entirely stripped of agency…. As *The Witch* progresses, it becomes clear that the campaign being waged against her family is targeted at freeing her so that she can join the coven in the woods." See "Female Freedom and Fury in *The Witch*," *The Atlantic*, 24 February 2016, http://www.theatlantic.com/entertainment/archive/2016/02/robert-eggers-the-witch-female-empowerment/470844/. I would suggest that Sims exaggerates both the lack of agency and the teleology of the film.

18. Martin, "'The Witch' Achieves Puritan American Horror."

19. Eggers loves that word "unguent," using it whenever he talks about the scene in the director's commentary track on the DVD edition of *The Witch* and in interviews. See, for example, Forrest Wickman, "All *The* Witch's Most WTF Moments, Explained: A Spoiler-Filled Interview with the Director," *Slate*, 23 February 2016, http://www.slate.com/blogs/browbeat/2016/02/23/the_witch_director_robert_eggers_on_the_real_history_behind_the_movie_s.html. The word signals his reliance on period sources—about which, more below—but it also is just a cool word.

20. Robert Eggers in the commentary track to the DVD edition of *The Witch*. The descriptor used for Satan—"cavalier"—has a political implication, because it associates Satan with royalists; the term was standard for the members of the king's army during the English Civil War (1640–1660). But it also reveals the slight anachronism of Eggers's sourcing, since the film is set in 1630, a decade before that. Indeed, much of Eggers's source material comes from a bit later than the film's setting, and especially from Puritan tracts and trial records nearer the time of the Salem trials (1692). There is a fairly broad consistency, however, in the material (both Puritan and witch-related) going back at least to Elizabethan times.

21. Eggers speaking in a question-and-answer session following a screening of *The Witch* in Salem, included on the DVD edition of the film. He makes a similar argument (starting with the title, but also in opening remarks) in *The Witch: A Primal Tale*, the making-of-the-film short also included on the DVD.

22. Mekado Murphy, "That (Very, Very) Old Black Magic in 'The Witch,'" *New York Times*, 18 February 2016, at nytimes.com.

23. Jordan Crucchiola, "How *The Witch*'s Director Made His Film So Terrifying," *Wired*, 20 February 2016, https://www.wired.com/2016/02/robert-eggers-set-design-how-he-made-the-witch-so-scary/.

24. Katie Rife, "*The Witch* Director Robert Eggers on Fellini, Feminism, and Period-Accurate Candlelight," *A.V. Club*, 23 February 2016, http://www.avclub.com/article/witch-director-robert-eggers-fellini-feminism-and—232450.

25. Matt Patches, "The Scariest Movie at Sundance: How Robert Eggers Made the Horrifying, Historically Accurate 'The Witch,'" *Grantland*, 29 January 2015, http://grantland.com/hollywood-prospectus/the-scariest-movie-at-sundance-how-robert-eggers-made-the-horrifying-historically-accurate-the-witch/. Eggers, when asked by Lauren Duca, "How much time did you spend immersed in this stuff?" answered, "Four years. But it wasn't full time." See Lauren Duca, "How Robert Eggers Wove the Nightmares of *The Witch* Out of Historical Documents," *Vulture*, 18 February 2016, http://www.vulture.com /2016/02/how-robert-eggers-researched-the-witch.html.

26. Rife, "*The Witch* Director Robert Eggers." For a sense of Eggers's extensive reading list on Puritan-era material culture, see Murphy, "That (Very, Very) Old Black Magic"; Emma Badame, "TIFF Interview: Robert Eggers and Anya Taylor Joy [*sic*] Talk *The Witch*," 21 September 2015, http://www.themarysue.com/tiff-interview-robert-eggers-and-taylor-joy-talk-the-witch/.

27. Brian Tallerico, "Cinematic Exorcism: Director Robert Eggers on 'The Witch,'" 17 February 2016, http://www.rogerebert.com/interviews/cinematic-exorcism-director-robert-eggers-on-the-witch

28. Eggers in *The Witch: A Primal Tale*.

29. Eggers in director's commentary track to the DVD edition of *The Witch*; here, he even notes the partial error that small boys would have been with their mothers, but they had too few settlers to make the gender separation clear in that case.

30. Eggers in the director's commentary track to the DVD edition of *The Witch*.

31. *Ibid.*

32. Lloyd E. Berry discusses the Puritan preference for the Geneva Bible in his "Introduction" to *The Geneva Bible: A Facsimile Edition* (Peabody, MA: Hendrickson, 2007).

33. Duca, "How Robert Eggers Wove."

34. Aaron Hillis, "How Director Robert Eggers Made 'The Witch" into a Genuinely Creepy Feminist Fable," *Vice*, 24 February 2016, http://www.vice.com/read/the-witch-director-robert-eggers-wants-to-terrify-people-into-believing-in-witches-again.

35. See John Cotton, *Spiritual Milk for Babes, Drawn out of the Breasts of Both Testaments*, esp. 2, 6–7, http://digitalcommons.unl.edu/cgi/viewcontent.cgi?article =1018&context=etas.

36. Murphy, "That (Very, Very) Old Black Magic." See Lewis Bayley, *The Practice of Piety: Directing a Christian How to Walk, that He May Please God*, 1631, http://www.documenta-catholica.eu/d_Bayly,%20Lewis%20-%20The%20Practice%20of %20Piety%20-%20EN.pdf.

37. Eggers, commentary track to the DVD edition of *The Witch*. See Charles E. Hambrick-Stowe, *The Practice of Piety: Puritan Devotional Disciplines in Seventeenth-Century New England* (Chapel Hill: University of North Carolina Press, 1982), 34–36.

38. Loren Rosson, "The Witch: Curses on Those Who Curse This Film," *Busybody* blog, 25 February 2016, https://rossonl.wordpress.com/2016/02/25/the-witch-curses-on-those-who-curse-this-film/. Eggers misremembers this as "from witch trials in Connecticut in the 1660s," while adding, "I wish I'd been a little more exact in my bibliography." See Duca, "How Robert Eggers Wove."

39. Eggers recalls merely that he found it in "a Jacobean pamphlet" and that he "thought it was nice and transportive"; see director's commentary on the DVD edition of *The Witch*. But that it was *A Most Certain, Strange, and True Discovery of a Witch* is clear, not only from the obvious resemblance, but from the fact that it is among the most widely reprinted frontispieces to a witch pamphlet from the period. The original is included in the range of witchcraft pamphlet frontispieces featured in the University of Glasgow Library's virtual exhibition "The Damned Art: The History of Witchcraft and Demonology," in the English section (http://www.gla.ac.uk /services/specialcollections/virtualexhibitions/damnedart/england/), although the rest of the collection merits perusal as well (and given Eggers's regular use of Continental materials—above all else in visualizing familiars like goats and hares—likely relevant to the film, too). Eggers also notes his use of collections of witch pamphlets and trial documents: "It's easy to find collections by contemporary historians of primary source materials, so I used a lot of those." Duca, "How Robert Eggers Wove." Among the handiest of those collections are Alan Charles Kors and Edward Peters, eds., *Witchcraft in Europe 400–1700: A Documentary History* (Philadelphia: University of Pennsylvania Press, 2001) and the classic earlier anthology, George Lincoln Burr, ed., *Narratives of the Witchcraft Cases 1648–1706* (New York: Harper & Row, 1914). The former, despite the title, includes significant American materials; the latter entirely focuses on the New World.

40. Patches, "The Scariest Movie."

41. *Ibid.* See also Murphy, "That (Very, Very) Old Black Magic." Among these sources, see especially Cotton Mather, *Memorable Providences, relating to Witchcrafts and Possessions* (1689) and, specifically on the Salem trials, *The Wonders of the Invisible World* (1693), both contained in Burr, *Narratives of the Witchcraft Cases*.

42. Eggers in *The Witch: A Primal Folktale*. Knap's 1671 possession is detailed in Samuel Willard, *A briefe account of a strange & unusuall Providence of God befallen to Elizabeth Knap of Groton* (1671), history.hanover.edu/texts/Willard-Knap.html. The closest connections to the film's depiction is in the form of the devil's temptations ("That the devil had oftentimes appeared to her, presenting the treaty of a Covenant, & preferring largely to her: viz, such things as suted her youthfull fancye, money, silks, fine cloathes, ease from labor to show her the whole world," 8) and that she cannot write her own name (when "hee … told her she must write her name in his booke, shee answered, shee could not Write, but hee told her he would direct her hand," 14). Knap also, in confessing her sins, mentions "profanation of the Sabbath &c." (15), one of the sins Thomasin also confesses early in the film. Willard in turn communicated his material to Increase Mather, who included the account in his *Remarkable Providences* (1684), included in Burr, *Narratives of the Witchcraft Cases*, with the Knap case appearing there on 21–23. (Increase Mather was Cotton Mather's father; witch belief apparently ran in the family.)

43. Wickman, "All *The Witch*'s most WTF Moments Explained."

44. Eggers in director's commentary to the DVD edition of *The Witch*. I have been unable to determine the source text (although the echoes of *Medea*, the tale of a much earlier witch, are clear).
45. *Ibid.*
46. Anya Taylor-Joy in *The Witch: A Primal Folktale*.
47. For a fascinating, very extended consideration of how each family member might be responsible for the witch of the film, see CraftD, "The Witch," *CraftD Movie Critiques*, 30 May 2016, https://craftdmoviecritiques.com/tag/witchcraft/.
48. Badame, "TIFF Interview."
49. The fungus hints at one of the other explanations of the Salem witch doings, although not one much favored by historians: ergot-induced hallucinations. Eggers knows that variation, too; he tells Forrest Wickman: "the rot on the corn is ergot, which is a hallucinogenic fungus, so if you wanted to take that route, you could." See "All *The Witch*'s Most WTF Moments," and, for a discussion of the ergot hypothesis, Demos, *Enemy Within*, 204–205.
50. R. Paul Stevens, *Doing God's Business: Meaning and Motivation for the Marketplace*, 47. The quotation from Calvin's *Institutes* is mis-cited, however; the actual passage on calling occurs at 3:10:6, not 3:11:6 as in Stevens's note. For a detailed account of Calvin's notion of calling and how it changed in Puritan usage, see also Robert S. Michaelsen, "Changes in the Puritan Concept of Calling or Vocation," *New England Quarterly* 26, no. 3 (1953): 315–36.
51. Stevens, *Doing God's Business* (Grand Rapids: William B. Eerdmans, 2006), 48.
52. Max Weber, *The Protestant Ethic and the Spirit of Capitalism* (1905; Gloucester, MA: Peter Smith, 1988), 110. Calvin's discussion of predestination can be found in *Institutes of the Christian Religion*, 1559 (http://www.sacred-texts.com/chr/calvin/inst/index.htm), 2:21–24. Weber's book has been as controversial as it has been influential. For a survey of the controversy it generated, see Ephraim Fischoff, "The Protestant Ethic and the Spirit of Capitalism: The History of a Controversy," in *The Protestant Ethic and Modernization: A Comparative View*, ed. S.N. Eisenstadt, 67–86 (New York: Basic Books, 1968) and, for examples of the controversy, the rest of the essays in the volume. For a more recent assessment, see William H. Swatos, Jr., and Lutz Kaelber, eds., *The Protestant Ethic Turns 100: Essays on the Centenary of the Weber Thesis* (Boulder: Paradigm, 2005). But it should be noted that, for Weber, the Calvinist sanction for worldly work leads, by a series of linkages, to the broader issue of the differential emergence of capitalist economies in parts, but not all, of Europe in the early-modern era. Thus, sanction for worldly work, combined with a strong Calvinist-encouraged ascetic emphasis (directly resulting in accumulation, rather than expenditure of wealth), along with more openness to new science, encourage the formation of the "Protestant work ethic" that, in turn, gives Protestant Europe the edge in the emergence of capitalism and later industrialism. Many of the challenges have been directed at these linkages, but they are irrelevant for our purposes. Whether Puritanism encourages capital accumulation matters less than the more root, and less contested, point that Calvinist doctrine sees "calling" in the full range of worldly work activities, not just in a calling to the priesthood.
53. For more on Puritan autobiographies and their form, see Owen Watkins, *The Puritan Experiences: Studies in Spiritual Autobiography* (New York: Schocken, 1972) and Patricia Caldwell, *The Puritan Conversion Narrative: The Beginnings of American Expression* (Cambridge: Cambridge University Press, 1983).
54. Weber, *Protestant Ethic*, 112.
55. Samuel Weber, "Money in Time: Thoughts on Credit and Crisis," in *The Cultural Life of Money: Culture and Conflict*, ed. Isabel Capeloa Gil and Helena Gonçalves da Silva, 23–46 (Berlin: Walter de Gruyter, 2015), 27.
56. Michaelsen, "Changes in the Puritan Concept of Calling," 328; the quoted passage is from English Puritan Richard Steele's aptly titled *The Tradesman's Calling* (1684).
57. Thomas, *Religion and the Decline of Magic*, 88. Michael Walzer sees it differently, arguing that "the anxiety of the Puritans led to a fearful demand for economic restriction (and political control) rather than to entrepreneurial activity." See Michael Walzer, "Puritanism as a Revolutionary Ideology," in *The Protestant Ethic and Modernization: A Comparative View*, ed. S.N. Eisenstadt (New York: Basic Books, 1968), 114. But Walzer seems again more concerned with the linkages to capitalism than with the self-evaluating process concerning one's personal salvation. For that basic premise, the evidence favors Thomas (and Weber, and the other Weber). Arjun Appadurai gives the argument a more contemporary twist, seeing it in terms of "derivatives": "the Calvinist approach to profit-making in this world—absent any possibility of certainty about one's station as saved or damned—is a derivative gamble in the face of radical uncertainty." See *Banking on Words: The Failure of Language in the Age of Derivative Finance* (Chicago: University of Chicago Press, 2015), 42.
58. Director's commentary to the DVD edition. Eggers is referring specifically to the way the family set-up in the house, sex-segregated when at the table, echoes that of the plantation. I am reading it more broadly here.

Bibliography

Appadurai, Arjun. *Banking on Words: The Failure of Language in the Age of Derivative Finance*. Chicago: University of Chicago Press, 2015.

Badame, Emma. "TIFF Interview: Robert Eggers and Anya Taylor Joy [sic] Talk *The Witch*." 21 September 2015. http://www.themarysue.com/tiff-interview-robert-eggers-and-taylor-joy-talk-the-witch/.
Baker, Emerson W. *A Storm of Witches: The Salem Trials and the American Experience*. Oxford: Oxford University Press, 2015.
Bayley, Lewis. *The Practice of Piety: Directing a Christian How to Walk, that He May Please God*. 1631 ed. http://www.documenta-catholica.eu/d_Bayly,%20Lewis%20-%20The%20Practice%20of%20Piety%20-%20EN.pdf.
Berry, Lloyd E. "Introduction." *The Geneva Bible: A Facsimile Edition*. Peabody, MA: Hendrickson, 2007.
Bitel, Anton. "Voices of the Undead: Robert Eggers on The Witch." *Sight & Sound* (4 July 2016), http://www.bfi.org.uk/news-opinion/sight-sound-magazine/interviews/robert-eggers-witch.
Boyer, Paul, and Stephen Nissenbaum. *Salem Possessed: The Social Origins of Witchcraft*. Cambridge: Harvard University Press, 1974.
Boyer, Paul, and Stephen Nissenbaum. "*Salem Possessed* in Retrospect." *William and Mary Quarterly* 3d series 65, no. 3 (2008): 314–24.
Burr, George Lincoln, ed. *Narratives of the Witchcraft Cases 1648–1706*. New York: Harper & Row, 1914.
Caldwell, Patricia. *The Puritan Conversion Narrative: The Beginnings of American Expression*. Cambridge: Cambridge University Press, 1983.
Calvin, John. *Institutes of the Christian Religion*. 1559 ed. http://www.sacred-texts.com/chr/calvin/inst/index.htm.
Campbell, Kenneth L. *Windows into Men's Souls: Religious Nonconformity in Tudor and Early Stuart England*. Lanham, MD: Lexington Books, 2012.
Cotton, John. *Spiritual Milk for Babes, Drawn out of the Breasts of Both Testaments*. 1646. Title varies somewhat in different editions. Online at University of Nebraska, Lincoln, Digital Commons, http://digitalcommons.unl.edu/cgi/viewcontent.cgi?article=1018&context=etas.
CraftD. "The Witch." *CraftD Movie Critiques*, 30 May 2016. https://craftdmoviecritiques.com /tag/witchcraft/.
Crucchiola, Jordan. "How *The Witch*'s Director Made His Film So Terrifying." *Wired*, 20 February 2016. https://www.wired.com/2016/02/robert-eggers-set-design-how-he-made-the-witch-so-scary/.
"The Damned Art: The History of Witchcraft and Demonology." University of Glasgow Library online exhibiton. http://www.gla.ac.uk/services/specialcollections/virtualexhibitions/damnedart.
Demos, John. *The Enemy Within: A Short History of Witch-Hunting*. London: Penguin, 2008.
Demos, John. *Entertaining Satan: Witchcraft and the Culture of Early New England*. Oxford: Oxford University Press, 1982.
Detweiler, Robert. "Shifting Perspectives on the Salem Witches." *History Teacher* 8, no. 4 (1975): 596–610.
Duca, Lauren. "How Robert Eggers Wove the Nightmares of *The Witch* Out of Historical Documents." *Vulture*, 18 February 2016. http://www.vulture.com /2016/02/how-robert-eggers-researched-the-witch.html.
Fischoff, Ephraim. "The Protestant Ethic and the Spirit of Capitalism: The History of a Controversy." In S.N. Eisenstadt, ed., *The Protestant Ethic and Modernization: A Comparative View*, 67–86. New York: Basic Books, 1968.
Garrett, Clarke. "Women and Witches: Patterns of Analysis." *Signs* 3, no. 2 (1977): 461–70.
Gaskill, Martin. "Witchcraft in Early Modern Kent: Stereotype and the Background to Accusations." In Jonathan Barry, Marianne Hester, and Gareth Roberts, eds., *Witchcraft in Early Modern Europe: Studies in Culture and Belief*, 257–287. Cambridge: Cambridge University Press, 1996.
Hambrick-Stowe, Charles E. *The Practice of Piety: Puritan Devotional Disciplines in Seventeenth-Century New England*. Chapel Hill: University of North Carolina Press, 1982.
Hillis, Aaron. "How Director Robert Eggers Made 'The Witch' into a Genuinely Creepy Feminist Fable." *Vice*, 24 February 2016. http://www.vice.com/read/the-witch-director-robert-eggers-wants-to-terrify-people-into-believing-in-witches-again.
Karlsen, Carl F. *The Devil in the Shape of a Woman: Witchcraft in Colonial New England*. New York: W.W. Norton, 1987.
Kors, Alan Charles, and Edward Peters, eds. *Witchcraft in Europe 400–1700: A Documentary History*. Philadelphia: University of Pennsylvania Press, 2001.
MacFarlane, Alan. *Witchcraft in Tudor and Stuart England: A Regional and Comparative Study*. 1970; 2d ed. London: Routledge, 1999.
Martin, Rachel. "'The Witch' Achieves Puritan American Horror Without The Gore." 6 March 2016. http://www.npr.org/2016/03/06/469383396/-the-witch-achieves-puritan-american-horror-without-the-gore
Michaelsen, Robert S. "Changes in the Puritan Concept of Calling or Vocation." *New England Quarterly* 26, no. 3 (1953): 315–36.
Murphy, Mekado. "That (Very, Very) Old Black Magic in 'The Witch.'" *New York Times*, 18 February 2016, nytimes.com.
Patches, Matt. "The Scariest Movie at Sundance: How Robert Eggers Made the Horrifying, Historically Accurate 'the Witch.'" *Grantland*, January 29, 2015. http://grantland.com/hollywood-prospectus/the-scariest-movie-at-sundance-how-robert-eggers-made-the-horrifying-historically-accurate-the-witch/.
Reklis, Kathryn. "On Media: Theological Horror." *Christian Century*, 11 May 2016, 58–59.

Rife, Katie. "*The Witch* Director Robert Eggers on Fellini, Feminism, and Period-Accurate Candlelight." *A.V. Club*, 23 February 2016. http://www.avclub.com/article/witch-director-robert-eggers-fellini-feminism-and-232450.

Rosson, Loren. "The Witch: Curses on Those Who Curse This Film." Busybody blog, 25 February 2016. https://rossonl.wordpress.com/2016/02/25/the-witch-curses-on-those-who-curse-this-film/.

Showalter, Elaine. "Hysteria, Feminism, and Gender." In Sander L. Gilman, Helen King, Roy Porter, G.S. Rousseau, and Elaine Showalter, *Hysteria Beyond Freud*, 286–344. Berkeley: University of California Press, 1993.

Sims, David. "Female Freedom and Fury in *The Witch*." *Atlantic*, 24 February 2016. http://www.theatlantic.com/entertainment/archive/2016/02/robert-eggers-the-witch-female-empowerment/470844/.

Stevens, R. Paul. *Doing God's Business: Meaning and Motivation for the Marketplace.* Grand Rapids: William B. Eerdmans, 2006.

Swatos, William H., Jr., and Lutz Kaelber, eds. *The Protestant Ethic Turns 100: Essays on the Centenary of the Weber Thesis.* Boulder: Paradigm, 2005.

Tallerico, Brian. "Cinematic Exorcism: Director Robert Eggers on 'The Witch.'" 17 February 2016. http://www.rogerebert.com/interviews/cinematic-exorcism-director-robert-eggers-on-the-witch.

Thomas, Keith. *Religion and the Decline of Magic: Studies in Popular Beliefs in Sixteenth and Seventeenth Century England.* Oxford: Oxford University Press, 1971.

Walzer, Michael. "Puritanism as a Revolutionary Ideology." In S.N. Eisenstadt, ed., *The Protestant Ethic and Modernization: A Comparative View.* New York: Basic Books, 1968.

Watkins, Owen. *The Puritan Experiences: Studies in Spiritual Autobiography.* New York: Schocken, 1972.

Weber, Max. *The Protestant Ethic and the Spirit of Capitalism.* 1905; rpt. Gloucester, MA: Peter Smith, 1988.

Weber, Samuel. "Money in Time: Thoughts on Credit and Crisis." In Isabel Capeloa Gil and Helena Gonçalves da Silva, eds., *The Cultural Life of Money: Culture and Conflict*, 23–46. Berlin: Walter de Gruyter, 2015.

Wickman, Forrest. "All *The Witch*'s Most WTF Moments, Explained: A Spoiler-Filled Interview with the Director." *Slate*, February 23, 2016. http://www.slate.com/blogs/browbeat/2016/02/23/the_witch_director_robert_eggers_on_the_real_history_behind_the_movie_s.html.

Willard, Samuel. *A briefe account of a strange & unusuall Providence of God befallen to Elizabeth Knap of Groton.* 1671. history.hanover.edu/texts/Willard-Knap.html.

The Witch: A New-England Folktale. Written and directed by Robert Eggers. A24 Films, 2015.

Emily Rose Died for Your Sins
Paranormal Piety, Medieval Theology and Ambiguous Cinematic Soteriology

KEVIN J. WETMORE, JR.

Losing control of a child to the evils of the world after he or she leaves home is every parent's nightmare. Losing control of a child to vicious, taunting demons utterly redefines that fear. *The Exorcism of Emily Rose* (2005) recounts the last days of a small-town Catholic girl who becomes possessed during her first semester at college. Tortured in body and mind, Emily Rose becomes a grotesque embodiment of evil. Her family's last hope for her—and their—salvation is engaging the parish priest to perform an exorcism, a rite that subsequently kills her. The film narrates her story in flashback, through the trial of Father Richard Moore, the priest who conducted the exorcism. In a letter penned just before her death, Emily reveals that she received a visitation from the Virgin Mary and was offered a choice: die in peace, or choose to die suffering and, through that suffering, inspire people to embrace Christianity. "People say that God is dead, but how can they think that if I show them the Devil?" she asks. *The Exorcism of Emily Rose* is a horror film, but—like Emily herself, who is possessed by the entity inside her—it also harbors a theological discourse that increasingly manifests itself as the film unfolds.

"Based on a true story," the trailer and advertisements for the film proclaimed, nodding obliquely at the story of Annaliesa Michel, a German girl who died during an exorcism in 1976,[1] and borrowing a marketing strategy used for decades to draw audiences to exploitation films. Scenes suggesting possession dominate the promotional materials: sinister figures and scenes of an increasingly terrified Emily fill the screen, along with repeated assertions that demons are possessing her and threatening the very souls of those around her. At the time of its release, the film was, in fact, frequently compared with *The Exorcist*. Much like its classic predecessor, the film's narrative is shot through with images designed to terrify and disgust the viewer (depictions of Emily eating bugs, having seizures, watching the people around her transform into demonic monsters, and seeing Satan in a storm). Its storyline, however, promotes a strongly Christian philosophy. It suggests that her death was purposeful—not only allowed, but mandated, by God as proof of the existence of supernatural evil, and by extension, the Divine—and designed to reinforce belief in God and Christ.

The film (intentionally or not) employs medieval theology in order to both create horror and promote Christianity. Emily's possession evokes the grotesque afflictions of medieval martyrdom: the purification of the soul through the torture of the body and mortification of the flesh. Both Emily's possessed body and the supernatural entities she perceives are presented as monstrous, and, as Timothy Beal observes in *Religion and Its Monsters*, the monstrous can be "a figure of divine revelation or an envoy of the sacred." Emily's possessed form is thus monstrous both in the mundane sense, as its graphic destruction generates visceral horror, and as a revelation from God. Audiences are meant to be horrified by the tortures inflicted on Emily's body and mind, but also—as a result of its encounter with them—to reconsider their ideas about the immanent presence of the divine and the diabolical in the physical world. In order to deliver its message, however, the film must overcome a substantial obstacle: the fact that the audience shares neither the precepts of its medieval theology nor the larger worldview with which they were interwoven.

The film uses defense attorney Erin Bruner (Laura Linney) to model and personalize this process of reconsideration. A self-professed agnostic, she is obliged by her role in the trial (and Father Moore's insistence on a plea of not guilty) to argue that Emily's possession may be just what he claims: a genuine instance of demonic possession, and thus an intrusion of supernatural evil into everyday life. As the trial progresses, her disbelief weakens in the face of Moore's testimony and that of expert witnesses she calls on his behalf. Moore also expresses his belief in the presence of supernatural evil directly to Erin, warning her that "there are forces surrounding this trial: dark, powerful forces. You must be careful. *Watch your step.*" Erin protests that she has nothing to fear ("I'm agnostic, remember?") but the priest is adamant: "Demons exist, whether you believe in them or not." Outside the courtroom, Erin begins to experience inexplicable disturbances that disrupt her sleep each night at 3:00 a.m.: the "witching hour" when Emily suffered her first attack and when, Father Moore explain, demons emerge from the darkness to mock and torment the faithful. By the time she delivers her closing argument, designed to convince jurors that Emily *may* have been the victim of demons, she has accepted that possibility herself. Erin thus completes, in the course of the film, the journey from unbelief to belief that, Douglas Cowan argues, lies at the heart of the exorcism-film subgenre: letting go of "the arrogance of rationality," discovering her faith, and accepting the reality of God.[2]

No such journey is possible for prosecuting attorney Ethan Thomas (Campbell Scott), who—more than Satan or any of his demonic minions—fills the role of Adversary. Thomas is selected for the case because he is a church-going man, but a Methodist, rather than a Catholic, and so, skeptical of Father Moore's dogmatic beliefs. The trial is thus framed in terms of his scorn for Catholic explanations of Emily's experiences, and his rejection of them in favor of scientific explanations. Thomas has no room in his worldview for miracles, demons, or actual divine presence, and prefers his religion to be intellectual, rather than phenomenological. He is a legalist, saying of the plea bargain his office offers Father Moore: "If he's a man of God, then personally I think he's even more subject to the laws of moral behavior and punishment. If it were up to me he'd get no deal at all." If Father Moore does not take the deal, then Thomas assures him that he will "seek the maximum." There is no room in Thomas's Christianity for mercy or forgiveness. He is both the least Christ-like character in the film and the one most contemptuous of Emily's and Moore's Catholicism itself.

The result is a film (and trial) that, *Rashomon*-like, presents Emily's possession from multiple perspectives, including Father Moore's and Ethan Thomas's. Emily's own perspective is never shown directly. Thomas claims that he is in court to speak for her, but he does not; he speaks for himself. Father Moore speaks for himself, as well. Emily's story is thus always mediated through others. The closest we come is when Father Moore reads a letter from Emily, which we see dramatized. Even then, they are Emily's words in Moore's voice. The film, cannily, never shows "what really happened" but offers dramatizations of possibilities.

Paradoxically, using the trial as a framing device results in the focus continually being pulled back to the ambiguity and uncertainty surrounding the actual possession. Alternate possibilities are shown in flashback, as well. We see Emily under demonic assault in her dorm room—struggling against an invisible adversary that tugs the covers off her and presses her down against the bed: overpowered, unable to move, and screaming in terror—but are then immediately shown the same scene with Emily, in the midst of an epileptic seizure, achieving the same body position and facial expression. Both narratives are possible. Unlike *The Exorcist*, and anticipating such films as *The Last Exorcism*, the possession in this film is not a certain thing. Regan MacNeil was obviously and definitely possessed—Emily Rose, perhaps not so much.

Despite the filmmaker's championing of a Christian interpretation of the events the film depicts, the "miracle" of Emily's deliverance and inspiration appears to be not so much a confirmation of the divine, as a tribute to the self-sacrifice of a human being, making Emily a female echo of Christ. The film asks audiences to accept the possibility of a non-scientific, non-medical explanation for what happened, and argues that one need not believe in the devil to believe in the reality of miracles and the possibility of redemption.

Emily Rose as Suffering Medieval Saint

Donna Yarri argues that *The Exorcism of Emily Rose* "raises a number of significant questions for religion: 'Do demons actually exist?' 'What does it mean to have a religious experience?' 'How does one prove or disprove spiritual experiences and what is the redemptive significance, if any, of suffering?'"[3] The answer in all these cases, of course, is that faith is a factor. Ethan Thomas offers the rational, scientific argument, while Erin Bruner, Father Moore, and especially expert witness anthropologist Dr. Sadira Adani (Shohreh Aghdashloo)—who testifies to the cultural reality of spirit possession and exorcism—argue that one must make a leap of faith in order to perceive and share in the divine.[4]

Emily's own experiences, the film illustrates, were shaped by her background: She came from humble origins—raised by her parents, along with three sisters, on a farm—and had experienced little of the wider world until she left for college. A devout Roman Catholic, very pious and spiritual, who attended Church-run schools all her life. Her experiences were, accordingly, framed by her faith. She was threatened, then possessed, by demons, then was granted a vision of the Virgin Mary and received the stigmata, the wounds of Christ. All of this, Father Moore contends, confirms her as a living saint and someone blessed by God. Emily experienced both the divine and the diabolical as genuine, real experiences. Indeed, she was the only one who saw the visions and who experienced the horrors of possession firsthand.

Emily embodies a particular trope of early Christianity, that of the suffering Chris-

The destroyed body of Emily Rose (Jennifer Carpenter) and Ethan Thomas (Campbell Scott), the unbeliever in *The Exorcism of Emily Rose* (2005). Is she a victim of faith, or a medieval martyr rejected by a Protestant prosecutor?

tian. As Judith Perkins observes: "The triumph of Christianity was, in part at least, a triumph of a particular representation of the Self."[5] That view of the Self was "the Christian as sufferer: to be Christian was to suffer and die."[6] Martyrs reject the idea that they are victims; early martyrs, in fact, championed "pain as empowering and death a victory," just as Emily does in her letter to Father Moore.[7] Indeed, the more tortured the body, the greater the Christian. The early and medieval Church focused on the torments done to the bodies of the Christian martyrs, as does the trial of Father Moore. Ethan Thomas similarly opens his case by showing before-and-after photos of Emily. Her high school portrait shows a lovely young woman, full of life; a photo taken on the day she died shows a broken body, emaciated and dirty, covered in blood, and missing teeth. The line connecting the two is evident in scenes throughout the film—the initial attack in Emily's dorm room, subsequent attacks in her hospital room and the campus chapel, and finally the exorcism itself—that show her limbs being twisted, her body bent backward seemingly to the point of snapping, and her face contorted in agony. She repeatedly throws herself out of beds, against solid objects, and (during the exorcism) through the glass of a second-story window and into the farmyard below. "She's burning up!" her father exclaims, after he and Father Moore have caught up with her, suggesting that, unseen, the demon is also, invisibly, tormenting her from within.

Such displays, though not uncommon in horror films, run counter to prevailing trends in religious representation. The modern convention is not to dwell on the physical details of suffering (lest they cause the audience to turn away, or distract them from the martyr's holiness), but for medieval audiences the details of suffering were the point, and proof of the sufferer's holiness. We are "lifted from suffering by accepting it," the early Christians believed.[8] Suffering brings salvation in the form of Christ's death, and, in the Catholic tradition, human suffering can be offered up to God. Emily, in this view, will come to accept her suffering and find it bearable, inasmuch as her suffering has a purpose—to bring others to Christ. She is empowered by her suffering, and by extension, she is empowered by her possession, which is also a rather medieval concept.

The 13th and 14th centuries saw a transformation in female spirituality and an increase in women's piety in the form of devotion to the Virgin Mary as well as to other female saints and mystics.[9] Convents saw an increase in women joining, along with an increase in the preparation of devotional material for laywomen. Ironically, Brian Levack suggests, because of this expanded emphasis on female piety, the Middle Ages also saw "a dramatic increase in the number of possessions."[10] Women "submitted themselves to a spiritual discipline that made unrealistic demands on them and led them to believe they were possessed by demons."[11]

A huge number of churches were dedicated to Mary Magdalene, a woman possessed by seven devils herself.[12] The ranks of female mystics and theologians also expanded, and "suffering mystics"—women who submitted willingly to bodily torments in the belief that their suffering release souls from Purgatory—proliferated. This category of female mystics, including historical figures such as Catherine of Sienna and Marie d'Aigu, experienced the divine through their torment, and thus took delight in it. During their lives, the type of spirit afflicting them remained an open question in the Church: was it holy or demonic? The signs are often the same: speaking in ancient or dead languages (as Emily does), levitation, bodily injuries and manipulations, trance-like states, an ability to go without food or water, superhuman feats of strength, and so on. It is only in the rejection of things holy that one can tell a demoniac from a saint.

Emily's descent into possession begins after she turns 18, entering the university— and a wider world of secularism, dating, and sexual awakening—for the first time. Unhappy and out of place at the university, unsettled by constant pressure to engage, intellectually and socially, with an unfamiliar world, she undergoes a spiritual crisis that ultimately leads to her possession. One of its most disturbing manifestations, in fact, occurs in a classroom. As she sits listening and taking notes during a science lecture, she witnesses the face of a fellow student turning demonic and terrifying, his mouth gaping into a round black maw and dark liquid pouring from his suddenly black, bottomless eye sockets. Fleeing the classroom and running into the dark rainy night, she watches the faces of everyone she passes flash into a similar demonic visage. Even the middle-aged women praying in the church where she seeks sanctuary transform, before her eyes, into demons, leaving her a terrified stranger in a "familiar" world that has suddenly become grotesque and terrifying. She finds a boyfriend who shares her values, but even he is a reminder that the complexities of courtship, marriage, and children lay in her not-so-distant future. In the Middle Ages, Levack notes: "Sexual desire and guilt for sexual transactions, both of which impeded the achievement of female sanctity, lay at the root of many female possessions in the Catholic areas" of Europe.[13] Emily's possession during her brief time at the university has similar roots.

Once it is determined she is possessed, Emily loses her agency. She might have experienced some level of freedom at college, but the patriarchal structures of the Catholic Church and rural America rule at home. Her family turns her over to Father Moore, their parish priest, and give him complete power over her, which he exercises by admonishing them to "do *exactly* as I say" and not engage directly with the entity that controls her. Though there are four other women in the household, her mother and sisters are absent from the exorcism and barely present for the trial. It is the priest, Emily's father, and her boyfriend who dominate the scene when she becomes possessed. *All* of them, however, are ultimately powerless in the face of Emily's spiritual experiences. They cannot help her, let alone save her from the spirits that possess her; indeed, they can barely hold her down during the exorcism. As the demons possessing Emily begin to emerge, she breaks the bonds that tie her to the bed and hurls those nearest her across the room. The others stand fast, chanting "and lead us not into temptation, but..." and the demons within her scream in response "but deliver us from EEEVIL!!" The lights go out and six cats—one for each demon—run into the room. They surround the priest and, as Emily growls at him. "One, two, three, four, five, six. One, two, three, four, five, six...," they attack, knocking Father Moore to the floor, allowing Emily and her demons to escape through the window.

The possessed, Levack notes, often belong to "subordinate groups in society," most notably women and the poor.[14] Both possession and extreme spirituality allowed women to transcend the social order and have power and authority over men in a manner no other situation could allow or create. It is as saint that Emily finally achieves control over her life. Through her possession and Mary's invitation to die in order to bring others to salvation, she transcends the secondary role accorded women by both the Church and her rural upbringing.

Emily Rose Died So That We Might Live: "Performing" Exorcisms, Mariology and Mimetic Soteriology

In his first letter to the Corinthians, Paul laments that he has become a *"theatron,"* a public display: "For it seems to me that God has put us apostles on display at the end of the procession, like those condemned to die in the arena. We have been made a spectacle to the whole universe, to angels as well as to human beings."[15] The martyrs who followed Paul, however, *wanted* to be spectacles; they sought to be put on public display in order to lead others to Christ. They played the roles of Christian and martyr, believing that if they played them well enough, their audiences might be moved to convert. Emily's possession and exorcism work the same way.

Possession and exorcism are first and foremost a performance, as Levack notes: "All possessions, not just those that were feigned or otherwise volitional, were theatrical productions in which the demoniacs and also their families, neighbors, physicians, pastors and exorcists played their assigned roles."[16] The words and actions of the demoniac are a performance by the demon meant dramatize its complete control over them. "We won't be dealing with Emily tonight," Father Moore tells Emily's boyfriend, and it quickly becomes clear what they *are* dealing with: not one demon, but six. The demons present themselves in turn, speaking through Emily: each in a different language and each in terms designed to designed to terrify the faithful and drive them to despair. One identifies itself by the ancient name of Belial, another names itself as Lucifer, and still others present themselves as the demons that possessed Cain, Nero, and Judas Iscariot. Father Moore, playing the role assigned to the exorcist, cautions the others not to be swayed by this ostentatious display of pure supernatural evil. His role in the drama is to remain resolute in the face of the demon(s), demonstrating unswerving faith in God's power to drive them out and invoking it through prayer, incantations, and the use of his crucifix and holy water. His will, even when combined with that of Emily's father and boyfriend, proves insufficient, and the exorcism fails, but the performance does not end. It only pauses, before entering a final act in which the Virgin Mary herself plays a pivotal role.

The Catholic Church promulgates four dogmas regarding Mary, the mother of Jesus: first, that she is the Divine Mother and *theotokos* ("God-bearer"); second, that she is a perpetual virgin; third, that she was born without the stain of original sin; and fourth, that she did not have a bodily death but was assumed into heaven.[17] In the eighties and nineties conservative forces within the Catholic Church advocated for the addition of a fifth and final dogma, that Mary is "co-redemptrix, mediatrix, and advocate." This role, posited during the Middle Ages and prominent in Catholic folklore for centuries afterward, thus gained official sanction. Women suddenly were perceived as having a role to play in salvation, and Mary herself was perceived by some as being Christ's equal as a redeemer of humankind.

The idea that martyrs other than Christ can inspire and bring people to salvation, hinted at throughout the film, takes center stage at the conclusion of the trial when Father Moore reads Emily's letter in court. She describes herself wandering across the mist-shrouded family farm the morning after the failed exorcism, developing stigmata, and seeing herself as if from the outside. Then, she reports:

> I heard a voice calling my name. It was the Blessed Holy Mother of God. And when I looked at her she smiled at me and said, "Emily, Heaven is not blind to your pain." I asked the Blessed Mother, "Why do I suffer like this? Why did the demons not leave me tonight?" She said, "I'm sorry, Emily, the demons are going to stay where they are." Then she said, "You can come with me in peace, free of your bodily form or you can choose to continue this. You will suffer greatly, but through you, many will come to see that the realm of the spirit is real. The choice is yours."
>
> "I choose to stay."

There is a good deal of medieval theology present in this conversation, particularly in the construction of Emily as a sort of savior of the lost—a minor co-redeemer. She chooses suffering and martyrdom, and she does so willingly, as a spectacle, just like Christ and the early martyrs. "Through her," the film's audiences are told, "many" people will come to God, or at least perceive Him as real.

Interestingly, the offer is made, not through Christ, but through the Virgin Mary. Emily will be able, like Mary, to intercede with God on behalf of people. Problematically, Emily's questions of why this all happened go unanswered, except for the implication that the ends justify the means. The idea of suffering for others is at the heart of this offer. If Emily chooses to go with Mary, she will no longer suffer, but her suffering will have been for nothing. If Emily chooses to suffer and then die, then her death will save others and give her experience meaning.

The family farm becomes Emily's own, private Garden of Gethsemane, where she asks that the cup be taken from her, but then willingly chooses to be sacrificed so that others may be saved. Father Moore, in the aftermath of her death, becomes her hagiographer—Paul to her Christ. He makes it his mission to tell her story, evangelize in her name, and use her life and death as an example of the spiritual reality of God and Satan. He gladly accepts the accusations of negligent homicide, declines to enter a plea of guilty, and makes no effort to mitigate or justify his actions other than asserting the reality of the possession and the necessity of the exorcism. "What I care about," he tells Erin, "is telling Emily Rose's story," and he does so: first by ensuring, through his "not guilty" plea, that a public trial takes place, and then by reading Emily's letter and so allowing her to "speak" for herself.

If, as Douglas Cowan suggests, the film could be called "The Conversion of Erin Bruner," it could equally be called "The Martyrdom of Father Richard Moore." Like all martyrs, he is put on trial and found guilty, but achieves victory through this seeming defeat. His martyrdom, however, is not physical but social, and he is martyred not for his faith in Christ but for his faith in Emily. She, like Christ, died for our sins, and he is more than willing to sacrifice himself for her.

Doubting Ethan Thomas, Antichrist

Emily Rose and Father Moore make the choices they make because they recognize that their deep, uncomplicated faith in God is becoming a rarity in the modern world. They set out act as witnesses to God's presence and engagement in the world, hoping to reach—and change the minds of—those who acknowledge neither. The rival attorneys both fall into that group, and Douglas E. Cowan sees the trial as "a set piece battle between contested worldviews: the rational, scientific view that Emily was psycho-epileptic and died because she stopped taking the medications designed to control her condition, and the religious view, which has not closed itself off to the potential reality of the unseen order, but that the prosecutor persistently derides as 'based on archaic, irrational superstition.'"[18] The prosecution's objection to the defense's arguments is ontological: that they are resting their case on the reality of spiritual experiences and the premise that the supernatural, both divine and diabolical, is present and active in our world.

Lead prosecutor Ethan Thomas, whose name is a combination of the Hebrew word for "strong" (Ethan) and the name of the doubting Apostle (Thomas) who would not believe in the resurrection until he touched the risen Christ himself, is selected to try Father Moore. He sings in his church choir and teaches Sunday school, but lacks Moore's faith in manifestations of the divine. He is a man of dogma and ritual, not mysticism and experience.

Emily has seen the very things Thomas has been told by his faith he must believe and accept, yet he does not believe she has actually had these experiences. He thus argues against a lived faith in favor of an intellectual, rationalizing one, asserting that science and rationality form the only acceptable evidence when one is dealing with religion. Like his namesake, he speaks as an apostle, but withholds actual belief until he can put his hands in the wounds. He is not interested in justice or mercy (Christian values) but rather in punishment for transgressions (legalism), and regards Father Moore with the contempt historically reserved for heretics.

The trial, however, is not a conflict between science and religion, since both Thomas and Moore are religious men. Rather, it is a conflict between different faith traditions and perceptions: Thomas's Methodism and Moore's Catholicism. Thomas's role in the trial seems to be not only to argue Moore's guilt, but to refute tenets of the Catholic faith. Moore sees Emily as a saint, but Thomas, like his namesake, doubts that any religious significance attaches to Emily's experiences: "Emily suffered because she was sick, not because she was a saint." As a Methodist he has a very different conception of saints than Father Moore.

Methodists have no mechanism for canonization, their perception of sainthood includes anyone who "exemplifie[s] the Christian life. In this sense, every Christian can be considered a saint."[19] Methodist doctrine holds that "we do not pray to saints, nor do we believe they serve as mediators to God."[20] Mary's (and Emily's) role as intercessor and co-redeemer likewise has no place in Methodist theology and thus in Thomas's religious universe. Whereas Father Moore sees Emily as both saint and mediator, therefore, Thomas sees her solely as a victim (of Catholicism).

Thomas likewise scoffs at the possibility of supernatural evil, and thus at exorcism. The Catholic Church, however, sees exorcism not as a sacrament, but a "sacramental": one of a class of "sacred signs that bear a resemblance to the sacraments. They signify effects, particularly of a spiritual nature which are obtained through the intercession of the Church."[21] The Catechism of the Catholic Church states: "Exorcism is directed at the expulsion of demons or the liberation from demonic possession through the spiritual authority which Jesus entrusted to his Church. Illness, especially psychological illness, is a very different matter; treating this is the concern of medical science. Therefore, before an exorcism is performed, it is important to ascertain that one is dealing with the presence of the Evil One and not an illness."[22]

So it is in *Emily Rose*. Doctor Graham Cartwright, a physician brought in by Father Moore to consult with Emily before the exorcism and be present during the rite, later tells Erin Bruner: "That girl was not schizophrenic, she was not epileptic, or any combination of the two. I've seen hundreds of people with those problems. They have terrible afflictions, of course, but they don't scare me.... I examined that girl before I drove back to the city. She was lucid and completely aware of the separate entity inside her. When she wasn't in its grasp, she was totally herself and completely normal, which contradicts the medical statement." Cartwright is killed in an accident before he can testify, leading Thomas to dismiss his claims, but Father Moore nonetheless met the Church's requirements for ensuring the possession was real and the exorcism called for—that it was, by the dictates of Catholicism, justified, necessary, and valid. The fact that the Catholic Church posits possession and exorcism as reality, however, is irrelevant to Thomas. Moore's faithfulness to his own tradition is, in Thomas's perception, a commitment to a false and misguided religion. It does not matter what Moore thought or what the Catholic Church believes—they are wrong.

Full of contempt for Catholic culture and theology, Thomas presents an overwhelming case, but justice, for him, is not tempered with mercy. The idea that our sins could, thanks to another's sacrifice on our behalf, already be forgiven eludes him, and his desire to see Father Moore go to prison for 20 years—at his age, a life sentence—remains undiminished. For Thomas, no forgiveness is possible, but the jury believes otherwise, thwarting his intentions by pairing their guilty verdict with a recommended sentence of time served. Judge Brewster's remarkable pronouncement—"You are guilty, Father Moore, and you are free to go"—sums up the legal paradox, but also the central message of Christianity: As sinners, we too are guilty, and we are free to go.

The end result is thus as ambiguous as the other aspects of the trial. We do not know if Emily was actually possessed; we do not know if she is actually a saint; we do not know if her vision of the Virgin Mary was objectively real, or simply real enough to an intensely devout young woman suffering from an altered mental state. Father Moore is found guilty, but it is no victory for Thomas, who sought punishment for Moore's sins. The jury, to the delight of the archdiocese, sees the guilty verdict itself as punishment enough. Moore's release from legal purgatory makes him, in fact, the first person freed by Emily's intercession.

Conclusion

Judged as a mainstream horror film, *The Exorcism of Emily Rose* is resolutely unconventional. It makes limited use of gore, jump scares, elaborate special effects, and other elements of contemporary horror, and the entire last section of the story passes without any sinister happenings or, indeed, any supernatural events at all. The exorcism itself is a failure—Emily is not freed from the possessing demons, and she dies.[23] The failure, however, is a victory in disguise, for Emily's death was the point all along. If she had been exorcized, no one would have believed it and she would have saved no one. In what was, perhaps, the ultimate parallel to Christ, Emily had to die. Erin Bruner and Father Moore visit Emily's grave, where he explains that the inscription on her tombstone is a quotation from Philippians 2:12 that she repeated to him the night she died: "Work out your own Salvation, with fear and trembling."

Erin Bruner's defense of Father Moore (which, like the exorcism, ultimately fails) is that we must remain open to the possibility of the reality of the diabolical and divine. In her closing statement she repeatedly uses the word "maybe" and the phrase "Isn't it possible?" The film—a medieval tale for a modern audience—takes a similar position. It does not ask viewer to believe in the devil, only to be open to the possibility of one. John Thavis states: "In an age in which Christianity is supposed to be the faith of reason, many are still fascinated by the possibility of miracles, apparitions, encounters with the devil and other signs of the supernatural."[24] *Emily Rose* argues we should move beyond mere fascination with such things and recognize them for what they are: *monstrums*: messages that break into this world from the realm of the divine. We need not abandon reason, but *Emily Rose* argues the cliché: God does indeed work in mysterious ways.

Notes

1. See Felicitas D. Goodman, *The Exorcism of Annaliese Michel* (Eugene, OR: Resource Publications, 1981).
2. Douglas E. Cowan, *Sacred Terror: Religion and Horror on the Silver Screen* (Waco: Baylor University Press, 2008), 252.
3. Donna Yarri, "Film Review: *The Exorcism of Emily Rose*," *Journal of Religion and Film* 10, no. 1 (April 2006), http://www.unomaha.edu/jrf/vol10no1/Reviews/emilyRose.htm. Accessed September 22, 2008.
4. *Ibid.*
5. Judith Perkins, *The Suffering Self: Pain and Narrative Representation in the Early Christian Era* (New York: Routledge, 1995), 11.
6. *Ibid.*, 24.
7. *Ibid.*, 122–23.
8. *Ibid.*, 130.
9. Carolyn Walker Bynum, *Jesus as Mother: Studies in the Spirituality of the High Middle Ages* (Berkeley: University of California Press, 1982). 18.
10. Brian P. Levack, *The Devil Within: Possession and Exorcism in the Christian West* (New Haven: Yale University Press, 2012), 173.
11. *Ibid.*
12. Bynum, *Jesus as Mother*, 137; cf. Luke 8:2 and Mark 16:9.
13. Levack, *Devil Within*, 175.
14. *Ibid.*, 184.
15. 1 Corinthians 4:9.
16. Levack, *Devil Within*, 30.
17. John Thavis, *The Vatican Prophesies* (New York: Viking, 2015), 92.
18. Cowan, *Sacred Terror*, 250–1.
19. "Do United Methodists Believe in Saints?" UnitedMethodistChurch.org, http://www.umc.org/what-we-believe/do-united-methodists-believe-in-saints. Accessed June 30, 2016.
20. *Ibid.*
21. *Catechism of the Catholic Church* (New York: William H. Sadler, 1994), 415.

22. *Ibid.*, 417.

23. This is in keeping with cinematic exorcisms, if we are honest. The exorcism in *The Exorcist* is also a failure, the demon only leaving the girl when Father Karras repeatedly punches her in the face screaming, "Come into me, come into me!" His training as a boxer serves him more effectively than his training as a Jesuit in helping Regan.

24. Thavis, *Vatican Prophesies*, 2.

Bibliography

Beal, Timothy. *Religion and Its Monsters*. New York: Routledge, 2002.
Bynum, Carolyn Walker. *Jesus as Mother: Studies in the Spirituality of the High Middle Ages*. Berkeley: University of California Press, 1982.
Catechism of the Catholic Church. New York: William H. Sadler, 1994.
Cowan, Douglas. *Sacred Terror: Religion and Horror on the Silver Screen*. Waco: Baylor University Press, 2008.
"Do United Methodists Believe in Saints?" UnitedMethodistChurch.org. http://www.umc.org/what-we-believe/do-united-methodists-believe-in-saints. Accessed June 30, 2016.
The Exorcism of Emily Rose. DVD. Dir. Scott Derrickson. Screen Gems, 2005.
Goodman, Felicitas D. *The Exorcism of Annaliese Michel*. Eugene, OR: Resource Publications, 1981.
Levack, Brian P. *The Devil Within: Possession and Exorcism in the Christian West*. New Haven: Yale University Press, 2012.
Perkins, Judith. *The Suffering Self: Pain and Narrative Representation in the Early Christian Era*. New York: Routledge, 1995.
Thavis, John. *The Vatican Prophesies*. New York: Viking, 2015.
Yarri, Donna. "Film Review: *The Exorcism of Emily Rose*." *Journal of Religion and Film* 10, no. 1 (April 2006). http://www.unomaha.edu/jrf/vol10no1/Reviews/emilyRose.htm. Accessed September 22, 2008.

"Is this my reward for defending God's church?"[1]

Monstrous Crimes and Monstrous Punishments in Witchfinder General *(1968),* The Devils *(1971) and* The Name of the Rose *(1986)*

JAMES J. WARD

In the memorable opening sequence of Francis Ford Coppola's 1992 version of *Dracula*, Romanian prince Vlad Țepeș (Gary Oldman), returning home from battling the Turks, discovers that his wife Elisabeta (Winona Ryder) has committed suicide after receiving false news of his death. Enraged when his court priest will not absolve Elisabeta of her sin, Vlad declares war on God. Driving his sword into the stone cross that towers above his wife's body, he releases a tide of blood that will compel him to live forever in trying to slake his unnatural thirst. Other than John Milton's description in *Paradise Lost* of Satan's defying, from the depths of Hell, the God who defeated him in the war of the heavens, it is hard to think of another display of spiritual rebellion as powerful as the image that Coppola brought to the screen.[2]

The allure of this dimension of unholiness, however expressed, has proven transcendent. The 20th century's most flamboyant practitioner of Satanic rebellion, the English mystic and charlatan Aleister Crowley, was thought to deserve a place on the Beatles' *Sgt. Pepper's Lonely Hearts Club Band* album cover in 1967 and has long been an acknowledged influence on both the musicianship and the lifestyle of Led Zeppelin's Jimmy Page. In their late '60s Satanic phase, the Rolling Stones professed "Sympathy for the Devil" and—at least until the disaster at Altamont occasioned a moment of introspection—were more than happy to traffic in the infernal associations that had surfaced as early as "Paint It, Black" in 1966. It was hardly by accident that director Taylor Hackford paid the royalties needed to use "Paint It, Black" on the soundtrack of *The Devil's Advocate* (1997), starring Al Pacino is high Luciferian mode. All the variations of Satanic rebellion—demonic possession, necromancy, celebration of the black mass, human sacrifice—had been commonplaces on the screen long before Jimmy Page wrote a score (which was not used) for Kenneth Anger's *Lucifer Rising* in 1973; Anger's scatological parody of the Eucharist in *Scorpio Rising* (1963) has remained far more notorious than the mélange of images, sounds, and celebrity cameos that constitute the later film. From major studio releases like *The Exorcist* (1973) and *The Omen* (1976) to such neo-exploitation fare as

The Devil's Tomb (2009) and *The Devil's Rock* (2011), anti–Christian and anti–Christological thought has provided an inexhaustible repository of themes and images that can be used across the entire spectrum of cinematic production. Even so incorrigible a provocateur and controversialist as Lars von Trier thought *Antichrist* (2009) an appropriate title for yet another of his psychosexual essays in self-loathing, self-mutilation, and self-abnegation.³

Diabolical evil, ritualistic magic, sexual excess and perversion—it was not as if the Church did not possess formidable weapons of its own to counter these malefic threats. No other institution possessed the authority, or exercised the surveillance over millions of ordinary people, that the medieval Christian Church did. Its clergy were unaccountable in the practice of their functions, its agents were everywhere, and its punishments for serious transgressions were brutal in this life and eternal in the next. Although extra-temporal in its self-definition, the Church asserted its control over the secular existence of the faithful with the promise of salvation and the threat of damnation; spiritual tenets and mystical ideas may have been paramount, but penalties and punishments were horrifically corporeal. The Church was, as Arthur Versluis has argued, "a centralized bureaucratic power insistent on the primacy of a single set of doctrines," whose modern equivalent is represented by the totalitarian dictatorships of the 20th century.⁴ Like these regimes, in its drive to enforce conformity in belief and practice the medieval Church admitted no limit to its authority and sanctioned imprisonment, torture, and murder for anyone who, in the face of reasonable persuasion, continued to assert an independent conscience.

The three films considered in this essay depict how far the medieval and early modern Church was prepared to go to suppress dissident thought and defiant behavior. Especially when tainted with demonic connotations, evidencing the monstrous powers of Satan and his minions, conduct of this kind was reciprocated with punishment that was equally, if not more, monstrous in its character and its inevitability. Like the Devil himself, dissidence and rebellion took multiple forms, all of them criminal in the view of the pulpit or the inquisitorial chamber. In these three films, the punishments fit the crimes, but in like measure the crimes are defined by the punishments they warrant.

Sexual Monsters in Holy Places

If Francis Ford Coppola set a high standard in depicting the ferocity with which love of God could turn to hate, Ken Russell had, 20 years earlier, upped the ante in showing the frenzy through which the adoration of Jesus Christ could transform into blasphemy, sacrilege, and erotic excess. Released in 1971, Russell's adaptation of Aldous Huxley's 1952 historical novel *The Devils of Loudun*, simply titled *The Devils*, remains one of the most admired, most reviled, and most contested films dealing with religious mania and its exploitation for non-spiritual ends.⁵ France, in 1634, was a country still recovering from 50 years of religious and civil warfare, the assassination of two monarchs in succession, and the refusal of many semi-independent towns to submit to the authority of the royal government in Paris. To prevent the country from again descending into chaos, Louis XIII and his chief minister, Cardinal Richelieu, were determined to break the resistance of these near-sovereign entities, among them the fortified town of Loudun, a Huguenot (Protestant) stronghold during the religious wars.

The history of Loudun's reduction—its walls were destroyed by royal engineers—is straightforward enough, but the personalities involved, and the political and religious dynamics that were at work, complicate the story. These formed the basis for both Huxley's novel and Russell's screen adaptation. Notoriously hard to see until the British Film Institute released a two-disc PAL edition in 2012, *The Devils* has accrued an extensive critical literature since its initial theatrical exhibition in the UK and the U.S. Most of this commentary falls into one or the other of two camps, either addressing the film in the context of Russell's oeuvre as a director or describing its divisive reception history, replete with allegations of censorship, intimidation, and intervention by both governmental and religious interests.[6] The historical events on screen tend to be quickly subsumed, as though most readers—or viewers of the film, for that matter—would have little interest in the complexities of the French wars of religion or in the state-building program initiated by Louis XIII that laid the foundations for the absolute monarchy of Louis XIV. Yet Russell's exposé of the methods by which religious fanaticism and social hysteria could be manipulated for ambitious political ends remains as relevant today as it was 45 years ago; as one recent observer notes, "W[arner] B[ros.]'s suppression of the film feels like primitive thought-policing and artistic censorship, withholding a vital piece of cinema from the public lest it do them the service of inspiring critical thought."[7]

The dominant figure in the historical events themselves, as well as in the film, is the Catholic priest Urbain Grandier, portrayed in the latter by Oliver Reed. Tolerant of Protestants who had remained in Loudun, fiercely protective of the town's independence, charismatic and licentious, Grandier was an obstacle to the alliance of state and church, represented respectively by the Baron de Laubardemont (Dudley Sutton), the king's commissioner, and by Father Mignon (Murray Melvin), a rival cleric, and Father Barré (Michael Gothard), an itinerant inquisitor. Elevated to political authority in Loudun upon the death of the town's governor, Grandier uses his predecessor's funeral to appeal for civic unity, while insulting the local notables with a display of his sense of self-importance. The most important of these is Sister Jeanne (Vanessa Redgrave), the Reverend Mother of the town's Ursuline convent. Ashamed of her severely hunched back and tortured by imaginings of a sexual relationship with Grandier, Sister Jeanne becomes the perfect vessel for the political intrigue that will culminate in his destruction. In one of her hallucinations Sister Jeanne confuses Grandier with the crucified Christ, who descends from his cross so that she can satisfy her carnal hunger, literally. While removed in time and space, the psychological havoc created by perverse sexual longings, first repressed and then indulged, puts *The Devils* in the company of such more overtly political films as Luchino Visconti's *The Damned* (1969), Bernardo Bertolucci's *The Conformist* (1970), and Pier Paolo Pasolini's *Salò, or the 120 Days of Sodom* (1975).

According to Oxford historian Robin Briggs, episodes of alleged demonic possession became particularly numerous in the early 17th century in England, France, and Germany, but also in the Low Countries and in Scandinavia. Catholic and Protestant polities were equally involved, even if specific regional or local circumstances influenced the outcome of individual accusations and interrogations.[8] Why the decades that produced the rational philosophy of Bacon, Descartes, and Pascal should have been the peak of the witch hysteria has been argued among scholars as various as H.R. Trevor-Roper, Carlo Ginzburg, Norman Cohn, Keith Thomas, and Brian Levack.[9] In the case of Loudun, memories of the recent wars, recurrence of the plague, and suspicions about the loyalties of Protestants gave rise to a collective psychosis that demanded ritual purification to purge the evils that had descended on the town and punishment of whomever was responsible.[10] Already once arrested on charges of immorality stemming from his love affairs, Grandier was a ripe target when the Ursuline nuns began confessing their imagined sexual relations with him.[11]

For many of these nuns, claustrophobia and loneliness, rather than sexual repression and erotomania—as Ken Russell would have it—explain the strange doings in Loudun. More on the mark were the public exorcisms enforced on the sisters and in the case of Sister Jeanne carried out with gynecological torture devices that could have been invented by Hieronymus Bosch.[12] While undergirded by an elaborate theology worked out over the preceding centuries, these rituals also partook of the bizarre and carnivalesque that formed so prominent a part of late medieval and early modern European life. The subsequent orgy scene reveals Russell at his most daring, with naked and semi-naked nuns writhing in ecstasy upon the carved figure of Christ while Grandier's local nemesis Father Mignon masturbates hysterically as he watches from the balcony above them. Falling somewhere between the most transgressive scenes in *Fellini Satyricon* (1969) and *Caligula* (1979), Russell's three-minute depiction of orgiastic release—commonly known as "The Rape of Christ"—remains omitted from the BFI "uncut" edition of *The Devils*.[13]

Sympathetic to the Protestant-hunting program of Louis XIII and Cardinal Richelieu, and envious of Grandier's sexual prowess and the privileges it allows him, his fellow churchmen are eager to collaborate in bringing the defiant curé down. If the methods of exorcism used on the bewitched sisters show Russell at his most grotesque, the prolonged sequence of Grandier's torture anticipated the sadomasochistic excesses Mel Gibson would allow himself in *Braveheart* (1995) and *The Passion of the Christ* (2004). The spectacle of Grandier's torture, where his legs are broken in the most excruciating fashion, followed by that of his execution, where he is burned at the stake without the customary last-minute garroting to spare him a final agony, are public festivals in which the participants fail to recognize that they are surrendering their liberties to an all-powerful state.[14] The film's closing scenes, looking over the ruins of Loudun's walls into a barren landscape populated with the rotting corpses of Protestants broken on the wheel, reveal a country that has reverted to the barbarism of the recent past rather than advanced to the brave new world its transvestite king and his invalid minister had imagined during the mincing court masquerade with which it began.[15]

Sex and Sadism in the Service of God

The Devils is set in a time of ascendant state authority and depicts in gruesome detail the futility of challenging its progress. *Witchfinder General*, describing virtually contemporaneous events on the other side of the English Channel, inhabits a world in which authority has disaggregated into its lowest common denominators—marauding bands of soldiers, local prelates and magistrates, and freebooting enforcers of religious and political conformity. As scholars have long pointed out, mid–17th-century England lagged behind its counterparts on the Continent in the persecution of witches even at the height of the European-wide "witch craze."[16] The witch hunt superintended by Matthew Hopkins and his confederate John Stearne in 1645 was the anomaly, accounting for two to three hundred arrests and as many as one hundred executions across several counties in eastern England, about one-fourth the number for the entire country. The

Father Grandier (Oliver Reed, tied to the stake) pays the price for defying the alliance of church and state in *The Devils* (1971) as Father Mignon (Murray Melvin, left) and Father Barre (Michael Gothard) order his execution.

Civil War still had a couple of years to run; Charles I was not put on trial, convicted, and executed until 1649, and fighting between royalists and parliamentarians continued for two more years. As with most wars in the early modern period, deaths on the battlefield were only part of the story. Additional fatalities caused by famine, plague, and the slaughter of non-combatants created a general sense of devastation and disorder.

The extremism of the times is evident in the opening scenes of Michael Reeves's *Witchfinder General*, retitled *The Conqueror Worm* for its U.S. release by American International Pictures (AIP) to capitalize on the studio's series of Edgar Allan Poe–themed films starring Vincent Price. Against the green English countryside, a terrified woman is dragged to the gallows by her neighbors; observing the result of his handiwork from a nearby hillside, with a look of grim satisfaction, is Matthew Hopkins (Price), the Witchfinder General. The film's production history records the trouble Reeves encountered in getting Price—his casting had been insisted upon by AIP, which co-financed the picture—to play out of character, dispensing with the over-the-top affectations that had become his trademark.[17] Operating in the parishes of East Anglia, Hopkins and Stearne (Robert Russell) are making a small fortune by identifying people in league with the Devil, subjecting those suspected to one or another ritual designed to "prove" guilt or innocence.[18] That the witchfinders' motivation is mercenary rather than political or religious is clear from the start. But Reeves also injects a powerful strain of sexual predation on Hopkins's part, evident in his interrogations of helpless young women, and depicts Stearne as an out-and-out sadist eager to torture victims of either sex.[19]

Summoned to the village of Brandiston by the local magistrates, Hopkins and Stearne focus their attention on Father John Lowes (Rupert Davies), whose political loyalties are in question. To spare her uncle the torment of having needles driven into his back to detect the Devil's mark, the clergyman's niece Sara (Hilary Dwyer) seduces a more-than-willing Hopkins, who proceeds to turn her into his concubine. In the meantime, Sara's lover, Richard Marshall (Ian Ogilvy), is off on campaign with Oliver Cromwell's Puritan army. The first half of the film ends with Stearne's rape of Sara, Lowes' execution once Hopkins loses interest in the defiled girl, and Marshall's discovery of the horrors the witchfinders have committed.

Witchfinder General takes some liberties with the historical record. Matthew Hopkins presides over so-called trials-by-water and hangings; but he is also instrumental in overseeing a particularly horrific burning alive, a punishment traditionally reserved for heretics. Swearing revenge for his lover's degradation at the hands of Hopkins and Stearne, Marshall sets out across the countryside to track them down. In the meantime, they persist in their monstrous trade, greedily pocketing the fees they charge from the villages they visit and satiating their appetite for lust and cruelty. Tricked and taken captive by Hopkins, Marshall refuses to confess to a charge of witchcraft even as the vicious Stearne pricks needles into Sara's back, reducing her to numbed madness. Turning to brand her with a hot iron, Hopkins orders Marshall released from his fetters so that he can witness Sara's suffering at close hand. Breaking free, Marshall throws Stearne to the ground, uses his boot to grind out Stearne's eye, seizes an axe, and in a homicidal frenzy hacks Hopkins into a bloody mess. When one of his fellow soldiers puts Hopkins out of his misery with a pistol shot, the emotionally shattered Marshall screams in despair, "You took him from me! You took him from me!"[20]

Every commentary on Reeves's film acknowledges the bleakness and nihilism of this final scene. Sara has been traumatized beyond any chance of recovery, and Marshall has been transformed into a madman even more bloody-minded than his captors.[21] There is no actual witchery in *Witchfinder General*, which is consistent with recent scholarly accounts of the English witch trials of the mid–17th century and which sets it apart from other similar-seeming British films from the same period.[22] While most of the latter traffic in demonic possession, sorcery, and reincarnation, *Witchfinder General* exposes the social and psychological pathologies that arise in conditions of civil war and political revolution—panic, prejudice, persecution, revenge and retribution. Paganism, necromancy, and—for the most part—nudity are missing; the corruption of power, the fear of marauding armies, and the total loss of moral bearings distinguish the film from the usual raft of late 1960s and early 1970s horror movies, despite an AIP promotional campaign that marketed it with a lurid parental warning and a "Not Rated" rating. While there is certainly something monstrous in Michael Reeves's film, the monstrosity is all too human.[23]

The Horror Within—Heresy and the Devil's Work

There is a charge of witchcraft, and a measure of deviltry, in *The Name of the Rose*, Jean-Jacques Annaud's 1986 adaptation of the 1980 novel by Umberto Eco. With a two-hour running time, the film omits much of the backstory to the criminal investigation that takes place inside a 14th-century monastery in the Alps. There is only a passing mention, for example, of the centuries-long struggle for dominance between the Popes in Rome and the Saxon Emperors in Germany, which is reflected in the monastery's fortress-like appearance.[24] Within the film's narrowed framework, however, Annaud's effort to get the historical details of late medieval monasticism right extends to the colors of the monks' robes, the physical effects of their ascetic lifestyle, and the claustrophobic repetition of their prayers and rituals; none of the brightly lit, if sterile, vaults and galleries at Loudun are on display here; nor are the hallucinations and contortions of the Ursuline sisters anywhere in evidence. Similarly, the primitive living conditions of the peasants whose village adjoins the monastery—and whose helplessness forms a backdrop to the power struggles being contested within its walls—could not be further removed from the high-spirited drinking and wenching that takes place in the taverns where John Stearne spends his time when he is not torturing witches.[25]

Behind the police procedural that foregrounds the plot in Eco's novel and Annaud's film, and in the latter draws its force from Sean Connery's performance as the Franciscan friar William of Baskerville, lie far deeper conflicts that go to the very core of the medieval Church. Accompanied by the novice monk Adso, played by a 15-year-old Christian Slater, William has arrived at an unnamed Benedictine monastery in the Alps to participate in a theological disputation to determine whether Christ, in his earthly ministry, owned the clothes he wore. This debate, with its allusions to the mind-numbing debates of the Scholastic thinkers of the preceding century, is fueled by a fierce struggle for the soul of the Church, fought between the Papacy and its stalwart defenders, the Benedictines and the Dominicans, on the one side and the mendicant orders, above all the Franciscans—for whom wealth, and with it power, were inimical to the message Christ had taught—on the other.

At an even deeper level, the issue is that of faith and reason—the question with which the Scholastics had to grapple once long-lost works of classical philosophy began to re-enter the mainstream of European thought in the 12th and 13th centuries. A corollary question asks whether Christian belief mandates hardship and self-abnegation, as the Benedictine brothers insist, or if humor, and even laughter, might be permitted to leaven a believer's piety. Laughter, Father Jorge de Burgos, the abbey's blind master librarian declares, is the work of the Devil and must be forbidden. But William of Baskerville, who knows a little of Aristotle, counters that the philosopher had taught that humor, too, could be an instrument of the truth. These arguments over doctrine and interpretation, which advance William's and Adso's investigation of the deaths of five monks in as many days, acquire immediate consequence with the arrival of Bernardo Gui (F. Murray Abraham), a representative of the Holy Office of the Inquisition who can barely control his appetite to punish each and all. The deaths of so many pious monks, in so short a time, betrays the presence of the Devil, and Bernardo quickly finds evidence of a Satanic ritual—a black cat, a black rooster, and an all-too-beautiful peasant girl who can only be a witch. Torture extracts a confession for the murders from the hunchbacked Salvatore, once a member of the suppressed Dolcinite order who now speaks in gibberish; the threat of torture does the same for the cellar master Remigio, who admits his connivings with the Devil; and the girl has already been doomed by her beauty and her defiant attitude, intolerable to the Dominican brothers who interrogate her. The verdicts, announced in the presence of Papal emissaries, are predictable and, as Bernardo Gui intones, "Anyone who disputes the verdict of an Inquisitor is a heretic."[26] Death by burning, the clever circumlocution by which the Inquisition eluded the Church's prohibition against shedding the blood of those who had once been among the faithful, is the inevitable punishment. Even after the punishments have been exacted, smoke from the smoldering funeral pyres seems to hang over the concluding scenes of the film.

The discussion here necessarily short-circuits the forensic methods with which

The Inquisitor Bernardo Gui (F. Murray Abraham, right center) uses the threat of torture to extract a confession of heresy from the cellar-master Remigio (Helmut Qualtinger, on his knees at left) in *The Name of the Rose* (1986).

William of Baskerville discovers the real murderer and the reason for his crimes. It is all a matter of books, of knowledge, and of skepticism and subversion—in short, the stuff of heresy.[27] The Church in the 14th century was at war with heretics and schismatics, and with rationalists within its own ranks; the Albigensian Crusade had been fought a hundred years earlier in Italy and France, and the Hussite movement would demand suppression a hundred years later in central Europe. The Papacy itself was soon to be shaken by the Great Schism, with rival Popes in Avignon and Rome pronouncing anathema on each other's followers, and the rulers of France, Spain, and the Empire mobilizing religious division and fear of damnation to advance their power-political objectives.[28] Himself once involved with the processes of the Inquisition, a realist about politics both inside and outside the Church, William of Baskerville has few illusions when it comes to the exercise of power to preserve authority that finds itself under attack. Casting dissident minorities like the Cathars and the Waldensians outside the body of the Church, and crushing them in their mountain strongholds with the military skills that had been honed in centuries of warfare against Slavs, Saracens, and Moors, was a manageable proposition; preventing the spread of impermissible ideas within the structures of the Church itself—the religious brotherhoods, the universities—was something more difficult, even in a time when the transmission of knowledge required years of painstaking work to translate a single manuscript.[29] While an entire library can easily enough be destroyed, as in *The Name of the Rose*, the ideas themselves can outlast the apocalypse.[30]

Conclusion

To perceive as comparable threats the recovery of a single forgotten work of ancient philosophy and the claims of demonic possession by the nuns of Loudun or the power of witches feared by the townspeople of Brandiston might seem too great a stretch. Yet all three instances, and a multitude more like them, could be branded as the work of the Devil, or at least as the maledictions of once-faithful believers whose minds and souls had been seized by an evil force and whose punishment was foreordained. If there was anything the late medieval and early modern Church was adept at, it was—to borrow from the title of a recent study—"playing the heresy card."[31] Heresy was a highly plastic term. It could embrace a solitary monk discovering that a pagan philosopher might have written words of import, words that—upon explication—could subvert Christian teachings. It could condemn innocent people whose only fault was somehow to have fallen out with their neighbors or to have crossed local secular or ecclesiastical authorities. It could lay waste to entire regions and could rationalize atrocities horrifying even by 20th- or 21st-century standards. It was synonymous with independence of mind and independence of action and, as such, was intolerable to those in charge, whether Popes, Inquisitors, Puritan zealots, or state-building administrators, for all of whom conformity and obedience were the highest virtues and dissent and defiance the gravest sins.[32] The horror was in the crime, whether in thought or deed; extirpating the crime required an equal horror, or even one greater. Otherwise, how was the universe to be kept in balance?

NOTES

1. Prince Vlad Țepeș (Gary Oldman) in *Bram Stoker's Dracula*.
2. Although scorned by most critics, Coppola's imagining of Dracula's origins is positively assessed in Cordula Lemke, "Dracula's Times: Adapting the Middle Ages in Francis Ford Coppola's *Bram Stoker's Dracula*," in *The Medieval Motion Picture: The Politics of Adaptation*, ed. Andrew James Johnston, et al., 41–5 (New York: Palgrave Macmillan, 2014).
3. While a number of such films clustered around the year 2000, their appeal has hardly waned in the decade and a half since. See Mick Broderick, "Better the Devil You Know: Antichrists at the Millennium," in *Horror Zone: The Cultural Experience of Contemporary Horror Cinema*, ed. Ian Conrich, 227–43 (New York: I.B. Tauris, 2010). For a useful overview of the connections between rock music and pop culture intonations of Satanism, with an emphasis on the Rolling Stones, see Sheila Whiteley, "Lucifer, Literature, and the Rise of the Rock Rebel," *Chapter & Verse: A Journal of Popular Music and Literature Studies* (2004), accessed January 28, 2016, http://www.popmatters.com/chapter/04win/whiteley.html.
4. Arthur Versluis, *The New Inquisitors: Heretic-Hunting and the Intellectual Origins of Modern Totalitarianism* (New York: Oxford University Press, 2006), 6 and *passim*. See also Jeffrey Richards, *Sex, Dissidence and Damnation: Minority Groups in the Middle Ages* (New York: Routledge, 1991), 42–73.
5. Russell's *The Devils* draws heavily on the stage adaptation of Huxley's novel by John Whiting, which was first performed in London in 1961 and in the U.S. in 1965. The production and reception history of *The Devils* has been reprised in Richard Crouse, *Raising Hell: Ken Russell and the Unmaking of* The Devils (Toronto: ECW Press, 2014) and in the 2002 television documentary by Paul Joyce, *Hell on Earth: The Desecration and Resurrection of* The Devils (British Channel 4 television documentary, 2002, accessed January 30, 2016, https://www.youtube.com/watch?v=Xeg1yIvalSo). As serious-minded an observer as Gerard Loughlin has called *The Devils* Russell's finest film. See *Alien Sex: The Body and Desire in Cinema and Theology* (Oxford: Blackwell, 2004), 133.
6. Examples of the former include Joseph Lanza, *Phallic Frenzy: Ken Russell and His Films* (Chicago: Chicago Review Press, 2007) and Kevin M. Flanagan, ed., *Ken Russell: Re-Viewing England's Last Mannerist* (Metuchen, NJ: Scarecrow Press, 2009). For the latter, see Sian Barber, "'Blue Is the Prevailing Shade': Re-Examining British Film Censorship in the 1970s," *Journal of British Cinema and Television* 6, no. 3 (2009): 349–69; Gordon Thomas, "'Nun-Lust, Torture-Porn, Church-Desecration, and Bad Taste': Reconnecting with Ken Russell's *The Devils*," *Bright Lights Film Journal*, April 30, 2012, accessed January 31, 2016, http://brightlightsfilm.com/nun-lust-torture-porn-church-desecration-and-bad-taste-reconnecting-with-ken-

russells-the-devils/#.Vq-zrLfSmM8; and Julian Petley, "Witch-Hunt: The Word, the Press, and *The Devils*," *Journal of British Cinema and Television* 12, no. 4 (2015): 515–38.
   7. Britt Hayes, "Don't Panic: *The Devils* Is an Exquisitely Powerful and Relevant Masterpiece," *Birth. Movies. Death* website, October 21, 2015, accessed January 31, 2016, http://birthmoviesdeath.com/tag/the-devils.
   8. Robin Briggs, *Witches and Neighbors: The Social and Cultural Context of European Witchcraft* (New York: Penguin, 1998).
   9. H.R. Trevor-Roper, *The European Witch-Craze of the Sixteenth and Seventeenth Centuries and Other Essays* (New York: Harper & Row, 1969); Carlo Ginzburg, *The Night Battles: Witchcraft and Agrarian Cults in the Sixteenth and Seventeenth Centuries*, trans. John and Anne C. Tedeschi (Baltimore: Johns Hopkins University Press, 1983); Norman Cohn, *Europe's Inner Demons: An Enquiry Inspired by the Great Witch-Hunt* (New York: Basic Books, 1975); Keith Thomas, *Religion and the Decline of Magic: Studies in Popular Beliefs in Sixteenth- and Seventeenth-Century England* (London: Weidenfeld & Nicolson, 1971); Brian P. Levack, *The Witch-Hunt in Early Modern Europe* (London: Longman Group, 1987).
   10. For the socio-psychological context of the Loudun "possessions," see Stephens, *Demon Lovers: Witchcraft, Sex, and the Crisis of Belief* (Chicago: University of Chicago Press, 2003).
   11. Left unexplained in *The Devils* are the specific circumstances of the Ursuline convent, only established in 1626 and populated in part by sisters from other parts of the Poitou-Charentes region. An uncloistered order until the 1620s, the Ursulines found themselves under increasing pressure from their superiors in Paris and Rome to adopt rules of austerity and strict observance. See Moshe Sluhovsky, "The Devil in the Convent," *American Historical Review* 107, no. 5 (2002): 1379–1411; Susan Ferber, *Demonic Possession and Exorcism in Early Modern France* (New York: Routledge, 2004), 135–47.
   12. The particular means of expurgation employed upon Sister Jeanne find some theological justification in Nancy Caciola, *Discerning Spirits: Divine and Demonic Possession in the Middle Ages* (Ithaca: Cornell University Press, 2003), 156–161.
   13. While missing from the film itself, "The Rape of Christ" footage—long believed lost until discovered by critic Mark Kermode—appears in Joyce, *Hell on Earth*.
   14. Cf. Michael Wolfe, *Walled Towns and the Shaping of Modern France: From the Medieval to the Early Modern Era* (New York: Palgrave Macmillan, 2009), 123–46.
   15. Russell's depiction of Louis XIII in drag-queen get-up appears a slight exaggeration of the actuality of his court. See Michael Sibalis, "Homosexuality in Early Modern France," in *Queer Masculinities, 1550–1800: Siting Same-Sex Desire in the Early Modern World*, ed. Katherine O'Donnell and Michael O'Rourke, 211–31 (New York: Palgrave Macmillan, 2005).
   16. See, e.g., E. William Monter, "Re-Contextualizing British Witchcraft," *Journal of Interdisciplinary History* 35, no.1 (2004): 105–11; and H.C. Erik Midelfort, "Witch Craze? Beyond the Legends of Panic," *Magic, Ritual and Witchcraft* 6, no. 1 (2011): 11–33.
   17. For the Reeves-Price interaction, see Steve Biodrowski, "*Witchfinder General* (1968)—A Retrospective," *Cinefantastique Online*, September 11, 2007, accessed February 8, 2016, http://cinefantastiqueonline.com/2007/09/witchfinder-general-1968. See also Justin Smith, "Vincent Price and Cult Performance," in *Cult Film Stardom: Offbeat Attractions and Processes of Cultification*, ed. Kate Egan and Sarah Thomas, 109–25 (New York: Palgrave Macmillan, 2013).
   18. These rituals, while not technically defined as "torture," are described in Diane Purkiss, *The Witch in History: Early Modern and Twentieth-Century Representations* (New York: Routledge, 1996), 234–47.
   19. A recent article argues the case, however, that in the practice of their "profession" Hopkins at least was something more than a depraved extortionist. See Sheilagh Ilona O'Brien, "*The Discovery of Witches*: Matthew Hopkins's Defense of His Witch-Hunting Methods," *Preternature: Critical and Historical Studies on the Preternatural* 5, no. 1 (2016): 29–58.
   20. In one interpretation, the brutality of Marshall's attack on Hopkins sublimates director Reeves's hostility toward his star, Vincent Price. See Leon Hunt, "*Witchfinder General*: Michael Reeves' Visceral Classic," in *Necronomicon Book One*, ed. Andy Black, 123–30 (London: Creation Books, 1996).
   21. *Witchfinder General* was Reeves's third, and last, film as he died a few weeks after its completion, evidently by is own hand. For critical evaluations, see Quentin Turnour, "*Witchfinder General*," *Senses of Cinema* no. 31 (April 2004), accessed February 10, 2016, http://sensesofcinema.com/2004/cteq/witchfinder_general; Benjamin Halligan, *Michael Reeves* (Manchester: Manchester University Press, 2003); Ian Cooper, *Witchfinder General: Devil's Advocates* (Leighton Buzzard: Auteur, 2011). For the larger context in which *Witchfinder General* is situated, see Marcus K. Harmes, "The Seventeenth Century on Film: Patriarchy, Magistracy, and Witchcraft in British Horror Films, 1968–1971," *Canadian Journal of Film Studies* 22, no. 2 (2013): 75.
   22. Most notably, see Malcolm Gaskill, *Witchfinders: A Seventeenth-Century English Tragedy* (Cambridge: Harvard University Press, 2005).
   23. David Sanjek, "Twilight of the Monsters The English Horror Film, 1968–1975," in *Re-Viewing British Cinema, 1900–1992: Essays and Interviews*, ed. Wheeler Winston Dixon, 195–209 (Albany: State University of New York Press, 1994); Leon Hunt. "Necromancy in the UK: Witchcraft and the Occult in British Horror," in *British Horror Cinema*, ed. Steve Chibnall and Julian Petley, 82–98 (New York: Routledge, 2002).

24. Constructed on a hillside outside Rome, the monastery's tower—which houses the scriptorium, where manuscripts are copied and illuminated—is generally acknowledged to have been modeled on the 13th-century Castel de Monte, erected by Emperor Frederick II to consolidate his hold over southern Italy and today a UNESCO World Heritage Site.

25. See the discussions of *The Name of the Rose* in Bettina Bildhauer, *Filming the Middle Ages* (London: Reaktion Books, 2011), 144–48 and Andrew B.R. Elliott, *Remaking the Middle Ages: Images of Cinema and History in Portraying the Medieval World* (Jefferson, NC: McFarland, 2011), 130–32.

26. In the director's commentary included on the 2004 DVD edition of *The Name of the Rose*, Jean-Jacques Annaud describes his fascination with the phenomenon of heresy in the Middle Ages. On the prominent role of the Dominicans in the Inquisition, see Christine Caldwell Ames, *Inquisition, Dominicans, and Christianity in the Middle Ages* (Philadelphia: University of Pennsylvania Press, 2009).

27. For an elaborate—the pun is intended—discussion of these aspects of the novel and the film, see Jeremy Strong, "Reconstructing the Rose, or How Joining the Dots (Generally) Makes the Picture." *Literature Film Quarterly* 39, no. 4 (2011): 297–305.

28. All this furnishes context for *The Name of the Rose*, as no doubt Annaud's script advisor, the noted medievalist Jacques Le Goff, would have made clear. See Richard Burt, *Medieval and Early Modern Film* (New York: Palgrave Macmillan, 2008), 166–67. For an overview of this period in the Church's history, see Michael D. Bailey, *Battling Demons: Witchcraft, Heresy, and Reform in the Late Middle Ages* (University Park: Pennsylvania State University Press, 2003) and Gary K. Waite, *Heresy, Magic, and Witchcraft in Early Modern Europe* (New York: Palgrave Macmillan, 2003).

29. On the military prowess of the Church in the 14th and 15th centuries, see David Chambers, *Popes, Cardinals, and Wars: The Military Church in Renaissance and Early Modern Europe* (London: I.B. Tauris, 2006).

30. Articulated by Brother Ubertino de Casale (in a scene-stealing performance by William Hickey), the theme of apocalyptic destruction runs as an undercurrent through the plot of Annaud's film. A large literature addresses the subject; for an introduction, see John Aberth, *From the Brink of the Apocalypse: Confronting Famine, War, Plague, and Death in the Later Middle Ages*, 2d ed. (New York: Routledge, 2010).

31. Karen Bollermann, Thomas M. Izbicki, and Cary J. Nederman, eds., *Religion, Power, and Resistance from the Eleventh to the Sixteenth Centuries: Playing the Heresy Card* (New York: Palgrave Macmillan, 2014); also see Andrew P. Roach, *The Devil's World: Heresy and Society, 1100–1300* (New York: Routledge, 2005).

32. Cf. Scott L Waugh, and Peter D. Diehl, eds.. *Christendom and Its Discontents: Exclusion, Persecution, and Rebellion, 1000–1500* (Cambridge: Cambridge University Press, 1996).

BIBLIOGRAPHY

Aberth, John. *From the Brink of the Apocalypse: Confronting Famine, War, Plague, and Death in the Later Middle Ages*, 2d ed. New York: Routledge, 2010.
Ames, Christine Caldwell. *Inquisition, Dominicans, and Christianity in the Middle Ages*. Philadelphia: University of Pennsylvania Press, 2009.
Bailey, Michael D. *Battling Demons: Witchcraft, Heresy, and Reform in the Late Middle Ages*. University Park: Pennsylvania State University Press, 2003.
Barber, Sian. "'Blue Is the Prevailing Shade': Re-Examining British Film Censorship in the 1970s." *Journal of British Cinema and Television* 6, no. 3 (2009): 349–69.
Bildhauer, Bettina. *Filming the Middle Ages*. London: Reaktion Books, 2011.
Biodrowski, Steve. "*Witchfinder General* (1968)—A Retrospective." *Cinefantastique Online*, September 11, 2007. Accessed February 8, 2016. http://cinefantastiqueonline.com/2007/09/witchfinder-general-1968.
Bollermann, Karen, Thomas M. Izbicki, and Cary J. Nederman, eds. *Religion, Power, and Resistance from the Eleventh to the Sixteenth Centuries: Playing the Heresy Card*. New York: Palgrave Macmillan, 2014.
Bram Stoker's Dracula. Dir. Francis Ford Coppola. 1992. Sony Pictures Home Entertainment, 2004. DVD.
Briggs, Robin, *Witches and Neighbors: The Social and Cultural Context of European Witchcraft*. New York: Penguin, 1998.
Broderick, Mick. "Better the Devil You Know: Antichrists at the Millennium." In *Horror Zone: The Cultural Experience of Contemporary Horror Cinema*, ed. Ian Conrich, 227–43. New York: I.B. Tauris, 2010.
Burt, Richard. *Medieval and Early Modern Film and Media*. New York: Palgrave Macmillan, 2008.
Caciola, Nancy. *Discerning Spirits: Divine and Demonic Possession in the Middle Ages*. Ithaca: Cornell University Press, 2003.
Chambers, David. *Popes, Cardinals, and Wars: The Military Church in Renaissance and Early Modern Europe*. London: I.B. Tauris, 2006.
Cohn, Norman. *Europe's Inner Demons: An Enquiry Inspired by the Great Witch-Hunt*. New York: Basic Books, 1975.
Cooper, Ian. *Witchfinder General: Devil's Advocates*. Leighton Buzzard: Auteur, 2011.
Crouse, Richard. *Raising Hell: Ken Russell and the Unmaking of* The Devils. Toronto: ECW Press, 2014.
The Devils. Dir. Ken Russell. 1971. BFI Video, 2012. DVD (PAL).

Elliott, Andrew B.R. *Remaking the Middle Ages: Images of Cinema and History in Portraying the Medieval World*. Jefferson, NC: McFarland, 2011.
Ferber, Susan. *Demonic Possession and Exorcism in Early Modern France*. New York: Routledge, 2004.
Flanagan, Kevin M., ed. *Ken Russell: Re-Viewing England's Last Mannerist*. Metuchen, NJ: Scarecrow Press, 2009.
Gaskill, Malcolm. *Witchfinders: A Seventeenth-Century English Tragedy*. Cambridge: Harvard University Press, 2005.
Ginzburg, Carlo. *The Night Battles: Witchcraft and Agrarian Cults in the Sixteenth and Seventeenth Centuries*, trans. John and Anne C. Tedeschi. Baltimore: Johns Hopkins University Press, 1983.
Halligan, Benjamin. *Michael Reeves*. Manchester: Manchester University Press, 2003.
Harmes, Marcus K. "The Seventeenth Century on Film: Patriarchy, Magistracy, and Witchcraft in British Horror Films, 1968–1971." *Canadian Journal of Film Studies* 22, no. 2 (2013): 64–80.
Hayes, Britt. "Don't Panic: *The Devils* Is an Exquisitely Powerful and Relevant Masterpiece." *Birth. Movies. Death* website, October 21, 2015. Accessed January 31, 2016. http://birthmoviesdeath.com/tag/the-devils.
Hunt, Leon. "Necromancy in the UK: Witchcraft and the Occult in British Horror." In *British Horror Cinema*, ed. Steve Chibnall and Julian Petley, 82–98. New York: Routledge, 2002.
_____. "*Witchfinder General*: Michael Reeves' Visceral Classic." In *Necronomicon Book One*, ed. Andy Black, 123–30. London: Creation Books, 1996.
Hell on Earth: The Desecration and Resurrection of The Devils. Dir. Paul Joyce. British Channel 4 television documentary (2002). Accessed January 30, 2016. https://www.youtube.com/watch?v=Xeg1yIvalSo. Also included on the special features disc in the 2012 BFI edition of *The Devils*.
Lanza, Joseph. *Phallic Frenzy: Ken Russell and His Films*. Chicago: Chicago Review Press, 2007.
Lemke, Cordula. "Dracula's Times: Adapting the Middle Ages in Francis Ford Coppola's *Bram Stoker's Dracula*." In *The Medieval Motion Picture: The Politics of Adaptation*, ed. Andrew James Johnston, Margitta Rouse, and Philipp Hinz, 41–56. New York: Palgrave Macmillan, 2014.
Levack, Brian P. *The Witch-Hunt in Early Modern Europe*. London: Longman Group, 1987.
Loughlin, Gerard. *Alien Sex: The Body and Desire in Cinema and Theology*. Oxford: Blackwell, 2004.
The Name of the Rose. Dir. Jean-Jacques Annaud. 1986. Warner Home Video, 2004. DVD.
Midelfort, H.C. Erik. "Witch Craze? Beyond the Legends of Panic." *Magic, Ritual and Witchcraft* 6, no. 1 (2011): 11–33.
Monter, E. William. "Re-Contextualizing British Witchcraft." *Journal of Interdisciplinary History* 35, no.1 (2004): 105–11.
O'Brien, Sheilagh Ilona. "*The Discovery of Witches*: Matthew Hopkins's Defense of His Witch-Hunting Methods." *Preternature: Critical and Historical Studies on the Preternatural* 5, no. 1 (2016): 29–58.
Petley, Julian. "Witch-Hunt: The Word, the Press, and *The Devils*." *Journal of British Cinema and Television* 12, no. 4 (2015): 515–38.
Purkiss, Diane. *The Witch in History: Early Modern and Twentieth-Century Representations*. New York: Routledge, 1996.
Richards, Jeffrey. *Sex, Dissidence and Damnation: Minority Groups in the Middle Ages*. New York: Routledge, 1991.
Roach, Andrew P. *The Devil's World: Heresy and Society, 1100–1300*. New York: Routledge, 2005.
Sanjek, David. "Twilight of the Monsters: The English Horror Film, 1968–1975." In *Re-Viewing British Cinema, 1900–1992: Essays and Interviews*, ed. Wheeler Winston Dixon, 195–209. Albany: State University of New York Press, 1994.
Sibalis, Michael. "Homosexuality in Early Modern France." In *Queer Masculinities, 1550–1800: Siting Same-Sex Desire in the Early Modern World*, ed. Katherine O'Donnell and Michael O'Rourke, 211–31. New York: Palgrave Macmillan, 2005.
Sluhovsky, Moshe. "The Devil in the Convent." *American Historical Review* 107, no. 5 (2002): 1379–1411.
Smith, Justin. "Vincent Price and Cult Performance." In *Cult Film Stardom: Offbeat Attractions and Processes of Cultification*, ed. Kate Egan and Sarah Thomas, 109–25. New York: Palgrave Macmillan, 2013.
Stephens, Walter. *Demon Lovers: Witchcraft, Sex, and the Crisis of Belief*. Chicago: University of Chicago Press, 2003.
Strong, Jeremy. "Reconstructing the Rose, or How Joining the Dots (Generally) Makes the Picture." *Literature Film Quarterly* 39, no. 4 (2011): 297–305.
Thomas, Gordon. "'Nun-Lust, Torture-Porn, Church-Desecration, and Bad Taste': Reconnecting with Ken Russell's *The Devils*." *Bright Lights Film Journal*, April 30, 2012. Accessed January 31, 2016. http://brightlightsfilm.com/nun-lust-torture-porn-church-desecration-and-bad-taste-reconnecting-with-ken-russells-the-devils/#.Vq-zrLfSmM8.
Thomas, Keith. *Religion and the Decline of Magic: Studies in Popular Beliefs in Sixteenth- and Seventeenth-Century England*. London: Weidenfeld & Nicolson, 1971.
Trevor-Roper, H.R. *The European Witch-Craze of the Sixteenth and Seventeenth Centuries and Other Essays*. New York: Harper & Row, 1969.
Turnour, Quentin. "*Witchfinder General*." *Senses of Cinema* no. 31 (April 2004). Accessed February 10, 2016. http://sensesofcinema.com/2004/cteq/witchfinder_general.

Versluis, Arthur. *The New Inquisitors: Heretic-Hunting and the Intellectual Origins of Modern Totalitarianism.* New York: Oxford University Press, 2006.
Waite, Gary K. *Heresy, Magic, and Witchcraft in Early Modern Europe.* New York: Palgrave Macmillan, 2003.
Waugh, Scott L., and Peter D. Diehl, eds. *Christendom and Its Discontents: Exclusion, Persecution, and Rebellion, 1000–1500.* Cambridge: Cambridge University Press, 1996.
Whiteley, Sheila. "Lucifer, Literature, and the Rise of the Rock Rebel." *Chapter & Verse: A Journal of Popular Music and Literature Studies* (2004). Accessed January 28, 2016. http://www.popmatters.com/chapter/04win/whiteley.html.
Witchfinder General. Dir. Michael Reeves. 1968. 20th Century Fox, 2007. DVD.
Wolfe, Michael. *Walled Towns and the Shaping of Modern France: From the Medieval to the Early Modern Era.* New York: Palgrave Macmillan, 2009.

Reckoning the Number of the Beast
Premillennial Dispensationalism, The Omen *and 1970s America*

BRAD L. DUREN

The end of the world has long been a source of fascination and conjecture. Desire to understand the unknown, particularly within the context of unfolding socio-political events, is evident in the histories of countless civilizations, with folklore and religion playing key roles in the formation of popular understandings. The United States is no exception. Infused with religious fervor and deeply influenced by a sense of mission from the time of their nation's founding, Americans have long sought to understand their place within what they see as the unfolding of a preordained historical destiny. Whether we examine the doctrines of New England Puritans who saw themselves as vanguards of prophetic fulfillment, the rhetoric of later social reformers who believed they were instruments of divine providence, or the perspectives of religious fundamentalists who interpreted every positive or negative news story within the context of scripture, strong religious elements have been persistent across American history. This tendency becomes even more evident during times of social and political crisis, when institutions threaten to buckle under the pressures of a chaotic world.

These themes have long been favorites of filmmakers, who have sought to reap box office benefits by incorporating religious ideas and imagery—particularly those of an apocalyptic nature—into their work. A film built on such religious elements, released at an opportune time, can not only reap financial rewards for its creators, but also send shockwaves through popular culture, becoming simultaneously representative of its time and transformative in its influence. Richard Donner's *The Omen* (1976) was such a film.

When *The Omen* arrived in movie theaters in June 1976, cinemagoers made it the top-grossing film of the week, and ultimately, one of the top-grossing films of the entire year. The story of Damien Thorn, a young boy who is actually the Antichrist, struck a chord with critics and film patrons alike. Its release coincided with both the cultural and political fallout of the tumultuous 1960s and the revival of horror films dealing with the cosmic battle of good and evil, which had been set in motion by Roman Polanski's *Rosemary's Baby* (1968) and gained momentum with the success of William Friedkin's *The Exorcist* (1973). What made *The Omen* different was its emphasis on the apocalypse—

"the end times," as evangelical Protestants refer to it—and the figure variously referred to in the Bible as "the Beast," "the abomination of desolation," and "the Antichrist." Specifically, it built on a fringe interpretation of biblical prophecy known as Premillennial Dispensationalism, which had gained acceptance among evangelicals over the previous century and recently begun to penetrate mainstream American culture.

The film depicts the very earliest stage of the apocalypse: the appearance of the Antichrist, unnoticed and unsuspected, on Earth. As Douglas Cowan notes, "it replicates in many ways the Antichrist's mysterious rise to power that Christian dispensationalists have been predicting," embroidering them with bits of "cinema horror" to strengthen its genre credentials.[1] Robert Thorn (Gregory Peck), an American diplomat in Rome, is grieving for his stillborn son when the hospital chaplain convinces him to adopt a newborn boy whose unmarried mother died giving birth. He accepts, and presents the infant to his unsuspecting wife Katherine (Lee Remick) as their newborn son. Thorn is soon appointed U.S. Ambassador to the United Kingdom, and during the first five years of his life in London, young Damien (Harvey Stephens) seems like a normal child. All of this changes at his fifth birthday party, when his nanny hangs herself in full view of the partygoers after shouting that "it's all for you, Damien."

With the unsolicited arrival of a mysterious replacement nanny, Mrs. Baylock (Billie Whitelaw), the Thorns' world grows steadily darker, and the disturbing events surrounding Damien grow more frequent. Father Brennan (Patrick Troughton), who warns Thorn that Damien is the "son of the devil," is impaled, in his own churchyard, by a falling lightning rod during a sudden storm. Katherine is badly injured when Damien, riding his tricycle in the halls of the ambassador's residence, causes her to fall from a second-floor balcony. When Thorn returns to Rome to investigate what happened the night Damien was born, he finds that a mysterious fire swept through the hospital maternity wing not long after he and Katherine brought the child home, destroying the records and killing most of the staff. He and an ally—photographer Keith Jennings (David Warner)—excavate the grave of Damien's mother, finding only the bones of a jackal, along with evidence that the Thorns' own son was murdered, before wild dogs drive them away. Concerned for Katherine's safety, Thorn arranges for embassy staff to bring her to Rome, but she is killed in a fall from the window of her fifth-floor hospital room (murdered, the film strongly implies, by Mrs. Blaylock) before the plan can be set in motion.

The rising death toll, and the evidence from the graveyard, leads Thorn to seriously consider Jennings' assertion that Damien is the Antichrist, and that his adoption was engineered by a shadowy cabal of Satanists. Travelling to Israel, Thorn and Jennings consult with an archaeologist (Leo McKern), who explains that the Antichrist will bear the "mark of the beast"—a birthmark in the shape of a triple "6"—and gives the ambassador a set of seven holy daggers capable of destroying him. Appalled at the idea of murdering a child, Thorn angrily discards the weapons. When Jennings attempts to retrieve them, he falls victim to yet another mysterious "accident," decapitated by a sheet of glass that slides off the bed of a passing truck.

After finding the telltale 666 birthmark beneath Damien's hair and being attacked by Mrs. Blaylock, who he is forced to kill in self-defense, Thorn finally accepts the horrifying truth about his son. He drags the now-screaming boy into a church in order to dispatch him on the altar. Alerted by the screaming and Thorn's erratic behavior, police officers enter the church, and—as Thorn raises the first dagger—shots ring out. The final scene of the film shows a state funeral for Thorn and his wife, attended by the President

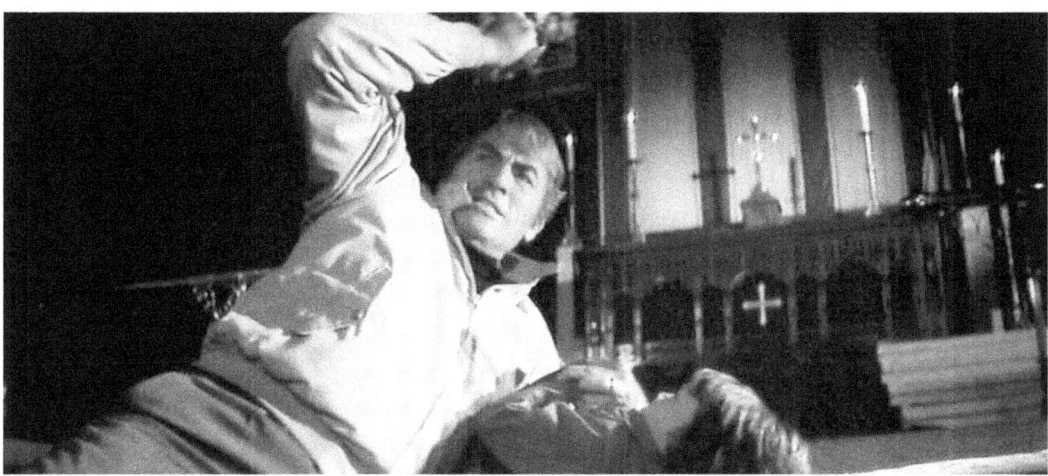

Robert Thorn (Gregory Peck) attempts to end Damien's (Harvey Spencer Stephens) life with a sacred dagger in *The Omen* (1976).

and First Lady of the United States. As the camera pans down, it reveals Damien, their newly adopted son, standing between them. He turns to face the camera, gives a little smile, and the credits roll. The Antichrist is alive and well and living in the White House.

What set *The Omen* apart from other religious horror films of the era was its clever, seamless weaving of Premillennial Dispensationalist views into a coherent narrative that captured both the imaginings and anxieties reflected in mid–1970s popular culture. As a result, it not only achieved success at the box office, but also helped to establish what was once a fringe interpretation of biblical prophecy as a valid interpretation of the end times. *The Omen* thus serves both as an historical artifact of its time—a window into the *zeitgeist* of mid–1970s America—and, even more importantly, as a vehicle for transforming (even within American Evangelical Christianity itself) popular conceptions of how the Antichrist would rise and the apocalypse would unfold.

Historical Moment: The 1970s and the Search for Meaning

No cultural artifact can be adequately understood in a vacuum, and the greater social significance of *The Omen* is best appreciated by placing the film within the historical and theological contexts of the mid–1970s. The social and political fallout from the struggles of the 1960s, both at home and abroad, created, for many Americans of the era, a sense that everything they knew and believed in was crumbling around them. Americans were in the midst of a national identity crisis, with once-trusted political and social institutions losing the prestige and respect they had once enjoyed. The lies and deceit perpetrated by the Nixon administration, and the blatant abuse of power by elected officials, diminished Americans' faith in government to levels not seen since the early years of the Great Depression. A sluggish economy, rampant inflation, and memories of gas shortages caused by the 1973 Arab oil embargo deepened Americans' sense of disenchantment and loss of purpose, leading to what President Jimmy Carter referred to in a famous 1979 speech as a "crisis of confidence."[2] The failure of the many utopian dreams of the 1960s (the war on poverty, the expansion of civil rights, etc.) and the loss of faith resulting from the political fallout of the Vietnam War and Watergate scandal resulted in a sense of political and cultural "aimlessness" that led many Americans to seek new sources of faith and hope amid a miasma of hopelessness.

A growing belief that the individual was the arbiter of truth also took its toll on religion, as Americans began abandoning traditional churches in droves—a trend that has continued to the present day. "Among all Americans, both Catholics and Protestants, the percentage who expressed a 'great deal' of confidence in organized religion plunged from 40 percent in 1967, the first year the question was asked, to 20 percent in 1979, about where it has remained ever since."[3] Even as the churches struggled between the rock of maintaining cultural relevance and the hard place of preserving orthodoxy, Americans continued to long for something tangible and stable in the midst of a troubled sea of uncertainty. They "yearned as fervently as ever for a direct encounter with the transcendent," David Frum observes, "but they chafed against the authority that had once guided them toward that encounter."[4] The antiauthoritarianism of the counterculture merged, in the late 1960s, with the traditional American skepticism of authority, leading many individuals to wonder if they had been deceived and manipulated by organized religion and its representatives. Were these all constructs, growing numbers of Americans wondered, merely designed to consolidate power and assert control? Was Marx right that religion was "the opiate of the masses?" Well-defined views of good and evil began, for many, to seem questionable at best and passé at worst. Still, the world around them manifested injustice and evil in numerous ways, suggesting that the need for a savior might indeed be real and that the answer to "Is God Dead?"—the question famously posed by the editors of *Time* on a 1966 cover—was "No."

Such widespread feelings of anxiety and uncertainty often lead to a search for meaning, and Americans began theirs by turning to science for solutions. Confession to a priest gave way to conversation with a therapist. The clear-cut, unchanging tenets of religious dogma morphed into the complex, continually evolving hypotheses of scientific research. Many, however, ultimately found such assertions unsatisfying—too simple, too cut and dried, to fill their spiritual needs. Who, an American of the mid–1970s might well have asked, is one to believe? The psychologist or the clergyman? The scientist or the bishop? Or are they are all wrong, obliging those in search of answers to seek them from some other authority, yet unknown?

The result of those existential questions was widespread apathy punctuated by a continued desire to believe something … anything. Where anxiety runs high, a fanaticism for certainty (be it religious or other) often reigns supreme. When science and modern, rationalized religion failed to satisfy, a return to the metaphysical, supernatural, and religious was bound to follow. As mainstream Christian churches suffered losses in membership, Americans shifted their focus to newer, more faddish expressions of spirituality. Everything from westernized versions of Eastern mysticism (part of a loose collection of spiritual beliefs referred to as "New Age" by detractors) to Transcendental Meditation and the Unification Church underwent growth spurts, and spiritual gurus of all stripes gathered followers and published books by the score. Even in the midst of these losses and defections from traditional religion, however, one segment of Christianity saw its numbers grow as Americans sought new spiritual directions: Christian fundamentalism.

A key element of post–1960s Christian fundamentalism was an intense focus on the

End of Days, and meticulous attention to the details of when, where, and how it would take place. While belief in an apocalyptic end to history has always been part of Christianity, there has been little consensus on how and when this would happen. Catholic, Orthodox, and most mainstream Protestant denominations have viewed these matters as a "great mystery," allowing for differences of interpretation while emphasizing that what mattered most was that God was in control, Christ would return, and the end would come. Specific details, such as the how and when of the "end times," who or what the Antichrist was, and the role of current events in the fulfillment of biblical prophecy, have been more the province of theologians than of the average lay person.[5] The fundamentalists of the early 1970s reversed that trend, a choice that resonated with Americans' perception that their society was rapidly unraveling and world events were growing ever more turbulent.

Fundamentalist Christian sects—delivering messages about the earthly presence of both God and the Devil, led by charismatic minister-showmen, and offering liturgical music that owed more akin to Joan Baez than to John Wesley—experienced a growth spurt in the fallout of 1960s America. A central element of this spiritual revival, critical to the pursuit of personal peace and spiritual enlightenment among these groups, was belief in an impending apocalypse during which believers and unbelievers, the righteous and the wicked, alike would face God's final judgment. These end-of-the world scenarios derived from a particular interpretation of biblical prophecy. Hal Lindsey seemed to tie it all together in his best-selling 1970 book *The Late, Great Planet Earth*.

Religious Roots: Premillennial Dispensationalism

Lindsey's work stands as an important link in understanding both the theological and cultural context of *The Omen*, because he not only attempted to link biblical prophecies of the "end times" to current events, but also claimed that these events were paving the way for the culmination of human history. The end was near in both sacred and secular senses, Lindsey argued, drawing on passages in Daniel, Ezekiel, 1 Thessalonians, and especially Revelation to support his position.

Utilizing a literalist interpretation of scripture and building on a school of thought known as premillennial, dispensational eschatology, Lindsey asserted that true Christians would soon be removed from Earth in an event known as the Rapture, paving the way for the rise of the Antichrist (a corporeal, supernatural being rather than—as some readings of Revelation suggested—a metaphor for secular evil) who would emerge from the world of international politics. The Antichrist would rule the world during a seven-year period known as the Great Tribulation, during which God would pour out His wrath on the unbelievers left behind, as well as make one last attempt to destroy the nation of Israel. At the end of that seven-year period, Christ would return, in the Second Coming, to defeat the Antichrist, reincorporate Israel into His rule, and set up His own kingdom from Jerusalem (the Millennial Reign of Christ) before creating a "new heaven and new earth," which would last for eternity.[6]

Lindsey's work struck a chord with a reading audience caught up in the disorder of post–1960s America. For many, it seemed that he was on to something significant. The idea that increased famine and pestilence was loose in the world seemed plausible, and the formation of the European Common Market—precursor of the European Union—

seemed to set the stage for a "United States of Europe" that would act as a new Roman Empire, providing for the rise to power of the Antichrist. The Soviet Union, with its massive stockpiles of nuclear arms, was a potential adversary in a future World War III (the "War of Gog and Magog" described in Revelation), and—while not formally uniting with them—it had supplied arms to Israel's enemies in the Six-Day War of 1967. While refusing to specify the timing of events, Lindsey claimed that biblical exegesis revealed a generation to be 40 years, meaning that 1988 would be "one generation" from the founding of modern Israel. This led some readers to contend that the Rapture would occur in or around 1988 and the Great Tribulation would then commence, a belief Lindsey himself embraced in his later works.[7]

Lindsey was no innovator. There had been millenarian groups in America since the colonial period, each claiming a special prophetic understanding of a world they believed to be collapsing around them. Those who carefully investigated the theological roots of Lindsey's ideas soon discovered that *The Late, Great Planet Earth* was just a modern repackaging of an eschatological narrative formulated, in the 1830s, by John Nelson Darby: an Anglo-Irish cleric who left the Church of Ireland (then a branch of the Church of England) and became the leader of a sect known as the Plymouth Brethren. Darby, whose ideas steadily gained popularity in America through the 19th century, originated virtually all of the key concepts that Lindsey drew together in *The Late, Great Planet Earth*, including the Rapture and the subsequent Great Tribulation in which those left behind suffer the scourges of a literal Antichrist for seven years.[8] His ideas—viewed with derision by mainstream Christians of the time—took root in the United States among the religious utopian communities of the 1840s, spread and gained popularity with the rise of the fundamentalist movement in the early 20th century.

Premillennial Dispensationalism, the formal name for Darby's belief system, provided believers with a sense of certainty—a confidence in their ability to anticipate, and interpret, major world events that, they believed, were foretold by Biblical prophecies. This providential perspective reassured Darby's followers not only that God had a plan, but that they were privy to its details and could be reassured that it was unfolding as He intended. It also "motivated believers to want to rescue others from damnation before the Second Coming," providing them with a sense of mission, as well as certainty.[9] Premillennial Dispensationalism remains the belief system of millions of Christian fundamentalists, and many outside fundamentalist circles have come to view the interpretations presented in *The Late, Great Planet Earth* as *the* accepted readings of biblical prophecy throughout church history, when in fact they were nothing of the sort. Theological debates aside, this ideology has, since the 1970s, transcended the pews of fundamentalist congregations. Other authors, like Salem Kirban in the 1960s, had ventured into the same narrative waters, but none achieved Lindsey's success in importing Premillennial Dispensationalism into the mainstream of American religious and popular culture.

The Late, Great Planet Earth became the first Christian prophecy book picked up by a secular publisher (Bantam Books, in 1973), and it sold even more briskly than titles with more obvious mass appeal, such as Alex Comfort's pathbreaking *The Joy of Sex* (1973). It was the best-selling non-fiction book of the 1970s and, despite its now-dated content, has continued to shape Americans' thinking about the future.[10] The book's success owed much to timing: Lindsey happened to release his book at the perfect cultural moment, and American book-buyers were fascinated by the resonances between his apocalyptic prophecies and their own widely shared sense of impending doom.

The Omen *as a Transformative Force*

It was amid this historical moment that *The Omen* found its way onto movie screens across the nation. According to producer Harvey Bernhard, the seeds of the story came from a conversation he had with Robert Munger, an advertising executive who had worked for World Wide Pictures, the film-production division of Billy Graham Ministries, and helped to secure the wide release of several films under that banner. Munger was not only a well-connected Hollywood ad man; he was also a born-again Christian, and, in the midst of their discussion, made a statement that Bernard found quite terrifying. What if, Munger asked, the Antichrist is alive today but he is a child and no one knows who he is? It was an inquiry that Munger regarded as both a serious question and a great film idea. Bernhard claimed that this idea prompted him to write a 15-page outline for such a story. After jotting down the short treatment, he contacted writer David Seltzer, and pitched him the story. After initially rejecting the project, Seltzer later changed his mind and accepted Bernhard's offer to write a screenplay based on Munger's idea, stating that it offered motivation to do something he had never done before—read the Bible.[11]

Ironically then, Seltzer's script is the work of someone with, at best, a superficial understanding of the conflicting interpretations of biblical prophecy. Though Seltzer claims it to be "steeped in the scriptures," interpretive liberties abound. The passage that ties all of the dramatic elements together—making the revelation of young Damien Thorn as the Antichrist convincing—is nowhere to be found in the Bible. It reads: "When the Jews return to Zion and a comet rips the sky, and the Holy Roman Empire rises; then you and I must die. From the eternal sea he rises, creating armies on either shore, turning man against his brother, 'til man exists no more." While he acknowledges the passage's lack of scriptural origin, Seltzer claims that it is derived from, and consistent with, scriptural imagery.[12] Regardless of its biblical status, the quote and the film mesh smoothly with the Premillennial Dispensationalism promoted by Lindsey and his followers.

Donner, as director, pushed for the events of the film to be staged so that viewers were free to interpret them either in secular or supernatural terms—as a string of bad luck and bizarre coincidences, or as the machinations of Satan and his acolytes. Seltzer, on the other hand had no interest in such deliberate ambiguities, stating in interviews that he took the project seriously and structured the film around the idea Damien was indeed the Antichrist.[13] Seltzer's biblically rooted certainty, rather Donner's finely tuned ambiguity, ultimately defined both the film and the advertising campaign. "You have been warned," posters proclaimed. "If something frightening happens to you today, think about it. It may be … *The Omen*." Seltzer's subsequent novelization of his script, over which Donner had no influence at all, leaned even more extravagantly on the apocalyptic ideas of Darby and Lindsey.

There are numerous embellishments to biblical prophecy in *The Omen*, however, that even some dispensationalists would find extraneous, such as erroneous references to the Antichrist as the son of Satan. In St. Paul's second letter to the Thessalonians, he is referred to as "the man of lawlessness" and the "son of destruction," but never the son of Satan. This presentation apparently resonated with post–*Rosemary's Baby* filmgoers, however, and has remained a fixture of Antichrist films ever since. The film's religious license extends to its portrayal of Catholic priests as supporters—in some cases, even devoted allies—of the Antichrist, which owes more to the views of Martin Luther and

The innocent face of the Antichrist, Damien (Harvey Spencer Stephens), in *The Omen* (1976). Here he walks between his new adoptive parents, the President (Gregory Peck) and First Lady (Lee Remick) of the United States.

his fellow Protestant reformers than to actual Catholic doctrine regarding the end times. A fundamentalist minister would have been a more theologically accurate choice, but one that would lack symbolic *gravitas* and, perhaps more important, fail to remind audiences of the grim-faced, heroic priests of *The Exorcist*. The ritual daggers that are, in the context of the plot, the only means of killing the Antichrist are also a product of Seltzer's creative license, not to be found in any interpretation of biblical prophecy. According to the Book of Revelation, it is Christ Himself who will bring down the Antichrist and consign him to everlasting hellfire for eternity.

More significant than any of these departures from the details of scripture, however, is the film's central narrative conceit: that Robert Thorn must, at all costs, destroy the Antichrist and avert the apocalypse. Framing the struggle between cosmic Good and Evil in this way implies that the outcome hangs in the balance, and can be determined by human actions: an idea that contradicts virtually all interpretations of biblical prophecy on the nature and role of the Antichrist. Scripture portrays the actions of the Antichrist as preordained by God, a necessary—if devastating—step on the road to the final unification of Heaven and Earth, the eternal punishment of the wicked, and the eternal reward of the righteous. To believers who take the prophecies of Revelation and other biblical texts seriously, neither the course nor the outcome of the End Times is in doubt. God will triumph, Christ will return to Earth, the faithful will be saved, and the Antichrist will be defeated. Only the identities of those who will be saved are in doubt, and delaying or diverting the actions of the Antichrist would presumably be anathema to anyone who longed for salvation and thus awaited the working out of God's ultimate plan. A true believer would rather anticipate the Rapture (expecting to be uplifted to Heaven), and—if left on Earth after it took place—acknowledge the presence of the Antichrist and pray for God's deliverance from his wrath.

Robert Munger, who served as a religious consultant on the film, was evidently untroubled by such contradictions. He contended, in numerous interviews, that the film was a true depiction of future events—a statement that is difficult parse, not just theologically, but rationally. Yet, it is his deep conviction that helped make *The Omen* such a resonant film. Darby's influence, via Lindsey, is readily apparent in the details of the finished film. Making Damien the son of an ambassador fits the dispensationalist belief that the Antichrist will arise from the world of politics, and setting the film in England aligns it with the contentions of Lindsey and others that a united Europe "'may well be the beginning of the ten-nation confederacy'—the revived Roman empire—'predicted by Daniel and the Book of Revelation.'"[14] What makes the film work for someone inclined to the dispensationalist viewpoint is not the specifics, but the overall message of the film: That the prophesied rise of the Antichrist is going to happen, and it will likely happen in our lifetime. This serves as a cinematic confirmation of belief for the already-convinced or the half-convinced, especially those who have just enough exposure to popular presentations of biblical prophecy to make the film seem believable.

Upon its release, critical reviews of the film were mixed, with some deriding it as nothing more than paranoid religious claptrap. Audiences, however, embraced the film, spawning a franchise that, to date, encompasses two sequels, a made-for-television reboot movie, and a 2004 remake that added very little to the original version and failed to generate the same level of audience excitement. The original, 1976 version of *The Omen* is now regarded as a horror classic, which John Kenneth Muir describes as "a powerful horror film, because it knowingly and cleverly interprets Christian belief."[15]

Muir's analysis of the film's success is broadly correct, but incomplete. While he recognizes the film's relationship to the cultural malaise of the mid–1970s, and the desire for certainty that leads individuals to search for answers in the divine, he unwittingly accepts the Premillennial Dispensationalist version of the end times as *the* standard Christian interpretation. "*The Omen* seeks to unnerve moviegoers, and tap into that irrational 'belief' zone in all of us," Muir continues. "What if the Bible is correct? What if all the signs of the Antichrist are happening around right now? Would we believe them? Heck, would we even notice?"[16] Such an analysis, however, misses the particular cultural influences of religion on the film. *The Omen* is a historical artifact: the product of a particular time in history, when Premillennial Dispensationalism—a once-obscure interpretation of biblical prophecy—merged with the cultural anxieties of the time, and so permeated both religious and popular culture that it does not, in retrospect, clearly stand out as a separate influence.

Premillennial Dispensationalist views of the end times have since become a central part of American evangelical Christianity itself. Even evangelicals who do not know who Hal Lindsey (let alone John Nelson Darby) is have been immersed, since the 1970s, in a culture of interpretation that accepts, with little reservation, the Premillennial Dispensationalist interpretation as the clear and correct reading of scripture. Christians outside the evangelical community, and even non–Christians unfamiliar with the details of biblical prophecy, are likely to be broadly familiar with elements such as the Antichrist, the Rapture, and the Great Tribulation. The ominous birthmark that confirms Damien's identity at last—"Here is wisdom. Let him that hath understanding count the number of the beast: for it is the number of a man; and his number is six hundred threescore and six"[17]—has to be explained to Thorn, and thus the audience. Now, it is lodged firmly enough in secular popular culture to be used, without explanation, on bumper stickers and as a punch line in cartoons. Premillennial Dispensationalism has been normalized, and *The Omen* was central to the process.

The process of normalization has created—particularly within the evangelical community—a market for fictional works that dramatize Premillennial Dispensationalist ideas more completely, and take its details more seriously, than did *The Omen*. The bestselling "Left Behind" series of novels by Reverend Tim LaHaye and Jerry Jenkins, for example, begins with the Rapture and follows a diverse band of characters through the Great Tribulation. The success of such stories, in print and on screen, has diminished the uniqueness of *The Omen*, but not its historical significance, It is a film that, even when it departs from the details of evangelical teachings about the end times, fits well enough with the underlying principles of those teachings that it could be screened within the worship spaces of many modern American churches without even a hint of controversy. Thus, one can say *The Omen* stands as a perfect example of film serving both as an historical artifact and a religio-cultural influence, a unique context making it worthy of additional attention from film lovers and historians alike.

NOTES

1. Douglas E. Cowan, *Sacred Terror: Religion and Horror on the Silver Screen* (Waco: Baylor University Press, 2008), 192.
2. The text of the speech, often called the "Malaise Speech" despite the fact that Carter never used the word, is available at Jimmy Carter, "'Crisis of Confidence' Speech," 15 July 1979, The Miller Center (University of Virginia), http://millercenter.org/president/speeches/speech-3402. Overviews of the 1970s as an age of malaise and uncertainty include David J. Schulman, *The Seventies: The Great Shift in American Culture, Society, and Politics* (Cambridge, MA: Da Capo Press, 2001) and Jefferson Cowie, *Stayin' Alive: The 1970s and the Last Days of the Working Class* (New York: The New Press, 2010).
3. David Frum. *How We Got Here, the 70's: The Decade That Brought You Modern Life—for Better or Worse* (New York: Basic Books, 2000), 149.
4. Ibid., 158.
5. For an accessible Catholic view of End Times theology that is critical of the Premillennial Dispensationalist perspective, see Paul Thigpen, *The Rapture Trap: A Catholic Response to "End Times" Fever* (West Chester, PA: Ascension Press, 2001). For a Reformed Protestant view, see R.C. Sproul, *The Last Days According to Jesus* (Grand Rapids: Baker Books, 1998).
6. Hal Lindsey, *The Late, Great Planet Earth* (New York: Bantam, 1973).
7. Ibid. Also see Hal Lindsey, *The 1980s: Countdown to Armageddon* (New York: Bantam, 1981).
8. For a short, yet thorough, overview on the life and influence of John Nelson Darby, see David S. New, *Christian Fundamentalism in America: A Cultural History* (Jefferson, NC: McFarland, 2012), 104–121. Modern clarions of eschatological doom like televangelist Jack Van Impe and the late Tim LaHaye, author of the popular *Left Behind* series of books and films, continue proclaiming variations of this same eschatological outline. They, like Lindsey, are the theological children of John Nelson Darby.
9. Martin E. Marty and R. Scott Appleby, *The Glory and the Power: The Fundamentalist Challenge to the Modern World* (Boston: Beacon Press, 1992), 53–54.
10. Cowan, *Sacred Terror*, 194.
11. *The Omen Legacy*, DVD, dir. Brent Zacky, 2001.
12. Ibid. Seltzer has changed his story over the course of four decades of interviews, so one is left to ponder what sources and/or interpretations inspired this poem and what influenced his take on biblical prophecy. It certainly fits nicely within a Premillennial Dispensationalist framework.
13. Ibid.
14. Ibid., 194.
15. John Kenneth Muir, *Horror Films of the 1970s* (Jefferson, NC: McFarland, 2002), 429.
16. Ibid.
17. Revelation 13:18 (King James Version).

BIBLIOGRAPHY

Cowan, Douglas E. *Sacred Terror: Religion and Horror on the Silver Screen.* Waco: Baylor University Press, 2008.
Cowie, Jefferson. *Stayin' Alive: The 1970s and the Last Days of the Working Class.* New York: The Free Press, 2010.
Frum, David. *How We Got Here, the 70's: The Decade That Brought You Modern Life—for Better or Worse.* New York: Basic Books, 2000.
Lindsey, Hal. *The 1980s: Countdown to Armageddon.* New York: Bantam, 1981.
_____, with C.C. Carlson. *The Late, Great Planet Earth.* New York: Bantam, 1973.
Marty, Martin E., and R. Scott Appleby. *The Glory and the Power: The Fundamentalist Challenge to the Modern World.* Boston: Beacon Press, 1992.
Muir, John Kenneth. *Horror Films of the 1970s.* Jefferson, NC: McFarland, 2002.
New, David S. *Christian Fundamentalism in America: A Cultural History.* Jefferson, NC: McFarland, 2012.
Noll, Mark A. *The Scandal of the Evangelical Mind.* Grand Rapids: William B. Eerdmans, 1994.
Schulman, Bruce J. *The Seventies: The Great Shift in American Culture, Society, and Politics.* Cambridge, MA: Da Capo Press, 2001.
Sproul, R.C. *The Last Days According to Jesus.* Grand Rapids: Baker Books, 1998.
Thigpen, Paul. *The Rapture Trap: A Catholic Response to "End Times" Fever.* West Chester, PA: Ascension Press, 2001.

The Fall of a Domestic Angel
Horror and Hierophany
in Rosemary's Baby *(1968)*

SUE MATHESON

Ranked second only to Alfred Hitchcock's *Psycho* (1960) as the best horror film of all time,[1] Roman Polanski's *Rosemary's Baby* (1968) popularized depictions of witchcraft, demonic activity, and the Devil on screen and generated a wave of supernatural horror movies that included *The Exorcist* (1973), *The Omen* (1976), *The Shining* (1980), and *The Blair Witch Project* (1999). Adapted from Ira Levin's 1967 horror novel, Polanski's blockbuster begins when a young couple—Rosemary (Mia Farrow) and Guy Woodhouse (John Cassavetes)—move into The Bramford, an old New York apartment building with a history of occult activity, and become friendly with their elderly neighbors, Minnie (Ruth Gordon) and Roman Castevet (Sidney Blackmer). Promised a successful acting career by Roman, Guy drugs Rosemary and hands her over a group of Satan-worshipping witches, who prepare her to be raped and impregnated by a supernatural being (later identified as the Devil). Afterward, the now-pregnant Rosemary finds herself imprisoned in her apartment, isolated from her friends, and increasingly ignored by her husband. She uncovers the secrets of her neighbors' religious cult, and, thinking they want her baby for ritual sacrifice, attempts to run away. Her effort to escape fails, and her husband, who is about to become a movie star, and her doctor, a member of the coven, take her back to The Bramford. When the baby is born, he is spirited away—but Rosemary, hearing him cry in the Castevets' apartment, attempts to rescue him. The film ends with her realizing her true role in the horrors around her: as the mother of the Antichrist.

Intrigued by Stephen Frankfurt's evocative poster, moviegoers flocked to theaters to "pray for Rosemary's Baby." Made for $2.4 million, the film became a runaway success by December 1969, grossing over $33 million in the United States alone. Typically, supernatural horror films focus on the intervention of the paranormal in natural events. *Rosemary's Baby*, however, became a *tour de force* for supernatural horror without any paranormal "machinery." Robert Evans, the film's producer, believes that Polanski's skill as a filmmaker was responsible for the overwhelming audience response to this film. Polanski, Evans says, "knew how to manipulate the mind on film and make it work."[2] Polanski himself attributes the success of his first Hollywood movie to its ambivalence regarding the supernatural. The film's only paranormal events are shown in a hallucinatory dream sequence, and he notes that Rosemary's experience "could have been all [a] question of her paranoia, of her suspicions during the pregnancy, and postpartum craze." There is, Polanski continues, "a subliminal moment when she remembers the eyes she saw with the dream, but other than that the film is totally realistic. There is nothing supernatural in the film, and everything that occurred could have happened in real life."[3]

Unsurprisingly, critical writing on *Rosemary's Baby* has focused on the film's framing of the social and psychological terrors attending marriage and childbirth. The mistreatment of married women features prominently in the conversation, as in Lucy Fife's contention that the film presents marriage as a structure to support "male selfishness," and Sharon Marcus' examination of Rosemary's "devastating recognition that her most intimate relationships have been the site of her exploitation."[4] Feminist critics have generally approached *Rosemary's Baby* from a gyneco-political standpoint, with Lucy Fischer describing it as a "Gynecological Gothic," echoing Rhona Bernstein's contention that the film reflects the "horrifying status of motherhood in American patriarchal culture."[5] Polanski's treatment of maternity, Karyn Valerius suggests, turns "horror to feminist ends," by presenting Rosemary's pregnancy, from conception to birth, as a nightmare of "violence, deceit, and [the] misappropriation of a woman's body by people she trusts."[6]

Broader discussions of the film's social and cultural message have been scarce,[7] and issues of religiosity associated with Rosemary's pregnancy have received no critical attention to date. This omission is particularly odd, given the visual and narrative emphasis that Polanski places, throughout the film, on Catholic tropes and gnostic traditions connected with the feminine mystery. This essay is a first step toward redressing that imbalance, examining Polanski's treatment of pregnancy as a site in which horror and *hierophany* intersect as the film charts the fall of a domestic angel.

From Domestic Angel to Walking Womb

Rosemary's pregnancy reanimates social and religious constructs belonging to the 19th-century Cult of Domesticity, a middle- and upper-class phenomenon in the United States and Great Britain that promoted "ideal womanhood," a value system based on the cardinal virtues of piety, purity, submission, and domesticity.[8] Equating "ideal womanhood" with motherhood, the Cult of Domesticity (also known as the Cult of Perfect Motherhood) determined the home to be a woman's "proper sphere." In the home, wives and mothers were expected to be "domestic angels," the guiding lights of their households, managing domestic affairs and providing moral guidance to their families. The domestic angel was expected, moreover, to raise sons who would have a direct impact on the success of the nation. Jeanne Peterson remarks in "No Angels in the House: The Victorian Myth and the Paget Women" that "[f]or some, the angel in the house is evidence of a 'golden age' of family life, an era when men and women had separate roles in the social hierarchy." "For others," Peterson continues, "she is a symbol of oppressed women trapped in the gilded cage of Victorian male domination." In either case, it should be noted, the domestic angel's salient characteristics are considered to be "innocence, piety, and dependency."[9]

On moving into The Bramford, Rosemary's socio-psychological profile does not appear to be that of a domestic angel—she makes the decision to change apartments, and she decides to befriend the Castavets. But having settled into her apartment and found herself pregnant, she becomes an "ideal" wife and mother, what Peterson would consider "an acquiescent, passive, unintellectual creature, whose life revolve[s] entirely around social engagements, domestic management, and religion."[10] Like an emblem of 19th-century middle class femininity in the 20th century, increasingly fragile and pale in her first trimester (domestic angels were considered delicate creatures), she becomes increasingly dependent on others. The Castevets and her husband decide what she will eat and drink, which doctor will attend her, what she will read, and with whom she will socialize. Roman Castevet even uses the Victorian cliché that he, his wife, and Guy "must see that she gets plenty of rest." Confined during her second trimester, Rosemary ceases to go out of her home and is socially isolated from her friends and peers.

Despite her compliance with social protocol, pregnancy does not turn out to be transcendent experience for Rosemary—physically, socially, or spiritually. Polanski's opening wide shot in *Rosemary's Baby*—a leisurely panoramic view of New York's skyline that pans past buildings and Central Park before the camera tilts down to survey the byzantine succession of rooftops belonging to the Dakota Apartment House on 72nd and 73rd streets—presages the dreadful nature of the events that are about to occur.[11] The camera's (and so, the viewers') gradual and winding descent from light to darkness eventually reveals the tiny figures of Rosemary and Guy entering that which Polanski himself considers "the real star of the picture."[12] As David Walsh remarks, Polanski intended The Bramford to be "a character in the story. He wanted it to be big and frightening and almost overwhelming."[13] Further establishing the importance of The Bramford (and its *mise-en-scène*) in the film's narrative, Polanski cuts to another wide shot of Rosemary and Guy inside the gated entrance of The Bramford's huge courtyard, which served as a carriage turnaround. The next, another wide shot, shows the couple walking with their real estate agent past a fountain sprouting gigantic iron calla lilies: white flowers associated with the Virgin Mary and The Annunciation that represent purity and innocence.

In 1969, Polanski noted that *Rosemary's Baby* is "full of intricate camera moves" that are not generally noticed because they are intrinsic or, as Polanski puts it, "relevant to the story."[14] Joe McElhaney remarks in "Urban Irrational: *Rosemary's Baby*, Polanski, New York" that the director has crafted "a film in which almost every detail within the image carries *potential* meaning."[15] Polankski's exacting attention to the nuances of interior space—his use of the Bramford's walls and corridors to frame the action taking place—creates a site of "enclosure and oppression in which finally a hospital broom closet, by contrast, seems more appealing"[16] When Rosemary and Guy walk from the courtyard into The Bramford, for example, Polanski immediately uses a reverse angle from inside the apartment's lobby for their entrance: the lobby's high narrow halls act as a frame within the frame, immediately constricting the navigable space onscreen to a third of what is shown to the viewer. This space is further reduced as the trio steps into the tiny cage elevator. One would expect stepping off the elevator into the hallway on the seventh floor to be a relief from the constriction experienced by the couple (and the camera) in the elevator, but the narrowness of the winding passageway in which Guy and Rosemary find themselves again restricts the viewer's gaze by enclosing sightlines.

Once Rosemary and Guy move into The Bramford, Polanski's framing of the action becomes even more restrictive. When the pair, one carrying a bag of groceries and the other a lamp, enter the apartment for their first night there, Polanski shoots their arrival from the apartment's point of view at the end of its long central corridor. In this interior shot, the apartment door creaks open to reveal the figures of the couple entering: as they approach the camera, the static frame cuts off first their heads and then the upper parts of their torsos as they advance to the end of the hall. Rosemary's headless body turns left and enters the bedroom with her grocery bag, Guy's (equally headless) enters the living room with the lamp. Rosemary is even more narrowly defined within the frame when she leaves the bedroom to enter the living room, being seen, at first, only from her knees down. As she moves towards the living room in the background of the shot, her figure diminishes in size, and, less constrained by the frame, becomes fully visible.

As a catalyst for a deeper, complicated range of audience responses to her unusually prolonged and restricted confinement, Polanski's careful inclosing of the action in The Bramford compounds the discomfort attending Rosemary's pregnancy and confinement for the viewer as well as the protagonist. The film's cinematographer, William Fraker, points out that Polanski's cramped frameworks in *Rosemary's Baby* are meant to involve the audience with the characters. When Minnie Castevet makes a phone call in Rosemary's bedroom, "I had a perfectly framed shot of her in the middle of the door frame," he says. "You could even see a little movement of her hair from a breeze coming through an open window. I called Roman over to the camera to see how we composed the shot. He said, 'No Billy. Move the camera to the left.' I kept moving it until he said, 'That's the shot.' I said, 'Roman, if we do this the audience won't see what she is doing.' 'Exactly,' he said. 'At the preview screening 500 people in the audience all shifted to the right in their seats trying to look around the door jamb and see what Minnie was doing.'"[17] As Rob Davies notes in "*Female Paranoia*: The Psychological Horror of Roman Polanski," Polanski's frames create settings that are "claustrophobic" in spite of the enormous size of the apartment.[18] Accordingly, Rosemary's experience of her pregnancy becomes the audience's as well—when watching *Rosemary's Baby* the viewer, visually curbed, hampered, and constricted, undergoes "the same loss of one's self" that she experiences.[19]

Socially isolated, Rosemary finds herself at the mercy of others as her pregnancy turns into "a Gothic spectacle" marked by her psychological descent into anxiety and then despair.[20] Episodes of forced actions, social and sexual restraint, entrapment, and confinement cause her self-image to crumble. Rosemary may be living in New York in the 20th century, but her horrifying experience of motherhood in The Bramford belongs to another place and time, giving form to the now-clichéd notion that women sacrifice their identities and freedom to fulfill their childbearing role.[21] As McElhaney notes, "the Castevets and their circle of acquaintances assume a function straight out of the world of European fairytales in which 'innocents' (Snow White or Hansel and Gretel, for example) are lured to their doom by deceptively kind, elderly people who are ultimately out for young blood" and "The Bramford becomes a variation on the gothic horror mansion: A place of mystery in a film in which "everything is marked by indeterminacy."[22]

It is no coincidence, then, that the warren of roofs created by the apartment block, first introduced from high in the air, resembles what Stephen Birmingham describes as "a miniature European town."[23] The Bramford thus evokes traditional ways of life that remain embedded in American culture despite the rapid social change that has taken place in the 20th century. Polanski's expressionistic and surreal treatment of The Bramford also communicates "inner-turmoil occurring within characters"—its interiors serve as "'cranial' spaces of inner-anxieties pertaining to relocation, religion, and heterosexual monogamy."[24] Supporting those anxieties, the topography of Rosemary's confinement also furthers traditional social, psychological, and religious attitudes towards expectant mothers, demonstrating that pregnancy (even today) remains largely an antique mystery,

Roman Castevet (Sidney Blackmer) asks Rosemary (Mia Farrow) to accept her own child and be a mother to it in *Rosemary's Baby* (1968).

defined and determined by ancient beliefs and traditions. Thus, past and present intersect and collide in Polanski's *mise-en-scène* as Rosemary attempts to update her gloomy, old-fashioned apartment into a bright and modern living space, but even white paint and sunny, yellow-flowered wallpaper are unable to render the stolid, 19th-century proportions and wainscoting in her apartment in The Bramford invisible.

As Rosemary's anxiety for the safety of her baby rises during her first trimester, Polanski's static framing carries on creating what become increasingly disturbing images of dismemberment as her due date approaches. Rosemary's apartment appears to be cheery and bright, but body parts of the figures blocked closest to the camera continue to be severed if the characters move too close to the edges of the picture. Parts of Rosemary's body, in particular, are lost or separated from one another. Increasingly, the image of dismemberment most often associated with Rosemary's pregnancy separates her brain from her body. This, too, is a throwback to the 19th century, when it was thought that pregnancy caused women's brains to atrophy: even in the late 1990s the British media "went to town on the incredible shrinking brain of the pregnant women: headlines declared she is "all stomach and no brain."[25] Illustrating such views, Polanski repeatedly cuts off Rosemary's forehead from the rest of her face with the camera, positioning the top edge of the frame just above her eyebrows. The first example of this image occurs just after she has been drugged and is lying on her bed, while Guy, shot from angles that provide ample headroom, prepares her for the Castevets' satanic ritual. During her dream sequence when she is tied to a mattress, her headroom is severely restricted, her forehead being again cut off by the top edge of the frame.

This framing device becomes an important motif that explains Rosemary's imprisonment in The Bramford after she announces her pregnancy. Just as Polanski's camera insists that Rosemary is functioning without a brain, those around her treat her as if she is mindless. Guy throws the book that Hutch gives Rosemary in the garbage because he does not want her "upsetting" herself. Unable to read what she wants and to make decisions for herself, Rosemary is reduced to being merely a vessel for the fetus she carries. Polanski's camera reinforces this most strongly when Rosemary, late in her last trimester, is seen packing her hospital suitcase for the maternity ward. In this image, she is framed as merely a heavily gravid torso, visible only from her shoulders down to her knees. Living in The Bramford, Rosemary has become little more than a walking womb.

Pregnancy and Hierophany—Passage to the Divine?

Polanski's attention to detail links the biological aspects of pregnancy to familiar social and psychological assumptions about it. His multi-layered *mise-en-scène* attention to the religious aspects of Rosemary's condition reconceptualizes and reorders the natural and the familiar. Polanski carefully prepares his viewer for this. When Rosemary begins to hallucinate before her rape, she learns that the "trip" she is on is "for Catholics only," and finds herself lying on scaffolding, transported while looking up at Michelangelo's *The Creation of Adam* on the ceiling of the Sistine Chapel. Conflicted and complex, her dream vision is not presented as a simple binary in which the forces of good (the sacred) and evil (the supernatural) are opposed: the ceiling of the Sistine Chapel displays demonic images as well as scenes from Genesis. Polanski then conflates elements of the supernatural and the sacred during her rape in what appears to be the basement of The Bramford. Directing the satanic ritual, Roman Castevet's creepy father, Adrian Marcato, returned from the dead and standing by a raised podium, oversees the rites performed by his son. As the unclothed members of the coven chant and Rosemary's legs are tied to bedposts, Castevet paints symbols on her naked torso, summoning a stranger whose scaly hands and elongated irises identify him as the Devil. At the rite's end, Rosemary is visited by a bejeweled Pope whose outstretched hand offers her a demonic amulet to kiss.

Catholic tropes throughout *Rosemary's Baby* express the intersection of the supernatural and the sacred with the ideology of pregnancy. In particular, the Virgin Mary's story (from the Annunciation to Christ's birth) functions as an ur-text. Throughout her pregnancy, the wardrobe of the Antichrist's reluctant mother, in various shades of blue (representing heavenly grace and servitude) and white (representing purity, innocence, and virtue), resembles that associated with the Virgin. Even Rosemary's dressing gown (sky blue edged with white lace) and bedroom slippers invite viewers to recognize her evocation of the *theotokos*—the Mother of God. At the film's end, she is told that, like Mary, she was chosen of all the women in the world by a supernatural being to be the mother of his "only living son." A "God-bearer," Rosemary, like Mary, is an *imago mundi*, a physical site in which earth, heaven, and the underworld are in communication. Pregnant, she houses "the breakthrough of the sacred (or the supernatural) into the ordinary world."[26] Throughout, Polanski's camera presents supernatural/sacred nature of Rosemary's rite of passage into motherhood as a *hierophany*—a manifestation of the sacred—via the homology of body-house-comos situated in The Bramford. As Eliade points out, traditional Man inhabits his body in the same way that he inhabits a house or the cosmos that he has himself created. As modes of being, body, house, and cosmos each offer means of access to one another by displaying, keeping, or being capable of receiving an opening (an *axis mundi*) that makes passage to another transcendent plane possible. Thus, even the most elemental hierophany offers its initiates passage from one mode of being or existential situation to another.[27]

In *Rosemary's Baby*, systematic correspondences convey this religious principle of human life. Rosemary and Guy's apartment reflects the belief that life is a maze through which the soul must travel, by appearing to be a literal maze itself. The central corridor offers a number of pathways and concealed cul-de-sacs, and leads into rooms that seem to be dead-ends. Maze-like, it requires those within to make choices, any of which can lead to error, confusion, entanglement, and finally entrapment if the puzzle presented is not properly solved. The apartment's passageways leading to dead ends are apt metaphors for the cosmos that Rosemary constructs for herself while living in The Bramford. Rosemary acts in error many times, her first mistake being her decision to move into the building. Others include accepting Minnie's invitation to dinner, befriending the elderly couple, eating the chocolate mousse that Guy urges on her, changing her doctor at the Castevets' insistence, allowing herself to be alienated from her friends and ignoring their advice, and drinking the "vitamin drink" that Minnie prepares for her daily. These "wrong" decisions increase her entanglement with the Castevets and tie her ever-more-tightly to her apartment. Just before giving birth, Rosemary does attempt to escape The Bramford to ensure her baby's survival, but New York poses the same problem: every path that she chooses to use to escape the Castevets also is a cul-de-sac. At Dr. Saperstein's office, she discovers that he belongs to the coven, like the Castevets who recommended him. When she bolts from his office into a telephone booth, she finds herself boxed in by a man (whom she mistakes for the doctor) waiting outside. Dr. Hill's office appears to offer her a route to safety, but there she is caged and handed over to Saperstein, Guy, and the witches, who march her back to The Bramford.

Robert Lima remarks, in "The Satanic Rape of Catholicism in *Rosemary's Baby*," that the film points to the continuity of gnostic practices in the present, and, in particular,

Minnie (Ruth Gordon) and Roman (Sidney Blackmer) Castevet in *Rosemary's Baby* (1968).

to those ceremonies associated with witchcraft.[28] Witchcraft, however, is not the only gnostic tradition at work. An antique tradition concerning gnostic knowledge and acts of transit, labyrinth walking also symbolizes the wandering of the soul in the material world. Unlike the maze, the labyrinth is a unicursal route, or single course, that signifies the initiate's endless search for meaning. Labyrinths whose paths lead to a divine symbolic image located at the center were placed in conspicuous places in churches throughout Europe. The best-known is that set into the floor of the Chartres Cathedral. It is split into four parts, and its pathway passes once through each part as it leads inexorably from the outside to the inside—that is from the entrance to the goal—before ending at a central space where, centuries ago, a metal plaque depicted "a most un–Christian tableau of Theseus killing the Minotaur with Ariadne holding the thread which was to show him the way home."[29]

As Rosemary's pregnancy progresses, it becomes evident that the path that she is following, like that of Theseus, is pre-determined and decidedly un–Christian; she cannot control (and refuses to alter by abortion) the events of her pregnancy. The viewer, who takes for granted that gestation leads inexorably from conception to childbirth, discovers that Rosemary's pregnancy defines her future as well as her present. Once Rosemary is confident her child will be born, preparations for motherhood—drinking Minnie's "vitamin" concoctions daily at 11 o'clock, preparing a nursery for her child, and packing her hospital suitcase well before she expects to be in the maternity ward—order her existence. As the activities of her second and third trimester become coherent, a corresponding pattern of transit from room to room in her apartment emerges. What appears at first to have been a puzzling warren becomes a unicursal pattern arranged in a series of intercommunicating planes. While Rosemary's fetus grows and takes shape within her, the inner workings of the apartment itself also take shape and are made manifest as the nature of this interior space becomes comprehensible. Internal passageways between rooms are revealed as the film's narrative progresses: first, the transit from the bedroom to the bathroom to the study which will serve as the baby's nursery is made apparent; then, the passageway between the kitchen and the living room is disclosed, exposing another circular multi-cursal design lying within the larger pattern; later, the overall scheme of the apartment itself is fully revealed when Rosemary discovers the hidden entry point that exists between her apartment and the Castevets.' In short, the development of Rosemary's fetus corresponds with the viewer's discovery of interconnecting passages, and, as hidden links between the rooms are uncovered by the camera and used by the characters, Polanski incorporates Rosemary's belly (a symbol of the Divine) into the body-house-cosmos. The womb itself not only becomes an *imago mundi*, a sacred Center in which and from which the world unfolds, but also an *axis mundi*, offering passage from one plane of existence to another.

Ordeal and Abjection

Deeply significant to the horror aesthetic, pregnancy in *Rosemary's Baby* is presented on every level as being an initiatory ordeal for women. After her baby is born, Rosemary finally arrives at her journey's harrowing end and learns the truth about the monstrous reality that has been hidden from her by her husband and her neighbors—Roger Ebert, who gave the film four stars in his 1968 *Chicago Sun-Times* review, remarks: "How the story turns out, and who (or what) Rosemary's baby really is, hardly matters." He continues: "When the conclusion comes, it works not because it is a surprise but because it is horrifyingly inevitable. Rosemary makes her dreadful discovery, and we are wrenched because we knew what was going to happen—and couldn't help her. This is why the movie is so good."[30]

The horror experienced by Rosemary and the viewer at the climax of the film has been attributed to Polanski's descralization of the infant. The viewer, however, has known throughout that he is a monster. The coven validates Rosemary's perception that her rape "is really happening" by placing a black cloth over her face to prevent her from witnessing her violation by the Devil. Physically and cognitively threatening, Rosemary's baby has been abject since his conception—his abjection confirmed at the movie's end when Rosemary realizes that he has the Devil's non-human eyes and Minnie (along with Laura-Louise, another member of The Bramford's coven) asserts that he also has his father's scaly hands and cloven hooves. The horror attending Rosemary's discovery of her diabolical child, however, pales beside the viewer's corresponding discovery that Rosemary herself, a Madonna immersed in the gross female biological processes of menstruation, pregnancy, and childbirth, does not recognize herself as a contaminated being.

As Peter Hutchings remarks, the abject—the object of horror—does not "respect borders, positions, rules"; rather, it upsets the social order that is created and managed through the division of objects and/or properties into distinct groups.[31] At the film's end, Rosemary, dressed in blue and white, breaches social and cultural taboos regarding childbirth. She stands in the Castevets' living room rocking her diabolical child when she should have been lying-in. As Eric Ives points out, a woman's confinement after the birth of her child is a "curious custom, part religious, part medical, part feminine mystery."[32] During the Renaissance in England, a woman's postpartum confinement kept her secluded until she was "churched," or purified, a month or more after the delivery of her child."[33] By the early 20th century, this lying-in period had ceased to be a religious mystery and had become a required period of bed rest in hospitals of up to 20 days even if there were no medical complications attending the birth.[34] Pre-partum, Rosemary was isolated like a monster; post-partum, she is revealed to be one—neither "churched" nor purified—roaming unrestrained amongst the members of her community.

Julia Kristeva argues that the mother is marked as abject (or discarded) at the instant of her infant's separation from her—first, at the moment of her baby's messy delivery when the child emerges from her body, and, second, at the separation of mother and child that occurs when the child is weaned.[35] But, paradoxically, in *Rosemary's Baby*, the mother's abjection continues when she and her child are reunited. The terrifying trajectory of Rosemary's desolation climaxes in Polanski's tableau of mother and child at the labyrinth's center in the Castevets' apartment. Evoking the audience's deepest feelings of horror, Rosemary meeting this child is like Theseus encountering the Minotaur, for the infant is something that "simply should not be."[36] However, in the living room that houses her baby's black bassinet, monstrosity is not vanquished. Discredited, deemed vulnerable to depression, anxiety disorders, eating disorders, panic disorder, social phobia, and psychosis, the Madonna figure succumbs to her maternal temperament. Her child, a gnostic demiurge, becomes her personal deity. Rosemary accepts her baby, because she is, as Roman Castevet points out, his mother.

Ultimately, the correspondences created by hierophany in *Rosemary's Baby* compound, complicate, and deepen the social and psychological horrors at work. Sold, body and soul, by her husband in a Faustian bargain for an "herb garden" and "a swimming pool" in Beverly Hills, Rosemary participates in her own horrifying damnation, a willing acolyte of the Cult of Domesticity which demands its followers be "religious, pure in heart and body, submissive to [their] husband[s] and God,"[37] even though, as Eliade points out, "[t]he mystery of childbearing ... woman's discovery that she is a creator on the plane of life, constitutes a religious experience that cannot be translated into masculine terms."[38] Polanski's closing shot of The Bramford, a visual echo of the viewer's initial descent into terror, ensures that the triplet of body-house-cosmos in *Rosemary's Baby* is recognized as a cul-de-sac—it returns the viewer to a bird's eye view of Guy and Rosemary's tiny figures entering The Bramford as Rosemary's voice-over is heard, singing a lullaby to her baby. At the film's end, The Bramford is "an architectonic structure, apparently aimless, and of a pattern so complex that, once inside it, it is impossible or very difficult to escape."[39] In it, there are no possibilities of passage to higher planes of being. Motherhood turns out to be a dead end, and the true relation between the world and woman is nothing more than sexuality, labor, and, ultimately, death. In *Rosemary's Baby*, motherhood is not the transcendent experience that the Cult of Domesticity promises it to be, for the domestic angel does not give her soul to God in the service of her family— in contemporary times, as Polanski says, "the Devil prevails."[40] At the end, they are, all of them, witches in The Bramford.

NOTES

1. See "The Greatest Films of All Time: Download the Date," *The Guardian* online, https://www.theguardian.com/news/datablog/2010/oct/16/greatest-films-of-all-time.
2. *Roman Polanski on Rosemary's Baby*.
3. Ibid.
4. Lucy Fife, "Human Monstrosity: Rape, Ambiguity and Performance in *Rosemary's Baby*," in *Hosting The Monster*, ed. Holly Baumgartner and Roger Davis, 43–62 (New York: Rodopi, 2008), 59; Sharon Marcus, "Placing Rosemary's Baby," *Differences: A Journal of Feminist Cultural Studies* 5, no. 5 (1993): 146–147.
5. Lucy Fischer, "Birth Traumas: Parturition and Horror in *Rosemary's Baby*," *Cinema Journal* 31, no. 3 (Spring 1992): 4; Rhona Bernstein, quoted in Fischer, 4.
6. Karyn Valerius, "*Rosemary's Baby*, Gothic Pregnancy and Fetal Subjects," *College Literature* 32, no. 3 (Summer 2005): 119, 116.
7. An important exception is David Frankfurter's "Awakening to Satanic Conspiracy: *Rosemary's Baby* and the Cult Next Door," in *Deliver Us From Evil: Boston University Studies in Philosophy and Religion*, ed. M. David Eckel and Bradley L. Herling (London: Continuum, 2008), 75–87, which claims that *Rosemary's Baby* foreshadows themes that became realized in the Satanic-cult panic that gripped the United States of the 1980s and 1990s.
8. The Cult of Domesticity has experienced resurgences of popularity, most notably in the 1950s and most recently as the New Domesticity in the 2010s.
9. M. Jeanne Peterson, "No Angels in the House: The Victorian Myth and the Paget Women." *American Historical Review* 89, no. 3 (1984): 678.
10. Ibid.
11. In *Life at the Dakota: New York's Most Unusual Address*, Stephen Birmingham remarks the Dakota Apartment House standing west of Central Park on 72nd and 73rd streets that Henry Hardenbergh designed was "essentially a huge hollow cube, roughly as tall as it was wide and long. To this basic structure were added elaborate embellishments—ledges, balconies, decorative iron railings and tall columns of bay windows climbing eight stories high" (34). Birmingham describes the capstone of the Dakota as being its "succession of roofs" which "resembles a miniature European town of gables, turrets, pyramids, towers, peaks, wrought-iron fences, chimneys, finals and flagpoles. The roof was shingled in slate and trimmed with copper, and it was peppered with windows of every imaginable shape and size—dormer and flush, square, round and rectangular, big and small, wide and narrow. Nestled among all this, Hardenbergh designed a rooftop promenade with gazebos and pergolas and canopied sunshades. The courtyard below would also be circled with an awning promenade" (35).
12. Roman Polanski, *Roman by Polanski* (New York: Morrow, 1984), 267.
13. Bob Fisher, "William Fraker Dances with the Devil," *Moviemaker*, October 7, 2008, http://www.moviemaker.com/articles-moviemaking/rosemarys-baby-william-fraker-roman-polanski-20081007.

14. Polanski, *Roman by Polanski,* 44.
15. Joe McElhaney, "Urban Irrational: *Rosemary's Baby*, Polanski, New York," in *City That Never Sleeps: New York and the Filmic Imagination*, ed. Murray Pomerance, Wheeler Winston Dixon, and Barry Keith Grant (New Brunswick: Rutgers University Press, 2007), 204 (emphasis added).
16. McElhaney, "Urban Irrational," 210, 202.
17. Fisher, "William Fraker."
18. Rob Davies, "Female Paranoia: The Psychological Horror of Roman Polanski," *FilmMatters* 5, no. 2 (June 2014): 18.
19. *Ibid.*
20. Valerius, "*Rosemary's Baby*, Gothic Pregnancy and Fetal Subjects," 116.
21. Simone de Beauvoir, *The Second Sex* (New York: Vintage, 1989), 477.
22. McElhany, "Urban Irrational," 211, 204.
23. *Ibid.*, 34.
24. Davies, "Female Paranoia," 19.
25. Claudia Aguirre, "Pregnancy Brain: Stereotype or Reality," *Headspace*, July 10, 2015, accessed July 25, 2016, www.headspace.com/blog/2015/07/10/does-pregnancy-brain-actually-exist/.
26. Mircea Eliade, *Myth and Reality* (Long Grove, IL: Waveland Press, 1998), 6.
27. Eliade, *Sacred and Profane*, 172–80.
28. Robert Lima, "The Satanic Rape of Catholicism in *Rosemary's Baby*," *Studies in American Fiction* 2 (1974): 212–222.
29. John James, "Mysteries of the Great Labyrinth, Chartres Cathedral," *Studies in Comparative Religion* 11, no. 2 (Spring 1977), http://www.studiesincomparativereligion.com /public /articles/The_Mystery_of_the_Great_Labyrinth-Chartres_Cathedral-by_John_James.aspx.
30. Roger Ebert, "Rosemary's Baby," rogerebert.com, http://www.rogerebert.com/reviews /rosemarys-baby-1968.
31. Julia Kristeva, *The Powers of Horror* (New York: Columbia University Press, 1982), 4.
32. Eric Ives, *The Life and Death of Anne Boleyn: "The Most Happy"* (Hoboken: Wiley-Blackwell, 2005), 184.
33. *Ibid.*, 184.
34. See Jan Nusche's discussion of postpartum practices found in *The Bride's Book—A Perpetual Guide for the Montreal Bride*, published in 1932, in *CMAJ* 167, no. 6 (September 2002): 675–676, https://www.ncbi.nlm.nih.gov/pmc/articles/PMC122038/.
35. Kristeva, *Powers of Horror*, 10.
36. Hutchings, *Horror Film*, 35.
37. "The Cult of Domesticity: Values Past and Present," *Owlcation*, 13 January 2016, accessed 31 July 2016, https://owlcation.com/humanities/The-Cult-of-Domesticity-Past-and-Present.
38. Mircea Eliade, *The Sacred and the Profane, The Sacred and the Profane: The Nature of Religion*, trans. Willard R. Trask (New York: Harvest, 1957), 194.
39. Cirlot, *Dictionary of Symbols*, 173.
40. Michael Ciment, et al., "Interview with Roman Polanski," in *Roman Polanski: Interviews*, ed. Paul Cronin, *Conversations with Filmmakers Series*, ed. Peter Brunette (Jackson: University Press of Mississippi, 2005), 46.

BIBLIOGRAPHY

Aguirre, Claudia. "Pregnancy Brain: Stereotype or Reality." *Headspace*, July 10, 2015. Accessed July 25, 2016. www.headspace.com/blog/2015/07/10/does-pregnancy-brain-actually-exist/.
Bernstein, Rhona. "Mommie Dearest: *Aliens, Rosemary's Baby* and Mothering." *The Journal of Popular Culture* 24, no. 2 (Fall 1990): 53–73.
Birmingham, Stephen. *Life at the Dakota: New York's Most Unusual Address*. New York: Random House, 1979.
Ciment, Michel, et al. "Interview With Roman Polanski." *Roman Polanski: Interviews*, ed. Paul Cronin, 31–46. Jackson: University Press of Mississippi, 2005.
Cirlot, J.E. *A Dictionary of Symbols*, 2d ed., trans. Jack Sage. London: Routledge & Kegan Paul, 1962.
"The Cult of Domesticity: Values Past and Present." *Owlcation*, 13 January 2016. Accessed July 31, 2016. https://owlcation.com/humanities/The-Cult-of-Domesticity-Past-and-Present.
Davies, Rob. "Female Paranoia: The Psychological Horror of Roman Polanski." *FilmMatters* 5, no. 2 (June 2014): 18–23.
De Beauvoir, Simone. *The Second Sex*. New York: Vintage, 1989.
Ebert, Roger. "Rosemary's Baby." rogerebert.com. http://www.rogerebert.com/reviews/rosemarys-baby-1968.
Eliade, Mircea. *Myth and Reality*. Long Grove, IL: Waveland Press, 1998.
_____. *Occultism, Witchcraft, and Cultural Fashions: Essays in Comparative Religions*. Chicago: University of Chicago Press, 1976.
_____. *The Sacred and the Profane: The Nature of Religion*, trans. Willard R. Trask. New York: Harvest, 1957.

Fife Donaldson, Lucy. "Human Monstrosity: Rape, Ambiguity and Performance in *Rosemary's Baby*." In *Hosting the Monster*, ed. Holly Baumgartner and Roger Davis, 43–62. New York: Rodopi, 2008.
Fischer, Lucy. "Birth Traumas: Parturition and Horror in *Rosemary's Baby*." *Cinema Journal* 31, no. 3 (Spring 1992): 3–18.
Fisher, Bob. "William Fraker Dances with the Devil." *Moviemaker*, 7 Oct 2008. http://www.moviemaker.com/articles-moviemaking/rosemarys-baby-william-fraker-roman-polanski-20081007.
Frankfurter, David. "Awakening to Satanic Conspiracy: *Rosemary's Baby* and the Cult Next Door." *Deliver Us from Evil: Boston University Studies in Philosophy and Religion*, ed. M. David Eckel and Bradley L. Herling, 75–87. London: Continuum, 2008.
Ives, Eric. *The Life and Death of Anne Boleyn: "The Most Happy."* Hoboken: Wiley-Blackwell, 2005.
James, John. "Mysteries of the Great Labyrinth, Chartres Cathedral." *Studies in Comparative Religion* 11, no. 2 (Spring 1977). http://www.studiesincomparativereligion.com/public /articles/The_Mystery_of_the_Great_Labyrinth-Chartres_Cathedral-by_John_James.aspx.
Hutchings, Peter. *The Horror Film*. Harlow, Essex: Pearson Education, 2004.
Kristeva, Julia. *The Powers of Horror*. New York: Columbia University Press, 1982.
Lima, Robert, "The Satanic Rape of Catholicism in *Rosemary's Baby*." *Studies in American Fiction* 2 (1974): 212–222.
Marcus, Sharon. "Placing *Rosemary's Baby*." *Differences: A Journal of Feminist Cultural Studies* 5, no. 5 (1993): 121–153.
McElhaney, Joe. "Urban Irrational: *Rosemary's Baby*, Polanski, New York." In *City That Never Sleeps: New York and the Filmic Imagination*, ed. Murray Pomerance, Wheeler Winston Dixon, and Barry Keith Grant, 201–213. New Brunswick: Rutgers University Press, 2007.
Nusche, Jan. "Lying-in." *CMAJ* 167, no. 6 (September 2002): 675–676.
Peterson, M. Jeanne. "No Angels in the House: The Victorian Myth and the Paget Women." *The American Historical Review* 89, no. 3 (1984): 677–708.
Polanski, Roman. *Roman by Polanski*. New York: Morrow, 1984.
Remembering Rosemary's Baby. Dir. Angie Bucknell. Criterion, 2012. DVD.
Rosemary's Baby. Dir. Roman Polanski. 1968. Criterion, 2012. DVD.
Valerius, Karyn. "*Rosemary's Baby*, Gothic Pregnancy and Fetal Subjects." *College Literature* 32, no. 3 (Summer 2005): 116–35.

"I have seen things that would make the angels weep. And they do weep"
The Devil and Scotland's *Religious Horrors in* Let Us Prey

ELEANOR BEAL

The last decade has been a strange and visceral time for horror. The supernatural and numinous aspects of the genre have gone stale, while "torture porn" emerging from America and parts of Europe has taken its place alongside the New French Extremity movement. Themes of cruelty and sadism run through the genre at almost every level, focusing on extreme physical pain, suffering, and entrapment. These films are deliberately designed to push the barriers of horror and good taste. Nevertheless, a number of them stand out for their attempts to explore, within their own national contexts and through their protagonists' physical pain, the philosophical and theological meaning of suffering. Brian O'Malley's *Let Us Prey* (2014) is a Scottish-Irish collaboration that reflects these trends in a different light. Creepy, brutal, and drenched in religiosity, it attempts to tackle what it sees as the Calvinistic horror and suffering inherent in its rural Scottish milieu.

Set in the small, remote town of Inveree, the story is deceptively simple and recognizably Gothic in formula. A young female police constable's first day in her new job coincides with the arrival of a mysterious stranger—the Devil himself, perhaps—who calls the townspeople to account for their carefully hidden sins. However, the film transcends this simplicity, opening out into a disturbing puzzle, the horrors intricately pieced together from the characters' pasts. By doing so, *Let Us Prey* sustains the central mystery but also causes the viewer to question the nature of the characters and their beliefs. Most of the characters represent some kind of power or authority in the town: the "justice keepers," Police Sergeant MacReady (Douglas Russell) and Police Constables Mundie (Hanna Stanbridge) and Warnock (Bryan Larkin); the doctor, Duncan Hume (Niall Greig Fulton); and the educator, Ralph Beswick (Jonathan Watson). However, the mysterious stranger's knowledge of their many dark secrets fuels their paranoia and sends them into a frenzy of violence, bodily mutilation, and torturous death.

Let Us Prey uses these characters—particularly MacReady, its central villainous figure—to address Scotland's religious fears by depicting the effects of a satanic Other on the mentality of a small Scottish community that harbors extreme Calvinistic views. The conflict is further emphasized by Fiona Watson and David Cairn's script, which subverts many horror tropes while uncovering terror in themes of Scottishness and Calvinism. Scottish Calvinism was famously given horrific form by the 19th-century author James Hogg, whose novel, *Private Memoirs and Confessions of a Justified Sinner* (1824), satirizes an extreme—and totally unrepresentative—form of the faith. Critics have long acknowledged the reliance of Scottish cinema on these literary narratives. As Alan Riach explains it, "Film is not only film. Both the complexities and the clichés were developed from literary forms and work alongside and in dialogue with them. Film is literature."[1] Like Hogg's novel, Watson and Cairn's horror script invokes a dark and twisted form of the religion's soteriological themes—predestination, election, justification and antinomianism—in order to explore and understand both Scottish identity and the country's relationship to the rest of Britain. *Let Us Prey* represents Calvinism—a belief that brands all humans as inherently and irredeemably sinful, condemned to Hell unless they are among the "elect" chosen by God for salvation—as a harsh and humorless creed with a stifling effect on Scottish culture. It reworks Calvinistic motifs and anxieties by placing them within the context of a present-day rural village whose inhabitants also battle with internal demons. As we shall see, however, this picture of Scotland's rural population as the last vestiges of an otherwise dead religion is also perpetually complicated in the film by its collaborative production and direction.

The first part of this essay explores how *Let Us Prey*'s representation of national and religious horror is subverted by its Irish production and direction, its use of Scottish and Irish locations to destabilize romanticized notions of a progressive Scotland beyond the grip of its Presbyterian past, and its casting of Irish actor Liam Cunningham as the Devil. Cunningham's performance, imbued with elements of Catholicism and supernaturalism, represents the film's strongest indictment of Calvinism. It evokes Scotland's past religious conflicts, as well as fears of an evil both external and internal. The second part of the essay focuses on the inhabitants of Inveree, and considers how the film uses Satanic and folkloric horror, along with the extreme violence of torture porn, to critique Calvinistic themes. In *Let Us Prey*, the body becomes the site of gruesome displays of spiritual violence that comment on Scotland's oppressive religious past by invoking religiously tyrannical characters that inflict pain and suffering on themselves and others. Thus, the body becomes a metaphor for the underlying religious forces that can always rise again.

The final segment of the essay focuses on the central character of Police Constable Rachel Heggie (Polyanna McIntosh). Woven through the scenes of terror and gruesome violence, which situate *Let Us Prey* firmly in the horror genre, is the story of a traumatized woman's search for justice and liberation from her past—a search that is complicated both by the appearance of the mysterious stranger and by the plague of prejudice and injustice that seems to be infecting the town. The film's Devil is a horrific reminder of the religious and national tensions that haunt the Scottish imagination, but he is also implicitly connected to Rachel's search for redemption. This is, in part, a reflection of O'Malley's fascination with re-mythologizing the Devil of his Catholic upbringing. "As a child growing up in Catholic Ireland," he recalls, "I was always confused by the Devil. We were told that he was evil, yet he only took the souls of sinners."[2] The Devil that O'Malley presents in *Let Us Prey*, however, is more heroic than horrific. Rather than conveying O'Malley's unconscious reverence or faith in his Catholic background, the film subverts Scotland's fears about not only Calvinism, but femininity, by visually incorporating multiple Western myths of the Devil, from his Romantic role as disenchanted outcast to his portrayal as a figure of justice and vengeance, and more specifically, to his connection with liberated femininity.

Old, but Not Forgotten, Religious Tensions

Let Us Prey begins with a biblical creation scene. The screen is filled with sublime imagery of enormous dark ocean waves and darkening thunderclouds. A murder of crows swarms and circles around a pinnacle of rock that rises from the crashing waves. The silhouetted figure of a man appears—seeming to emerge from the blackness of its surface—and stands defiantly amidst the storm. The pulsating sound of a doom-rock soundtrack kicks in as he makes his way across the rock accompanied by the swarming crows. The threatening preternatural imagery is repeated in another shot of the ocean waves, this time filmed in reverse motion, causing it to appear as though the sea is being unnaturally sucked back through the gaping chasm formed by two adjacent cliffs. This uncanny reversal of the ocean's natural trajectory once again reveals the dark figure of the man, as he proceeds to walk out of the chasm and the sea like an unholy version of Moses.

Satanic horror films are rich in paranoid fear of the Other. The sea from which this Other emerges in *Let Us Prey* is represented in sexually symbolic terms: as an archaic and monstrous mother from which the Devil is "unnaturally" birthed. This linkage establishes a connection between the feminine and the Satanic—one the film returns to in the relationship between the Devil and Rachel Heggie—and ties both to the primitive past. It simultaneously suggests deep rooted anxieties about foreign Others—Protestant Scotland's historic fears about Irish Catholics—as a brooding, defiant, and distinctly Irish Devil appears on the coastline and makes his way to a small Highland town.

Historically, Scotland has a cultural kinship with Ireland formed by their shared origins, Gaelic language, and cultural experiences as annexes to a politically dominant

The Devil (Liam Cunningham) rising from the ocean in *Let Us Prey* (2014).

England. This kinship is reflected in Piers McGrail's cinematography, which paints a beautiful and haunting picture of rolling hills, a glowing sunset and an epic skyline that, though filmed in Ireland, establishes both countries as lands of shared natural beauty. However, traditions of Catholic-Protestant conflict in Scotland have been overt, most notably in Glasgow, which supplies the scenery for the town of Inveree. From the 19th century forward, Irish Catholics were settling in Scotland as it was aligning itself with the Protestant values of northern Britain. The Scottish Presbyterian church, in particular, was instrumental in advertising animosity against cultural and religious groups it felt were trying to destroy Scotland and its values from within. Critics and historians have often noted that sectarian rivalry, though it has diminished over time, still exists in areas of Scotland such as Glasgow, where it is demonstrably present in "ethno-tribal" and religious forms of prejudice.[3]

This ambivalent relationship is demonstrated most obviously in the film's opening scenes which continue to evoke Scotland and Ireland's historic, ethnic and religious tensions through the use of space and location. The coastal landscapes are those of Galway, Ireland, used to represent the isolated west coast of the Scottish highlands. Summoning Scottish fears of an Irish Catholicism that menaces from within, the mysterious stranger moves inland, the scenery becoming shadowed by a darkly threatening storm as the camera tracks his movements. As the horrifying acts of the past begin to form an increasingly central anxiety in the film, they are accentuated by repeated images of a single, portentous crow in flight against this infernal sky. His destination, visible in the distance, is a sprawling Scottish city, but the image of a modern city is destabilized and complicated by the simultaneous vision that *Let Us Prey* offers of its remote rural locale. Rather than a typically "parochial" and pastoral fictionalization of a Scottish village, Inveree is composed of shots of urban Glasgow in which rundown apartment buildings, deserted petrol stations and cafes provide an eerie backdrop of decay and empty commercialism. Later scenes add images of cobbled streets and claustrophobic spaces, accentuating a mythology of "backward," disconnected Scottish life. The film thus conforms to Gothic tradition by projecting its horrors onto the rural village where the remote landscape and rugged natural environment are transformed into a site for anxiety and alienation.

Rather than support the stereotypical social construction of the rural village as a place of ignorance and prejudice, however, *Let Us Prey* discredits this trope through its use of urban imagery. Further symbolic images of barbed wire dripping blood against a black screen connect Christian imagery of the crucifixion with the material and moral decay of the modern urban city. The sense of threat thus created is increased by the juxtaposition of symbolic images of ancient, dark mysticism and Christianity with scenes of urban violence and degeneration.

The opening scenes of *Let Us Prey* strongly suggest that Inveree is an uncanny mirror of the historic attitudes and religious conflicts of Glasgow. Thus, the village reflects both the deep-seated prejudices of the modern city against outsiders and city dwellers' stereotypical fears of the remote Scottish highlands as a place where old ideas and traditions, such as the marking of the Sabbath, still survive, and where old fears and grievances about Catholics and Jacobites may have been repressed but not forgotten. This destabilization of Scotland's Romantic notions of the self and the land establishes the Scottish landscape as something that is simultaneously alien and familiar, in keeping with the film's efforts to present a society at once contemporary and haunted, normal and monstrous.

Let Us Prey, therefore, is not just interested in relocating Scotland's past conflicts and reinvesting them with supernatural dread. Rather, the film reinscribes the Devil into contemporary Scottish culture by moving the narrative away from the supernatural and mystical toward the horrifying physical affects and displays of power that come from the inhabitants' extreme beliefs. Religious hubris is a common theme of Scottish horror, where it is considered the monstrous outcome of Calvinist doctrines of predestination and the elect. The ambiguity in the film comes from the fact that it remains unclear whether the characters' displays of religious power and suffering are the outcome of the Devil's presence or their own deep psychological hatred and pain. As the film progresses, it increasingly draws from this latter genre by presenting brutal and ambiguous displays of self-immolation and atonement.

Horror and the Devil's Justice

The Wicker Man (1973) was perhaps the first horror film to mythologize Scottish folklore and religion in its portrait of Summerisle, a remote, idyllic island in the Outer Hebrides whose inhabitants worship the ancient pagan gods of their ancestors. A devout Christian police sergeant, sent from the mainland to investigate the disappearance of a local girl, realizes too late that the islanders' rituals include human sacrifice—and that he is the next offering.[4] *Outcast* (2010), about a member of an ancient, magical Celtic race hiding from her murderous ex-lover, tapped into a similar fascination with Scotland's pagan and religious past, as did *Lord of Tears* (2013), a low-budget horror film about a man haunted by childhood visions of the Owl Man, a creature from Scottish folklore. Like these narratives, *Let Us Prey*'s horror arises from a people and community whose physical and emotional isolation deforms their beliefs. *Let Us Prey* never departs, in this respect, from being a genre film that draws heavily from Scotland's folk horror tradition, but it twists this tradition, along with horror genre conventions, in powerful and interesting ways, depicting a supernatural terror from the past that takes over the community, creating chaos and madness.

Let Us Prey presents a series of characters who, through faults of their own, find themselves trapped at the Inveree police station on a dark and stormy night, experiencing the justice of the deeply devout Sgt. MacReady and constables Jack Warnock and Jennifer Mundie. The first of these is Ralph Beswick, who begins the film already incarcerated in for beating his wife. The second is Caesar (Brian Vernel), a young joy rider and general delinquent, who is arrested for running a man down with a stolen car. The man, who is the mysterious stranger, subsequently disappears, only to be found later by Mundie and Warnock, covered with scratches and carrying only a notebook. The cast of characters is completed by Doctor Hume (Niall Grieg Fulton), who is brought in by MacReady to examine Caesar's victim and help identify him. The stranger is placed in cell six and it is by this number that he is identified throughout the rest of the film. Once all these characters are gathered at the police station, strange and mystical things begin to happen. The demonic in *Let Us Prey* is insinuated through shadows and seemingly innocent everyday objects such as a matchstick, a brick in a cell wall, and a ticking clock. These mundane objects take on occult and ritualistic significance in the presence of Six. The point is significant, suggesting that sources for evil exist not only in the realm of the supernatural, but are already embedded in the rational and the everyday.

The film underscores the horror of Scotland's isolation by focusing, for the rest of its running time, on one setting: Inveree's police station. A natural site for investigation, the station connects with the film's central mystery—Six's identity—but also becomes the setting for events that lead viewers to question the nature of the other characters. The locus of these developments is the character of Rachel Heggie, who finds herself transferred back to the village after leaving years before to escape its lack of opportunities, suffocating poverty, and atmosphere of religious oppression. The film highlights the locals' intolerance toward Rachel, whose desire to help the town change and improve is seen as a threat, and evidence of her "uppity," modern, and outsider ways. Rachel is not, however, the only one trapped by Inveree. Whether by choice or circumstance, the locals are similarly caught—disconnected from the outside world. Each of them has a dark past, and Inveree is a town where such secrets are kept carefully concealed.

Inveree functions, in this respect, as a synecdoche for Scotland—a nation haunted by the ghosts of its past. Tom Nairn proposes, in "The Three Dreams of Scottish Nationalism," that "[Scotland] is doubly dominated by her dead generations. At bottom there is the bedrock of Calvinism, the iron abstract moralism of a people who distrusts this world and itself; then overlaying this, the sentimental, shadow-appropriation of this world and itself through romantic fantasy. Naturally these strata are also in conflict with each other much of the time [but] present in some form in everything distinctly Scottish."[5] While three hundred years have passed since Scotland was in the grip of an oppressive Presbyterianism, the potency of fear and horror surrounding the severity of the religion remains central to Scottish culture. Indeed, scholarly interest in Scottish Gothic and horror has long acknowledged the connections between the country's Calvinistic ethic and the oppressed and self-oppressing tendencies of literary and cinematic characters. As Cairns Craig puts it: "Calvinism was the foundation of key institutions—religion, education—through which Scottish identity was shaped, and through which it maintained its distinctness during Scotland's participation in the British empire: whether for or against Calvin's conception of human destiny, no Scot could avoid involvement in the imaginative world that Calvinism projected."[6]

No one who watches *Let Us Prey* could doubt that Calvinism makes a crucial contribution to its themes and concerns. As much as Six gives rise to the occult happenings in the film and seems to torment his victims with mystical forces, almost all the horror stems from the extreme and unswerving fundamentalism of the town's people. The psychological (and ultimately physical) destruction of Inveree's inhabitants is punctuated by only brief supernatural images; the real nightmare and sense of foreboding comes from the people's suffocating, yet corrupted, moral judgment. For Craig, the key to understanding Scottish issues lies in understanding the level to which Calvinistic "God-fearing" influences the construction of Scottish subjects. As Craig tells it, "there is no more powerful term of approbation in the language of Scottish Presbyterianism; suffering and death are as nothing to maintaining the virtue of 'God-fearing.'"[7] The film emphasizes ideas of God's ultimate sovereignty through the characters' commitment to the hardness of their lives and their belief in sustaining strict systems of authority and discipline. When the errant Caesar is placed in a cell opposite his teacher, Beswick, the older man lectures him on how a dwindling emphasis on authority and discipline are the cause of a failing education system. Furthermore, Beswick suggests, it is only through the harsh administering of religious principles that the "natural order" can be re-established. These identifiably Calvinistic sentiments are also echoed by MacReady, a smug, self-righteous

"Christian man" who considers his God-fearing to be the only quality that he needs to run a controlled and, more importantly, quiet "ship." He is especially defensive of his police station and the particular brand of "justice" that he and his officers carry out there. Shortly after Caesar is brought in, Rachel witnesses MacReady's equation of "authority" and violence, when he brutally elbows the young man in the stomach causing him to vomit on her shoes.

The film connects the dreadful acts committed by the characters to Calvinism's emphasis on ideas of fate and Total Depravity. This Calvinistic concept, sometimes known as Total Inability, emphasizes man's inherent sinfulness, but also the impossibility for ordinary "natural" men and women to understand the gospel's message or God's will. They are spiritually helpless, and if God does not decide to intervene and administer grace, then they are inevitably and irrevocably lost. Thus, according to Craig, the God of Calvinism is not only cruel and fearsome Himself, but creates fearful subjects who are terrified of retribution and damnation and, at the same time, driven to console themselves about their lack of power and salvation by becoming as fearsome as their God. This they do by inspiring God-like fear in their fellow humans.

As Rachel tries to find her footing in her new job, she succeeds in finding only a broken law-enforcement system filled with horrific misappropriations and redirections of power that have the single intention of making someone else feel pain and powerlessness. The first to feel Six's occult justice is Dr. Hume, who attacks and attempts to kill Six, his patient, after declaring that the stranger "knows everything." MacReady orders the doctor confined to a cell, dispatches Warnock and Mundie to Hume's house to inform his wife, and then (without explanation) leaves the station to return to his own home. Left unattended, Six questions Beswick about his abuse of his wife, and Caesar about an unreported hit-and-run accident that left a girl gravely injured. He drives Beswick to suicide, and Caesar to a confession that Rachel, distracted by the return of Warnick and Mundie, does not hear. The constables reveal that Hume has murdered his entire family by conducting gruesome surgeries in an attempt to extract their souls from their brains. The film less-than-subtly suggests, through Hume's descent into violent madness, that the realms of rational science are of no use against the horror of the irrational, which lies not in the supernatural, but within man himself, fed by his religious beliefs. The film's horror continues in this vein, with each character being led into an encounter with Six that causes them to reveal their own acts of religiously motivated madness, then give in to their rage and despair as he ruthlessly eggs them on toward oblivion.

Temporarily absent from the escalating madness, Sgt. MacReady nonetheless stands at the center of Inveree's corrupt world. It is he who, despite representing the Law, promotes an insidious antinomian form of belief in the town. A militant and politically extreme form of Presbyterianism, antinomianism opposes itself to religious and moral law, contending that men are free from the obligation to carry out works of moral good because the gospel dispensation of grace makes faith alone necessary for salvation. The film's scathing indictment of MacReady's Calvinistic notions of predestination and the elect are its strongest criticism of the dysfunctional character of Scottish community. This indictment takes the form of MacReady's disproportionate sense of self-justification and "God-fearing," which continues to unfold over the course of the narrative.

MacReady's return to his house, however, reveals his own deeply buried secret: that he has beaten his young male lover to death. A flashback—the film's most troubling scene—shows him seducing the young man, only to then attack him in a brutal display of violence, savagely reducing his face to a bloody pulp. Disturbed by Hume's claim that Six "knows everything," MacReady now sets about the gruesome task of concealing the body. We learn that this is not his first victim, but the latest in a dark tradition, as his open refrigerator displays carefully packaged body parts, on top of which lies the mangled spectacle of a severed head.

Returning to the station with a shotgun and a can of gasoline, MacReady kills Warnock, Mundie, and Caesar, wounds Rachel, and sets the station afire. With each new attack, the camera focuses on the victim's head and face, registering the gory devastation wrought by MacReady's shotgun and his victims' horrifying realization of their imminent death and inevitable damnation.[8] The film's dramatization of the psychological and spiritual destruction of each character by the horrors of Calvinism is supplanted by scenes of frightful physical violence, both sadistic and masochistic. Some of the characters' deaths—such as Beswick's suicide—are explicitly acts of self-directed violence, but *Let Us Prey* suggests that even outwardly directed acts of violence are, ultimately, a form of self-destruction. MacReady's serial murders, for example, are products of his attempt to repress sinful difference within: self-hatred that takes the form of monstrous and transgressive violence against others.[9]

It is MacReady's rampage through the station, however, that renders his religiously rooted masochism explicit. He is naked to the waist, with lengths of barbed wire wrapped around his shirtless torso so that the barbs gouge viciously into his flesh. More barbed wire is wrapped around his head, cutting into his temples and causing blood to flow over his face in a horrific evocation of Christ's scourging and crucifixion.

The self-mutilation depicted in this indelibly gruesome image is MacReady's attempt to atone for his sinful nature. The Passion imagery also, however, acts as an implicit critique of the Calvinistic belief that Christ died not for all sinners, but only for the elect, so that they might repent and come again to believe in a redeeming God. The dreadful

Sgt. MacReady (Douglas Russell) parodying Christ in *Let Us Prey* (2014).

determinism of Calvinism's Limited Atonement is parodied and subverted in MacReady's belief that he can be returned to God's grace not through Christ's sacrifice, but by monstrously becoming his own Christ. Thus, as Craig argues, Calvinism "creates its own antagonist in a form which is equally Calvinist, for the only individual capable of surviving a repressive society of this kind is one who accepts a terrible—a fearful—isolation, one who engages in a terrible fearful extension of the self, an aggrandisement of the ego, until the individual is transformed from a God-fearing into a fear inspiring creature-a diabolically "fearful" presence to all who live within the boundaries of our ordinary and fear-haunted society."[10] The "fear-inspiring creature" that MacReady becomes is, nevertheless, eliminated from the film, proving that, in Scottish horror, no one wins against the Devil. Targeting the self-righteous individualism that can arise from Calvinism's curious doctrine of the elect, *Let Us Prey* exacts revenge. It does so rather differently, however, in that this revenge does not come through the Devil's supernatural powers, but through Rachel. It is Rachel, rather than Six, who brings MacReady down in a triumphant and brutal scene inside the burning station. When she flings the half-empty fuel can at him, he reflexively blasts it apart with his shotgun and is instantly engulfed in a ball of fire. MacReady, dying, recites a Bible verse, to which Rachel responds "Amen," and shoots him—exorcising *Let Us Prey*'s religious trauma and acting as the film's "final girl."

The Final Girl: The Devil's Fantastic Liberations

It is the Scottish male that often stands as the defining feature in the landscape of Scottish identity, and Scottish horror fiction has not done much to change this. In response, *Let Us Prey* attempts to craft an alternative to masculine modes of horror and renewal and, in so doing, links its depiction of the apocalypse to a narrative of femininity and trauma. Both horror and fantasy elements operate in the plot, but they become concentrated in the central figure of Rachel. Throughout the film, she is framed as the counterpoint to evil. She challenges conventions of gender difference by being professional and tough, but also compassionate. Furthermore, she disrupts the relationship between masculinity and roles of detection and protection. She passionately wants to believe that the law provides protection for the vulnerable and victimized, and the film strongly suggests that this desire relates to some hideous event in her past, leading to her constant battle against the effects of her victimization. In the course of the narrative, this event is revealed to be an instance of extreme childhood abuse.

Clues within the narrative suggest that we should also interpret *Let Us Prey* as an exploration of female gothic trauma. As Six insinuates to Rachel throughout the film, the night's apocalyptic events are really all about her. They are also about her overcoming her trauma and suffering. As is central to the female Gothic, the line between the supernatural and the psychological becomes permeable, with the result that supernatural horrors can be read as psychological manifestations and paranoid fears that become materially manifest. The Inveree police station can, therefore, be interpreted as an uncanny mirror of Rachel's fears of entrapment and threat. Indeed, nearly all of the events that occur during the film lead back to Rachel's trauma—in which she was trapped, violated, and shamed—while simultaneously making it real to her in new and horrifying ways that range from the callous and uncaring suspicions of the police to her fears about not being taken seriously as a woman in the authoritative role of protector. These fears are realized in the narrative, most strikingly in the revelation that each one of her colleagues is willing to kill her in order to cover up their own, earlier crimes.

The film's notion of Scotland as a kind of earthly purgatory for the sinful is thus integral to its construction of a Calvinistic female horror narrative. In Calvinism's system of grace and damnation, the lot of women is particularly demoralizing, particularly if notions of fate are taken into account. If everything that happens is predestined and ordained by God, then Rachel's sexual abuse becomes a form of divine punishment—a reflection of her sinful nature—that she is obliged to accept without complaint. This, in effect, is the narrative that *Let Us Prey* attempts to undermine by making her the "final girl" and granting her the agency and the power of self-determination.

In the final scene of the film, the burning police station forms an infernal backdrop to Rachel's last confrontation with Six, who emerges from the flames and uses the burning corner of his notebook to light a cigarette before sitting down on the police station steps to open it and slowly draw a line through the names of MacReady, Mundie, Warnock, Beswick, Hume, and Caesar. The off-screen sound of cawing crows further adds to the dramatic and preternatural effect. As Six lists the crimes of the characters, the scene shifts between their names on the pages of his book and shots of their bodies inside the police station as they are engulfed in a supernaturally black and sinewy substance. The disembodied cawing increases in volume, harshness, and pitch before it is silenced by Six when he suddenly snaps the book shut.

The ending of the film points toward Six's rehabilitation by drawing upon a distinct history of Romantic literature, in which Satanic figures feature as symbols of rebellion and liberation. The film uses the symbol of a feather to suggest a connection between Six and Rachel. Falling from the wing of the crow that accompanies Six into Inveree, the feather subsequently appears on Rachel's pillow at the beginning of the film, and again is seen falling when Six appears in front of Caesar's car. In Victor Hugo's epic *La fin de Satan*, published posthumously in 1886, a feather falls from the wing of Satan while he battles with God, and takes the form of a beautiful angel called Liberty. Liberty goes on to encourage humanity to rebel against the symbolic prison of the Bastille, which keeps mortals from their freedom. The Devil's intervention in *Let Us Prey* illustrates a similar impulse for liberation and redemption. As Six finishes marking off the names, he turns the page over to reveal a blackly inked drawing of Rachel, surrounded, like some dark angel, by crow feathers. He reinforces the importance of this image as he slowly traces his thumb over the feathers. When Rachel cries, "I never asked you for anything!" Six insists, "Oh, I think you did. I think you begged." The camera cuts to an image from the past: young Rachel fleeing from her captivity. As the camera follows her flight, we can see Six watching her from the background as he stands in the garden of the house. The satanic pact, the film suggests, was made by Rachel and Six well before the events of the film, and it was made to free Rachel from her imprisonment.

The film's final shot is a close up of Rachel and Six sharing a passionate kiss in front the burning doorway of the station before the camera pans out to take in more of the scene. Before the final scene, Rachel's face was fully lit by the light of the fire, its illumination suggesting that she possessed uncorrupted virtue. As the characters embrace, however, both are cast in full shadow, becoming silhouettes against the backdrop of the fire and presenting the audience with a diabolic religious tableau. It is interesting to note that, despite its evil connotations, the symmetry of the shot suggests a perfect partnership in which neither is subject to the other. Rachel and Six's bodies are positioned to mirror each other—both in profile and fully facing each other, one hand placed on the other's cheek—and both bodies equally placed in the center of the shot. Rachel, who uses language reminiscent of both the wedding vow and the Lord's Prayer to invoke the image of "heaven and hell forever and forever," also suggests a marriage between two equal halves. The religious myth the film favors is not the last temptation of Christ, but Rachel's transformation into Lilith, companion of Lucifer. This transformation recalls the fascinating satanic heroines of 19-century literature: romantic female rebels that give themselves to the Devil so as to escape the inferior position to which they have been doomed. Similarly, in *Let Us Prey*, when Rachel says "yes" to Six she is, in fact, also saying no to her traumatic past and the stifling control exercised over her by family, social authorities, and religion. As the shot slowly pans out, the frame takes in only the carnage of the burning station before the screen goes black and the credits roll. The effect is that the external world has been completely erased, while inside the station the sinful characters that represented Scotland's corrupted institutions of the law, science and medicine, education, and religion are dead bodies burning to ash.

Notes

1. Alan Riach, *Representing Scotland in Literature, Popular Culture and Iconography: The Masks of the Modern Nation* (New York: Palgrave Macmillan, 2005), 195.
2. "Interview with Director Brian O'Malley (Let Us Prey)," March 26, 2015, ThrillandKill.com, accessed June 19, 2016, http://www.thrillandkill.com/interview-with-director-brian-omalley-let-us-prey/.
3. For a more in-depth analysis of the debate on the social implications of Scotland's sectarian history, see Thomas Martin Devine, *Scotland's Shame? Bigotry and Sectarianism in Modern Scotland* (Edinburgh: Mainstream Publishing, 2000).
4. For more a more detailed discussion of *The Wicker Man* see Melanie Wright's chapter in *Religion and Film: An Introduction* (New York: I.B. Tauris, 2008), 70–106.
5. Tom Nairn, "The Three Dreams of Scottish Nationalism," *The New Left Review* I/49 (1986): 8.
6. Cairns Craig, *The Modern Scottish Novel: Narrative and the National Imagination* (Edinburgh: Edinburgh University Press, 1999), 37.
7. Ibid., 38.
8. This is an interesting point about *Let Us Prey*, since all of the barbaric deaths that occur are focused on the head. Hume mutilates his son's head to extract his soul. Beswick, is suddenly compelled to beat his own head in by running at the bars of his prison cell. Warnock kills Hume by driving his head through a table leg. Warnock is shot in the face and Mundie is virtually decapitated by MacReady.
9. Despite my argument here, the alignment of the character's self-hatred with homosexual urges that are also played in his urges to serially kill, is duly noted as problematic. This is especially true if we consider that these scenes seem to emphasize the brutality of these crimes in precisely the exploitative way that it refuses to do with Rachel's abuse. This no doubt deserves some interrogation, although, unfortunately, I do not have the space to do it here.
10. Craig, *Modern Scottish Novel*, 38.

Bibliography

Craig, Cairns. *The Modern Scottish Novel: Narrative and the National Imagination*. Edinburgh: Edinburgh University Press, 1999.
Devine, Thomas Martin. *Scotland's Shame? Bigotry and Sectarianism in Modern Scotland*. Edinburgh: Mainstream Publishing, 2000.
"Interview with Director Brian O'Malley (*Let Us Prey*)." *Thrill and Kill*, March 26, 2015. http://www.thrillandkill.com/interview-with-director-brian-omalley-let-us-prey/.
Jackson, Rosemary. *Fantasy: The Literature of Subversion*. London: Methuen, 1981.
Nairn, Tom. "The Three Dreams of Scottish Nationalism," *The New Left Review* I/49. May-June (1968): 3–18.
Riach, Alan. *Representing Scotland in Literature, Popular Culture and Iconography: The Masks of the Modern Nation*. Hampshire and New York: Palgrave Macmillan, 2005.
Wright, Melanie. *Religion and Film: An Introduction*. New York: I.B. Tauris, 2008.

PART II

The Boundaries of Good and Evil

God's Bloody Hand
The Horrible Ambiguity of Religious Murder in Bill Paxton's Frailty

MARK HENDERSON

Although *Frailty*, Bill Paxton's 2002 directorial debut, did not make much of a popular splash upon its initial release, it did earn critical acclaim, cult status, and eventual, belated appreciation from viewers. Upon the film's release, Roger Ebert praised it for its compelling combination of horror and sadness, focusing upon a fanatical father's tortured sense of rectitude and his sons' isolated vulnerability and helplessness. Ebert also called attention to the jarring ambiguity created by the film's sudden plot twists, and was particularly haunted by how it appears to fictionally portray "where the logic of the true believer can lead."[1] Indeed, *Frailty*'s enduring power as both a horror film and a psychological thriller lies in the horrible ambiguity with which it presents fanatical, religious murder. The film is thus a departure from the more familiar God-good/Devil-bad dichotomy exemplified by such classics as *The Exorcist* (1973), *The Omen* (1976), and *Rosemary's Baby* (1968). It presents a scenario that is far more complex: God as serial murderer—or rather, serial murder as sanctioned by God.

Frailty begins with Agent Wesley Doyle (Powers Boothe) entering FBI headquarters in Dallas, Texas, to find a strange man, Fenton Meiks (Matthew McConaughey), waiting for him in his office. Doyle has been working extensively on the "God's Hand Killer" serial murder case, and Fenton claims that his recently deceased brother, Adam, is the killer Doyle seeks. Fenton begins to recount the extraordinary events of his childhood: One morning, he relates, his father (played by Paxton himself) claimed that an angel of God had visited him in a vision and bestowed upon him and his two sons the mission of seeking out and slaying demons. Fenton was skeptical (to say the least), but the younger Adam enthusiastically believed. As it turned out, "demon-slaying" involved the seemingly random kidnapping and murder of many innocent people—murders committed by the father in front of both Fenton and Adam. Several complications lead to the father killing the town sheriff in order to keep their mission a secret, after which Fenton felt compelled to turn on his father and kill him (apparently to stop the murders). The situation changes abruptly, however, when, in the present-day framing story, Doyle's visitor confesses that he is not Fenton Meiks, but younger brother Adam; that Fenton, not Adam, is the God's Hand Killer; and that Doyle is yet another name on the latest demon list. Adam continuing the work of his late father, kills Doyle with the same ax that his father had used to destroy demons, but is never suspected of the murder; he is, in fact, a county sheriff.

To be sure, *Frailty* plays with viewers' sensibilities—baiting the audience into writing off the Meiks boys' father as a murderous and psychotic religious zealot, only to then reveal that his apparent gift for finding demons disguised as people is genuine after all. Added to the stunning revelations of angelic visitations, the existence of demons, and the father's ability to see the crimes of those demons upon touching them, is the apparent divine intervention that prevents Adam from being found out. Those who have spoken with him face-to-face are inexplicably unable to remember what he looks like, and there is convenient distortion on all surveillance-camera footage in which he might appear. This intervention might lend validation to the brutality practiced by Adam and his father, and to vindicate (against any secular skepticism) the pair's religiosity, but such validation and vindication remain miserably unsettling at the film's conclusion. God exists, but is that God good? Such an uncomfortable resolution was presented a decade or so earlier by Michael Tolkin with his surreal 1991 drama *The Rapture*, in which a fanatically religious mother (Mimi Rogers) who believes in the imminent Rapture is similarly vindicated by its actual arrival. But *Frailty* presents this uneasiness more specifically within the realm of horror, with less of a focus on human agency and free will, and within a much more specifically *American* context.

At the conclusion of *Frailty*, Adam Meiks is revealed to be a county sheriff, and his uniformed, masculine stance is iconically heroic—almost Western. This final, archetypal American image will serve as the ultimate focus of this essay, as it speaks to the disturbing ambiguity behind American religious identity—in terms of both history and symbolism—from the enduring mixed emotions concerning the doctrine of Manifest Destiny, to the divisive nature of current politics (particularly when it comes to the evangelical vote). The classic God/Devil dichotomy is too simplistic for such a troubling history/identity; a darkly behaving God—a modern-day version of the Old-Testament Jehovah, who is both owned and feared—is perhaps more appropriate. Nietzsche and Kirkegaard provide a useful theoretical basis for trudging through (and perhaps out of) such a complicated and distinctively American horror. Both thinkers are, after all, notorious for (and often discarded because of) their apparently dangerous amorality—Nietzsche arriving at his conclusions by way of a strong, class-conscious hostility toward religion, and Kierkegaard arriving at similar conclusions by way of religious faith. This combination, therefore, provides an effective foundation from which to explore the conclusion of *Frailty* through questions concerning the American Gothic.

The Monstrous Proves Divine

At the outset, viewers of *Frailty* are led to believe that the Meiks boys' father is delusional—an extreme example of the stereotypical southern, down-on-his-luck, blue-collar "Jesus freak." Given his situation (a widowed auto mechanic raising two sons on his own in a small home), the father appears to justify Marx's summation of religion as the "sigh of the oppressed creature" and the "*opium* of the people"[2] through his religious mania. The film thus begins by apparently assuming, and even relying on, a generally skeptical attitude, grounded in class-consciousness, toward religion. The audience is clearly and purposefully driven to the conclusion that the father, as a victim of the slippery slope of religion-as-consolation, is both tragic and monstrous. He is, after all, a man who kills apparently innocent people with an ax in front of his own two children, displaying a chilling confidence in the moral rectitude of doing so.

Only two of the elder Meiks' angelic visitations are shown in the film, and both of them undercut the father's credibility. The first instance, in which light appears to brilliantly play off of the angel figurine atop a trophy, seems so open to natural explanation as to make the father seem gullible and exaggerating. The second instance is even more alarming, suggesting not just naiveté but the possibility of bona fide psychosis. At work, while repairing a vehicle's transmission, the father has a vision of an archangel with a flaming sword descending upon him from the ceiling of a cathedral. It is from this sword-bearing angel that the father supposedly gets his list—the names of the demons he must destroy. The staging of the scene implies, however, that his damaged psyche has conjured the hallucination from his surroundings, morphing the underside of the car chassis into a cathedral ceiling and the sparks falling from a nearby grinder into an angel with a fiery sword. The audience is thus encouraged to agree with the apparently sane and rational son, Fenton, who at one point tells his father: "Maybe you just dreamed it. Maybe you ain't right in the head."

Gradually, however, the father begins to reveal an unexpected, moral rationale for his extreme convictions. When Adam, the younger son who believes and hero-worships his father, creates an imitation of his father's list consisting of various bullying enemies, the father makes a distinction between *destroying* demons and *killing* people. While burying the first "demon," a woman, who he kills in front of his sons, he tells Fenton: "Don't cry for her. [...] She wasn't human. [...] I didn't kill her. [...] I destroyed her. She was a demon. [...] This is our job now, son. You've got to accept that." And when Fenton's mounting outrage over further "destructions" leads him to call the sheriff on his father, the father sees no other choice but to kill the sheriff. He is, however, remorseful for having to do so, telling the sheriff before striking the killing blow, "May God welcome you, and keep you." While burying the sheriff, he tearfully yells at Fenton: "That man is dead because of you!"

This capacity for genuine remorse and moral discernment unfolds from the initial and intentionally misleading close-up of the father before he leads the sheriff off to kill him. He appears to menacingly ask Fenton, "Whaddaya think, kiddo? Does it have to be done?" There is almost a smile on his face when he says this, and an ominous beat taken between the two sentences. But what comes across as pure malice proves to actually be alloyed with a strong-but-regretful sense of necessity. Nothing can interfere with the urgency of this divine mission, even if murder (as opposed to "destruction") becomes necessary. The killing of the sheriff thus turns out to be an act of moral self-sacrifice on the part of the father—a considerable narrative development from the possible, initial suspicion that he is more purely, psychotically murderous. He genuinely believes in his mission and even proves capable of experiencing moral dilemmas, making him a potentially more sympathetic character.

The biggest shock of *Frailty*, of course, is that the father not only becomes more sympathetic as a character, but turns out to have been sane and correct all along. This narrative turn occurs when, after "Fenton" reveals himself to Agent Doyle to be Adam, he touches Doyle's arm during a struggle and proves that he, like his father, can "see" the crimes of people who are in fact demons. It turns out that Doyle has actually stabbed his own mother to death and is one of the more recent additions to Adam's list of names. As

The death of Pa Meiks (Bill Paxton), slain with his own axe by the demon/son he cannot bring himself to destroy, is a turning point in the lives of both Meiks boys.

a child, then, Adam was not merely hero-worshipping his father when he claimed that he also could see the demons' crimes; in fact, he could, and very much still can. When Adam says, "God will protect me" before killing Doyle with the ax, the seemingly divine interventions which leave him inexplicably undetected and unsuspected certainly appear to prove this conclusion true.

The audience is also shocked to find out that Fenton apparently is a demon himself—that the angel had included Fenton one of the lists given to the father. The moral agony experienced by the father for not killing Fenton, then, was very real, not a ploy to merely frighten Fenton into believing. This loving lack of resolve adds yet another layer of sympathy for the father as a character. Furthermore, this love for his son turns ultimately tragic; it leads to Fenton's killing him with an ax-blow to the chest. It is clearly implied that the dying words that the father whispers to the distraught Adam concern both Fenton's status as a demon and the father's wish for Adam to carry on his work of demon-slaying (begun when Adam dispatches Brad White, the "demon" who Fenton was instructed to destroy before killing his father instead).

Fenton, for his part, accepts his status as a demon; while burying his father in the rose garden, he says to Adam, "[I]f you ever *destroy* me, promise me you'll bury me here" (emphasis added). The killing of his father suddenly appears to be less the heroic dispatching of a deranged murderer and more a demonic, villainous thwarting of a divine agent. Later, the tortured adult Fenton is seen drinking and listening rather significantly to Johnny Cash's "Peace in the Valley," a song with lyrics hinting at a man who has lived a long and tortured, bestial life looking forward to the deliverance provided by death.

The scene of these two axings—of Fenton's *killing* his father, followed by Adam's destroying White—highlights the film's most central and lingering ambiguity, over which there is potential for confusion: the true identity of the God's Hand Killer. This moniker harkens back to the father's earlier explanation of he and the two boys being "God's hands" (with, oddly, no evidence of the authorities who had dubbed the killer as such being aware of this connection). Initially, Adam (calling himself "Fenton") tells Agent Doyle that the God's Hand Killer is his brother "Adam" (by whom he means the real Fenton), encouraging the audience believing that the (real) Adam is the killer, and attempting to deflect suspicion from himself. Adam, however, makes a clear distinction to Agent Doyle between the "demons" buried in the rose garden and the dead human bodies found in Fenton's basement (and the other bodies found elsewhere, neither in the garden nor in the basement).

Fenton, then, is the God's Hand Killer, his victims being those in the basement and found at other locations earlier in the case. Also, Fenton's murders appear to be a psychotic offshoot of the trauma and confusion resulting from his own status as a demon and having to witness his father's demon-slayings as a child. Before his death—presumed to be suicide, but actually destruction at Adam's hands—he deliriously telephoned Adam, saying that demons are destroying the world. But Fenton *is* one of those demons. His killings are demonic; his father's and Adam's demon-slayings are divine. Fenton's killings are done out of retaliation against God while the slayings perpetrated by Adam and his father are sanctioned by God. And yet the divine sanction behind the latter fails to render the destruction any less horrifying. Distinctions between *killing* versus *destroying* aside, what Fenton *and* Adam are doing (and what their father did during his lifetime) both amount to serial murder.

Nietzsche and Kierkegaard: An Unlikely Fit

Given that they arrive at a similar, horrifying conclusion while coming from the opposite poles of religious belief, it is instructive to look to both Nietzsche and Kierkegaard. Their philosophies approach the prospect of religious faith with very different, even opposing, attitudes; yet both focus on an amoral fulfillment of power and transcendence. The ruthless, beyond-good-and-evil strength of Nietzsche's ideas find, in those of Kierkegaard, an unexpected confirmation rooted in the very thing that Nietzsche considers both a delusion and a hindrance: Abrahamic faith. Nietzsche's opinions on Christianity, for instance, seem to diagnose the father's religiosity without necessarily condemning the violence that results from it; Nietzsche merely resents the hypocrisy behind such religious violence. Kierkegaard, however, seems to find no such hypocrisy in this violence; such violence can, he believes, be *continuous* with religious faith.

Nietzsche sees religion—Abrahamic faith in particular—as the bitter outgrowth of a position of inferiority, or what he calls "*ressentiment*" (or "resentment")[3]; it is "*the slave revolt in morality*,"[4] the expression of "a profound discontent with the actual [by] [h]e who *suffers* from it."[5] The kicker for Nietzsche, however, is how this pitiable position in fact manages to eschew pity through an ironic elitism. Such faith is not an anti-elitism, but a *counter*-elitism in which the inferior call themselves "good" rather than "weak"— not out of a lofty wish for spiritual transcendence, but rather a more base desire to "revenge themselves on their masters."[6] The "Kingdom of God" which they await is "*their* kingdom," and their "faith," "hope," and "love"[7] are flowery euphemisms for the apocalypse/Rapture.

More ironically and more hypocritically still, these members of the lower classes apparently do not even want actual freedom, but merely a *new* master, "God," in whose existence Nietzsche sees a confirmation of "the instincts of the subjugated and oppressed"[8] to be further subjugated and oppressed, a "*slavery* in a higher sense."[9] Finally, most incredibly, and least pitiably, the ultimate ambitions of these lower classes appear to be no less terrible than those of their superiors; the "certain sense of cruelty towards oneself and others" in such faith confesses the "will to persecute."[10] For the downtrodden, it is apparently not a matter of ending persecution altogether, but merely vengefully altering in tit-for-tat fashion who does the persecuting and who is persecuted, maintaining a kind of grisly, historical power-struggle pendulum.

The surprising continuity between the ideas of Nietzsche and those of Kierkegaard comes through Nietzsche's call for a philosophy "beyond good and evil," that "resist[s] accustomed value feelings in a dangerous way,"[11] and Kierkegaard's interpretation of true faith as placing the chosen individual beyond the normal moral conventions of human society. This evokes the faith that God asks of Abraham in Genesis 22, when He calls upon the patriarch to make a sacrifice of his beloved son Isaac—the story that is the subject of Kierkegaard's *Fear and Trembling*. Even Nietzsche makes (if perhaps grudgingly) an admiring distinction between the "terror and reverence" evoked by the "divine justice"[12] of the Jewish Old Testament and what he sees as the weaker and more dishonest doctrines of the Christian New Testament. Thus the connection between Nietzsche and Kierkegaard perhaps turns out to be not as surprising as one might have expected. The Nietzschean beyond-good-and-evil finds itself echoed in Kierkegaard's conclusion that Abraham was "greater than all"[13] because of his ultimate willingness to sacrifice his young son to God. It is the nature of Abraham's ultimate faith in God that Kierkegaard apotheosizes, and he does so because of the leap from the rational that such faith requires—willingness to renounce common sense, pride, and the closest bonds of worldly love for what defies "worldly understanding,"[14] and thus "believe the absurd."[15] Kierkegaard renders virtuous the "strength of will"[16] to tackle such absurdity—*true* faith, not the "pitiable, luke-warm [...] caricatures of faith."[17] It is, for him, the equivalent of Nietzsche's will-to-power. Adam, taking after his father, makes this leap as well. At the beginning of the film, when he is still pretending to Fenton, he says to Agent Doyle: "Sometimes truth defies reason."

The story of the binding of Isaac is specifically mentioned by Adam, after he has revealed himself to Agent Doyle. Adam sees sacrifice as a mission handed down to him, since his father's love for Fenton had led to both his failure and his death. The angst that Abraham experiences when asked to sacrifice Isaac is echoed in the elder Meiks' sometimes-apparent remorse for having to involve his children in the murders, as well as in his unwillingness to believe that Fenton is a demon. As he explains before his sons witness his first murder of a demon, "Fenton, if I could spare you this, I would." The divine sanction behind the father's actions makes him appear, like Kierkegaard's Abraham, "wild" and "horror"-inspiring.[18] For a man supposedly chosen by God to slay demons—monsters—the father himself appears monstrous for carrying out this divine work. And that monstrosity is created by the abandonment of the rational resulting from his leap of faith; as Kierkegaard mentions specifically, faith seems a "monstrous [...] paradox" for it begins "precisely where thinking leaves off."[19] The man of faith becomes a monster; the monstrous proves divine.

God's American Hand

Although divine agency proves to be a reality in the world of *Frailty*, the film's use of this central plot twist begs for a more metaphorical interpretation. Certain instances in the film, in fact, point toward a metaphorical reading. When asked by his children why the demons have to be buried in the rose garden near their house, the father replies: "I chose it. Just like He chose us, I suppose." One scene shows his children watching an episode of the Christian animated series *Davey and Goliath* in which the child Davey, having broken his arm, asks his father why God let it happen. The father replies, "What God lets you do is decide for yourself what you will do." All along, then, there is the strong sense that the father might be simply validating his monstrous actions with God's imaginary blessing. In fact, this sense carries through even beyond God's involvement being proven true. This lingering ambiguity reveals the possibility that some more symbolic statement of historical-cultural criticism or social commentary is afoot.

Within the context created by his faith, Fenton and Adam's father sees himself and his family as *exceptional*: God's chosen ones, who in preparation for the imminent Rapture must destroy demons by morally questionable means. This exceptionalism, however, apparently places him and his sons beyond the sway of human law and human morality—all for a greater cause. Given the distinctively American flavor of *Frailty*, associations with the doctrines of American exceptionalism and manifest destiny are perhaps unavoidable. The events of the film take place, after all, in Texas (opening at the FBI headquarters in Dallas, then moving on to the small fictional town of Thurman, where the Meiks family lives), a Southern state that is also a *Western* state. This Western-ness is reinforced by the concluding image of Adam as a small-town lawman who has ostensibly won the day—the heroically successful "good guy." These Western tropes and iconography, combined with the film's apocalyptic religiosity—especially the religious murder—potentially call critical attention to the problematic history, doctrine, and myth behind American national identity.

John L. O'Sullivan's 1845 coining of the concept of "manifest destiny" lent divine sanction to the call for American westward expansion, describing the continental-United-States-to-be as "allotted by Providence for the free development of our yearly multiplying millions."[20] The "our," of course, refers those of European descent—certainly not the Native Americans and Mexicans who happened to stand so inconveniently in the way of their "destiny." If fulfillment of that "destiny" requires the eradication such groups, the Judeo-Christian overtones of divine sanction are there to unburden the American expansionist conscience of any resulting guilt and moral crisis. The movement behind such a doctrine becomes, for believers, "God's plan incarnate,"[21] thus minimizing genocide and other atrocities as apparently necessary. Richard Slotkin describes the myth of "regeneration through violence" that lies behind the myth of the frontier as "the structuring metaphor of the American experience." Such violence, he argues, was the means by which even the first colonists regenerated "their fortunes, their spirits, and the power of *the church and nation*"[22] in the New World.

According to Frederick Jackson Turner, "The western man believe[s] in the manifest destiny of his country,"[23] and, given the geography and landscape of *Frailty*, Fenton and Adam's father is certainly positioned to be a Western man. Indeed, Paxton says that he had the classic Western film *The Searchers* (1956) in mind while shooting the scene in which the father finds the supposedly magical ax and gloves.

The Meiks boy's father (Bill Paxton) initially finds the "magic weapons" used for discovering and slaying demons in *Frailty* in an isolated shed that is singularly illuminated by sunlight through a cloudy sky—suggesting divine agency, selection and endowment of supernatural power in *Frailty* (2001).

It is with this ax (named "Otis") and these gloves (the removal of which apparently allows for the "seeing" of the demon's sins) that the father, as a Western man, will achieve his "regeneration through violence" by cleansing the world of demons. His increasing social withdrawal, which also engulfs his two sons, is a consequence of the secrecy of his divine mission. This withdrawal is also consistent with what Turner describes as an important effect of the frontier—an antisocial regression from complex society "into a kind of primitive organization based on the family."[24] Such self-imposed isolation, as well as that imposed upon those with close ties to these individuals—such as the Meiks boys—can, however, ultimately work both "for good *and* for evil."[25] Obviously, the purpose of this extreme individualism for the Meiks' father is to avoid any of the community's secularly moral judgments, which could potentially thwart his absurd faith-based mission.

The *Searchers*-esque landscape provides an appropriate backdrop for the film's horrific power by evoking the morally ambiguous influence of the American frontier. It is what Alan Lloyd-Smith would describes as an "affectless or threatening landscape suggest[ing] a dead Mother Nature's implacable gaze," an environmental symbolism suggesting a debilitating (if unconscious) guilt for the historical sins and evils beneath the "American Imaginary."[26] Its ominous yet blank nature (very much like the Purgatory in *The Rapture*) simultaneously provides the morally ambiguous Western man with both an ennobling arena for righteous adversity and a *tabula rasa* for reinvention and regeneration. The elder Meiks (along with the adult Adam and, to a less obvious degree, Agent Doyle) all fit the mold of Robert Lamar Turner and Robert J. Higgs' archetypal Western leader: the "military and […] political figure whose instincts and rapid decision-making processes can mean the difference between life and death."[27] Against such perilous and empty landscapes, such a man—whose actions would, anywhere else, disturb and outrage with their dark and amoral ingenuity—becomes virtuous and heroic.

Frailty distracts the audience with Agent Doyle. Paxton says that he had thought of the character as the "iconic FBI guy" trying to crack the case; hard-boiled and tough-talking. His Texas accent and swagger, however, make him more specifically Western, complete with such cool and slurred, John Wayne–esque one-liners as—when he gives "Fenton" the handcuffs to put on himself before letting him into his unmarked car—"Put 'em on, or I'll put 'em on for ya." But it is Adam who turns out to be the Western leader *par excellence* of the film. He utters his final line, "God's will has been served" (answered with "Praise God" by his pregnant spouse-secretary Becky, who embraces him from the side), while standing resolute in his immaculate sheriff's uniform beneath both an American flag (directly above him) and a Texas flag (just to his left), representing both iconic American heroic success and iconic Western heroic success.

Given the supernatural abilities afforded to him by God, Adam is not merely a dark Western hero, but a dark Western *superhero*. This presence of the supernatural is validation for what had initially seemed the evil-minded humoring of a child's (Adam's) imagination on the part of the father—when he assents to the child Adam's enthusiastically asking if their mission, complete with the "magical weapons" of the ax and the gloves, makes them "like superheroes." He is, consistent with the "American monomyth" described by John Shelton Lawrence and Robert Jewett, a combination of "the selfless servant who impassively gives his life for others and the zealous crusader who destroys evil."[28] Purging the land of demons is certainly an exhaustive calling and an act of community redemption, but what *Frailty* highlights through Adam (and his father before him) is a troubling contradiction *within* the myth of the American superhero. Whatever horrific acts he commits in accomplishing his zealous crusade are conveniently validated by the ennobling selfless-servant reputation, rendering his true motivations suspect.

A telling counterpoint to the closing shot of Adam is the film's theatrical release poster. After all, composer Brian Tyler's ominous main theme plays as the camera dollies away from this heroic and clichéd pose, implying that one is not to be as satisfied, settled, and happy with this conclusion as might be expected. The poster features a close-up of Adam's face, half-shadowed in darkness, with the illuminated side suggesting angelic purity while still remaining eerie. It is angelic, demonic, and enigmatic all at once—evoking the horrible ambiguity of a terrible American God, the second coming of "the 'God of Israel,' the national God" grudgingly respected by Nietzsche for His unapologetic, wanton cruelty and destructiveness.[29] This is the God of a people whose doctrines of destiny and exceptionalism produce "as much need of the evil God as of the good God."[30] It is the God of Jonathan Edwards' sermon "Sinners in the Hands of an Angry God," in which the only thing keeping sinful man from "sudden unexpected destruction"[31] in the fiery pit is "the mere arbitrary will, and uncovenanted, unobliged forbearance of an incensed God."[32] Such a face, and such a representation, of God brings attention to the enduring dialectic between the American Dream and the American Gothic—between the sanitized, picturesque, and optimistic myths of American history and the messy, dark, and uncomfortable truths behind them.

Two moments in *Frailty* particularly highlight this American Dream/American Gothic dichotomy. The audience's first flashback glimpse of Adam's 1979 boyhood in Thurman shows an idyllic small town, complete with school bus, corner drugstore, and church—the stuff of nostalgic Americana. Later in the film, however, "Fenton" tells Agent

Doyle that after the first demon-slayings "My happy and secure world had just been flipped over, and there were dark things under there—very dark things." Beneath the endearingly sunny veneer lies a dark underbelly, and beneath both lies the sanction of religious doctrine. The regenerative symbolism of the Dream evokes the Resurrection, excusing and validating the dark and terrible Gothic acts associated with its fulfillment. The historical American spirit, then, resembles that of Kierkegaard's Abraham, whose consolation for the moral crisis over the deed demanded of him is "the promise that all nations of the earth should be blessed in his seed."[33] The country's status as a lone superpower with a global imperial/cultural reach would thus blunt an American Abraham's pangs of guilt over the means used to achieve that end. Hindsight, and knowledge of the result, cause the coarse and brutal practicality of those means to be hailed as noble, virtuous, and definitively American. D.H. Lawrence's summation of the "essential American soul" as "hard, isolate, stoic, and a killer"[34] becomes a badge of honor.

Conclusion

According to Leslie Fiedler, American literature is, "bewilderingly and embarrassingly, a gothic fiction, nonrealistic and negative, sadist and melodramatic—a literature of darkness and the grotesque in a land of light and affirmation."[35] He ties this conclusion to the United States' "certain special guilts," including "the slaughter of the Indians" and "the abominations of the slave trade"[36]—both consequences of American westward expansion. The same observation can be applied to American film, or even films that are about American or employ American tropes. Indeed, many of the subtexts in *Frailty* are consistent with the American Gothic. Central to the film is the terrible uncertainty over whether or not the "greater good" (the American Dream) is worth the ugly sacrifices necessary to achieve it. According to Fiedler, "tell[ing] where the American dream ended and the Faustian nightmare began" given the prospect of "total freedom"[37] becomes difficult, even impossible. This is the "guilt and anxiety [...] of the Break-through,"[38] of firmly cutting ties with one's European, pre–American past, even one's colonial past, and venturing off into the regenerative unknown West, only to be persistently haunted and even driven by the ideals and validations of one's colonial, religious Puritanism.

This haunting Americanness is central to the divine horror that *Frailty* inspires. The film's subtle employment of Western tropes and idyllic American clichés, as well as the violent manipulation of those tropes and clichés, link religious serial murder with the unspoken historical dark side of America's creation, establishment, and perpetuation. The God at work in *Frailty* is thus a sobering commentary on the uneasy truth of the American identity—not only the doctrines behind America's multilayered historical guilt, but the uneasy persistence of religious belief—including zealous belief—even in the midst of so-called secular American modernity. The value of the evangelical vote and the idea of American exceptionalism, for instance, persist in today's politics, even on the liberal side. With no more tangible, literal West to conquer, settle, and tame, the continued existence of the doctrines that fueled westward expansion is a double-edged sword—both reminding the collective American consciousness of its past sins *and* remaining enough of a serious threat to keep one's guard up against one's national self. Perhaps, of course, to do better.

Notes

1. Roger Ebert, "*Frailty*," RogerEbert.com, April 12, 2002, http://www.rogerebert.com.
2. Karl Marx, *Contribution to the Critique of Hegel's* Philosophy of Right: *Introduction* (New York: Penguin, 1983), 115.
3. Friedrich Nietzsche, *On the Genealogy of Morals* (New York: Modern Library, 1992), 472.
4. *Ibid.*, 470.
5. Friedrich Nietzsche, *The Anti-Christ*, in *Twilight of the Idols and The Anti-Christ* (New York: Penguin, 1990), 137.
6. Nietzsche, *Anti-Christ*, 139.
7. Nietzsche, *Genealogy of Morals*, 484.
8. *Ibid.*, 143.
9. *Ibid.*, 185.
10. *Ibid.*, 143.
11. Friedrich Nietzsche, *Beyond Good and Evil* (New York: Penguin, 1990), 202.
12. *Ibid.*, 255.
13. *Ibid.*, 50.
14. *Ibid.*
15. *Ibid.*, 54.
16. *Ibid.*, 65.
17. *Ibid.*, 66.
18. *Ibid.*, 45.
19. *Ibid.*, 82.
20. John L. O'Sullivan, "Annexation," *United States Democratic Review* 17, July-August 1845, 5.
21. Anders Stephanson, *Manifest Destiny: American Expansion and the Empire of Right* (New York: Hill and Wang, 1995), 40
22. Richard Slotkin, *Regeneration through Violence: The Mythology of the American Frontier, 1600–1860* (Norman: University of Oklahoma Press, 1973), 5 (emphasis added).
23. Frederick Jackson Turner, *The Frontier in American History* (Charleston, SC: Bibliobazaar, 2008), 180.
24. *Ibid.*, 33.
25. *Ibid.*, 38 (emphasis added).
26. Alan Lloyd-Smith, *American Gothic Fiction* (New York: Continuum, 2004), 93.
27. Robert J. Higgs and Ralph Lamarr Turner, *The Cowboy Way: The Western Leader in Film, 1945–1995* (Westport, CT: Greenwood Press, 1999), ix.
28. Robert Jewett and John Shelton Lawrence, *The Myth of the American Superhero* (Grand Rapids: William B. Eerdmans, 2002), 6.
29. Nietzsche, *Anti-Christ*, 139.
30. *Ibid.*, 138.
31. Jonathan Edwards, "Sinners in the Hands of an Angry God," *The Norton Anthology of American Literature*, 8th ed., ed. Nina Baym (New York: W.W. Norton, 2013), I:210.
32. *Ibid.*, 214.
33. Søren Kierkegaard, *Fear and Trembling*, trans. Alastair Hannay (New York: Penguin, 1985), 51.
34. D.H. Lawrence, *Studies in Classic American Literature* (New York: Viking, 1961), 62.
35. Leslie Fiedler, *Love and Death in the American Novel* (Normal, IL: Dalkey Archive, 1966), 29.
36. *Ibid.*, 143.
37. *Ibid.*
38. *Ibid.*, 129.

Bibliography

Ebert, Roger. "*Frailty.*" April 12, 2002. RogerEbert.com. http://www.rogerebert.com. Accessed May 15, 2016.
Edwards, Jonathan. "Sinners in the Hands of an Angry God." *The Norton Anthology of American Literature*, 8th ed., ed. Nina Baym, I: 209–220. New York: W.W. Norton, 2013.
Fiedler, Leslie. *Love and Death in the American Novel*. Normal, IL: Dalkey Archive, 1966.
Frailty. Dir. Bill Paxton. Lions Gate, 2002. DVD.
Higgs, Robert J., and Ralph Lamar Turner. *The Cowboy Way: The Western Leader in Film, 1945–1995*. Westport, CT: Greenwood Press, 1999.
Jewett, Robert and John Shelton Lawrence. *The Myth of the American Superhero*. Grand Rapids: William B. Eerdmans, 2002.
Kierkegaard, Søren. *Fear and Trembling*. Trans. Alastair Hannay. New York: Penguin, 1985.
Lawrence, D.H. *Studies in Classic American Literature*. New York: Viking, 1961.
Lloyd-Smith, Alan. *American Gothic Fiction: An Introduction*. New York: Continuum, 2004.

Marx, Karl. *Contribution to the Critique of Hegel's* Philosophy of Right: *Introduction. The Portable Karl Marx*, trans. and ed. Eugene Kamenka, 115–124. New York: Penguin, 1983.
The New Oxford Annotated Bible with the Apocrypha, Revised Standard Edition. New York: Oxford University Press, 1977.
Nietzsche, Friedrich. *The Anti-Christ*. In *Twilight of the Idols and The Anti-Christ*, trans. R.J. Hollingdale, 123–199. New York: Penguin, 1990.
———. *Beyond Good and Evil.* Trans. and ed. Walter Kaufmann, 179–435. New York: Modern Library, 1992. Print.
———. *On the Genealogy of Morals. Basic Writings of Nietzsche.* Trans. and ed. Walter Kaufmann. New York: The Modern Library, 1992. 437–599.
O'Sullivan, John L. "Annexation." *United States Democratic Review* 17 (July-August 1845): 5.
Slotkin, Richard. *Regeneration through Violence: The Mythology of the American Frontier, 1600–1860*. Norman: University of Oklahoma Press, 1973.
Stephanson, Anders. *Manifest Destiny: American Expansion and the Empire of Right*. New York: Hill & Wang, 1995.
Turner, Frederick Jackson. *The Frontier in American History*. Charleston, SC: Bibliobazaar, 2008.

No Religion or Too Many
Problematizing God Told Me To

FERNANDO GABRIEL PAGNONI BERNS

The social and cultural upheavals of the 1960s and 1970s in the United States had a profound influence on the decades that followed, drawing attention to social issues that had, until that time, remained under the radar. Turmoil reigned: Activism aimed at curbing gender inequality, racial injustice, and the excesses of capitalism, as well as promoting sexual freedom, environmentalism, and alternative religions, came into full bloom, and caused many to see these decades as characterized by organized protest.[1] The assassinations of reformist leaders such as John F. Kennedy, Robert Kennedy, and civil rights activists Medgar Evers, Martin Luther King, Jr., and Malcom X added to the growing tensions of the times. By the mid–1970s, the Watergate scandal and the resignation of President Richard Nixon had led many Americans—even those outside the counterculture—to regard traditional politics and politicians with suspicion. American interventions overseas were, in the aftermath of the Vietnam War, increasingly seen as a meaningless waste of young lives rather than a necessary sacrifice in defense of freedom. The moral and political certainty that once characterized the American national identity had, by the mid–1970s, become a thing of the past. And although Christopher Gair argues that "a great deal of the music, literature, art, and film that challenged mainstream values was a product of, rather than a reaction against, the material wealth enjoyed by much of the nation,"[2] the era's sense of unrest—and of an imminent, inter-generational shift in power—was widespread in popular culture.

Darkness and cynicism—a sense that established institutions were beyond redemption, and the future was uncertain at best—pervaded many of the films of the era. *The Graduate* (1967) lampooned the empty hypocrisy of middle-class values, *The French Connection* and *Dirty Harry* (both 1971) excoriated the futility of the legal system, and *Deliverance* (1972) reimagined rural America as a nightmare world of random violence. Still others explored the religious dimensions of this conflicted era—such as *Race with the Devil* (1975), *The Omen* (1976), and *The Sentinel* (1977)—but none made a stronger and more terrifying link between everyday fears, existential horror, and the divine than *God Told Me To* (1976).

Written and directed by Larry Cohen, the film focuses on a city plagued by a series of murders linked only by the killers' claims that God compelled them to take the lives of their victims. Bleak and heavy with ambiguity, the film has no clear resolution to its narrative. It is, in this respect, a reflection of its era, when the Age of Aquarius—with its dreams of a utopian future of peace, equality, and harmony—had passed, and Americans were struggling against disillusionment and pessimism.

This struggle is apparent in Cohen's depictions of both traditional faiths (particularly Catholicism) and the new religions embraced by the counterculture. *God Told Me To* depicts America as a land in the midst of losing its moral compass—abandoning religion and traversing a path toward evil—and suggests that God has ceased to be relevant to the American soul.[3] Individuals carrying out horrifying acts in the name of God (a possibility seldom raised, let alone addressed, in theological discussions with lay audiences) are at the center of Cohen's film. Richard E. Wentz argues that people do "bad things in the name of religion because they have taken a phantom of reason and fashioned it into an absolute."[4] As a result, William Cavanaugh suggests, religion "appears to have a particular tendency toward absolutism, and therefore, violence."[5]

Cohen's modern-day urban horror tale suggests that those who commit the film's violent acts are trapped in the "absolutes" of their traditional understandings of Catholicism, and insist on blindly following God's traditional designs in a world where secularism and unconventional religions possess as much (or more) cultural influence as the established church. It also suggests that a strong commitment to traditional religion and (*passé*) values could be problematic. The film's multiple killers are obeying abhorrent commands from God. Thus, amid a scenario in which traditional religions and moral standards are in crisis, the film criticizes religion as an institution that overrides the wills of individuals. This essay, then, explores the ways in which Cohen's film derives its horror from depictions of embattled, traditional Catholicism within the cultural landscape of the 1960s and 1970s, as it confronts countercultural thinking and alternative views of traditional religious doctrines.

He Made Me Do It: Morals in a World of Gray

God Told Me To, also known as *Demon*,[6] was Larry Cohen's fifth film and his second horror production after his 1974 hit *It's Alive*. The title credits are backed by a soundtrack of sacred music—including church bells—that evoke a traditional, familiar religious atmosphere, but the opening of the film quickly moves into unfamiliar territory.

Cohen's film uses New York City as its principal setting. The first shot of the film establishes a jungle of tall buildings and glass, and the second, a chimney spitting gray smoke. The third, complementing the others, is one of city streets filled with cars and the sound of impatient horns. This string of bleak images suggests that, much as the countryside is—in popular imagination—the place for transcendence, the city is a landscape of oppression, entrapment, and ruthless individualism.

The grimness of Cohen's cityscape reflects the ecological concerns that were urgent topics of discussion in the 1970s.[7] It mirrors—along with films such as *Silent Running* (1972) and *Soylent Green* (1973)—the death of the counterculture's once-vibrant 1960s dream that "an ecologically viable relationship to the natural world will characterize the future age, when humans will live more harmoniously on earth,"[8] and evokes the pessimism and brutal individualism of the decade that followed. Emerging press coverage of global pollution and competition for scarce resources also marked the end of the idea that continual, technology-driven progress would improve human welfare. Rather than helping to empower humanity, technology (represented in Cohen's film by the city) came to be seen as a destructive force that consumed scarce natural resources and polluted the environment, leaving humanity in a more tenuous situation than it had ever existed in before.

God is seemingly absent from Cohen's corrupt, polluted city. As if to emphasize the absence of the divine, Cohen shoots the city streets from a "God's-eye" point-of-view: an overhead, downcast gaze that invites viewers to conclude that God is, in fact, observing the world that humans are busily destroying ... but declining to save either the planet or its inhabitants.

In the film's first minutes, a passerby is killed by a rifle shot fired from the top of a water tank. Other shots, and other deaths, quickly follow: a massacre in which men and women are killed indiscriminately, seemingly at random, by sniper Harold Gorman (Sammy Williams). Detective Peter Nicholas (Tony Lo Bianco) risks his life by climbing the water tank and talking to Gorman, who explains, before jumping to his death, that he is killing people because God ordered him to. Gorman's killings are the first in a chain of bizarre situations in which otherwise exemplary citizens go on killing sprees, murdering innocents, because they, like Gorman, believe God commanded them to do so.

This notion of God commanding humans to kill raises the famous Euthyphro Dilemma—is something moral because God commands it, or does God command it because it is moral?—and the problem of abhorrent commands. The two are inextricably linked: If God's commands, no matter how arbitrary, define moral goodness, then it is conceivable that God could command us to kill innocents indiscriminately. Atrocities committed in the name of God, throughout history and down to the present day, show this to be no mere philosophic matter. The architects of sectarian violence—from the slaughter of Muslims and Jews by Christian knights after the capture of Jerusalem in 1099, through the mob violence against French Calvinists on St. Bartholomew's Day, 1572, to the Srebenica Massacre in 1995—routinely see themselves as agents of God. The possibility that God *could*, in fact, order such actions bring what ethicists call the "vacuity objection" into play: "When we call God 'good,' we tend to think that such an ascription means something, that it features determinate content that at least resembles ordinary language. But if the ascription is consistent with God being horrible, his issuing of abhorrent commands and the like, then the attribution is vacuous."[9] Goodness then becomes meaningless—a linguistic/social/cultural construction rather than an "essence."

The idea of *God* appearing before a person and commanding something seemingly in conflict with the laws of morality recalls the biblical story of Abraham, whom God directs to kill his own only son, Isaac, as a sacrifice. A similar scene in *God Told Me To* shows a happily married man shooting his wife and seven-year-old son one afternoon without apparent motive, but with the feeling that God guided his hand and even his aim— ensuring that he not fail in blowing the boy's head off. The idea that a believer *should* be willing to kill his own son if God tells him to is implicit in the biblical story: Seeing that Abraham possesses the radical obedience that faith demands, God stays his hand and tells him to release his son. Religious radicalism on such a level seems extreme in an era defined by skepticism about traditional religions. It also taps into social anxieties surrounding the hideous killings perpetrated by the followers of Charles Manson—a figure who was, for them, a legislator of morality. Interestingly, Cohen's film prefigures another notorious series of murders: the "Son of Sam" killings perpetrated in 1977 by New York City resident

David Berkowitz, who claimed he was answering the ulterior commands of his neighbor's dog, an ancient demon disguised as a black Labrador retriever. The possibility that people might start killing at random because God (or dog) commanded was a troubling side-effect of a decade in which traditional morals were becoming grey zones and justifications for traditional moral judgments were being placed under the microscope.

The arbitrariness, disorder, and chaos that the vacuity objection introduces into the moral framework of the universe also meshed with the cultural zeitgeist of the 1970s, suggesting that there was no reason or larger plan underlying the events of the era, and that God's commands were rooted in nothing but divine caprice.[10] The random nature of the shootings in *God Told Me To* underscores this sense of a world without reason or meaning. The people killed are merely bystanders, innocent citizens in the wrong place and time. That the killer commits his crimes from the top of a water tank visually links his gaze—and his utter lack of concern for the suffering of his victims—to that of the distant, indifferent God implied in the opening scenes. At a time when satanic horror films presented the Devil as an agent of disorder, chaos, internal conflict, and dissidence, Cohen's film raised the alarming possibility that God could also be such an agent. In doing so, it calls into question not only the essential "goodness" of God, but also the nature of a civil society that has framed its identity around its trust in that divinity. The United States, Cohen suggests, is so devoid of moral sense that its citizens are no longer capable of distinguishing between morality and immorality, good and evil, or God and the Devil anymore.

It is not by chance that the film's main character is a police officer—an arbiter of good and evil. Even he, however, is a man in the brink of losing his moral compass. Indeed, Peter Nicholas' story could be read as a parable about society losing *its* moral bearings. It is quickly established that Nicholas has been raised as a Catholic and studied in Catholic schools. He continues to practice his faith: attending masses on Sundays, praying, and confessing his sins. The walls of his house are adorned with Catholic sym-

The sniper Harold Gorman (Sammy Williams) on the water tank in *God Told Me To* (1976).

bols—crucifixes and a framed portrait of the Virgin Mary—and his wife Martha (Sandy Dennis), attests that he has a strong faith in God.

Peter is also, however, carrying on an affair with a young woman, Casey Forster (Deborah Raffin)[11]—a burden for him, even though Martha knows about her. Trapped in a disintegrating marriage, Peter is unwilling, mostly due to his Catholic background, to divorce Martha, and so fails to either sustain his marriage or fully embrace the new morality of the 1970s. Peter is a man trapped in a moral gray zone, indicative of the turning point between the two decades. The sexual freedom and emphasis on self-gratification offered by the changing sexual morality of the 1960s and '70s invites him to embrace divorce, but his Catholic upbringing ties him to his marriage. Martha, more in step with the rapidly changing times, is ready to grant him his freedom, or to renegotiate the terms of their marriage—accepting, and allowing him to continue, his affair with Casey—she asks only that Peter make a decision. This, however, proves to be the one thing he is incapable of doing. The film oscillates between depicting Peter as a man with a strong sense of morality and using him as a narrative device through which to tell the story of a decade turning ethically gray.

Peter's search for the reason behind the killings leads him to a mysterious barefoot man with long, unkempt blond hair who appears to be conveying God's commands to the killers. Peter insinuates, in one of the film's first scenes, that there may have been a "supernatural" hand guiding Gordon's killings. Casey, his lover, strongly dismisses this idea—"Are you gonna tell me all those people were meant to die?"—but her words leave her position ambiguous. Is she dismissing the idea that God could order the murder of innocents, or dismissing the existence of God—of meaning and purpose in the universe—altogether?

As the investigation progresses, however, Peter becomes increasingly confident that divine intervention is involved. The improbable coincidence of so many innocent citizens suddenly stabbing, strangling, and shooting both friends and strangers generates suspicions that are reinforced by his first meeting with the main suspect, Bernard Phillips (Richard Lynch). Phillips is a strange androgynous being bathed in a supernatural blinding glow, whose appearance leaves the detective willing to accept the presence of something beyond the material, everyday world. This interpretation fits easily with Peter's inner desire to find some cosmic order in life, and so resolve his ongoing struggle with his faith. If Bernard really is behind the killings, then at least there is a figure of order in the world, even if what this particular figure asks contradicts traditional morality.

Bernard's physical appearance suggests the sexless quality traditionally ascribed to angels, or an androgynous-seeming depiction of Jesus.[12] Feminist theology similarly proposes that God could be a woman or, at least, a non-gendered being. The film also hints at the possibility—floated in a spate of books from the late 1960s and early 1970s—that ancient "gods," even Jesus himself, may have been aliens who came to Earth millennia ago.[13] Bernard's mother (Sherry Steiner) states that she was abducted by a UFO many years ago, and that Bernard was a product of the aliens' artificial insemination of her. The film never fully endorses her story, but another character—old Elizabeth Mullin (Sylvia Sidney)—claims that she, too, was abducted and inseminated by aliens in the past. She tells Peter that nobody believed her story of abduction, even when she was a pregnant virgin—a revelation that links her story of alien abduction with the classical rendition of the nativity of Jesus.

Peter's disenchantment with, and doubts about, the institutions he was raised to

Peter (Tony Lo Bianco) faces Bernard (Richard Lynch), who emits a divine glow in *God Told Me To* (1976).

revere and the "truths" he was taught to believe in becomes increasingly acute as he digs deeper into the investigation. In one scene, he urgently questions Mrs. Mullin, a Catholic—asking her whether the Church gives her aid and comfort. Seeking reassurance that the Church is a source of goodness, he finds none. Mrs. Mullin states that she wants to kill herself, but cannot do so because she is Catholic. She cannot, in other words, control her life and her body—Catholic dogma keeps her, and other suffering people, trapped within their miserable existences by holding the threat of eternal damnation over them—confirmation of the 1960s–70s image of traditional religion as indifferent to human suffering.

Another key scene reveals that one of Peter's fellow police officers (Andy Kaufman) is among the "chosen ones" commanded to kill people—in this case, citizens attending a St. Patrick's Day parade—at random. The scene of Kaufman's unnamed character opening fire on his fellow officers as they march is shot in slow motion, depicting the killings in excruciating, morbid detail. For a brief second, he shoots directly at the audience, suggesting that the innocent viewer, too, is at risk. In another scene, Peter's lieutenant is stabbed to death by a drug-dealing pimp (George Patterson). The two are in a corrupt business partnership until the lieutenant is obliged to make some arrests to please his boss. The pimp takes advantage of the paranoid climate surrounding the "God told me to" murders to kill the lieutenant and pass off the murder as yet another random killing. Kaufman's cop-turned-killer and the corrupt lieutenant add an additional dimension to the film's notion of moral decay, suggesting that even agents of "law and order" have lost sight of the boundary between black and white, and the legal strictures designed to maintain it.

The sight of a uniformed cop turning on parade-goers echoes images of state-sponsored violence against rights protestors in the 1960s, the "police riot" against demonstrators at the Democratic National Convention in 1968, and the shooting of student protestors at Kent State University by members of the Ohio National Guard in 1970. The Kent State incident was one of the events that symbolized the death of 1960s idealism and, as Adam Lowenstein argues, "marked a crisis point for contemporary fears that America [was] divided against itself"[14] rather than united against an external Other. Soldiers charged by the government with protecting American citizens were now shooting them instead, seemingly with the government's endorsement.

Peter's obsession with the idea that the murders were a product of divine intervention is, for him, a search both for material proof of God's existence and for solid ground on which to base a sense of morality. If God is really behind the murders, issuing commands that do not reflect a human sense of goodness, Peter's view of morality will—along with virtually everyone else's—be altered forever. God and ethics would, in other words, be divorced from one another, rendering morality arbitrary and artificial. Peter, himself on morally unstable ground, needs to know the answer. Only after he has it will he be able to make choices that would be proscribed by traditional ethics.

Religion in the 1970s: Multiculturalism and Disenchantment

The 1960s were a spiritually complex era, called "the secularisation decade" by some historians, and a time of "spiritual awakening" by others.[15] The 1970s deepened that complexity. As Erling Jorstad observes: "in a vivid expression of irony and paradox, American life during the 1970s became both more religious and more secular."[16] Americans increasingly abandoned the pursuit of social justice in order to concentrate on issues of individual significance.[17] The religious landscape itself was also undergoing significant changes: notably a decades-long shift from religion-as-communal-experience to religion-as-personal-journey. Organized, scheduled services that strengthened bonds between friends and neighbors gave way to individual searches for enlightenment.[18]

The result was a plurality of faiths. Catholicism and mainstream Protestantism had been challenged, since the early 1950s, by new (or newly energized) religions such as Mormonism, Seventh Day Adventism, and Scientology. The Judeo-Christian center of the American religious landscape had initially held firm, but by the mid–1960s the "fringe sects" (as mainstream believers thought of them) were rapidly gaining ground.[19] Catholicism persisted, but was transformed by the reforms initiated by the Second Vatican Council, along with a surge in Catholic immigrants from Europe and elsewhere.[20] Liberal and moderate Protestant denominations such as Prebyterianism and Methodism suffered substantial declines in membership in the 1970s, while evangelical churches—with their literalist interpretations of the Bible, conservative morality, and ecstatic worship services—flourished, becoming the self-described home of 25 percent of American Protestants by 1973.[21]

The changing religious landscape meshed readily with the emerging youth-oriented counterculture. Among Protestants, the "Jesus Revolution" offered "a traditional, evangelical Christianity with a hippie twist,"[22] while other forms of countercultural Christianity embraced Jesus' teachings about simplicity and charity as a form of reaction against the materialistic and increasingly technologized 1960s.[23] Members of the counterculture, early exponents of self-actualization, also became enthusiastic students and promoters of Eastern religious traditions. They explored Buddhism and Yogism, filled the ranks of the Hare Krishnas and the Unification Church (sects far beyond the Judeo-Christian "fringe" of the 1950s), and adopted Eastern symbols and spiritual practices as "alternatives to the perceived decadence of the West."[24] More generalized, diffuse forms of "spirituality" also found numerous adherents, especially among the young, who found them preferable to older, more established forms of religion that they associated with rigid traditionalism, and culturally conservative dogmas. Collectively, the new religions functioned both as a critique of, and as a form of rebellion against, the established socio-political order and its bourgeois values—none more so than Satanism.[25]

Satanism's appeal to the counterculture was rooted in an image of the Devil that was at least as old as Milton's *Paradise Lost:* that of a charismatic rebel standing in opposition to a staid establishment. Winstead explains that, "[t]hough used interchangeably, Satan and Lucifer actually represent two different images of the Devil."[26] While Satan manifested himself in monstrous form, a corporeal embodiment of his sin against God and a mark of his evilness, Lucifer (Latin for "light bearer") was the Supreme Archangel of God's armies, who was cast out of Heaven because he wanted to grant knowledge to humanity and thus free them from ignorance. Where Satan embodies the idea that misbehavior is evidence of weakness—a willingness to choose the easy way over the hard, or self-gratification over service to others—Lucifer equates misbehavior with strength: a willingness to defy convention and make bold leaps into the unknown.

It was Lucifer—not Satan—that the counterculture embraced. God, in the "new" reading of the Lucifer story, was the tyrannical ruler imposing capricious and irrational demands on humans and insisting that they obey without question. The religions constructed in his name were seen by many as oppressive in their own right, allies of equally oppressive secular authorities. Their countercultural critics saw them as creators and defenders of restrictive family structures, gender roles, and racial barriers; enemies of sexual and sensual pleasure; and opponents of paths to enlightenment other than the narrowly bounded one that they themselves offered. In the language of the time, they were part of the Establishment. Lucifer, by contrast, was an explicitly oppositional figure: a rebellious, questioning, proponent of physical and spiritual liberation.

The image of the Devil as Satan—as a tempter, corruptor, and manipulator of the innocent, and an agent of evil—persisted, however, alongside the counterculture's Lucifer. His growing presence in horror and fantasy films of the 1960s and 1970s marked a cultural shift in which "individuals no longer felt compelled to take personal responsibility for their actions, but rather pointed an accusing finger at external forces."[27] The presence of Satan in horror films capitalized on the sense of chaos created by political scandals such as Watergate and the unpopular war in Vietnam, as well as the discontent created by once-marginalized Others (African Americans, Native Americans, Latinos, women, and homosexuals) campaigning for a place in the public agenda. As Winstead suggests, horror films of the era "reflected the widely held belief of evil run amok, for what else could possibly explain the sudden upheaval of traditional morals and values?"[28] The catchphrase "The Devil made me do it" served as an all-purpose comic excuse for Flip Wilson, the African American comedian who popularized it on an award-winning album and NBC television variety show, but it also had darker implications. It suggested that the will of the individual could be overridden by that of the Devil, and that deeds performed under the Devil's influence could not be laid at the feet of those who actually committed them.

This seeming abandonment of personal responsibility was, more broadly "a rejection of the concept of free will."[29] In a context of sociocultural chaos, where traditional values were malleable and alternative religions overwrote the morality of established ones, the existence of someone with the power to control others offered a kind of relief: reassurance that the world itself was simple, and someone *else* was making things complicated. The Devil became an ideal scapegoat to blame for the topsy-turvy morals of the era, and all of humanity's wrongdoing—a reason for the chaotic violence that, increasingly, seemed to dominate everyday life. The novelty of Cohen's film lay in shifting these abhorrent commands from Satan to God.

So Many Religions to Choose From

Bernard's appearance simultaneously evokes both the stereotypical image of the hippie, and the standard image of Jesus, thus underlining a key intersection between the counterculture and traditional religion. Framing Jesus as a spiritual revolutionary, a common interpretation in the 1960s, repositions him—almost by definition—as a hippie figure. The image of Jesus as a flower child with a subversive message of love and acceptance, challenging staid authority figures, was central to the Jesus Movement, but also to stage musicals such as *Jesus Christ Superstar* (1970) and *Godspell* (1971). When Peter asks a hotel doorman (James Dukas) about a barefoot young man with long hair, the latter states that "people like that got no business in here," mistaking him for a hippie. A fruit vendor (Armand Dahan) also warns against people like him, whom he believes are always looking for "something to steal," while the mother of one of the killers assures him that her son has no friends of that kind. The hostility of these (uniformly middle-aged) onlookers toward him closely reflects many older Americans' perception of hippies as subversive, unpatriotic, and—because of their embrace of drugs, promiscuity, and anti-war rhetoric—potentially dangerous.

The wrath of God is finally poured out, not on Peter, but on others. Bernard does not kill Peter, and there are (truly ambiguous) hints throughout the film that the two of them may in fact be brothers. They are linked by the fact that both of their mothers were allegedly abducted and raped by aliens, and by their shared commitment to the Catholic faith. The film also hints—again ambiguously—that Peter shares, or has gained, Bernard's ability to control others' minds. Late in the film Peter confronts Zero, the pimp who killed the lieutenant. Peter looks intently at him, and—without any mediating action—Zero slashes his own throat with a knife. The film closes with a freeze frame of Peter smiling into the camera, and the revelation that he has been committed to a mental institution, suggesting that he was either saved (and transformed into a figure of Godlike powers) by his strong faith, or driven insane by it. The ending—and the moral—of *God Told Me To* thus becomes a mirror of the point of view that the viewer brings to the film, and a reflection of whether they interpret the 1970s as a decade of secularism or of religious fervor.

The film is similarly ambiguous about Bernard's true nature: he may speak for God, or actually *be* God, or perhaps is an alien from another world whose telepathic powers oblige people to do as he desires. The possibility that Bernard is an alien that people mistake for God highlights the desperation of at least some in 1970s America to grasp onto a normative religious dogma—a rock of certainty in a society saturated with secularism or alternative religions. Even if he is ordering his followers to kill, the film implies that (some) people will find his divine, not-to-be-questioned command a welcome relief from the sea of multiculturalism and moral grayness framing the 1970s.

The possibility that God might command abhorrent acts is ethically troublesome, since it blurs divine intervention and divine caprice into a single cause, which complicates the engagement of morality and religion with one another. God traditionally defines our moral frame, teaching and mandating what is right and what is wrong. If, however, God commands the deaths of individuals on a whim, or for reasons that cannot be elucidated, the whole moral framework collapses. God would be no longer representative of a clear-cut definition of good and evil, and our human actions would have no moral guidance at all. This complication is fully in keeping with the culture of the 1960s and 1970s, in which Americans had described themselves as living not in a "Christian country," as they had in prior decades, but in a "post–Christian" or "secular" one.[30] Traditional moral principles seemed *passé*, outmoded, and incapable of dealing with issues such as abortion, LGBT rights, or divorce. Laws and forms of social discourse based on Christian moral principles might no longer be appropriate in a society where "there was no consensus on key ethical questions, and where the rights of a variety of groups, Christian and non–Christian, needed to be recognized."[31] With an ambiguous god-like creature commanding people to kill innocents, the traditional figures of God and Satan overlap, thus reconfiguring the solidity of moral ethics and principles in a post–Christian era in which religious dogmas were no longer monolithic.

Conclusion

God Told Me To mirrors the anarchy of an era that generated an intense rage against the *status quo* and was marked by disenchantment with traditional religions. Through the film, the Catholic Church is marked as a site for oppression rather than a space for happiness. Martha, for example, chastises Peter, who is Catholic, for the lack of joy in his heart. If God's mission was to fulfill men and women's hearts with joy, Jesus and traditional religion seem, in the film, to be unable to do so. Alternatives that *could* do so—including Neopaganism, New Age, and the idea that "God" was a member of an advanced alien species—flourished. In the context of the 1970s, the film denies that God is metaphysically relevant to morality at all. "God language," David Weaver-Zercher contends, "no longer made sense to modern ears"[32] as the utopic 1960s slipped into the bleak 1970s. Peter tries to hold onto his traditional beliefs, swimming against the cultural tied, but the film frames him as a dinosaur and, as such, he must ultimately vanish.

God Told Me To dramatizes two seemingly opposite but actually complementary trends unfolding in the United States during the 1970s. Corrupt policemen shooting innocents and God Himself commanding people to commit abhorrent deeds are both reflections of a society losing its moral compass. They dramatize, in the starkest possible terms, the death of 1960s optimism and belief in the possibility of a better future and the emergence of the disillusionment that dominated the 1970s. Simultaneously, they embody the era's sense of religious plurality: The existence of more—and more diverse—faiths than had ever existed before, all seemingly equal and each claiming to offer believers a path to enlightenment. The sense of uncertainty that pervades this world—embodied in Peter, who spends the entire film struggling to plot his own path through it—makes *God Told Me To* feel as relevant today as it did when first released. The horror of the random, senseless murders it depicts has been eclipsed by real-world horrors whose magnitude would have been unimaginable in the mid–1970s. The motive behind them, however, remains disturbingly familiar. Disillusionment with once-revered authorities and institutions remains intense, the challenge of choosing between the unsatisfying old and the uncertain new remains profound, and individuals willing to slaughter the innocent—firm in their conviction that they were commanded to by God, who will look on them with favor for doing so—are more numerous, and more terrifying, with each passing year.

Notes

1. Rodney Carlisle and Geoffrey Golson, eds., *America in Revolt during the 1960s and 1970s* (Santa Barbara, CA: ABC-CLIO, 2008), xvii.
2. Christopher Gair, *The American Counterculture* (Edinburgh: Edinburgh University Press, 2007), 4.
3. Donald Musser and Joseph Price, eds., *New & Enlarged Handbook of Christian Theology: Revised Edition* (Nashville: Abingdon Press, 2003), 124.
4. Richard E. Wentz, *Why People Do Bad Things in the Name of Religion* (Macon: Mercer University Press, 1993), 70.
5. William Cavanaugh, *The Myth of Religious Violence: Secular Ideology and the Roots of Modern Conflict* (New York: Oxford University Press, 2009), 25.
6. The film was distributed by Roger Corman's New World Pictures. Corman tried to cash in on the "satanic panic" craze of '70s genre cinema and retitled the film *Demon* in some markets and issued posters that were reminiscent of the posters for *The Omen*.
7. Together with cinematic "folk horror," the subgenre of "nature-run-amok," in which animals or group of animals attack humans due to different motives, was other of the cycles of horror in tap into social anxieties of that era.
8. Sarah Pike, *New Age and Neopagan Religions in America* (New York: Columbia University Press, 2003), 145.
9. David Baggett and Jerry Walls, *Good God* (New York: Oxford University Press, 2011), 154.
10. *Ibid.*, 48.
11. She is first seen first walking the streets among the potential victims of sniper Gorman. She is holding a book titled *The Philosophy of Andy Warhol*, highlighting her connection to the countercultural art scene of the era and (perhaps) acknowledging Cohen's admiration of Warhol's avant-garde filmmaking, which privileged ambiguity rather than logical narrative. Her ties to the avant garde and the counterculture set her apart from the more grounded Peter, whose job encourages a more conservative point of view.
12. David Hillman, *Hermaphrodites, Gynomorphs and Jesus: She-Male Gods and the Roots of Christianity* (Berkeley: Ronin, 2013), 134.
13. The idea of "ancient astronauts" being mistaken for gods by ancient pagan cultures was popularized by Erich Von Daeniken in *Chariots of the Gods?* (1968; New York: Bantam, 1973). The specifically Christian interpretation of the alien-emissary theory played with in the film was outlined in works such as Paul Misraki, *Flying Saucers Through The Ages* (London: Neville Spearman, 1965); Barry Downing, *The Bible and Flying Saucers* (Philadelphia: Lippincott, 1968); and Robert Dione, *God Drives a Flying Saucer* (1969; New York: Bantam, 1973).
14. Adam Lowenstein, *Shocking Representation: Historical Trauma, National Cinema, and the Modern Horror Film* (New York: Columbia University Press, 2005): 115.
15. Callum Brown, "The Secularisation Decade: What the Sixties Have Done to the Study of Religious History," in *The Decline of Christendom in Western Europe, 1775–2000*, ed. Hugh McLeod and Werner Ustorf, 29–46 (2003; Cambridge: Cambridge University Press, 2011); Robert S. Ellwood, Jr., *Sixties Spiritual Awakening* (New Brunswick: Rutgers University Press, 2003).
16. Erling Jorstad, *Popular Religion in America: The Evangelical Voice* (London: Greenwood, 1993), 27.
17. Neil Hamilton, *The 1970s* (New York: Facts on File, 2006), 232.
18. Bruce J. Schulman, *The Seventies: The Great Shift in American Culture, Society, and Politics* (New York: DaCapo Press, 2001), 96–101.
19. Robert Wuthnow, *The Restructuring of American Religion: Society and Faith Since World War II* (Princeton: Princeton University Press, 1988), 159.
20. James Fisher, *Catholics in America* (New York: Oxford University Press, 2000), 153.
21. Schulman, *The Seventies*, 92–93.
22. Larry Eskridge, *God's Forever Family: The Jesus People Movement in America* (New York: Oxford University Press, 2013), 1.
23. Preston Shires, *Hippies of the Religious Right* (Waco: Baylor University Press, 2006), 9.
24. Schulman, *The Seventies*, 96–97; Harold Netland, *Encountering Religious Pluralism: The Challenge to Christian Faith & Mission* (Downers Grove, IL: InterVarsity Press, 2001), 107.
25. Antoinette Winstead, "The Devil Made Me Do It! The Devil in 1960s-1970s Horror Films," in *Vader,*

Voldemort and Other Villains: Essays on Evil in Popular Media, ed. Jamey Heit (Jefferson, NC: McFarland, 2011), 31.
  26. Winstead, "The Devil Made Me Do It," 30.
  27. *Ibid.*, 34.
  28. Winstead, "The Devil Made Me Do It," 29.
  29. *Ibid.*
  30. Thomas McLeod, *The Religious Crisis of the 1960s* (New York: Oxford University Press, 2008), 2.
  31. *Ibid.*
  32. David Weaver-Zercher, "Theologies," in *Themes in Religion and American Culture*, ed. Philip Goff and Paul Harvey (Chapel Hill: University of North Carolina Press, 2004), 33.

Bibliography

Baggett, David and Jerry Walls, *Good God: The Theistic Foundations of Morality*. New York: Oxford University Press, 2011.

Brown, Callum. "The Secularisation Decade: What the Sixties Have Done to the Study of Religious History." In *The Decline of Christendom in Western Europe, 1775–2000*, ed. Hugh McLeod and Werner Ustorf, 29–46. 2003. Cambridge: Cambridge University Press, 2011.

Carlisle, Rodney, and Geoffrey Golson, eds. *America in Revolt during the 1960s and 1970s*. Santa Barbara, CA: ABC-CLIO, 2008.

Cavanaugh, William. *The Myth of Religious Violence: Secular Ideology and the Roots of Modern Conflict*. New York: Oxford University Press, 2009.

Dione, Robert. *God Drives a Flying Saucer*. 1969. New York: Bantam, 1973.

Downing, Barry. *The Bible and Flying Saucers*. Philadelphia: Lippincott, 1968.

Ellwood, Robert S., Jr. *Sixties Spiritual Awakening*. New Brunswick: Rutgers University Press, 2003.

Eskridge, Larry. *God's Forever Family: The Jesus People Movement in America*. New York: Oxford University Press, 2013.

Fisher, James. *Catholics in America*. New York: Oxford University Press, 2000.

Gair, Christopher. *The American Counterculture*. Edinburgh: Edinburgh University Press, 2007.

Hamilton, Neil. *The 1970s*. New York: Facts on File, 2006.

Hillman, David. *Hermaphrodites, Gynomorphs and Jesus: She-Male Gods and the Roots of Christianity*. Berkeley: Ronin, 2013.

Jorstad, Erling. *Popular Religion in America: The Evangelical Voice*. London: Greenwood, 1993.

Lowenstein, Adam. *Shocking Representation: Historical Trauma, National Cinema, and the Modern Horror Film*. New York: Columbia University Press, 2005.

McLeod, Thomas. *The Religious Crisis of the 1960s*. New York: Oxford University Press, 2008.

Musser, Donald and Joseph Price. *New & Enlarged Handbook of Christian Theology: Revised Edition*. Nashville: Abingdon Press, 2003.

Netland, Harold. *Encountering Religious Pluralism: The Challenge to Christian Faith & Mission*. Downers Grove, IL: InterVarsity Press, 2001.

Pike, Sarah. *New Age and Neopagan Religions in America*. New York: Columbia University Press, 2003.

Schulman, Bruce J. *The Seventies: The Great Shift in American Culture, Society, and Politics*. New York: DaCapo Press, 2001.

Shires, Preston. *Hippies of the Religious Right*. Waco: Baylor University Press, 2006.

Thomas, Paul. *Flying Saucers Through The Ages*. London: Neville Spearman, 1965.

Von Däniken, Erich. *Chariots of the Gods?* 1968. New York: Bantam, 1974.

Weaver-Zercher, David. "Theologies." In *Themes in Religion and American Culture*, ed. Philip Goff and Paul Harvey, 5–38. Chapel Hill: University of North Carolina Press, 2004.

Wentz, Richard E. *Why People Do Bad Things in the Name of Religion*. Macon: Mercer University Press, 1993.

Winstead, Antoinette. "The Devil Made Me Do It! The Devil in 1960s–1970s Horror Films." In *Vader, Voldemort and Other Villains: Essays on Evil in Popular Media*, ed. Jamey Heit, 28–45. Jefferson, NC: McFarland, 2011.

Wuthnow, Robert. *The Restructuring of American Religion: Society and Faith Since World War II*. Princeton: Princeton University Press, 1988.

Demons to Some, Angels to Others
Eldritch Horrors and Hellbound Religion in the Hellraiser Films

Lúcio Reis-Filho

Stephen King once famously said, "I have seen the future of horror, and his name is Clive Barker."[1] More to the point, King saw the moment where horror's past and future merged in Barker's *Hellraiser* (1987), creating one of the most distinctive and chilling pieces of horror cinema of its decade, and spawning a franchise still active today.[2]

Hellraiser has deep roots in the supernatural literature of myth and legend. Director John Landis and critic Paul Kane both consider the film a sadomasochistic take on the myth of Pandora's Box, an artifact converted by Barker into a mysterious device that contains unimaginable pain and suffering.[3] Kane also draws a connection between the film and the legend of Faust, given that the overarching theme of both tales is a bargain with the Devil. Barker's first commercially released film, *Hellraiser* is a skillful merging of two versions of the myth: Marlowe's, about a scholar who trades his soul to Mephistopheles for knowledge and is sucked into the pits of Hell, and Goethe's, in which the protagonist escapes damnation by cheating the Devil. To these, *Hellraiser* adds elements borrowed from the later work of H.P. Lovecraft, master of the literary "weird fiction" subgenre.

One of the most influential horror writers of the 20th century, Lovecraft created tales of elder gods and powerful supernatural beings that have been banished from Earth and wait impatiently to return. These stories, which have come to be called the "Cthulu Mythos," culminate in deadly encounters between these gods and hapless human beings who stumble across them and discover, to their horror, a universe far darker and more hostile than they had ever imagined. Innumerable writers have elaborated on this pseudo-mythology, both during Lovecraft's own lifetime and in the decades following his death. Among them was his disciple August Derleth (1909–1971), who took the mythos in new directions. Derleth's stories transformed Lovecraft's bleak cosmic vision into a traditional and naïve moral struggle between good and evil,[4] a schema that allowed Derleth to harmonize the mythos with his own Christian beliefs.

Based on Barker's 1986 novella *The Hellbound Heart*, *Hellraiser* borrows Lovecraft's signature elements: dreadful mythology, arcane religion, forbidden lore, dream worlds, and an amoral universe. Film theorist Andy Black cites the links between the two in his praise of Barker as an "auteur [who] appears to be mining the rich seam of Lovecraftian creativity ... featuring the now-familiar 'other dimensional' Cenobites, grotesque monsters and labyrinth corridors/caves."[5] William Latham extends the connection between the two, describing *Hellraiser* (1987) as "the first attempt anyone had really taken to create a universe in a horror story since Lovecraft."[6]

This essay develops and expands on Black's observations, demonstrating the ways in which the balance between Lovecraftian and Derlethian elements in the *Hellraiser* universe shifts over the course of the series, blurring the boundaries between good and evil without completely abandoning the dichotomy. The first entries in the *Hellraiser* series echo central tenets of Lovecraft's horror fiction and philosophy, but Derleth's influence is present from the beginning. Initially, it manifests itself only in climactic battles between good and evil, but over the course of the first four films the depictions of good and evil become steadily more polarized. The Cenobites shift, in the process, from complex, amoral figures to beings of pure evil: agents of violence and chaos. The next five installments take place in a universe structured by Derleth's conventional, dichotomous view of good and evil, and unfold as conventional crime stories and self-referential horror films onto which elements from the *Hellraiser* mythos have been grafted. Derleth's dichotomous, moralistic, worldview dominates, and only a few vestigial traces of Lovecraft's dark, amoral universe remain.

The Hellraiser *Universe Unfolds*

Hellraiser opens in the gloomy attic of an old house, where Frank Cotton (Sean Chapman)—a hedonistic criminal who believes he has experienced everything—opens a mystical/mechanical puzzle box, known as the Lament Configuration, which he purchased in Morocco. The box is "the key to a doorway between the seen and the unseen," Douglas E. Cowan explains, "the boundary along which vastly different orders of reality occasionally and violently collide ... it is a means to summon the Cenobites, beings who exist in a dimension where pleasure and pain come together as one, and the all-too-thin line between the two is torn relentlessly apart."[7] Promised that the box would deliver a new realm of sensual pleasures, Frank cloisters himself in his attic and solves its puzzle, bringing forth the Cenobites: a communal order of mutilated and modified, black-robed figures—explorers in the extremes of bodily experience—who rend flesh, rip out organs and tear souls apart in the pursuit of ecstasy.[8] Frank observes: "Some things have to be endured and that's what makes the pleasures so sweet,"[9] but for him, the price of opening the box is high. The Cenobites transform the attic into an inter-dimensional slaughterhouse, filled with chains and hanging pieces of human flesh, and proceed to destroy his body and drag his soul to the underworld.

After his apparent death, Frank's brother Larry Cotton (Andrew Robinson) and his wife Julia (Clare Higgins), who had an illicit affair with Frank shortly after their marriage, inherit the house and move in. But when Larry cuts his hand carrying a bed up the stairs, his blood drips onto the attic floor where Frank was dismembered, and brings his brother back to life as a withered, decaying corpse. Julia discovers her former lover, and Frank promises that they can be together once again ... if only he can regenerate. He tells her that "every drop of blood is more flesh on my bones," and urges her to harvest more blood for him so that he can fully return to life. Still obsessed with him, she agrees, and begins luring unsuspecting men to their doom. As the story unfolds, Larry's adult daughter Kirsty (Ashley Laurence) eventually unravels the murderous plot, and must then defeat not only her uncle and stepmother, but also the Cenobites, who return to Earth to reclaim his soul. She ultimately uses the box to dispatch the demons back to Hell, one by one, and with the danger seemingly past, the interior of the house crumbles.

"Franchise" was a buzzword in horror filmmaking during the 1980s, and multiple sequels were expected to follow films that achieved success at the box office. *Hellbound: Hellraiser II* (1988) was created to surpass its predecessor, but in the process, downplayed or ignored significant elements of the original film.[10] The story, which opens immediately after the actions closing the first film, shifts the setting from Earth to Hell. Kirsty wakes up in a mental hospital whose director, Doctor Channard (Kenneth Cranham), is a demonology expert who has been searching for the Lament Configuration as part of a quest to acquire demonic powers. Replicating the events that resurrected Frank, he brings Julia back to life, restoring her body with the flesh and blood of several captured victims. After he encourages a semi-catatonic patient—a puzzle-obsessed child named Tiffany (Imogen Boorman)—to solve and open the Lament Configuration, a gateway to Hell is opened, and Julia, Channard, and Kirsty slip into the Cenobite realm, shifting the narrative back to the supernatural realm.

Hellbound establishes that the Cenobites were once human before being transformed into demonic servants of the dark god Leviathan—a revelation that touches a chord of humanity in Pinhead and several other Cenobites. When they uncharacteristically attempt to defend the "innocents" (Kirsty and Tiffany) against Julia and Channard, both of whom have perverted the amoral mandate of the order, the complex narrative arc shifts to that of a more simplistic tale of good versus evil. As if to signal an end to the divine ambiguity of the Cenobites, Pinhead and the others are destroyed.

The resurrection of Pinhead for a third film, however, was inevitable. The plot of *Hellraiser III: Hell on Earth* (1992) is set in motion by Pinhead's return, set loose on Earth to wreak havoc. Consistent with then-emerging trends in horror filmmaking, the film substituted naturalistic urban settings for elaborate secondary worlds, and transformed Pinhead into "a canny and intriguing serial killer or indefatigable psycho stalker."[11] This film was even more expansive than the second, with special effects artist Bob Kane relishing its broadening "to a point where it is now *Hell on Earth*, where we are wrecking an entire city," and attributing the change to the franchise's move to the U.S., "where everything is done on a grander scale."

"In many ways," Cowan observes, the fourth film in the series, *Hellraiser: Bloodline* (1996), "is the most ambitious of the franchise, seeking to weave together the numerous strands of the emerging *Hellraiser* mythology and to account both for the box's origin and future."[12] The film covers 400 years, and traces the evolution of the Lament Configuration through three different periods of history. The three temporal segments are connected by the Lament Configuration itself—its creation, present life, and future. After being the center of *Hell on Earth*, Pinhead is now relegated to the sidelines, replaced by his predecessor in Hell, the demon Angelique (Valentina Vargas). He reassumes his role as the main villain in the final, futuristic segment, however, joined by the Twin Cenobites, whose heads are conjoined like a twisted yin and yang symbol; the Chatter Beast, a huge, toothy half-man, half-dog creature; and a reconfigured Angelique.

Bloodline portrays the Cenobites as imperialistic villains, determined to turn the whole of Earth into a yawning gateway to Hell.[13] In keeping with the franchise's shift to clear-cut morality tales, Pinhead and Angelique appear as latter-day Olympian gods, moving human beings around like pieces on a gigantic chessboard, using them for their own entertainment and pleasure. "The Garden of Eden. A Garden of flesh," Pinhead says of the Earth as he looks down on it from orbit, plotting to open the gateway between Earth and Hell once and for all.[14] At the final battle, the protagonist Paul Merchant (Bruce Ramsay) sets a trap for him and destroys the space station, sending the demon back where it came from.[15]

The remaining five films (to date) completely reshaped the *Hellraiser* series, drawing so little of substance from the Cenobite mythos that they connect only superficially to the first four films. They are also, for the most part, independent from one another, telling self-contained stories that neither advance the mythos nor deepen the series' shared universe. What little commonality they do possess is rooted in storytelling tropes such as dream imagery and non-linear time, along with a moralistic tone that evokes Derleth's vision of the Cthulu mythos, rather than Lovecraft's. Humans are at the center both of the later films and—as in Derleth's writings—at the center of the universe, their actions watched and scrutinized by supernatural beings. Pinhead delights in revealing himself after his victims have irrevocably damned themselves, ushering them to Hell to be punished for transgressions committed on Earth.[16] The lesser Cenobites are, similarly, reduced to silent killers and sinister figures that foreshadow death.[17]

The fifth through ninth films in the franchise—*Hellraiser: Inferno* (2000), *Hellraiser: Hellseeker* (2002), *Hellraiser: Deader* (2005), and the low-budget *Hellraiser: Revelations* (2011)—follow plotlines that more closely resemble everyday crime stories than tales of supernatural horror: killers are tracked, mysteries are solved, and wrongs are redressed.[18] The elements of the Cenobite mythos that *do* appear in the films have a forced or disjointed quality; and any suggestions of torture, horror or madness "could simply be explained away as [human] guilt ... without any involvement of the Cenobites at all."[19]

The *Hellraiser* series thus undergoes, in these later films, a process of decay common to many long-running film franchises. Elements that prove popular with audiences are given steadily greater emphasis, but rendered in ways that reduce them to their superficial, formulaic essentials. Details that gave the early installments depth and complexity are, simultaneously, pruned away to make room for the marquee elements audiences are assumed to want. The later *Hellraiser* films tend, therefore, to resemble other horror films of their era more than they do the richly textured early installments of their own series.

The Horrors of the Cenobites

The Cenobites—demonic, yet highly disciplined—blur the boundaries between the horrific and the divine. They are "angels to some, demons to others," as Pinhead, the Lead Cenobite, explains. Much like the monastic orders after which they were fashioned, they are bound by strict codes of behavior, and practice inducing extreme pain and pleasure as a form of transcendence. Powerful beings, they may only exercise their will when others have transgressed by solving the puzzle box known as the Lament Configuration, thus opening a schism in time and space that connects their world with our own.

The monstrous body modifications of the Cenobites, carried out in their ecstatic quest for the extremes of pain and pleasure, bring to the films a strong element of "body horror": a "hybrid genre that recombines the narrative and cinematic conventions of the science fiction, horror and suspense films."[20] Its narratives seek to inspire revulsion—

Pinhead (Doug Bradley) and the Cenobites, featured throughout the *Hellraiser* series.

and in its own way, pleasure—through explicit representations of violence, in which the human subject is dismantled and demolished.[21] Through its uses of body horror, the *Hellraiser* franchise moves beyond the mere "uncanny" evoked by classic horror narratives, and transgresses the boundaries of manipulation of the human face and form, creating entities that induce both fascination and fear. Rather than creating a society of "freaks" that lurk at the margins, the extreme physical difference of the Cenobites signals power and control. Pinhead, the films' principal Cenobite character, exemplifies this complex identity through the feature that gives him his nickname: a grid of horizontal and vertical incisions scar his corpse-pale, hairless head, with a nail extending outward from each intersection.

The term cenobite signifies membership in a communal religious order[22]—in *The Hellbound Heart*, the aptly named Order of the Gash. *Hellraiser*'s Cenobites are complex entities—leather-clad theologians attempting to shift the moral order; hierophants ushering new congregants into the presence of the holy; and amoral sentionauts seeking higher levels of consciousness—and Pinhead functions, in *Hellraiser* and its first sequel, as an "impartial demonic referee."[23] He and the other members of his order thus blur the lines between opposites. Even as their grotesque appearances and sadistic behavior suggests that they are creatures of pure evil, they are, in fact, seekers of enlightenment who refuse to be limited by the Judeo-Christian moral universe.[24]

Hellraiser's depiction of the Cenobites as disinterested and amoral entities mirrors the image of the Old Ones in Lovecraft's writings. While Barker's depiction of the demons as heavily mutilated and scarified cell-dwelling monks is quite different from the appearances of Lovecraft's elder gods, their existential underpinnings are similar. The Cenobites are priests from a dark house, just like those who serve Cthulhu; and like the Old Ones, they are morally complex, only appearing to lay claim to what is already theirs.

The Cenobites provide narrative continuity across the *Hellraiser* series as the films become increasingly stand-alone in nature. The mysterious Pinhead, whose richness of language and dark ironic humor were enhanced by the performance of Shakespearian actor Doug Bradley, was immediately popular despite his brief screen time in the first installment, becoming an enduring icon of the horror genre and the only character to appear in all nine entries released to date.[25] He and the other Cenobites acquired additional depth and shading in the next two films. *Hellbound: Hellraiser II*, for example, establishes that the Cenobites were once human before being transformed into demons by the dark god Leviathan. As agents of its will, they become servants to Hell, their orders coming from the all-seeing, all-knowing deity, and their efforts are all in the name of the god. This plot device gives the Cenobites a complexity that sets them apart from the real villains of the film.

In its original depiction of demons, the *Hellraiser* series drew upon the provocative imagery associated with the "splatterpunk" aesthetic and the extreme expressions associated, in of the fetish scene from the 1970s and 1980s, with the sadomasochistic and body-piercing subcultures.[26] Noticeably absent are the elements made familiar in traditional descriptions of Satan: "the serpent's features, the hooves and goat's head, even the red skin, horns and wings which connote chaos."[27] Equally significant, the first two *Hellraiser* films not only challenge the popular conception of what a demon is, but also subvert the deeply rooted Christian belief that demons are embodiments of evil.

Historically, the word "demon" comes from the Ancient Greek *daimon*, from the verb *daiein*, "to distribute." In a wide range of classical sources *daimon* could mean "the power controlling the destiny of individuals." Thus, a *daimon* was both the distributor of destinies and the destiny itself. The Christianization of the Greek-speaking world did much to popularize the idea of demons as exclusively evil spirits, and to attach a negative connotation to the word, as Charles Stewart notes[28]: "The already many-stranded traditional conception of *daimones* was reoriented by the Judeo-Christian story of Satan who, in an act of hubristic jealousy, attempted to place his throne higher than God's. In recompense, he was cast down from the heavens, along with his conspiring angels who became demons.... Demons in the Christian world were unequivocally evil, associated with matter, sin, corruption, and the body, as opposed to the values of Christian purity, restraint, and spirituality overseen by God and Christ."[29] The *daimones* were a nameless, ill-defined plurality of supernatural beings. In *Hellbound*, which retains the premise of the first film, the Cenobites come close to that original meaning of the word. They are not evil, despite their monstrous appearance. In contrast, the transformation of the villainous Doctor Channard represents the shift of the *daimones* from elements of a philosophical cosmology to elements of a moral one, the *demones*, or demons.

By introducing a Cenobite with immoral, rather than amoral, character, however, *Helbound* also reduces the narrative complexities of the story to a mere struggle between good and evil—albeit one which takes place within the hellish realm of the Cenobites. The identity of Pinhead's former self (Captain Elliot Spencer, who served in World War I) is revealed, causing him to revert to his human form and lose his demonic powers. Seeing an opportunity to seize power in Hell, the Channard Cenobite conjures surgical blades, which extend from his hands like the appendages of Lovecraftian monsters, and uses them to kill Pinhead and his followers as they attempt to rebel.[30] The introduction of a simplistic moral binary into the world of the Cenobites sets the franchise on a path of transition from its original Lovecraftian complexities toward more conventionally moralistic horror, with the Cenobites as key markers of that change.

The shift is fully realized in *Hellraiser III: Hell on Earth* (1992), which features Pinhead's reincarnation.[31] As Doug Bradley noted:

> Principally, in the first two films, we established very strongly that he worked through the Lament Configuration box.... The whole of *Hellraiser III* is driven by the questions of how Pinhead is reincarnated, and what happens when he is. This time we meet a Pinhead who is freed from the rules, the laws and the constraints of the Lament Configuration, and *Hell on Earth* tells you he's out there, on the streets. This also is a more sinister, a more glibly malevolent character, who this time is prepared to—and does—get his hands dirty.[32]

Pinhead obeys no authority other than his own moral compass in *Hell on Earth*. He is "unbound"—his demonic essence (a term now used pejoratively) freed to wreak havoc—and no longer listens to his former master, Leviathan. "Pinhead has broken away from Hell. I tried to make him a real person, much more vicious but also much more realistic," said director Anthony Hickox.[33] The character becomes an anarchic figure who delights in violence, staging a massacre in a rock club and slashing down hundreds with his hooks purely for his own amusement. Both Muir and Kane criticize the transformation of the Lead Cenobite into an indiscriminate mass murderer. David McWilliam agrees, noting that Pinhead is now less interested in torture than bloodletting. He is no longer the disciplined priest of pain of the first two films, but a slasher-film-franchise icon similar to Freddy Krueger (*Nightmare on Elm Street*), Michael Myers (*Halloween*), and Jason Voorhees (*Friday the 13th*).[34] The divine has become mundane.

Each successive installment in the franchise has gradually reshaped the *Hellraiser* series, while drawing little from the Cenobite mythos. When the Lament Configuration is taken in *Hellraiser III: Hell on Earth*, Pinhead attempts to regain it, using his new powers to create pseudo-Cenobites by fusing the transmuted flesh of his victims with electrical appliances.[35] These lesser Cenobites are ingenious monsters—unstoppable, bulletproof, each with their own special powers—and they add science fiction to the list of genres the series samples from.[36] They are not, however, evil by any conventional definition, and thus unable (as Cenobites originally were) to trouble the boundaries separating evil from good. Scenes featuring Pinhead, or the Cenobites in general, grow progressively scarcer as the series continues, and new creations appear only in hallucinatory glimpses. The villains are human psychopaths who end up meeting their fates in the hands of Cenobites who, this time, offer nothing but a cruel death. Following what became a pattern in the later films, Pinhead delights in revealing himself at the end, after his victims are irrevocably damned, adding a moralistic tone absent in the original concept.[37] He is no longer an amoral entity—an impartial referee—but a moral guardian, or a judge who leads sinners to their doom.

Light and Dark, Good and Evil

Humans occupy a central, privileged position in the Judeo-Christian worldview, but a peripheral, insignificant one in the Cthulu mythos created by Lovecraft. The Bible evokes the vastness of the visible universe in order to reassure humans that they occupy a special place within it. The question posed in Psalm 8: "What is man, that Thou art mindful of him?" is purely rhetorical. The answer has been made clear in Genesis: Man is God's greatest creation, who was made in His image, and for whom He made the Earth and all it contains. The central theme of the New Testament—that God sacrificed His only son to redeem humankind—only reinforces humans' privileged status. Humans in the Judeo-Christian universe draw the continual attention of God, Satan, and all their legions. Lovecraft, in contrast, uses the vastness of the universe and the insignificance of humans to terrify his characters and unsettle his readers. Earth remains a (mostly) congenial space for humans in Lovecraft's fiction, but those who venture past it into the vast darkness beyond risk death, madness, and the burden of knowledge they can never un-know. The greatest of all those burdens is the knowledge of humans' utter insignificance in Lovecraft's dark cosmos, where their lives are as irrelevant to the elder gods as the lives of insects are to us.

According to Kane, *Hellraiser* shares its roots with films—such as *The Exorcist* (1973) and *The Omen* (1976)—that are deeply and explicitly rooted in a Judeo-Christian worldview.[38] Framed as stories of conflict between God and the Devil, with Earth (and the film's human characters) as the battleground, these earlier films present good and evil as clearly defined, sharply polarized extremes. This dichotomy is evident in *Hellraiser*'s portrayals of Kirsty and Julia as "light" and "dark" characters respectively, embodying "a universal duality" that, in the Western world, is traditionally associated with good and evil, angels and demons.[39] Angelic Kirsty is, when she first appears, "virtually in soft focus, her face bathed in light like an angel. Even her name is Christ-like." Julia, on the other hand, first appears wearing white blouses, but switches to orange and finally to dark blue as the film proceeds,[40] the darkening of her clothing reflecting the darkening of her character. The actions of the two women become equally polarized as the film moves toward its climax. Julia emerges as a seductress who lures men to their deaths in order to harvest their blood, and Kirsty as a virtuous "final girl" whose only goal is survival. The film then moves toward a final battle—a conclusion that is absent in the novella—between the forces of good and evil, in which Kirsty banishes the demons to Hell.

Beneath these Judeo-Christian surface elements, however, the underlying structure of *Hellraiser* owes more to Lovecraft than to Derleth. Kirsty is good, and Julia is evil, but the final battle is not a moral contest but a struggle for control of the portal that the Lament Configuration opens between Earth and Hell. Frank is dragged to Hell at the beginning of the film not because he is evil but because he solves the puzzle-box and opens the portal. When the Cenobites come after him the second time, they do so in order to reclaim their lost "property," not to administer divine punishment. Kirsty's moral purity does not, in itself, protect her from the Cenobites. The Cenobites save her from being stabbed by her uncle, but—because she, too, opened the Lament Configuration deliberately—they then attempt to claim her soul. She ultimately thwarts them, and sends them back to Hell one-by-one, not because she is "good," but because she is skilled at manipulating the box. *Hellbound*, as Paul Kane notes, makes this point explicit: Hell is not a world of punishment for wrongs done in life, and individuals are not automatically sent there when they die. They could have a perfectly pure existence and still fall victim to this particular Hell. All they need to do is open the box.[41]

The Hell briefly glimpsed in *Hellraiser* and fully depicted in *Hellbound* is, not surprisingly, far removed from the fire-and-brimstone image deeply rooted in Christian thought; indeed, it bears little resemblance to any vision of Hell ever seen before. It is "a vast labyrinth ... surrounded by little realms where individuals suffer in their personal, perpetual torments."[42] This vision of an orderly Hell and individualized torments echoes that outlined by Dante, but the first two films' imagery owes little to Gustave Doré's famous gothic illustrations for *Inferno*. Instead, they fuse elements from the work of European graphic artists M.C. Escher and H.R. Giger into a dream-like world of awe-inspiring grandeur and Cyclopean architecture: "There are no caves in this Hell, only corridors, steps and dark storm clouds on the horizon. The captives aren't packed into small confines, but given the space of their own personal Hells. This Hades is not the epitome of chaos, but of order.... Finally, this Hell shares the view that torment should be forever. Working through your bad deeds or repenting will not earn you a way out—karma has nothing to do with it. The only means of exit is to escape, as Frank does in the first film."[43] Lovecraft—who wrote about characters helpless in the face of forces beyond their comprehension, and believed that "atmosphere, not action, is the great desideratum of weird fiction"[44]—would have been proud.

Casual dismissal of the Christian worldview, and mockery of its symbols and rituals, is evident throughout the early films in the series. Frank's body is "resurrected," in *Hellraiser*, by blood taken from others: Holy Communion turned inside out. Captured by the Cenobites at the climax of the film, he mockingly declares "Jesus wept" and opens his arms open wide in imitation of Christ on the cross before his physical body is, for the second time, torn to pieces. The final battle of *Hell on Earth*, set in a Catholic church, makes Pinhead himself the agent of mockery. The priest holds up a crucifix, Pinhead intones "Thou shalt not bow down before any graven image" and the metal cross melts in the cleric's hand. He then pulls two long nails from his head and pierces his palms with them, in imitation of the stigmata, raising his arms and proclaiming (as Jesus did): "I am the way."[45] As the window behind him shatters and the church begins to collapse, Pinhead pulls off a piece of his own flesh and forces the helpless priest to eat: "This is my body, this is my blood. Happy are they who come to *my* supper." Merchant, meeting Pinhead for the first time in *Bloodline*, exclaims "Oh, my God!" and the Lead Cenobite responds, disdainfully: "Do I look like someone who cares what God thinks?"

This line, Cowan suggests, completes "the narrative arc that has been building since the first film: the fear that the gods to whom we pray or make offerings, whose altars we adorn with service and sacrifice, whose rules we follow and to whose promises we cling, simply don't matter."[46] It evokes Lovecraft's *cosmicism*, both as a metaphysical position (an awareness of the cosmic insignificance of humanity in a boundless universe), and as an aesthetic one (a literary expression of this insignificance, which minimizes human character by displaying the titanic gulfs of space and time).[47] Pinhead's observation, in the futuristic seg-

Pinhead (Doug Bradley) turns the Holy Communion upside down in *Hell on Earth* (1992).

ment of *Bloodline*, that "there are more humans alive at this moment than in all [Earth's] pitiful history," and that the humankind shares "the same faithless hope in light," illustrates the character's *indifferentism*. Humans are tiny, insignificant specks in an often-hostile universe that does not care what they do or do not. Lovecraft's pessimistic cosmic views were tied to his dismissal of the metaphysical claims of religion. In *A Confession of Unfaith* (1922), he wrote: "A mere knowledge of the approximate dimensions of the visible universe is enough to destroy forever the notion of a personal godhead whose whole care is expended upon puny mankind."[48] Thus, as Lovecraft sloughed off any belief in a deity as scientifically unjustified, he was left with the awareness that humankind was (probably) alone in the universe. Gazing at a view-screen image of Earth aboard the space station in *Bloodline*, Pinhead sums up this chilling perspective of human existence: "Glorious, is it not? The creatures that walk on its surface, always looking to the light, never seeing the untold oceans of darkness beyond." This cosmic wide view grants Pinhead the role of an eternal (and evil) Old One, waiting to step out of the dark. He acknowledges as much in *Bloodlines*, the film that completes his transformation from a morally ambiguous figure in whom darkness and light blur together to an unambiguously evil, oppositional one. "Darkness, he intones, "is where you'll find me."

Such nods to Lovecraft largely disappear from the series after *Bloodline*, as the Cenobites become more traditionally demonic, and the plots are re-oriented around Derleth-style moral dichotomies. A central Lovecraftian conceit remains in the background of the series, however—linking all the *Hellraiser* films and persisting even as their plots, characters, and genre associations change. Each installment in the series forces its human characters to confront a universe more vast and terrifying than they had ever imagined, filled with creatures more horrific than their worst nightmares. The characters' bodies are constantly at risk (the films are filled with pain, dismemberment, and death) but their naive assumptions about the universe, and the rules that govern it, die first.

Conclusion

The first four entries in the *Hellraiser* series have a distinctly Lovecraftian approach to horror. Indeed, the original film and its sequel might be considered highly innovative pieces of the Lovecraftian cinema, which borrow the dreadful mythology, arcane religion, forbidden lore, dream worlds, and amoral universe common to the writer's work, along with tenets from the philosophy of cosmicism. Each of these earlier films, however, features a conclusion marked by a struggle between good and evil, in which good is clearly triumphant. This reflects Derleth's, rather than Lovecraft's, interpretation of the Cthulu mythos, transforming Lovecraft's bleak cosmic vision into a traditional black-and-white moral struggle. The polarization of good and evil in the films becomes even more pronounced in the third and fourth films, made after *Hellraiser* moved to the United States, and the last five films completed the transformation. Peeling off Lovecraftian elements such as the depiction of an amoral universe and dropping important elements of the original concept, they are Americanized and Christianized, adopting a distinctly moralistic tone. They also reflect a shift from external to internal horror, placing their anomalous phenomena—whether natural (blood murders) or supernatural (the Cenobites)—within the distraught, or drug-addicted, mind of the protagonist. Once agents of a vast, amoral universe who bring humans face-to-face with their own insignificance,

Pinhead and the Cenobites have been transformed into moral guardians—dispensers of both punishment and universal enlightenment.

NOTES

1. Paul Kane, *The* Hellraiser *Films and Their Legacy* (Jefferson, NC: McFarland, 2006), 5.
2. *Ibid.*
3. John Landis, *Monsters in the Movies: 100 Years of Cinematic Nightmares* (London: Dorling Kindersley, 2011); Kane, *Hellraiser Films.*
4. Andrew Migliore and John Strysik, *Lurker in the Lobby: A Guide to the Cinema of H.P. Lovecraft*, 2d ed. (Portland, CA: Night Shade Books, 2006), 103.
5. Andy Black, "Crawling Celluloid Chaos—H.P. Lovecraft in Cinema," *Necronomicon—The Journal of Horror and Erotic Cinema* 1 (1996): 199–201.
6. Cited by John Kenneth Muir, *Horror Films of the 19890s* (Jefferson, NC: McFarland, 2011), 580.
7. Douglas E. Cowan, *Sacred Terror: Religion and Horror on the Silver Screen* (Waco: Baylor University Press, 2008), 61.
8. David McWilliam, "Cenobites," in *The Ashgate Encyclopedia of Literary and Cinematic Monsters*, ed. Jeffrey Andrew Weinstock (Dorchester: Ashgate, 2014), 74; John Kenneth Muir, *Horror Films of the 1980s* (Jefferson, NC: McFarland, 2007), 582.
9. Muir, *Horror Films of the 1980s*, 581.
10. Kim Newman, *Nightmare Movies: Horror on Screen since the 1960s* (London: Bloomsbury, 2011), 381–383.
11. Muir, *Horror Films of the 1990s*, 9.
12. *Ibid.*, 88.
13. *Ibid.*, 458.
14. *Ibid.*, 456.
15. *Ibid.*, 458.
16. McWilliam, "Pinhead," 467.
17. McWilliam, "Cenobites, 74.
18. Kane, *Hellraiser Films*, 167.
19. *Ibid.*, 161.
20. Kelly Hurley, "Reading Like an Alien: Posthuman Identity in Ridley Scott's Alien and David Cronenberg's Rabid," in *Posthuman Bodies*, ed. Judith Halberstam and Ira Livingston (Bloomington: Indiana University Press, 1995), 203.
21. *Ibid.*
22. Cited in Kane, *Hellraiser Films*, 39.
23. http://www.stufftoblowyourmind.com/blogs/monster-of-the-week-the-cenobites.htm and Bradley in Anthony C. Ferrante, "Hellraiser: Inferno Attempts a New Twist on the Franchise—for One Thing, There's Not Much of the Star Cenobite," *Fangoria*, November 2000, 28.
24. *Ibid.*
25. David McWilliam, "Pinhead," in *The Ashgate Encyclopedia of Literary and Cinematic Monsters*, ed. Jeffrey Andrew Weinstock (Dorchester: Ashgate, 2014), 466.
26. Peter Hutchings, *Historical Dictionary of Horror Cinema* (Metuchen, NJ: Scarecrow Press, 2008), 29.
27. Kane, *Hellraiser Films*, 90.
28. Charles Stewart, "Demons and Spirits," in *Encyclopedia of Ancient Greece*, ed. Niger Wilson (Routledge: New York, 2010), 216.
29. *Ibid.*
30. McWilliam, "Cenobites," 74.
31. Kane, *Hellraiser Films*, 127.
32. Bradley cited by Jones, "Hellraiser III: Creating the Cenobites," in *The Hellraiser Chronicles*, ed. Stephen Jones, 54–85 (London: Titan Books, 1992).
33. Jones, "Hellraiser III: Creating the Cenobites."
34. McWilliam, "Pinhead," 467.
35. Kane, *Hellraiser Films*, 127.
36. Muir, *Horror Films of the 1990s*, 234–235.
37. McWilliam, "Pinhead," 467.
38. Kane *Hellraiser Films*, 35–37.
39. Jean Chevalier and Alain Gheerbrant, *Dicionário de Símbolos*, 27th ed. (Rio de Janeiro: José Olympio Editora, 2015), 568.
40. *Ibid.*, 37.
41. Kane, *Hellraiser Films*, 87.
42. Muir, *Horror Films of the 1980s*, 661.
43. Kane, *Hellraiser Films*, 88.

44. H.P. Lovecraft, "Notes on Writing Weird Fiction," *The H.P. Lovecraft Archive*, October 20, 2009, accessed October 8, 2016, http://www.hplovecraft.com/writings/texts /essays/nwwf.aspx.
45. John 14:6, which reads in full: "I am the way, the truth and the light. No one comes to the Father, but through me."
46. Cowan, *Sacred Terror*, 92.
47. Joshi, *I Am Providence*, 484.
48. Lovecraft cited in Joshi, *I Am Providence*, 124.

Bibliography

Black, Andy. "Crawling Celluloid Chaos—H.P. Lovecraft in Cinema." *Necronomicon—The Journal of Horror and Erotic Cinema* 1 (1996): 109–122.
Chevalier, Jean, and Alain Gheerbrant. *Dicionário de Símbolos*, 27th ed. Rio de Janeiro: José Olympio Editora, 2015.
Cowan, Douglas E. Sacred Terror: *Religion and Horror on the Silver Screen*. Waco: Baylor University Press, 2008.
Ferrante, Anthony C. "Hellraiser: Inferno Attempts a New Twist on the Franchise—for One Thing, There's Not Much of the Star Cenobite." *Fangoria*, November 2000, 26–31.
_____. "Hellraiser IV: Bloodline—To Hell and Back." *Fangoria*, April 1995, 40–45.
Hurley, Kelly. "Reading Like an Alien: Posthuman Identity in Ridley Scott's Alien and David Cronenberg's Rabid." In *Posthuman Bodies*, ed. Judith Halberstam and Ira Livingston, 203–22. Bloomington: Indiana University Press, 1995.
Hutchings, Peter. *Historical Dictionary of Horror Cinema*. Metuchen, NJ: Scarecrow Press, 2008.
Jones, Stephen. "Hellraiser III: Creating the Cenobites." In *The Hellraiser Chronicles*, ed. Stephen Jones, 54–85. London: Titan Books, 1992.
Joshi, S.T. *I Am Providence: The Life and Times of H.P. Lovecraft*, Vol. 1. New York: Hippocampus Press, 2013.
Kane, Paul. *The Hellraiser Films and Their Legacy*. Jefferson, NC: McFarland, 2006.
Landis, John. *Monsters in the Movies: 100 years of Cinematic Nightmares*. London: Dorling Kindersley, 2011.
Lovecraft, H.P. "Notes on Writing Weird Fiction." *The H.P. Lovecraft Archive*, October 20, 2009. Accessed October 8, 2016. http://www.hplovecraft.com/writings/texts/essays /nwwf.aspx.
McWilliam, David. "Cenobites." In *The Ashgate Encyclopedia of Literary and Cinematic Monsters*, ed. Jeffrey Andrew Weinstock, 74–75. Dorchester: Ashgate, 2014.
_____. "Pinhead." In *The Ashgate Encyclopedia of Literary and Cinematic Monsters*, ed. Jeffrey Andrew Weinstock, 466–468. Dorchester: Ashgate, 2014.
Migliore, Andrew, and John Strysik. *Lurker in the Lobby: A Guide to the Cinema of H.P. Lovecraft*, 2d ed. Portland, CA: Night Shade Books, 2006.
Muir, John Kenneth. *Horror Films of the 1990s*. Jefferson, NC: McFarland, 2011.
_____. *Horror Films of the 1980s*. Jefferson, NC: McFarland, 2007.
Newman, Kim. *Nightmare Movies: Horror on Screen Since the 1960s*. London: Bloomsbury, 2011.
Stewart, Charles. "Demons and Spirits." In *Encyclopedia of Ancient Greece*, ed. Niger Wilson, 216. Routledge: New York, 2010.

Redeeming the Demon-Child and the Eco-Horror Fairy Tale
Ambivalent Theosis and Ambiguous Eucatastrophe in Guillermo del Toro's Hellboy *Films*

DANIEL OTTO JACK PETERSEN

Prelude: The Gospel of Monstrosity

It is no secret that Guillermo del Toro is one of the most consistently spiritual directors in contemporary cinema. Regarding his own religious background, del Toro quips: "I mercifully lapsed as a Catholic, I say. But as [Luis] Buñuel used to say, 'I'm an atheist, thank God.' You know, there is always 'once a Catholic, always a Catholic' in a way."[1] Given such frankly acknowledged ambivalences, del Toro's interpreters have noted the "submerged religious discourse that is part of a sustained quest for the spiritual in his work, whereby art, storytelling and the sublimity of horror take on would-be religious connotations."[2] This self-aware tension between former faith and present disbelief (half-belief?) is perhaps why del Toro repeatedly couches his monstrophilia in religious language. For example, he remarks of his penchant for monsters: "It's a spiritual reality as strong as when people say, 'I accept Jesus in my heart.' Well, at a certain age, I accepted monsters into my heart."[3] When his personal collection of monster memorabilia was being exhibited at the Los Angeles County Museum of Art last year, he spoke of the vast array of grotesque and outré objects as "spiritual relics; they have the same value as a relic for me,"[4] proclaiming with passion: "I love monsters the way people worship holy images."[5] Indeed, he professes to be something of an evangelist for monsters: "It's a spiritual call for me. It's a vocation. So the work I'm doing here is evangelical. I'm praising the gospel of monstrosity because monsters have always been an incredibly important component of art. You have always had people creating the stained-glass windows; you always have people carving gargoyles."[6] He avers that monsters are an "intrinsic part" of humanity's "spiritual means"[7] and, noteworthy for the purposes of this essay, del Toro sees this worshipful, vocational monster evangelism as something he articulates "not only with this exhibition but in my movies."[8]

Though each of del Toro's films is a work of hybridized genres, from "art house" to blockbuster action-adventure, horror is certainly the central genre within which he situates himself. Horror is the one generic quality that is present in every single one of his films. Given his claims for the kinship of spirituality and monsters above, it is no wonder del Toro makes strong religious claims for horror storytelling: "Within the genre lies one of the last refuges of spirituality in this, our materialistic world."[9] Supernatural horror, he suggests, "is the only tool we have nowadays to explain spirituality to a generation that refuses to believe in dogma or religion. [...] Creature movies, horror movies, create at least a belief in something beyond."[10] Del Toro links the shudders and shivers ("frisson") that horror provides directly to religious experience: "At its root, the frisson is a crucial element of this form of storytelling—because all spiritual experience requires faith, and faith requires abandonment: the humility to fully surrender to a tide of truths and wills infinitely larger than ourselves."[11] Del Toro's conviction is that this surrender of faith puts us in touch with a fuller reality. "It is in this abandonment that we are allowed to witness phenomena that go beyond our nature and that reveal the spiritual side of our existence."[12]

I argue in this essay that the theological tensions and ambiguities of del Toro's films, in this case *Hellboy* (2004) and *Hellboy II: The Golden Army* (2008), open up the possibility that "accepting" Jesus and Monsters into one's heart need not be mutually exclusive. Specifically, the Christian doctrine of the sinner's adoption (or *theosis*)—that is, "ontological participation of the human in God"[13]—can provide a way of theologically reading the eponymous hero's character development in *Hellboy*. In *Hellboy II: The Golden Army* J.R.R. Tolkien's concept of "eucatastrophe" and Catholicism's "sacramental ontology," which emphasizes "the sacramental presence of supernatural grace in natural realities,"[14] can provide a theological reading of the ecological/magical themes of this sequel.[15]

Ambivalent Theosis in Hellboy

Mike Mignola's monster-rife *Hellboy* comic book series is lovingly adapted to the screen by del Toro. The director goes so far as to say that the *Hellboy* films are his most personal works thus far and that the eponymous character "is a fictional embodiment of himself."[16] Hellboy is a half-human, half-demon character who cannot physically hide his demonic heredity since he is completely red of skin, horned (though he files these down to stumps), tailed, hooved (in the comics at least), and possesses a massive stone right hand. Hellboy and his clandestine troupe of fellow monsters, such as the anthropo-amphibian Abe Sapien and the pyrokinetic Liz Sherman (who is also Hellboy's romantic love interest in the films), are harbored by a cabal of associates and overseers—the B.P.R.D. (Bureau of Paranormal Research and Defense)—as secret protectors of humanity against other monstrous aggressors. This stance as ally rather than enemy to the humans is fostered by Hellboy's relationship with his adoptive human father, Professor Bruttenholm (pronounced "Broom" and often abbreviated to this spelling, a convention this essay will follow). The wise and kind-hearted Broom took Hellboy in as a small child when the half-demon toddler was summoned to Earth from Hell by occultic means, as portrayed in the opening scene of the film. Broom is a devout Catholic, making his adoption of the demon-child all the more surprising. The adult Hellboy appears to have absorbed his adoptive father's faith, at least implicitly. In his work for the B.P.R.D. Hellboy shoots bullets filled with holy water (from a gun he calls the Good Samaritan) at unholy monsters and uses amulets containing bone fragments of saints to ward off demons—the repurposed tools of an exorcist. Indeed, though Hellboy's stone right hand is prophesied to

The Ogdru Jahad unleashed upon the Earth by Hellboy's Right Hand of Doom.

bring about the doom of the world, he uses it instead, in scene after scene, to crush entities of spiritual darkness and harbor innocents (memorably kittens and babies).

Hellboy's commitment to humanity is tested time and again when the evil forces that would use him invoke his prophetic destiny as the Beast of the Apocalypse who unlocks the "bottomless pit" to unleash forces of ancient cosmic chaos. In the climactic moment of the film, in order to rescue Liz, Hellboy begins to finally give in and bring about the apocalypse. At the sorcerer Rasputin's command, Hellboy utters his "true name," Anung Un Rama, which causes his horns to grow out to their full majestic arc, a fiery crown hovering between them. As he inserts his stone right hand into the lock of an interdimensional portal, Cthulhu-esque elder gods, the Ogdru Jahad, are released in dark glory and descend toward earth, vast tentacles reaching toward the portal. Before the opening of the final lock, however, Hellboy's companion, Agent Myers, intervenes with words of assurance regarding his adopted identity by which he can resist this destiny. As we'll see, Hellboy changes his mind about becoming the Beast of the Apocalypse he is constantly foretold to be.

Digging deeper into the theological possibilities the film opens up for this reversal of the demon-child figure, we see that del Toro's adaptation emphasizes what could be construed as distinctly Catholic reasons for Hellboy's redemptive behavior. At the beginning of the film we hear a voiceover of Broom saying: "What is it that makes a man a man? Is it his origins, the way things start? Or is it something else, something harder to describe?" Already there is an emphasis on Hellboy's human side in the asking of what makes a "man" rather than a demon. There is also an emphasis on the process of an individual's formation over and against any sense of being locked into a static, essentialized identity. As Broom says of Hellboy to Agent Myers later in the film: "He was born a demon. Can't change that. But you will help him, in essence, to become a man." By the end of the film, after Hellboy has stood firm in his decision to be a force for good rather than evil, Myers's voice is heard echoing the opening words from Broom: "What makes a man a man? A friend of mine once wondered. Is it his origins? The way he comes to life? I don't think so. It's the choices he makes. Not how he starts things ... but how he decides to end them."

This emphasis on Hellboy's choices connects to the Catholic doctrine of the dignity and freedom of humans. As some have noted, what makes Hellboy heroic is simply his choice *not* to be evil[17] and del Toro "makes this even more explicit" than in Mignola's comics series.[18] The Catechism of the Catholic Church asserts: "God created man a rational being, conferring on him the dignity of a person who can initiate and control his own actions."[19] Hellboy's adoptive father obviously counts on this dignity being conferred to his half-human adopted son. Indeed, Broom's "naming, adoption, and tutelage of Hellboy [...] imply the belief that any essentializing ontology can be undone by choice."[20] But what is the nature of this freedom of choice? Is it individualistic self-determination or something more complex?

This question leads to another of the film's theological themes: spiritual adoption. While it is possible to characterize Hellboy's decision as humanistic self-determination,[21] this seems to do little justice to the ambivalence del Toro has carefully worked into the film regarding faith. In the climactic scene described above, when Hellboy is about to open the final lock that will usher in the Lovecraftian gods and their reign of horror, Agent Myers throws Broom's rosary to Hellboy, who catches it in his left hand of flesh. It burns the shape of the cross there. Myers then shouts to him: "Remember who you are!" He reminds Hellboy: "You have a choice. Your father gave you that." Heeding this call to true selfhood, Hellboy dramatically breaks off his horns, thus closing the portal. Rasputin remonstrates with him: "What have you done?" Hellboy laconically replies: "I chose."

This can be read as S.T. Joshi does: "The message we are to derive from this series of incidents is not that Hellboy himself is acknowledging faith in the Catholic Church; although Bruttenholm is himself a devout Catholic, Hellboy's attraction to the rosary is largely a matter of devotion to his "father," Bruttenholm. Myers's cry is meant to recall to Hellboy that he is half-human and therefore should show some sort of devotion to his species rather than to the extra-dimensional monster seeking to destroy the world and all its inhabitants."[22] Yet surely it is more true to the tensions in del Toro's filmmaking to acknowledge that the "conflation of human and divine fathers is not accidental here and although del Toro may have rejected the confining dogma of Catholicism, he continually explores questions of faith."[23] Rather than mere self-determination or devotion to one's species, theologically (following the cue of fatherhood/Fatherhood that del Toro has signaled here), we may see Hellboy's choice as emblematic of the Catholic doctrine of *participation* in the very life of God (or *theosis*) through adoption into the Trinitarian family of Father, Son, and Holy Spirit. Following this emblem then, it is receiving the gift of his adoption and son-ship that determines who Hellboy is and what he may or may not choose to do. This may be seen to resonate with a participatory theology in which the "increasing resemblance to God comes about in the human soul through the exercise of the virtues, which is simply the life of the Trinity participated by the human person."[24]

Even in a secular humanist reading, Hellboy's is a freedom of choice achieved through community and nurture, not one of purely individualist self-determination. Catholic theology goes further. It underwrites the choice Hellboy's adoptive father gives him by supplying an ontological realism for such loving community, grounding it in the eternal life of the Trinity from which all creation proceeds,[25] rather than merely characterizing Hellboy's choice as something like species in-group behavior. That the choice was *given* to Hellboy through his adoption, a gift he may simply receive with gratitude, is crucial to a theological rather than merely humanistic interpretation. At one point in the film, Rasputin asks Broom if he would like to learn Hellboy's "true name." Broom replies: "I know what to call him. I call him ... Son." Participation in the life of the Trinity (the eternal love between the Father, Son, and Holy Spirit, to which *Hellboy*'s recurring emphasis on the father-son relationship alludes) is, theologically, a stronger force than mere self-determination:

> The dispositions called virtues are not a matter of heroic self-mastery or the sedimentation of a quality of self-sufficiency in the individual soul. Precisely to the contrary, the virtues grow from the passions, and the passions are a matter of self-surrender, of decentring, of moving outside the self. What we love possesses us, and not vice-versa. The theological virtues, as Aquinas says, become necessary at the point at which human nature becomes insufficient for achieving that for which it longs, which is the ultimate happiness of participation in God's life.[26]

In order to make the choice he made, Hellboy had to surrender to others, to the love of his friends and to his father's will that he become a man (that is, a fully formed person of virtue despite his origin). Hellboy was not sufficient in himself to do this. He had to become possessed by what he loved (a subversion of demon-possession) so that he could move outside himself into that spiritual experience that we have already seen del Toro describe precisely as a surrender to truths and wills larger than ourselves. Thomas Aquinas was convinced that every love participates in the likeness of Divine Love and so "it seems every love causes ecstasy," which Aquinas defined as being "placed outside oneself."[27] Such ecstatic experience is how del Toro characterizes the effect of horror that comes through, in his own words, "abandonment: the humility to fully surrender."[28] Thus, though it may come as a surprise, we can see how horror and theological accounts of free will and love coincide in Hellboy's journey.

Furthermore, if the conflation of human and divine fathers in the film is not accidental, then neither is the centrality of the image of the cross burnt glowingly into Hellboy's hand and thereby just as glowingly into the audience's minds. The image of the crucifix is traced from the opening scene of the film in which we see a large crucifix at the abbey ruins, and where we are first introduced to Broom's ubiquitous rosary, right through key moments of the film such as Broom's death, the funeral where Hellboy wears the sacred heirloom, and finally, the climactic scene of the filial gift of Hellboy's choice.[29] That the image of the cross accompanies Hellboy's self-surrender just as he is being called on to exercise his demonic royalty—his own supernatural princely crown flaming over his head—is supremely appropriate. Hellboy in essence chose a very different line of royalty and exercise of kingship. As Joseph Ratzinger (not yet Pope Benedict XVI) wrote of Christ: "His crucifixion is his coronation; his coronation or kingship is his surrender of himself to men."[30] Hellboy is empowered by his father's adoption and love to participate in what the cross of his father's rosary memorializes: the crucifixion "is the expression of the radical nature of the love which gives itself completely, of the process in which one is what one does, and does what one is; it is the expression of a life that is completely being for others."[31] In Hellboy's choice, just as Myers's voiceover at the end of the film declares, he is what he does and does what he is, in being for others. This makes him the man he has become despite his origins. And just as Myers declared to Hellboy during the crucible of his decision, his father gave this choice to him and he need but be thankful and accept it. "Worship follows in Christianity *first of all* in thankful acceptance of the divine deed of salvation. The essential form of Christian worship is therefore rightly called '*Eucharistia*,' thanksgiving."[32]

The cross may look like a tiny symbol when dangling from the rosary or burnt into Hellboy's hand, but its significance is as cosmically inflected as the vast and ancient Ogdru Jahad entities descending from deep space. Ratzinger noted that the Book of Hebrews in the New Testament looks at the cross in relation to the Jewish feast of reconciliation and "expounds it [the cross] as the true cosmic reconciliation feast" such that "the hour of the cross is the cosmic day of reconciliation, the true and final feast of reconciliation."[33] It is truly an epic battle of worldviews staged in the hour of Hellboy's decision whether to throw in with his demonic destiny or with the rewritten identity his father's adoption has provided for him. It is the question of faith in a cosmic feast of self-giving love or faith in cosmic domination by indifferent forces of chaos. All of del Toro's work shows him to be very alive to this struggle between worldviews.

A final element of Hellboy's cosmic scope is its focus on divine hiddenness. Rasputin had earlier taunted Broom, just before murdering him: "Your God chooses to remain silent. Mine lives within me." And then we see something coil just beneath his skin. Later, after Hellboy has broken off his horns he stabs Rasputin with them. We again see something coiling just beneath the skin of Rasputin's forehead as he says to Hellboy: "You've killed me ... an insignificant man. But you have brought forth ... a god." Rasputin's boast to both Broom and Hellboy is made good when a hellish Lovecraftian theophany occurs as a tentacled horror bursts forth from Rasputin's stomach and grows to gigantic size, resembling the Ogdru Jahad that have been blocked from entering Earth. The monster crushes Rasputin and his lover Ilsa before Hellboy battles and dispatches it. (This is again done somewhat self-sacrificially as the thing swallows Hellboy, enabling him to detonate a set of explosives from within its stomach. As with other explosions, Hellboy survives with a characteristically wry one-liner about how he's going to feel it in the morning.) The contrast between the significance or lack thereof that the deities of their respective faiths bestow on Hellboy and Rasputin couldn't be starker. To participate in the "divine life" of the Lovecraftian gods is to be furnished with abundant visual and material "proof" of their existence, but it is also to be mutilated and crushed once you serve no more purpose, much like a nihilistic worldview sees the universe discarding sentient life in the end. Conversely, the Catholic doctrine of participation in the divine life outlined above is predicated on "Aquinas's foundational presupposition that grace builds on, and does not destroy, nature."[34] Participation in Trinitarian life diminishes neither God nor the human, for God is not in competition with his creation on the Catholic view. The divine life works in and through human life. Broom's God (and Hellboy's God?) does not remain silent after all, but speaks in a very different language than that of spectacular domination and subjugation, instead coaxing the free-will participation and ennobling of his creatures, manifesting his love through theirs. We might even be so bold as to claim that del Toro's film thereby opens the door to theodicy.

Ambiguous Eucatastrophe in Hellboy II: The Golden Army

Though S.T. Joshi claims that *Hellboy II* "does not raise any profound religious or philosophical issues beyond that contained in the original film,"[35] others have noted that it is "deliberately more ambiguous" than its precursor,[36] developing and complicating the first film's themes. *Hellboy II*'s central premise that the creatures of myth and fairytale are endangered species in our secularized modern world involves the film with the intertext of Lord Dunsany's 1924 novel *The King of Elfland's Daughter*.[37] Del Toro thereby not only takes a step away from the theme of Lovecraft's cosmic pessimism but also a tentative step in the direction of the "more hopeful philosophy" of J.R.R. Tolkien.[38] Tolkien alleged that "eucatastrophe"—the term he coined for the happy ending (or, more correctly, the "good catastrophe")—is "the true form of the fairy-tale, and its highest function"[39] because eucatastrophe is the narrative shape of the Christian gospel.[40,41] Del Toro's work, we might say, is a halfway house between cosmic pessimism and eucatastrophe.[42]

The Catholic visual references in *Hellboy II*, while less obvious than the rosaries and crucifixes of *Hellboy*, are nevertheless present. The Troll Market sequence, for example, reveals beneath the Brooklyn Bridge a bazaar so replete with a variety of richly grotesque and inventive creatures that it is frequently compared to the polyxenological cantina scene in *Star Wars*. Among the market's most memorable characters is one called Cathedral Head, who sports an actual miniature Gothic cathedral growing out of his stonelike head. The architectural crown is redolent, says del Toro, of clergy: "The cathedral gives him a church-like position," he comments.[43] Another instance of Catholic-informed imagery is the scene featuring an eyeless Angel of Death with "eyes scattered across its wings like stars in the night."[44] It is an image, says del Toro, "rooted in medieval illustrations, which show angels with four wings and eyes in the wings. I just love that image, and I keep it in my head."[45]

Catholic-tinged ideas are woven more deeply into this film, however, than any particular image. The "Ebbing of Elfland" (to borrow a chapter title from Dunsany's novel) in *Hellboy II* can be read as a loss of the sacred. The capitalistic marketing and selling of holy artifacts from ancient cultures in the opening of the film does not represent the secularist casting down of lifeless idols as has been suggested,[46] but rather the devaluing (then re-valuing as commercial possessions) and subjugation of non–Western worldviews.[47] The elven Prince Nuada's critique of the insatiability of human greed that rapes the land merely to build more shopping malls echoes a Heideggerian critique of modernity as "an epoch dominated by the implacable drive to reduce all of reality to a resource for human use and exploitation," even to the point that, as Heidegger memorably put it, "nature becomes a gigantic gasoline station."[48] Though the giant numinous forest god of a later scene, which we will discuss below, is "relegated to myth" by human indifference, it is nevertheless "a reminder of what was once possible for humanity and what has replaced those possibilities."[49] In other words, the felling of deities in *Hellboy II* is not a skeptical ideological cleansing (*pace* Wetmore), but rather is elegiac,[50] the totality of the film forming something of a jeremiad for lost worldviews and, just possibly, a call for the renewal of something that can preserve and develop what was best about them.

Yet despite the sense of loss and elegy that permeates the film, *Hellboy II* features elements of eucatastrophe—including hints of its characteristic "sudden joyous 'turn'"[51]— beneath the bewilderment and uncertainty. The final "turn" of del Toro's ambiguous exemplification of eucatastrophe comes when the last frame of the film comically freezes the look of shock on Hellboy's face as he learns that Liz is pregnant with twins, adding a note of exuberance to the Annunciation of Liz's pregnancy earlier in the film. Before discussing that, however, we do well to take note of *Hellboy II*'s rather poignant instance of proto-eucatastrophe in the scene where the spilled green "blood" of a mortally wounded forest god, an elemental and the last of its kind, turns an urban setting into a beautiful "pastoral paradise."[52] The event is distinctly sacrificial in that "this transformation of the landscape is the disintegrated body of the forest god."[53] Just prior to this death and transformation, the giant elemental looms menacingly over the city, crushing cars and pavement, its sheer proximity unsafe for the humans below. When Hellboy comes to the city's defense and shoots the elemental in the heart, we witness vividly and with no small sense of wonder that the death of the Forest Creature allows for the regeneration of the urban landscape. As the creature's blood falls and body disintegrates, the city streets become verdant: grass and ferns overlay pavement, vines bedeck tall buildings, and an orchid sprouts from the head of the creature, launching sparkling crystals into the air. And yet, this magical regeneration is ignored by the crowd of humans in their rush to denounce Hellboy.[54]

Though Hellboy saves the crowd from the elemental, they accuse him of ill will and harm. This echoes the complaint of "too much magic" made by the villagers living contiguous to Elfland in Dunsany's novel.[55] Humanity's indifference to this sudden turn of "good catastrophe" surrounding them is as ugly as the forest god is beautiful. The "intense beauty of the elemental's death—undoubtedly the most inspired scene in the film—is lost on them […] they are too absorbed in their own xenophobia and anthropocentric self-interest to experience or appreciate the momentary transformation of their world."[56]

Transformation and regeneration are well-chosen terms for the effect of the forest god's blood on the cityscape, especially since del Toro intended a theological resonance. "[The] destruction of the metamorphic green god results in a momentary Edenic greening of the city, '[m]oss and roots cover the pavement, walls, and abandoned vehicles. Hummingbirds flutter out from the newly grown moss mounds, green grass overtakes the pavement. In the end, most of the building looks like the Garden of Eden.'"[57] Tony Vinci concurs that the scene is "a retelling of the Eden story," except that in this version, instead of humans being cast out of paradise, "they cast paradise out of the world."[58] Against

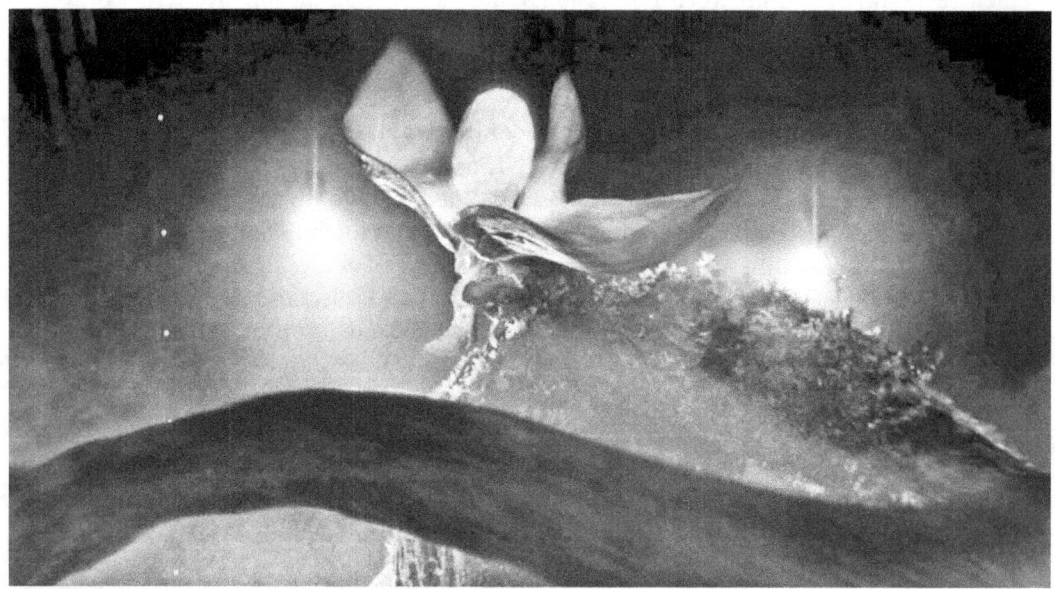

The Forest God, or Tree Elemental, awakening in *Hellboy II: The Golden Army* (2008).

Kevin Wetmore's suggestion that the "death of the last Forest God changes nothing beyond its immediate environment,"⁵⁹ we may see that, despite the negative reaction of the crowd in the film, it is the *audience* of the film that may be provoked to be more self-critical. "The sequence makes the audience aware of itself as potentially monstrous, more akin—as humans—to the hectoring crowd (one of whom throws a stone that bloodies Hellboy's face) than to Hellboy. In so doing, the film bequeaths the potential for self-reflection to the moviegoing audience."⁶⁰ Not only self-reflection but "other-reflection" is made possible for the audience by this scene. The gift of the beauty of the transformation lingers with the viewers who have tasted the possibility of eucatastrophe, a sudden turn communicating "a fleeting glimpse of Joy, Joy beyond the walls of the world, poignant as grief,"⁶¹ "a piercing glimpse of joy, and heart's desire, that for a moment passes outside the frame, rends indeed the very web of story, and lets a gleam come through,"⁶² a gleam from beyond the regnant materialistic Western worldview. So here the monster serves its revelatory function (*monstrum*, an omen or portent, from *monstrare*, to show or reveal). The forest god, monstrous to the New Yorkers, "is shot and disintegrated, but in this process he reveals to everyone that New York could be different"; the scene "allows human characters to see different possibilities through an empathy with the damaged and displaced body of the monster."⁶³

That the death of the forest god is effected by a huge gun Hellboy calls "Big Baby" (which features a kitschy picture of a rosy-cheeked baby on its stock), whilst he is saving a living human baby, ironically echoes the theme of newborn life at the film's emotional, and potentially philosophical, core. Hellboy's bloody-browed rejection by the crowd in this scene is Christlike, full of tension in his tender care for those who reject him. The city crowds "do not know enough to recognize Hellboy as their savior."⁶⁴ Hellboy is their potential savior at a far deeper level than the protection of one innocent, however, and in a way that may have wider effect than the death of the forest god. Hellboy and Liz's union provides a transformative seed "incarnated" into the world rather than merely the temporary surface overlay achieved by the blood of the tree elemental. The ending of the film sees the small band of "freaks" quitting the BPRD and thus ceasing their aid of the human attack on Faërie as well as refusing to join elven forces in attacking humans. Hellboy and his troupe appear to opt for an as yet only sketched but potentially eucacatastrophic third way: a new family centered around the birth of yet another hybridization, their children who are in essence half fairy (the elven folk consider Hellboy a creature of their ilk) and half (pyrokinetic) human, closing a circle with the first film's emphasis on Hellboy's own origins, and opening out to an undisclosed future.⁶⁵

The conflict between Faërie and Earth in *Hellboy II* renders the decision to "remember who you are" from the first film "thoroughly ambiguous" in the sequel.⁶⁶ Hellboy's human father and his small community of fellow monsters helped make him a "man" (in one scene he relishes that Liz calls him the best *man* she knows), but now his adoptive humanity is set against his otherworldly nature in an impasse of conflict. Prince Nuada tells Hellboy to choose which "holocaust" he will back, that of magical creatures (who imbue ecology with its vitality) or that of humanity. Thus in the sequel, rather than by merely remembering, the continuance of Hellboy's unified identity must be cast forward into the hope for a united world. Refusing to participate in the stark and mutually destructive division of Faërie and Earth, Liz and Hellboy combine the two worlds in their physical union and its fruit. "Combination is redemption in all of [del Toro's] films and it is through making new bonds out of suffering that a way forward is found."⁶⁷ Given that

Hellboy's adoptive father Broom was a "mediatory figure" between the rational and otherworldly,[68] Hellboy can be seen now as potentially continuing that role at an ontological level through his hybridized elven/human children.[69] Perhaps this provides a way for us to understand the monstrous eucatastrophe that del Toro says *Hellboy II* is: "It is a Beauty and the Beast story where at the end they kiss and they both turn to beasts."[70]

On a theological reading of the second *Hellboy* film, then, the participation in divinity of *theosis* must broaden ontologically to cover all of creation, human and nonhuman. In their promulgation of "sacramental ontology," the *la nouvelle théologie* movement of 20th-century theologians insisted on a divinely imbued and non-instrumentalized view of creation[71] that resonates with the hopeful ecological ethics of *Hellboy II*. Due to the doctrines of Creation and Incarnation, the sacramental ontology, or "participatory ontology,"[72] of Catholic theology sees the whole world and each thing in it as potentially a mediatory being for the divine presence. As Hans Urs von Balthasar averred: "the infinite Creator has equipped it [created being] with the grace of participation in the inexhaustibility of its origin."[73] Thus rather than nature being a giant gas station or shopping mall, each member of each ecosystem is a conduit of divine presence *by being itself* and thereby resists reduction to mere human use. As Balthasar elaborates: "It bears in itself a wealth that cannot be consumed like a finite sum of money. You are never finished with any being, be it the tiniest gnat or the most inconspicuous stone. It has a secret [*geheime*] opening, through which never-failing replenishments of sense and significance ceaselessly flow to it from eternity."[74]

If we conflate the ecological and otherworldly as del Toro's film does, then in this all-inclusive sacramental vision God becomes, as Tolkien joyously averred, "Lord, of angels, and of men—and of elves"[75]; we might add, *and of monsters*. And why not? Sometimes, as David Williams notes, "it is only through [a] monstrous combination of contrarieties that the supralogical truths about divinity and humanity can be communicated."[76] Indeed, modern Roman Catholic writers of Gothic-tinged fiction, from Chesterton to Flannery O'Connor, have found the grotesque to be an essential feature of a sacramental vision of the world. Balthasar encapsulated the Catholic sacramental vision in what appears to be an almost accidental connection to the monstrous when he wrote that "creation as a whole has become a monstrance of God's real presence."[77] "Monstrance" (the name for the vessel that elevates the consecrated Host of the Eucharist in Catholic liturgy), like "monster," as noted above, is rooted in the word *monstrare* (to show or reveal). Thus, the very fabric of existence may be seen as monstrous in its sacramental capacity to "shine forth" its own depths, to once again borrow Heideggerian terminology,[78] rooted in the inexhaustible divine nature of its Creator.

With this vision in mind, let us glance once more at the Troll Market scene in *Hellboy II*. Though its Boschian and "Goya-esque monsters" are alive with an exuberance that notably "contains little or none of Bosch's tortured Catholic imagery," it is precisely Catholic sacramental ontology that can underwrite it as "a playful celebration of imagined otherness"[79] where what "the viewer sees is a kind of rhizomatic proliferation of forms and beings that stretch into the far distance."[80] Sacramental ontology can fulfill the inscription—"Unus Mundus," one world, a Jungian concept[81]—above the entrance to the Troll Market by truly unifying the world(s) at the level of being itself. All things participate in the divine essence and show it forth by sheer virtue of existing, and all may partake in the divine life of the Trinity by the descent of Incarnation and the ascent of *theosis*[82] that the Incarnation accomplishes.

These suggestions seem quite the contrary of Kevin Wetmore's claim that *Hellboy II* performs a "subtraction," that is, "the removal of any religious elements and the domestication of the magical and mysterious. In short, del Toro demystifies the magical world, transforming it into just another border region of our own."[83] At any rate, it is simply not unequivocally true that "del Toro does what Lovecraft and Dunsany already began in their narratives: removing the supernatural, un-deifying the gods, and reducing the border between magic and mundane, domesticating the horror."[84] It is certainly the case that del Toro's works keep Elfland and the human world in unresolved tension. Yet they also provide hints of a promise for their reconciliation rather than any sort of reductionism that merely "domesticates" the otherworldly into the mundane. These hints of eucatastrophe, furthermore, are given (at least in part and ambiguously) through Christian theological imagery.

Postlude: The Hoard Unlocked and Unleashed

In one of his notebooks, next to a card with a Hellboy drawing from Mike Mignola, del Toro's handwriting can be seen recording the following: "NUMINOUS, INSCRUTABLE, INDIFFERENT, MYSTERIOUS, RECONCILIATION, TRANSMUTATION. [...] 'The decisive question for man is this: Is he related to something infinite or not?' Jung asked himself this in his writings and man combats the void and Cosmic indifference looking for the answer."[85] Such ruminations are yet further indications that "the argument with his former faith is an ongoing dialectic that is fundamental to his art."[86] Victoria Nelson goes so far as to claim: "Where his hero the twentieth-century master Luis Buñuel could proudly proclaim, 'I am an atheist and a Catholic, thank God!' Guillermo del Toro can say, 'I am a heretic and a Catholic, thank God!'—and mean it."[87]

Here we might do well to note Tolkien's claim that the fairy tale unlocks all the things of the world that we have taken for granted in such a way that they can't be thereafter safely locked away again. He says we "locked them in our hoard, acquired them, and acquiring ceased to look at them."[88] The fantastical imagination can undo this and upset our tidy worldviews. "Creative fantasy [...] may open your hoard and let all the locked things fly away like cage-birds. The gems all turn into flowers or flames, and you will be warned that all you had (or knew) was dangerous and potent, not really effectively chained, free and wild; no more yours than they were you."[89]

Films like del Toro's can open up even theological concepts again and unleash them as dangerous, potent, wild, and free things that can't be owned or domesticated. Del Toro echoes Tolkien when he elucidates the spiritual potential of the genre of horror, which he alleges finds its roots in fairy tales.[90] Following directly from his remarks about horror's ability to reveal to us the spiritual side of our existence, which we noted at the beginning of this essay, del Toro describes what happens when we surrender to the horror tale in terms remarkably similar to Tolkien's in regard to fantasy. "We dislocate, for a moment, the rules of our universe, the laws that bind the rational and diminish the cosmos to our scale. And when the world becomes a vast, unruly place, a place where anything can happen, then—and only then—we allow for miracles and angels, no matter how dark they may be."[91] *Anything* can happen: miracles, angels, demon-children redeemed, monsters and humans reconciled, the world re-sacralized and re-enchanted. Or so the fantastical horror tale whispers to our hearts, with shudders and shivers.

Notes

1. S.T. Joshi, "The Magical Spirituality of a Lapsed Catholic," in *The Supernatural Cinema of Guillermo del Toro: Critical Essays*, ed. John W. Morehead (Jefferson, NC: McFarland, 2015), 12.
2. Keith McDonald and Roger Clark, *Guillermo del Toro: Film as Alchemic Art* (New York: Bloomsbury Academic, 2014), 76.
3. Victoria Nelson, *Gothicka: Vampire Heroes, Human Gods, and the New Supernatural* (Cambridge: Harvard University Press, 2012), 220.
4. Jacki Manksy, "Director Guillermo del Toro Shares the Monsters in His Closet with the Public," Smithsonian.com, August 1, 2016, accessed November 30, 2016, http://www.smithsonianmag.com/arts-culture/guillermo-del-toro-shares-monsters-in-his-closet-with-public-180959957/?no-ist.
5. Jordan Reife, "Guillermo del Toro: 'I love monsters the way people worship holy images,'" *The Guardian*, August 3, 2016, accessed November 30, 2016, https://www.theguardian.com/film/2016/aug/03/guillermo-del-toro-bleak-house-home-lacma-exhibit.
6. Mansky, "Director Guillermo del Toro Shares."
7. *Ibid.*
8. *Ibid.*
9. Guillermo del Toro and Marc Scott Zicree, *Guillermo del Toro: Cabinet of Curiosities: My Notebooks, Collections, and Other Obsessions* (London: Titan Books, 2013), 66.
10. McDonald and Clark, *Alchemic*, 182.
11. Del Toro and Zicree, *Cabinet*, 66.
12. *Ibid.*
13. William T. Cavanaugh, "A Joint Declaration? Justification as Theosis in Aquinas and Luther," *The Heythrop Journal* 41, no. 3 (2000): 265.
14. Hans Boersma, "Nature and the Supernatural in *la nouvelle théologie*: The Recovery of a Sacramental Mindset," *New Blackfriars* 93, no. 1043 (2012): 34.
15. While attempting a theological reading of these films, I acknowledge that it certainly is characteristic of del Toro to present moments in his films "where a Christian-inflected view of the cosmos is juxtaposed with events that seem to question and undermine its power and relevance" (McDonald and Clark, *Alchemic*, 182). I here argue only that this questioning and potential undermining goes both ways in del Toro's films. Indeed, various worldviews are simultaneously espoused and interrogated in his exuberantly intertextual filmmaking, nihilism and Paganism and scientism no less than Christianity.
16. McDonald and Clark, *Alchemic*, 16.
17. Tony M. Vinci, "Remembering Why We Once Feared the Dark: Reclaiming Humanity Through Fantasy in Guillermo del Toro's *Hellboy II*," *Journal of Popular Culture* 45, no. 5 (2012): 1052.
18. Rebecca Janicker, "Myth and Monstrosity: The Dark Realms of H.P. Lovecraft and Guillermo del Toro," in *The Transnational Fantasies of Guillermo del Toro*, ed. Ann Davies, et al. (New York: Palgrave Macmillan, 2014), 53.
19. *Catechism of the Catholic Church* (London: Geoffrey Chapman, 1999), Section 1731.
20. Vinci, "Remembering," 1046.
21. Glenn Ward, "'There Is No Such Thing': Del Toro's Metafictional Monster Rally," in *The Transnational Fantasies of Guillermo del Toro*, ed. Ann Davies, et al. (New York: Palgrave Macmillan, 2014), 22.
22. Joshi, "Magical Spirituality," 17.
23. McDonald and Clark, *Alchemic*, 182.
24. Cavanaugh, "Joint," 273.
25. *Ibid.*, 268.
26. *Ibid.*, 274.
27. *Ibid.*, 275.
28. Del Toro and Zicree, *Cabinet*, 66.
29. Cf. Ward, "No Such Thing," 19.
30. Joseph Ratzinger, *Introduction to Christianity* (London: Search Press Limited, 1969), 152.
31. *Ibid.*, 214.
32. *Ibid.*, 215, emphasis in the original.
33. *Ibid.*, 216, 218.
34. Cavanaugh, "Joint," 278.
35. Joshi, "Magical Spirituality," 18.
36. McDonald and Clark, *Alchemic*, 181.
37. *Ibid.*, 181–182. See also Kevin Wetmore, "At the Mountains of Mexico: The Echoes and Intertexts of Lovecraft and Dunsany," in *The Supernatural Cinema of Guillermo del Toro: Critical Essays*, ed. John W. Morehead (Jefferson, NC: McFarland, 2015), 22–40.
38. Vinci, "Remembering," 1041.
39. J.R.R. Tolkien, *The Tolkien Reader* (New York: Ballantine, 1966), 85, 86.
40. *Ibid.*, 88.

41. On eucatastrophe as "tragedy baptized," a sub-genre of comedy, vs. the existentialist novel of the absurd engendered by nihilism, see Christopher Toner, "Catastrophe and Eucatastrophe: Russell and Tolkien on the True Form of Fiction," *New Blackfriars* 89, no. 1019 (2008): 77–87.

42. Tolkien, like del Toro, saw the connections and overlaps between horror and the fairy tale and thought this was entirely healthy, even for children (Tolkien, *Reader*, 56). Indeed, Tolkien's own great work of fantasy, *The Lord of the Rings*, includes strong elements of horror and frisson. Fabulous creatures such as Tolkien's giant spiders, Black Riders, Balrog, orcs, and dragons are some of the most famous monsters of the 20th century. It is also sufficiently ambiguous as to whether Tolkien's epic fantasy has a happy ending or good catastrophe that scholars argue whether it contains a clear eucatastrophe or not. Cf. Kevin R. West, "Julian Of Norwich's 'Great Deed' and Tolkien's *Eucatastrophe*," *Religion & Literature* (2011): 40. Although del Toro says that Tolkien's works never called to him (Wetmore, "Mountains," 30), he and Tolkien are not so far apart in their distinctive engagements with dark fantasy and fairy tale. This makes del Toro's (ultimately abandoned, though credited) involvement with *The Hobbit* films all the more intriguing.

43. Guillermo del Toro, "Director's Notebook" special feature, *Hellboy II: The Golden Army*, DVD, directed by Guillermo del Toro (Universal Studios, 2008).

Victoria Nelson, in a chapter entitled "Cathedral Head," considers this character "emblematic of the larger world of this director's work, which uniquely infuses Old Goth elements into the Gothick in a weird and very heterodox re-Catholicizing of the faux Catholic" (Nelson, *Gothicka*, 220). (Her book also includes a chapter entitled "Faux Catholic" that outlines Gothic literature's appropriation of Roman Catholic trappings.) In this sense, Cathedral Head could be a nickname for del Toro himself. Etienne Gilson called scholastic theology a "cathedral of the mind" and del Toro's work exemplifies this again and again in outré and "heterodox" echoes. For the Gilson quote, see Alister McGrath, *Christian Theology: An Introduction* (Chichester: John Wiley & Sons, 2017), 26.

44. Del Toro and Zicree, *Cabinet*, 214.

45. *Ibid.*, 219. Del Toro keeps the image, that is, in his Cathedral Head (see previous endnote), which is no doubt adorned with myriad other Christian Gothic images and notions. "There are monsters side by side with angels in cathedrals for a reason," says del Toro. "They occupy the same parcel in the imagination of mankind that angels occupy" (Nelson, *Gothicka*, 220). In his Angel of Death, del Toro doesn't merely juxtapose the monster and the angel, but merges them (this merging actually being a return to biblical representations of angelic beings such as the multi-winged and poly-ocular excess of the Cherubim in Ezekiel 10 or the heavenly Four Living Creatures in Revelation 4).

46. Wetmore, "Mountains," 36.

47. Vinci, "Remembering," 1047.

48. Matthew T. Eggemeier, "A Sacramental Vision: Environmental Degradation and the Aesthetics of Creation," *Modern Theology* 29, no. 3 (2013): 341, 343.

49. Vinci, "Remembering," 1049.

50. This elegiac tone is consistent with *The King of Elfland's Daughter*, though Dunsany's novel portrays Christianity as the enemy of Faërie rather than its ally against secular modernity.

51. Tolkien, *Reader*, 86.

52. Ann Davies, "Guillermo del Toro's Monsters: Matter Out of Place," in *The Transnational Fantasies of Guillermo del Toro*, ed. Ann Davies, et al. (New York: Palgrave Macmillan, 2014), 38.

53. Davies, "Matter," 38.

54. Laura Podalsky, "Of Monstrous Masses and Hybrid Heroes: del Toro's English-Language Films," in *The Transnational Fantasies of Guillermo del Toro*, ed. Ann Davies et al. (New York: Palgrave Macmillan, 2014), 113.

55. Lord Dunsany, *The King of Elfland's Daughter* (London: Gollancz, 2001), 208.

56. Vinci, "Remembering," 1048.

57. McDonald and Clark, *Alchemic*, 183, quoting from Guillermo del Toro and Mike Mignola, *Hellboy II: The Art of the Movie* (Milwaukie: Dark Horse Books, 2008).

58. Vinci, "Remembering," 1048.

59. Wetmore, "Mountains," 25.

60. Podalsky, "Masses," 114.

61. Tolkien, *Reader*, 86.

62. *Ibid.*, 87.

63. Davies, "Matter," 38, 39–40.

64. Podalsky, "Masses," 112–113.

65. Del Toro's Catholic background may in part account for the fact that one of his "preoccupations" is a "fascination for female fecundity and pregnancy" (Hutchings, "Adapt or Die," 89), as well as his traumatic encounter with a pile of dead fetuses at a hospital as a young man, which he credits as the decisive moment he came to believe (at least as a young man) that there was no human soul (Joshi, "Magical Spirituality," 15). Indeed, del Toro's imagination may be characterized as occupying a disquieting space between the glory and promise of the Virgin Birth and the disillusioning horror of a pile of aborted foetuses.

66. McDonald and Clark, *Alchemic*, 174.

67. *Ibid.*, 69.
68. *Ibid.*, 182.
69. Some critics have seen Hellboy and Liz's union, supported by the amphibious Abe Sapien and the ghostly Johann Kraus, as a "queering" of the nuclear family (McDonald and Clark, *Alchemic*, 74), creating a "family of 'freaks'" (180, 184). Yet other critics find the union to be a conventional move "upholding the sanctity of the patriarchal family" (Podalsky, "Masses," 111). These ostensibly contradictory interpretations again show the tensions and ambivalences built into del Toro's works, which, I would argue, come out of the wrestlings of del Toro's own heart and mind as evidenced not only in his films, but in his essays, interviews, and notes.
70. *Ibid.*, 173
71. See Boersma, "Nature and the Supernatural."
72. Hans Boersma, *Heavenly Participation: The Weaving of a Sacramental Tapestry* (Grand Rapids: Eerdmans, 2011), 24.
73. Eggemeier, "Sacramental Vision," 353.
74. *Ibid.*
75. Tolkien, Reader, 89.
76. Nelson, *Gothicka*, 221.
77. Eggemeier, "Sacramental Vision," 358.
78. *Ibid.*, 343.
79. McDonald and Clark, *Alchemic*, 53.
80. *Ibid.*, 179.
81. *Ibid.*, 178.
82. Boersma, "Nature and the Supernatural," 34.
83. Wetmore, "Mountains," 37.
84. *Ibid.*, 38.
85. Del Toro and Zicree, *Cabinet*, 223.
86. McDonald and Clark, *Alchemic*, 77.
87. Nelson, *Gothicka*, 236.
88. Tolkien, *Reader*, 77.
89. *Ibid.*, 78.
90. McDonald and Clark, *Alchemic*, 185.
91. Del Toro and Zicree, *Cabinet*, 66; cf. Vinci, "Remembering," 1057.

BIBLIOGRAPHY

Boersma, Hans. *Heavenly Participation: The Weaving of a Sacramental Tapestry*. Grand Rapids: Eerdmans, 2011.
Boersma, Hans. "Nature and the Supernatural in *la nouvelle théologie*: The Recovery of a Sacramental Mindset." *New Blackfriars* 93, no. 1043 (2012): 34–46.
Cavanaugh, William T. "A Joint Declaration? Justification as Theosis in Aquinas and Luther." *The Heythrop Journal* 41, no. 3 (2000): 265–280.
Davies, Ann. "Guillermo del Toro's Monsters: Matter Out of Place." In *The Transnational Fantasies of Guillermo del Toro*, ed. Ann Davies, Deborah Shaw, and Dolores Tierney, 29–43. New York: Palgrave Macmillan, 2014.
Del Toro, Guillermo, and Marc Scott Zicree. *Guillermo del Toro: Cabinet of Curiosities: My Notebooks, Collections, and Other Obsessions*. London: Titan Books, 2013.
Dunsany, Lord. *The King of Elfland's Daughter*. London: Gollancz, 2001.
Eggemeier, Matthew T. "A Sacramental Vision: Environmental Degradation and the Aesthetics of Creation." *Modern Theology* 29, no. 3 (2013): 338–360.
Hutchings, Peter. "Adapt or Die: Mimicry and Evolution in Guillermo del Toro's English-Language Films." In *The Transnational Fantasies of Guillermo del Toro*, ed. Ann Davies, Deborah Shaw, and Dolores Tierney, 83–97. New York: Palgrave Macmillan, 2014.
Janicker, Rebecca. "Myth and Monstrosity: The Dark Realms of H.P. Lovecraft and Guillermo del Toro." In *The Transnational Fantasies of Guillermo del Toro*, ed. Ann Davies, Deborah Shaw, and Dolores Tierney, 45–60. New York: Palgrave Macmillan, 2014.
Joshi, S.T. "The Magical Spirituality of a Lapsed Catholic." *The Supernatural Cinema of Guillermo del Toro: Critical Essays*, ed. John W. Morehead, 11–21. Jefferson, NC: McFarland, 2015.
McDonald, Keith, and Clark, Roger. *Guillermo del Toro: Film as Alchemic Art*. New York: Bloomsbury Academic, 2014.
Nelson, Victoria. *Gothicka: Vampire Heroes, Human Gods, and the New Supernatural*. Cambridge: Harvard University Press, 2012.
Podalsky, Laura. "Of Monstrous Masses and Hybrid Heroes: del Toro's English-Language Films." In *The Transnational Fantasies of Guillermo del Toro*, ed. Ann Davies, Deborah Shaw, and Dolores Tierney, 99–120. New York: Palgrave Macmillan, 2014.

Ratzinger, Joseph. *Introduction to Christianity*. London: Search Press Limited, 1969.
Tolkien, J.R.R. *The Tolkien Reader*. New York: Ballantine, 1966.
Vinci, Tony M. "Remembering Why We Once Feared the Dark: Reclaiming Humanity Through Fantasy in Guillermo del Toro's Hellboy II." *Journal of Popular Culture* 45, no. 5 (2012): 1041–1059.
Ward, Glenn. "'There Is No Such Thing': Del Toro's Metafictional Monster Rally." In *The Transnational Fantasies of Guillermo del Toro*, ed. Ann Davies, Deborah Shaw, and Dolores Tierney, 11–28. New York: Palgrave Macmillan, 2014.
Wetmore, Kevin. "At the Mountains of Mexico: The Echoes and Intertexts of Lovecraft and Dunsany." In *The Supernatural Cinema of Guillermo del Toro: Critical Essays*, ed. John W. Morehead, 22–40. Jefferson, NC: McFarland, 2015.

Binary Opposition, Subversion and Liminality in Francis Lawrence's *Constantine*

CATHERINE BECKER

Throughout history, religious forces are depicted as binary oppositions. From the first lines of Genesis to the last lines of Revelation, pairings like Heaven and Hell, God and Satan, angel and demon, dark and light, are pervasive. These binaries are unequivocally bound to one another, intertwined despite, or perhaps through, their opposition: If God had not defeated Satan and cast him from Heaven, Satan would not fight to usurp God. These acts frame the two as eternal enemies and motivate their battle for cosmic supremacy. Traditionally, God is supreme, and Satan merely strives to assume his authority. What would happen, though, if the Devil could seize God's power, or if evil could run rampant? Modern horror filmmakers frequently pose this question, building on Ferdinand de Saussure's original linguistic conception to pair light/dark and good/evil against one another, and to tie those powers together in their battle for humanity and control,[1] but they approach the linguistic pairing in reverse—focusing not on the dominion of God but on the threat posed by evil—and using classical oppositions are to elicit tension.

One such example is Francis Lawrence's 2005 film *Constantine*.[2] A symbiotic relationship—in which God and Satan are absolutely opposed, yet inextricably intertwined—is crucial to the narrative. The film's tension, however, is built not only on this pairing, but also on the role humanity plays within it. If the film were simply about a battle between Heaven and Hell, there would be no horror, but *Constantine* presents humans as simultaneously at the mercy of the supernatural forces, and vital elements in the fight between them. Peace on Earth depends on "the balance": a pact between God and Satan to use only tacit influence in their eternal contest for human souls. When the forces of evil begin to abrogate that agreement, all Hell literally breaks loose, and it falls to the cynical, chain-smoking title character and his small band of confidants to avert the Apocalypse. This essay, then, examines the precarious balance between good and evil, Earth and the eternal, as those binaries are established, subverted, and (finally) restored in *Constantine*, and the critical, liminal role of humans in the eternal battle between Heaven and Hell, as characters blur and cross the boundaries that are so critical to keeping binaries intact.

A Man on the Brink of Hell

Based on the DC Comics graphic novel *Hellblazer*, *Constantine* narrates the lives (and deaths) of John Constantine (Keanu Reeves) and twins Angela and Isabel Dodson (Rachel Weisz). John is nominally a private investigator, but his real, self-appointed task is maintaining the balance between the forces of Heaven and Hell by policing the interactions of their representatives on Earth: the middle ground where humanity precariously dwells. Constantine, while powerful, is acutely troubled. As a child, he heard voices and saw demonic or heavenly presences in the world that were invisible to others: "things," he says, "that nobody should have to see." These visions led to a childhood fraught with well-intended medical interventions that made the problem worse, and, eventually, to his attempted suicide as a teenager. In the film's version of Catholic theology, taking one's own life is an unforgivable sin, and John, clinically dead before doctors revived him, thus spent that time in Hell. Two minutes passed as if they were a lifetime, and he returned to Earth knowing precisely what awaited him when (absolution being beyond his reach) he was sentenced to a true eternity in Hell at the end of his natural life.

Facing the imminent arrival of that end due to a diagnosis of terminal lung cancer, Constantine spends his days hunting down half-demons who have entered the earthly plane and (in his words) "deporting those bastards back to Hell." After one such battle, he asks the half-angel Gabriel (Tilda Swinton), one of Heaven's representatives on Earth, for a temporary reprieve from the cancer, so that he can continue his work. Gabriel turns down his request, and warns him that his exorcisms—carried out in an attempt to win God's favor and thus buy his way out of Hell—will not bring him redemption.

Constantine's greatest challenge, and his last chance to escape the fate that awaits him in Hell, comes to him from an unlikely source. Angela Dodson, a Los Angeles police detective, asks him to investigate the suicide of her twin sister Isabel, who leapt to her death from the roof of the psychiatric hospital where she had been confined. Other forces, Angela insists, must have been at work: Isabel was a devout Catholic who would never have knowingly taken her own life. He initially refuses, but changes his mind when Angela is attacked by demons soon after leaving his office.

Constantine saves Angela and, as he investigates the Isabel's death, learns that both sisters shared, as children, his ability to see the true forms of angels and demons. Angela, by steadfastly refusing to believe in the visions, gradually suppressed them, but Isabel embraced them and, as a result, became a powerful psychic. Her powers brought her to the attention of the forces of Hell and made her a vital but unwilling pawn in a plot set in motion by Mammon, the son of Satan. Dissatisfied with the way his father is ruling Hell, Mammon intends to cross into the earthly plane and establish a kingdom of his own, triggering the Apocalypse and unleashing Hell on Earth. In order to do so he requires a powerful psychic whose body will serve as a vessel within which he can make the otherwise forbidden crossing between planes. His half-demon minion Balthazar locates the Dodson twins and, when Isabel dies, turns his attention to Angela.

Constantine gradually realizes that the powers working to bring Mammon to Earth include Gabriel, who thinks that God is too forgiving of humans and too willing to grant them entry to Heaven. The terrors of Mammon's rule over Earth will, Gabriel believes, severely test the faith and moral compass of all humanity, making it possible to identify those truly worthy of salvation.³ Constantine defeats Mammon's demonic minions in the final battle, but is defeated, in turn, by Gabriel. Realizing that he is out of options, he does the unthinkable and cuts his wrists, knowing that Satan (Peter Stormare) will appear in person to gloat over his death and collect his soul. When Satan arrives, John reveals the plot, causing Satan to banish his son to Hell and casually defeat the once-powerful Gabriel (after God withdraws the rebellious half-angel's divine protection). Satan grants Constantine one favor as a gesture of gratitude for the information and—in his first genuinely selfless act—John asks for Isabel's soul to be released from Hell. Satan complies, only to discover that he no longer has a claim on Constantine's soul. God, in recognition of his final sacrifice, has absolved John of his sins.

Binaries Established

The opposing binaries that structure the universe and the plot of *Constantine* are visually reinforced throughout the film. Heavenly entities are accompanied by images of light and order, while hellish entities are accompanied by images of darkness, decay, and chaos. Gabriel first appears in a majestic church, beside a roaring fire, and a second, unnamed angel is shown amid the chaos of death, wings protectively spread as it kneels beside the body of a fallen psychic, keeping watch. When Gabriel reappears in the final scenes, the filmmakers arrange the shots in ways that expressly avoid placing Gabriel in the same frame with the gory battle scene unfolding in the next room. Demons, in contrast, are represented as conglomerations of insects, skeletal shape-shifters, or winged bringers of darkness. When the true nature of the demon Balthazar (Gavin Rossdale) is revealed, his unctuous, well-kept figure transforms into that of a skeletal monster. On his death, he turns to ash, his surroundings destroyed along with him. Satan too, is an image of decay, with putridity beneath his clean exterior and a tar-like substance oozing from his feet with every step.

The film's construction of visual oppositions is equally apparent in its depictions of Heaven and Hell. When John and Angela travel to Hell, they find themselves in a dry, ruined, sepia-toned version of Los Angeles, whose gutted structures are filled with skull-less demons, ready to attack intruders. Husks of burnt-out cars litter the landscape, fiery winds whip to and fro, and smoky dark clouds dot the orange sky. Beneath this outer, earth-like layer of Hell is a writhing pit of souls and a lake of fire and sulfur that vividly evokes descriptions found in the Bible. The film's brief glimpse of Heaven is, by contrast, a lush and beautiful vision of the city, picturesque and serene.

The oppositions given form in these images are derived from ideas deeply rooted in the Judeo-Christian tradition—notably the first chapter of Genesis, which establishes the light/dark and good/evil binaries.⁴ Each of these pairings carries with it a hierarchy—sometimes explicitly stated, sometimes merely inferred—whose origins reach back to foundational religious texts such as the Dead Sea Scrolls and the first chapters of Genesis.⁵ Order is superior to chaos, as light is to dark, day to night, and the sun to the moon. God and Satan—goodness and evil—coexist, but the power of the former exceeds that of the latter. God, in the Judeo-Christian worldview, allows evil to exist, but maintains power over it.

Demons are never clearly described in the Bible, and often go unnamed. According to scholars, this is troublesome for attempts to clearly define these supernatural entities.

John Constantine (Keanu Reeves) crosses into Hell in *Constantine* (2005).

Three of the four Gospels, for example, describe Jesus encountering a man whose erratic behavior suggests that he is possessed. When Jesus asks, "Who are you?" a voice from within the man responds, "My name is Legion, for we are many," an assertion of power, but not of identity.[6] It is only in non-canonical works that demons are described in detail. The Book of Enoch—composed between the third century BC and the first century AD—includes the first references to fallen angels who mated with human women, creating demonic offspring. Their half-demon children are associated, according to some scholars, with the *nephilim* referenced in Genesis and other early books of the Bible.[7] Biblically based literary works such as Dante's *Inferno* and Milton's *Paradise Lost* add further details, and the latter assigns names and personalities to Satan's principal lieutenants. The depictions of demons in *Constantine* draw elements from all these sources: from the Bible, demons' ambiguous form and shape-shifting abilities; from Enoch, the idea of "half-breed" angels and demons that walk the Earth; from Milton, the personality of Constantine's nemesis Balthazar.

Catholic theology, meanwhile, provides the matrix that ties these diverse elements together. Articulating, for Angela, the details of the hidden supernatural world whose existence she rejected along with her visions, John explains that full-fledged demons and angels are not allowed to cross to the earthly plane, but that angelic or demonic half-breeds can walk among humans, whispering in their ears with the goal of winning souls for Heaven or Hell. This worldview reinforces the traditional Catholic idea that Earth is a microcosm of a larger, unseen universe, and that humans and their salvation are both central to the Heaven/Hell binary and critical to the eternal contest between God and Satan.

Binaries Subverted

Binary pairings are, as Jacques Derrida suggests, inherently hierarchical; one entity in a pairing is inevitably privileged over the other. Derrida posits an "inside and an outside," and contends that the debased in the pairing is "always present within the inside, imprisoned outside the outside."[8] This concept lies at the heart of the Judeo-Christian worldview, in which good/God/Heaven is privileged, while evil/Satan/Hell is perpetually subordinate. Satan's eternal goal, then, is to subvert, and somehow break free of, God's privilege. This notion is made explicit in the Book of Revelation, which declares that "Satan will be released from his prison, and will come out to deceive the nations that are at the four corners of the earth."[9] Milton's *Paradise Lost* similarly affirms:

> For this infernal pit shall never hold
> Celestial spirits in bondage, nor the abyss
> Long under darkness cover.[10]

In neither narrative, however, is God ousted from His privileged position. Satan and his legions gain temporary dominion over the Earth in Revelation, but the dominion of God and Christ is restored in the end. Milton's version of Satan successfully tempts Adam and Eve, bringing about the Fall and their subsequent expulsion from Paradise, but he succeeds only because God—having granted humans free will—stands back and allows them to exercise it. *Constantine* fits smoothly into this tradition, and the filmmakers lean heavily on Miltonian and apocalyptic imagery to depict the end times and the rising of Satan. The film's narrative goes further, however: raising the possibility that, this time, the hierarchy might be dissolved, and evil allowed to win.

The first scenes of the film introduce an object capable of bringing about such dissolution: the legendary "Spear of Destiny" with which a Roman soldier pierced Christ's side during the Crucifixion.[11] The film's treatment of the spear reflects the medieval Christian understanding of holy relics as artifacts imbued with great power that—because they can be bought, sold, given, and stolen like any other material objects—confer their powers on whomever currently holds them. The first scenes of *Constantine* show a Mexican man finding the Spear of Destiny, inadvertently beginning a chain of events that will eventually allow Mammon to be set loose upon the Earth. Control of the spear, powerful both because of its association with the Crucifixion and because Christ's blood still coats its blade, gives the legions of Hell leverage not only to break free from the divine hierarchy, but to dissolve it altogether—making their bid for dominion over the Earth a greater threat to the Christian worldview than a traditional Satanic uprising that is doomed (by definition) to fail.

John's first indication that something is deeply wrong comes when he experiences a "soldier demon" attempting to gain access to the earthly plane. The inability of demons to cross from Hell to Earth is as fundamental to the structure of *Constantine's* supernatural universe as gravity is to the material universe. Meeting one face-to-face on the streets of Los Angeles suggests, therefore, that laws he had assumed to be immutable are being rewritten, and old certainties undermined. He recounts the story to one of his associates, a relic dealer named Beeman (Max Baker), as the two debate the abilities of demons to use humans as chess pieces. Beeman dismisses the possibility, saying: "No, we are finger puppets to them, John, not doorways."[12] As the film progresses, however, it becomes apparent demons *are* using humans as doorways—as literal vessels through which to gain access to Earth. Beeman realizes, while studying passages from a Latin translation of the Bible, how Mammon plans to cross to the earthly plane, but he is cornered and killed by demons as he tries to alert Constantine.

Father Hennessy (Pruitt Taylor Vince), another of Constantine's associates, suffers a similar fate. Able, like John and the twins, to hear voices and identify spirits, he relies on a holy relic and his heavy consumption of alcohol to mute the voices and keep himself sane. When John requests that he listen to the "ether," the priest submits and removes his protective relic in order to do so. Although he is able to confirm that Isabel is in Hell and identify her role in the demonic plot, he receives the mark of Mammon, which overwhelms his usual protections against the supernatural. Driven mad, he drowns himself while the demon Balthazar looks on. Like Beeman, Hennessy realizes too late that Mammon's plot represents an entirely new kind of threat to humanity—that old rules no longer apply, and old protections are no longer adequate.

Angela, too, realizes that the reality she took for granted is dissolving before her eyes. Unlike John, she has spent much of her life denying the existence of the supernatural creatures her psychic powers revealed to her. Forced to confront such creatures first-hand, she recognizes simultaneously that they are real—that her visions of are not manifestations of insanity—and that her sister (who embraced her own visions and accepted the existence of the supernatural) was not crazy. This reaffirmation of sanity is balanced, however, by more disturbing implications. A devout Catholic with a deeply rooted faith in the inherent power of Heaven and a 20th-century skepticism about the existence of Satan, she learns—in a single scene—that demons exist not only in stories and Bible verses but also in the corporeal world, and that they are able to interfere with human lives. Worst of all, she discovers that the all-protecting, all-powerful God in whom she believes is inactive and seems to have no providential role, allowing the forces of Hell to run rampant.

The worldview that Angela has built her life around thus dissolves in the time it takes her to be attacked by demons and rescued from them by John. When the dust has settled, she confronts a world in which neither God nor angels have any apparent interest in her welfare. She experiences, firsthand and with a vengeance, Freud's *uncanny*: the "sense of unfamiliarity at the very heart of the familiar."[13] Indeed, as she grapples not only with the shift but also with her newly accepted powers, that sense of disorientation becomes the center of her redefined world.

The sense of unraveling is further reinforced when John and Angela discover the message left by Isabel before her death. In it, Isabel points Angela to 1 Corinthians 17, a chapter that does not exist in the Bible, but according to John, exists in Hell's scriptures. He recounts how in the last four chapters, the story of Revelation is re-told, in this instance with a demonic reign. John and Angela then discover how Mammon plans to cross to the earthly plane, using Angela—whose psychic powers enable her to bridge both worlds—as a gateway and the Spear of Destiny as the necessary divine assistance. As the forces of evil continue to press for total subversion, Angela is kidnapped to facilitate Mammon's grotesque rebirth. She becomes the demon's unwilling pawn, and thus a party to his attempt to bring death and ruin to her world.

John's growing awareness of the personal and cosmic stakes in the battle he is fighting is matched by a growing awareness that his powers are inadequate to the task. The forces of Hell, he realizes, could only have made such gains if the forces of Heaven had—for whatever reason—permitted it. He thus finds himself confronting soldier demons in the open, knowing that he can count on neither protection nor intervention from God. He ultimately succeeds, but only barely, and at enormous cost.

Betwixt and Between

Constantine may be the story of an eternal struggle between two nearly infinite cosmic realms, but it takes place almost entirely on Earth. That paradoxical fact, and the agreement of the two principal combatants to forswear direct action, places the focus of the narrative squarely on figures—supernatural as well as human—for whom the boundaries between the earthly plane and the infinite realms beyond are fluid and permeable.

The positioning of humans in the cosmic struggle between good and evil has been a central Judeo-Christian theme since Genesis, when Satan convinced Eve to eat the fruit of the tree of knowledge.[14] *Paradise Lost* echoes this theme when Satan suggests it is better to lay waste to God's favorite creations, or seduce them to evil, than to settle for merely reigning in Hell.[15] Humans are thus caught between the supernatural forces that vie for their souls: integral to the struggle, in that they are both the means of keeping score and the ultimate prize, yet impotent, in that they have no power to engage directly in the fight.

Humanity as a whole occupies a similar position in the film—"stuck in the middle"[16] between infinitely more powerful forces—but John and Angela are exceptions to the pattern. Their ability to see the true forms of angels and demons make them continually aware of the struggle. Just as their shared awareness sets them apart from (most) other humans, however, their sharply different responses to it sets them apart from one another. John spends his life embracing, honing, and using his powers, while Angela denies hers until they practically disappear. His experience enables him to recognize supernatural forces at work, and, in his role as gatekeeper, he is able to take an active role in protecting the boundary between worlds, and influence the balance of angelic and demonic forces on Earth.

Angela's naiveté and her refusal to believe in evil present a striking contrast to Constantine's world-weary cynicism. John continuously tries to protect her, but—particularly early in the story—her inexperience leaves her prone becoming a pawn, a victim, or both. In one early scene, when John goes to question the demon Balthazar, he gives her a protective relic and tells her to remain in the car. Unaware of the magnitude of the forces in play around her, and the danger they pose to her—she takes off the relic, follows him, and is abducted by demons. Eventually, however, as Angela becomes more familiar with the presence of the supernatural, she is able to play an active, rather than passive role. Unlike Henessey and most others who share her gift, she is able not just to see angels and demons as they truly are, but to anticipate and predict their actions. Her powers—like John's though to a lesser degree—mark her as a pivotal figure in the battle between good and evil.

Angela and John's ability to cross between planes—traversing, and so blurring, the boundaries between the human and the supernatural realms—reinforces their uniqueness among humans and enhances their ability to alter the course of supernatural events. John first crosses into Hell to confirm Isabel's damnation, returning with her hospital bracelet as evidence that her soul resides there. He later crosses a second time, with the assistance of Papa Midnite (Djimon Honsou), a retired witch doctor turned nightclub owner, whose club serves as a neutral meeting ground for soldiers on both sides of the cosmic war. When Angela crosses the first time, she is endowed with the knowledge of cosmic forces. When she returns the second time, Mammon accompanies her, using her body as a vessel. Once on Earth, he strains against her abdomen from within until the contours of his face are visible beneath her distended skin, threatening to burst forth at any moment in a grotesque parody of birth.

Crossing between planes in the world of *Constantine* requires the use of objects that are, themselves, liminal: apparently earthly—even mundane—to the casual observer but immensely powerful to those who, like John, are aware of their supernatural capacities. John makes his first crossing by immersing his feet in water, a trans-dimensional lubricant, and holding a cat: a creature that, he tells Angela, exists in both worlds. Immersing her in a filled bathtub, he facilitates her own first crossing by holding her beneath the surface until she nearly drowns, enabling her to temporarily slip across the border between this life and the next. He later seeks out Papa Midnite, who owns "the chair," once used to electrocute condemned inmates in New York's Sing Sing Prison, to assist in his second crossing. The device, having held the bodies of hundreds of condemned men at the moments their Hell-bound souls departed the earthly plane, became a kind of unholy relic, serving as a gateway for those seeking to cross between planes voluntarily. Even Mammon—who, like his soldier demons, should be confined to Hell—facilitates his own crossing between planes by acquiring a relic (the Spear of Destiny) that allows him to channel the power of God. Consistent with the film's (loosely) Catholic view of relics, these instances of borrowing and crossing suggest objects can, at least for brief moments, confer cosmic powers on individuals who would not otherwise be able to wield them.

Liminal figures—those creatures belonging to both planes, and yet fully to neither—extend this notion of the interrelationship between worlds as they further blur the boundaries separating traditional binary oppositions. The characters of Gabriel and Balthazar, half-angel and half-demon respectively, are both rooted in Judeo-Christian narrative traditions: Gabriel shares the name and many of the qualities of the biblical archangel, and Balthazar could easily be one of the lesser devils of Milton's *Paradise Lost*. Far from being indifferent supernatural figures, however, both are deeply involved in Earthly events. Balthazar, for most of the film, is the physical manifestation of evil, the arbiter for Hell on Earth. It is he who orchestrates Hell's minions, bringing about the deaths of Beeman and Father Hennessy and unleashing demons on Angela after her sister's death. Simultaneously, however, he continues to carry on the traditional role of all Earth-dwelling half-demons: seeking out vulnerable individuals and subtly influencing them toward evil.

Gabriel, on the other hand, is "the Angel of Revelation: the blower of the trumpet blast, that, at the end of time, will shatter the bonds of the physical world and awaken the sleeping souls of the blessed to everlasting life."[17] The Gabriel of *Paradise Lost* also serves as the protector who stands watch over the Garden of Eden, and who fails to prevent Satan from penetrating the garden's defenses and tempting Eve.[18] In both cases, Gabriel is a gatekeeper, although a poor one. In the film, Gabriel's ability to blur boundaries tips the scales of a battle that, for the half-angel, is a means of redressing human failings. Joining forces with Mammon, Gabriel aligns with evil in order to create good—to help humans reach their full potential—arguing that "it's only in the face of horror that [humans] can indeed find your nobler selves."[19] Like the Gabriel of the Book of Revelation, the Gabriel of *Constantine* is the one to awaken humanity to a new reality. Unlike the biblical angel, however, the cinematic half-angel is not content to serve as God's agent on Earth, just as Bathazar is not content to serve *his* (nominal) master, Satan, preferring instead to follow the rebellious Mammon. Both use their liminal status—their rootedness in both the earthly and the supernatural planes—in an attempt to permanently alter the relationship between the two realms, even as John and Angela use their own liminality to stabilize the rapidly crumbling hierarchy.

The Sacrifice: Binaries Restored

Constantine reaches its climactic moment when Gabriel bests John in the final battle. Everything seems lost, and evil is on the verge of victory, when John finally understands sacrifice and cuts his own wrists in order to summon Satan to his side. John's act is the last, most startling subversion of the rules governing the cosmic conflict: a human manipulating Satan rather than the other way around. As soon as Satan appears, however, the traditional hierarchy begins to reassert itself, and we see not only Satan's power, but also God's power over him.

Satan (Peter Stormare) attempts to retrieve John's soul in *Constantine* (2005).

Each of the divine combatants demonstrates the consequences of rebellion to their wayward offspring: Satan sends Mammon back to Hell, and God withdraws His protection from Gabriel, leaving the fallen angel vulnerable to Satan's retaliation. Only when Satan tries to drag John to Hell does God actually exert his power. Recognizing John's penitence, He snatches the mortal from Satan's grasp, restoring the divine hierarchy and leaving the audience to ponder the attempts (albeit messy) by evil to manipulate the (super)natural order of things. In this one moment, God establishes His power without even showing Himself. Satan's only recourse is to cure John of his cancer and grant him additional time on Earth, hoping that he will once again make choices that condemn his soul to Hell. Satan leaves, impotent in the face of God's power.

John's sacrifice here mirrors that of the Christ. Biblically, Christ dies to save humankind, and, in *Constantine*, so does John. He gives up his last hopes for Heaven to save humanity and Isabel. He could have asked for more time, but like Christ, he chooses instead to die so that she might live. His act is not only the pivotal moment in his shift from cynicism to selflessness—for which God rewards him with redemption—but also the ultimate expression of his role as gatekeeper. John has fulfilled his task of protecting humanity from cosmic forces. The hierarchy is restored and, although opposition remains, the apocalypse is held at bay.

Notes

1. Ferdinand de Saussure first posed the term binary opposition to understand his Structural theory of the linguistic sign in which he considers words as gaining meaning from their opposites. For example, the lack of light is what creates an understanding of darkness. Saussure and his successors found binary pairings to order thought and establish hierarchies. Jacques Derrida was the first to describe the pairing as hierarchical
2. *Constantine*, dir. Francis Lawrence, 2005, Warner Bros. Entertainment, 2005. DVD.
3. Matthew famously describes Christ, during the Second Coming, dividing the deserving from the undeserving "as a shepherd separates the sheep from the goats." Matthew 25:31–46, New Revised Standard Version (hereafter NRSV).
4. Genesis 1:1–19, NRSV.
5. Kenneth L. Hanson, "The Dead Sea Scrolls and the Language of Binary Opposition: A Structuralist/Poststructuralist Approach," *Australian Journal of Jewish Studies* 22 (2008): 31.
6. Luke 8:30–31, NRSV.
7. *The Book of Enoch*, trans. August Dillman, ed. R.H. Charles (Oxford: Clarendon Press, 1893).
8. Jacques Derrida. *Of Grammatology* (Baltimore: Johns Hopkins University Press, 1976), 35.
9. Revelation 20, NRSV.
10. John Milton, *Paradise Lost*, Book I, lines 657–659.
11. The wounding is described in John 19:34. The spear—also referred to as the "Holy Lance" or the "Lance of Longinus" (after the centurion who supposedly wielded it)—subsequently became the subject of elaborate legends. Three or four separate relics purporting to be the spear circulated in Europe during the Middle Ages.
12. "Little Talks" (*Constantine* DVD extra).
13. Andrew Bennett and Nicholas Royle, *Literature, Criticism and Theory* (London: Pearson Education Unlimited, 2004), 34.
14. Genesis 3:1–6, NRSV.
15. Milton, *Paradise Lost*, line 368.
16. "The World Behind the World" (*Constantine* DVD extra).
17. Ptolemy Tompkins, "Gabriel's Moment," *Angels on Earth* 13, no. 2 (2007).
18. Milton, *Paradise Lost*, Book 4.
19. "Gabriel's Road to Salvation" (*Constantine* DVD extra).

Bibliography

Bennett, Andrew, and Nicholas Royle. *Literature, Criticism and Theory*, 3d ed. Harlow: Pearson Education Limited, 2004.
The Book of Enoch. Trans. August Dillmann. Ed. R.H. Charles. Oxford: Clarendon Press, 1893.
Constantine. Dir. Francis Lawrence. 2005. Warner Bros. Entertainment, 2005. DVD.
Derrida, Jaques. *Of Grammatology*. Baltimore: Johns Hopkins University Press, 1976.
Hanson, Kenneth. "The Dead Sea Scrolls and the Language of Binary Opposition: A Structuralist/Poststructuralist Approach." 1*Australian Journal of Jewish Studies* 22 (2008): 26–55.
Milton, John. *Paradise Lost*. Ed. Stephen Orgel and Jonathan Goldberg. New York: Oxford University Press, 2008.
Tompkins, Ptolemy. "Gabriel's Moment." *Angels on Earth* 13, no. 2 (2007): 28–32.

Monsters of God
Negotiating the Sacred in Stake Land

RHONDA R. DASS

"In desperate times false gods abound. People put their faith in the loudest preacher and hope they're right. But sometimes they're wrong, dead wrong."—Martin, *Stake Land*

Post-apocalyptic movies depict survivors of global catastrophe coping with life after the collapse of civilization and, often, the near-total destruction of humanity. Typically focusing on mere survival, or at most on the rebuilding of the institutions and structure necessary to recreate a semblance of "normal" life, they seldom depict—let alone address the nuances of—religion. The rare examples that *do* depict religion as part of life in the post-apocalyptic world typically focus on the survivors' loss of faith in the divine, and their perception that God has failed humanity by not intervening to stop the disaster that has befallen them.[1] *Stake Land* (2010), directed by Jim Mickle and co-written by Nick Damici, is a rare exception to the pattern. Set in a post-apocalyptic America that has been decimated by a vampire pandemic, it depicts traditional religious institutions breaking down and new ones forming as the boundaries between the sacred and the profane are renegotiated in tandem with the new world order.

Stake Land opens with a vampire hunter, known only as Mister (Nick Damici), rescuing teenaged Martin (Connor Paolo) from the vampires that have just slaughtered his parents. Mister becomes Martin's protector and mentor, teaching him the skills required to survive in the post-apocalyptic world, along with the finer points of hunting down and killing vampires. Martin travels with Mister on the long road from the vampire-ridden American South to safety in Canada, now known as New Eden. He narrates their story and those of the other survivors who join them along the way, as well as the group's encounters with a violent religious sect known as the Christian Brotherhood.

The post-apocalyptic world through which Mister and Martin travel bears little resemblance to the one that existed before the plague. The social institutions and cultural norms of the old world have been reduced to tatters by the vampire onslaught, and the new ones that will take their place are only gradually coming into being. Jebedia Loven (Michael Cerveris), the leader of the Christian Brotherhood, already controls much of the eastern United States, and is actively working to create a new society with himself as absolute and unquestioned ruler. The Brotherhood casts the vampires plaguing the country as agents of God who feed on the sinful, and uses the creatures as part of a campaign to "purify" what remains of the human race. Mister harbors no such ambitions—his interest in vampires extends only to killing as many as possible—but his actions establish him as an alternative to Jebedia, and his band of followers as the nucleus of post-apocalyptic society very different than that sought by the Christian Brotherhood. The collision between the two groups thus becomes a struggle not just for survival, but for the right to shape the society slowly emerging from the ruins of the vampire apocalypse.

Both groups are actively engaged in renegotiating what pioneering sociologist Emile Durkheim called the boundary between the sacred and the profane. The realm of the sacred, Durkheim argued, encompasses the extraordinary and awe-inspiring; the profane, on the other hand, comprises the mundane and the everyday. The boundary between the two is not fixed, but fluid, and the rituals used to maintain it are socially negotiated. *Stake Land* illustrates that process in a time of social and cultural crisis—a world where the old religious order has dissolved but not yet disappeared, and a new one has begun to coalesce but not yet solidified. This essay is an examination of *Stake Land's* dramatization of that process: an exploration of the ways in which symbols, objects, words, and actions are shaped into a new understanding of the sacred, and ordinary individuals like Mister and Martin emerge as apostles of a new religion for a post-apocalyptic world.

The Sacred and the Profane

Durkheim argues that the sacred and the profane can only be understood in relation to one another. The sacred encompasses things set apart and accorded special treatment: that which transcends everyday existence and is seen as extraordinary, potentially dangerous, awe-inspiring, or even fear-inducing. This includes beliefs, practices, and objects connected with the divine, but is—crucially, for the purposes of this essay—not limited to them. A purely secular place or object can be rendered sacred if it evokes feelings of awe and reverence, or is imbued with intense emotional significance. The regimental flags that 19th-century armies carried into battle were sacred objects to the men who fought—and the idea that battlefields are "sanctified" by the blood of the men who fought there reaches from Lincoln's address at Gettysburg to the 1995 controversy over plans to build a Disney theme park near Manassas, Virginia. Anything can become sacred if a community marks it as such, but its status is specific to the community, and thus to a particular time and place. Different societies, and different religious communities within a single society (or even a single faith), may draw the boundaries of the sacred differently, and redraw them over time. Neither the extent nor the contents of the world of the sacred are immutable, then, and neither can be determined once and for all.

Once defined, the sacred becomes the focus of beliefs and practices designed to insulate it from the world of the profane and prevent it from being contaminated by mundane things. The boundary between the two is maintained by taboos and admonitions. Awareness of those taboos, and mastery of the rituals associated with sacred objects, is thus prerequisite for interaction with them. The sacred, unlike the profane, must always be approached mindfully—never casually. The taboos and rituals that surround the sacred are, themselves, signposts of the community's beliefs, and individuals' deference to them serves as public affirmations of those beliefs. A group, Durkheim explains, will hold up a sacred object as a symbol of the group itself, and the reverence felt for the object derives from the respect held for the values of the group, rather than from feelings about the object itself. The veneration of sacred objects—whether tinged with the divine, like a Christian crucifix, or purely secular, like a national flag—is thus, ultimately, veneration of the group.[2]

It is no surprise, therefore, that communities in crisis often venerate, with renewed fervor, that which they hold sacred—practicing familiar rituals with more than the normal attention to detail, and policing taboos with more than the usual sharpness. Such vigorous reaffirmations of community identity and celebrations of shared values take place, not just in response to direct, specific threats such as conquest or active persecution, but in the wake of any disruptions that leave it feeling threatened or embattled. They serve as a stabilizing reaction to the mysterious, the extraordinary, or "anything that is ominous, and anything that motivates feelings of disquiet or fear."[3]

Vampires and the Dissolution of the Old World

The monsters of *Stake Land* are a continuous presence in the background of the film, and a continuous reminder that old rules, taboos, and assumptions have broken down. The first vampire appearing in the film, revealed when Mister meets and rescues Martin, is startling proof that the America in which *Stake Land* takes place—though superficially familiar—has been profoundly transformed. The vampire has just mortally injured both of Martin's parents and is perched in the rafters of the barn with their infant in his hands, blood smeared across its pale, distorted face. Its hair is wild and unruly, but its body and clothing hint at its former status as a civilized human. It and the other vampires in *Stake Land* are true monsters, their physical appearances harking back to the early days of vampire lore when Nosferatu—with his skull-like visage, pale skin and sunken eyes—was the stereotypical vampire.[4] They retain their basic human form, but their bodies harden, and their brow ridges and fangs steadily grow as they age, giving them an ever-more grotesque, distorted appearance.[5] The more time that has passed since their transformation into vampires, the more horrific their faces and the more monstrous their appearance.

The vampires are animalistic in their postures, as well, and are often seen crouching or positioned on all four limbs. The savagery of their attacks upon their human prey clearly sets them apart from the suave, sophisticated vampires we have come to associate with horror films in the latter half of the 20th century.[6] Far from being a covert subculture of intelligent, nearly immortal beings capable of hiding among us—embodiments of the culturally fraught concept of difference among humans—they are not even capable of speech, communicating instead through primal screams and incomprehensible sounds. *Stake Land* treats them as utterly, irredeemably Other: possessing humanoid form, but completely beyond the human experience.[7] They are the agents of not just the fall, but the utter dissolution, of the pre-apocalyptic world.

We have learned, from catastrophes both natural and human-made, that civilization is terrifyingly fragile. Scott Poole argues, in *Monsters in America*, that America's embrace of zombie culture is a reflection of our anxieties about its potential, imminent collapse: "The very complexity of modern society, the intricate support systems that keep the lights on, the water running, the gas pumping, and the ATMs dispensing cash, has given a special twist to the theme of apocalypse in modern America…. These fears were transferred after 2001 to the possibility of some kind of high tech terrorist attack that would render modern conveniences inoperable.... Zombies represented the end of the world, the complete breakdown of human society, and the cannibalization of humanity."[8] The linking of monsters with the apocalypse, Poole argues, is not new. Bram Stoker's *Dracula* also deploys the specter of an impending apocalypse—the gradual conquest of England by Dracula and his vampiric "children," but averts it through the last-minute triumph of man over monster.[9] Modern zombie-apocalypse tales like *World War Z* and *The Walking Dead* deny humans their triumph, and explore what happens as civilization crumbles under the onslaught of monsters. The hybrid zombie-vampire monsters of *Stake Land* combine the two apocalyptic threats into a single horrific being—one sufficient to overcome human resistance, topple civilization as we know it, and leave in tatters the social fabric that it once supported.

All this has come to pass, in the world of *Stake Land*, before Martin's story begins. The characters experience disquiet and fear on an epic scale, and—with vampiric monsters roaming the countryside at will—the mysterious and the extraordinary have become part of the survivors' everyday lives. The ubiquity of the vampires, the steady dwindling of the human population, and the inability of individuals to defend themselves from the monsters around them, render life in post-apocalyptic America both precarious and ominous. Reaffirmation of the old values, and retrenchment around old concepts of the sacred, are no longer sufficient. Once-isolated survivors are slowly organizing themselves into communities, however, and—as Durkheim would predict—those communities are gradually creating new definitions of the sacred, and new rituals, that (like the old ones) reaffirm their values and provide cohesion.

Jebedia Loven and the Christian Brotherhood

"They said they were Christians."—Sister, *Stake Land*

The Christian Brotherhood is a religious sect, but despite their name and their embrace of what they see as a divinely ordained mission, little connects them to the culture of the pre-apocalyptic world. The Brotherhood's members see vampires as sacred beings, and use them to carry out "God's work" of converting non-believers and killing those who resist conversion. "Behold, the children of salvation," Jebedia declares at one point. "They come at my calling and feed on the unfaithful."

Jebedia spouts fire-and-brimstone rhetoric like a Southern evangelist, but he directs the Brotherhood's rooting out of the "unfaithful" as if it were a military campaign. He functions like a dictator rather than a benevolent leader, and although his rhetoric is suffused with religious fervor, his actions are self-serving and cruel. Jebedia sanctions the objectification of women, classifies members of the Brotherhood by their ethnic "purity," sets roadblocks and vampire-laden traps for its enemies, and employs terroristic methods against "sinners." Residents of the towns that Mister and his group pass through on their way north repeatedly warn them to stay clear of the Brotherhood, and their first-hand encounters with Jebedia and his followers give them ample reason to heed the advice, with each successive encounter becoming more violent.

The Brotherhood controls much of the eastern seaboard, its territory spreading as the story unfolds. Radio broadcasts—suggestive of both elaborate infrastructure and a high degree of organization—introduce viewers to the Brotherhood and punctuate Martin's narrative as Mister and his pilgrims move northward on their journey to New Eden. The Brotherhood even practices aerial warfare, using airplanes to drop vampires into outposts of civilization that have taken refuge behind walls and barricades, destroying them from within. Mister and his followers hear rumors claiming that aerial vampire attacks were used to topple the national government, along with suggestions that the Brotherhood was the real culprit. If true, these rumors implicate the Brotherhood in hastening the demise of civilization—destroying it in order to create a power vacuum that will allow them to become the future rulers of the region.

Jebedia and his followers freely appropriate the symbols of the old, pre-apocalyptic world, and just as freely modify them to suit their own needs. Their principal symbol is based on the traditional Christian cross, with an additional vertical piece extending downward from each end of the crossbar, forming a shape reminiscent of a trident. This deliberate alteration of the most potent of Christian symbols—a significant redefinition of the sacred—is rendered even more striking by the trident's distinctly non–Christian associations with the Greek god Poseidon, Roman gladiators, and the Devil. The Brotherhood uses this altered cross to mark the geographic and social boundaries of their world. Scrawled on buildings, it indicates Brotherhood-controlled territory. It is also tattooed onto the back of Jebedia's scalp, and incorporated into the design of the hooded robes worn by his followers. The Brotherhood's cloth masks—like their robes, an appropriation from the pre-apocalypse Ku Klux Klan—are divided into three strips that mimic the three legs of the trident-like cross, covering the wearer's face while allowing him to see through the spaces between.

Recognizing the powerful associations that certain once-sacred symbols held in the world before the vampire plague, the Brotherhood uses them to set traps for its enemies. A vampire dressed in the costume of a shopping-mall Santa Claus, a once-sacred symbol of childhood innocence and trust, becomes bait designed to lure to their doom those who are *too* innocent and trusting.[10] Later, the Brotherhood sets another, even more elaborate trap: a large and seemingly empty tent—like those used in evangelical revival meetings—with what appear to be murdered worshipers scattered among the seats and a baby's cries issuing from a bassinet positioned near the altar. When Mister and his followers enter the tent to rescue the baby, however, they find only a tape recorder in the bassinet. The trap is then sprung, and the "dead" in the audience leap up to capture them. This repurposing of once-sacred items for the purely mundane purpose of baiting and trapping enemies mirrors the Brotherhood's creation of a new realm of the sacred that exalts both vampires and themselves. It also suggests the extent to which their nominally religious mission is intertwined with—and perhaps used as mere cover for—a drive for power over their fellow humans that is all too familiar from the pre-apocalyptic world.

Mister and Martin

Even before the two become sworn enemies, Mister is Jebedia's opposite. He is a loner who accepts followers grudgingly, out of a sense of obligation, rather than a charismatic leader eager to build a movement and, perhaps, a kingdom. Where Jebedia is a vicious thug who presents himself as a pious servant carrying out God's will, Mister is a decent man who makes no attempt to disguise, or apologize for, the ruthless violence he

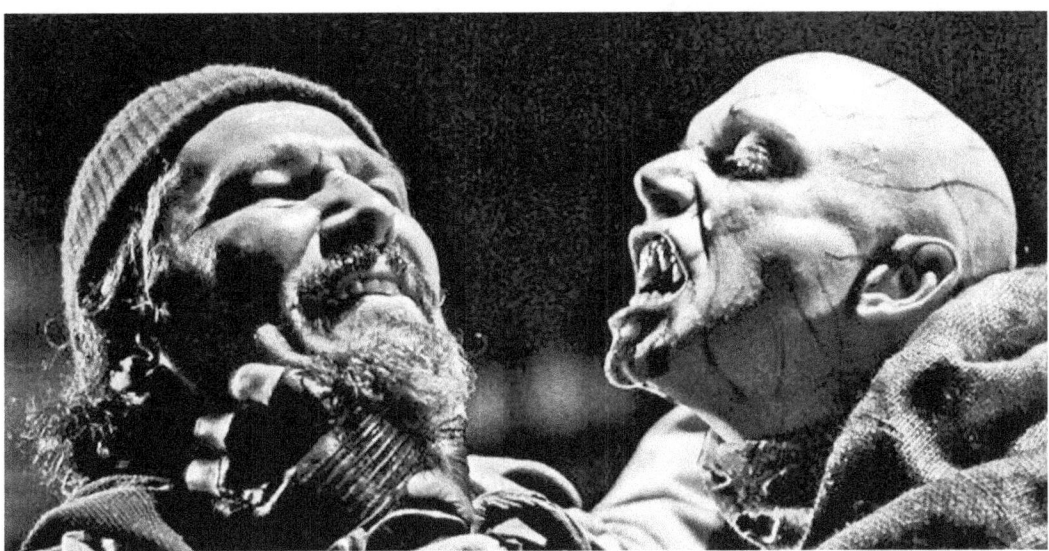

Mister (Nick Damici) stares evil in the face as he confronts Jebedia Loven (Michael Cerveris) in *Stake Land* (2010).

inflicts on those (man or monster) who prey on the weak. Mister—who lies, cheats, drinks, deals in marijuana, and is intimate with women whose names he does not even know—is lacking in virtue when measured against the standards that pre-apocalyptic religions venerated, and the Christian Brotherhood professes to live by. Yet he is revered by the townspeople he encounters along his journey—the same people who fear and avoid Jebedia. In a world where society and culture are in the midst of being renegotiated, and the standards of the old world have ceased to be the measure of an individual, Mister is revered not only for the courage and skill with which he dispatches vampires, but for this actions toward those closest to him, such as Martin and Sister (Kelly McGillis).

Mister, unlike Jebedia, has no intention of establishing a new understanding of the sacred, let alone an entire new religion. Over the course of the narrative, however, he clearly does the former, and *Stake Land* ends with suggestions that he may, without realizing it, have set the stage for the latter. The center of this new vision of the sacred—and of Mister's post-apocalyptic life—is vampire-killing. Seen purely in functional terms, as the eradication of a natural enemy that threatens humankind's safety, it would appear to be a profane act, as mundane and everyday as the work of an exterminator. The vampire threat to humankind is so profound, however, and Mister's dedication to his work so single-mindedly intense, that it is transformed into a sacred act, one that defines the small community around him and, gradually, the larger community of those touched by him.

Mister's approach to vampires is motivated by something deeper and more profound than the need for bare, personal survival. It is an act of sacrifice through which, in the name of the common good, he repeatedly and willingly puts his own life at risk so that the risk to others' lives may be reduced. Over the course of his travels he has many opportunities to avoid vampires, but he repeatedly chooses to engage them, intentionally bringing about confrontations with vampires that would otherwise have ignored him. He hunts vampires not because he has to, but because he sees doing so as his responsibility—as his mission. His treatment of vampire-killing as a life-defining calling, not just a practical act of survival, pushes it into the realm of the sacred. It is an implicit affirmation of a new set of values for the post-apocalyptic world: one that calls upon humans to push back against the chaos brought by the vampires (and their human allies, the Christian Brotherhood), not simply hide from it and hope that it passes them by.

Durkheim argues that the symbols a culture chooses to embrace are a crucial part of how it expresses its core values to the world; as cultures change and values shift, old symbols fade and new ones take their place.[11] Mister signals his own identity as a protector of humankind—and an agent of ruthless, righteous violence against any being, human or vampire, that threatens its survival—by adopting the skull as his visual signature. Skulls adorn the necklace he wears, cover the lock buttons in his car, and decorate the instruments he uses to kill. His actions, in this respect, parallel Jebedia's in that they appropriate elements of a dying culture and repurpose them as part of a new one. Unsettling in the (comparatively) peaceful and orderly world of pre-apocalyptic America because of its association with death, the skull becomes—for Mister and his followers—a symbol of death specifically to humankind's *enemies*, and thus of resistance and hope.

Likewise adorned with skulls, the weapons that Mister carries cross the line separating profane tools from sacred objects. Mister's meticulously detailed, scrupulously observed rules for their preparation and use further affirms their status. His rituals transform the killing of vampires from an everyday (and thus profane) improvisational act necessary ensure a lone individual's survival into a sacred calling pursued by select, selfless individuals on behalf of their friends, neighbors, and (in a broad sense) all surviving humans. Rituals ensure that the "correct" method of vampire killing is preserved and spread, eliminating the waste of lives that the trial-and-error efforts of individuals would inevitably bring.

The film depicts these rituals in a series of scenes illustrating Mister's training of Martin: He introduces the boy to the tools and weapons of the vampire-killer's trade, and works with him in daylight until the movements they will perform in the dark are second nature. The process begins when Mister opens the trunk of his car and, after handing Martin a spear, says, "Welcome to Stake Land." Over time, Martin learns the use of all the ritual objects to be used in killing vampires, each more ornate and complex than the one before. The relationship between the two, however, goes beyond that of an apprentice learning skills from his master; rather, it approximates that of a novice being indoctrinated into a religious order. When Martin is set against his first vampire he is dressed in ways that set him apart from others and conform to the stringent requirements of Mister's rituals. His costume may be improvised protective gear—a football helmet and shoulder pads—but they are *Stake Land*'s version of a priest's vestments.

Martin is not simply trained in the most efficient means of killing vampires, however—he is also instructed in Mister's grimly practical values and worldview. Mister explains that vampires can be classified into various types according to their teeth, and demonstrates that the teeth (pulled from the jaws of newly dead vampires) serve as a kind of credential for vampire killers. When the pair is interrogated at the first safe town they encounter, Mister shows the guards his bag of teeth and their demeanor instantly changes. Mister and Martin are quickly admitted to the community, and Mister is given (without charge) the goods and services he asks for, solely on the strength of his standing as a vampire-killer. His skill and efficiency—seemingly confirmed by his abundant collection of teeth—establish him as a sacred figure, capable of doing what ordinary humans cannot. Martin quickly grasps the power of such a reputation in the fragmented social world of post-apocalyptic America. When questioned about Mister by a resident of a town where they have stopped, he takes the opportunity to brag about Mister's vampire-killing prowess and emphasize his own role in assisting Mister's work. He carefully omits (as does Mister himself) the fact that Mister pads his vampire-killing record by harvesting teeth from already-dead vampires, as well as those he has actually killed.

Even as he absorbs his master's habit of not telling the entire truth, Martin learns the core of his philosophy: That the lives of their small group, and those of the other remnants of humanity, are at stake in the fight against the vampires and must be protected. By the end of the film, he will carry both types of teachings—Mister's methods and his values—far beyond their small group of survivors, sharing them with others willing to learn, to follow, and so, to serve.

Negotiation of the Sacred

"They renamed their town 'Strivington.' It said it all. It gave me hope for people. It gave me hope for New Eden. Sometimes hope is all you got."
—Martin, *Stake Land*

The renegotiation of the sacred in the post-apocalyptic world of *Stake Land* involves not just Mister and the Christian Brotherhood, but a multitude of sects and would-be leaders. The near-collapse of civilization and the undermining, or eradication, of traditional religious communities leaves the survivors with no clear place to turn for reassurance that the world will be brought to some new form of normality. Those searching for some form of salvation can choose among many who promise it, each of whom claims to offer a path to redemption, and none of whom enjoys a privileged position or unquestioned support among the survivors. Their sheer number of such would-be saviors lowers their standing, rendering them commonplace and, ironically, profane. The behavior of organizations like the Brotherhood—which presents itself as Christian, but freely engages in violence, intimidation, and oppression—lowers it further. The true tension in the film—between the alternate visions of the future offered by Jebedia and Mister—is played out against this backdrop.[12]

Negotiating a new definition of the sacred amid the reality of the post-apocalyptic world is about defining the morals and values of the survivor communities. Jebedia and his Christian Brotherhood represent the old morality, with its obsession with moral purity, and sin. Their determination to punish sinners by setting vampires on them only accelerates the toll taken by the monsters, further diminishing the human race's chances of survival. The townspeople Mister and his group encounter reject the Christian Brotherhood so thoroughly that they refuse even to have them spoken of in their establishments. Mister and his followers—both the few who travel with him and those who support him, but stay behind—are more warmly received. They offer a new morality and a new set of values for the post-apocalyptic world, where formerly perceived vices such as alcohol, drugs, and sex are balanced by generosity and deeds done for the common good. Mister's behavior—particularly his familiarity with violence and ruthless efficiency in dispatching those be believes unworthy of life—would have framed him as a disreputable outcast in the pre-apocalyptic world. In the post-apocalyptic world, however, he becomes a true Monster of God and an ideal savior for the human race.

The gradual falling away of the old world and its values, and the need to embrace a new understanding of the world, are explored, in *Stake Land*, through the character of Sister—the first follower, after Martin, to join Mister. A Catholic nun, she symbolizes—both visually and spiritually—the pre-apocalyptic world, particularly people of faith and their understanding of the sacred, She is, initially, almost painfully innocent, never considering that the world she knew has changed forever. She is genuinely shocked when two members of the Christian Brotherhood attack and attempt to rape her ("They said they were Christians!" she exclaims). She gradually adjusts her assumptions about the world, however, coming to accept—if not embrace— the set of values embodied by Mister and adopted by Martin.

Sister (Kelly McGillis), a former nun, grows accustomed to her new life following Mister in *Stake Land* (2010).

On the first night that he, Martin, and Sister travel as a group, Mister sets a trap for any vampires that may be in the area. He anoints a teddy bear with Martin's blood to lure the creatures in, and as he sits and watches, a vampire is drawn into the trap. Sister recognizes the creature as Sister Agatha, once her friend; but her exchange with Mister reveals her growing acceptance of killing as necessary and her gradual shift away from the traditional teachings of the Church.

> SISTER: "We thought she was dead."
> MISTER: "She is."
> SISTER: "What are you going to do?"
> MISTER: "I'm going to kill that thing."
> SISTER: "Go with God."

Once the deed is done, Sister leaves the pair in order to gather flowers for Sister Agatha's grave: an indication that she has not fully let go of her old attitudes, let alone come to terms with Mister's belief that vampires are vermin in humanoid form. Out of deference to her, Mister treats the body differently than those of the other vampires he has killed, waiting until she is out of sight before harvesting the fangs, and digging the grave for it without waiting for her to ask.

Visibly upset by Mister's killing of the Sister Agatha–vampire, Sister asks Mister how many he has killed. When he answers "Not enough," she presses him further, asking him whether he has also killed survivors and specifically mentioning the two members of the Brotherhood who tried to rape her. When Mister flatly states his belief that "In my book, rapists have no right to live," she nods her head in agreement and, when he returns to his slaying of vampires, shows minimal reaction to the carnage. Her apparent equanimity suggests that she is coming to terms with a new set of values tailored to the post-apocalyptic world: one in which vampires' human form does not make them human, and lethal, proactive violence takes the place of forgiveness.

The spiritual transition that Sister undergoes during her travels with Mister is symbolized by her gradual shedding of the symbols of her former life in the church. Her nun's habit—torn and soiled from her encounter with the Christian Brotherhood—is gone after her encounter with Sister Agatha. Later, she removes the cross she wears around her neck and gives it to Martin when he runs from the Brotherhood. When she leaves her small statuette of the Virgin Mary behind on the dashboard of a vehicle, it is as if she is leaving behind the last vestiges of her belief that humanity embodies the purity and innocence represented in the symbol of the Virgin. Doing so, she also leaves behind the old culture in which she was raised, and becomes part of the new one that has begun to coalesce around Mister and Martin.

Conclusion

The survivors of the apocalypse are, in *Stake Land*, struggling to negotiate a new understanding of the sacred, and to craft a code of morals and values that will be a reflection of their new, post-apocalyptic lives. Searching for a new worldview, the survivors confront two possibilities, each drawing on elements of the past but incorporating them into new visions of the sacred and radically different approaches to the future. They are offered, in effect, a choice between the cross of Jebedia Loven or the skull of Mister.

Jebedia declares, "We'll get you some religion. Bring you to God and the right way," and shows mercy only to those who adhere to his narrow vision of "right," but this approach wins him few converts among the remaining human population. The survivors see themselves reflected neither in the elements of the past that the Brotherhood upholds through its religious practices and symbols, nor in its belief that vampires are sacred beings through which the Brotherhood does God's work on Earth. Mister's ritualized violence, and vision of resistance—both to vampires and to the Brotherhood—as a sacred calling, resonates with them far more deeply and intensely. It leads them, over the course of the film, to elevate Mister and his followers toward the realm of the sacred. Mister is not yet, by the end of the film regarded as divine, but he is well on his way down the path that will advance him in that direction—signaled by his triumph over Jebedia. "I am your God now!" Jebedia declares in the climax of *Stake Land*, only to have Mister drive him backward onto a stake held by Martin. Mister, by killing him, not only slays his own greatest (human) enemy, but symbolically eradicates of the affront to the sacred that Jebedia and his movement represented.

Having killed a man who called himself God, Mister shows no desire to claim the role for himself. Handing his skull necklace on to his disciple, Mister passes out of the story and into legend, leaving Martin to tell the tales, perform the rituals, and thus perpetuate a new vision of the sacred that reflects the values of humanity in the post apocalyptic world. Along with Mister's vampire-killing rituals, however, Martin has also learned the value of embroidering the stories he retells, rendering it possible that—as generations pass—Mister may yet be transformed, in the memory of his disciples, from a flawed man into a sacred, even godlike, figure.

NOTES

1. Sometimes in such films, religion itself is shown failing. *The Day After* (1983), set in Lawrence, Kansas, during and after a "limited" nuclear war, includes a scene of Sunday-morning services in a bomb-damaged church. The pastor breaks down, sobbing inconsolably, during the scripture reading, his faith overwhelmed by the enormity of the destruction around him.

2. Emile Durkheim, *The Elementary Forms of the Religious Life*, trans. Karen E. Fields (1912; New York: Free Press, 1995).
  3. *Ibid.*, 392.
  4. *Nosferatu* was released in 1922 and was one of the earliest representations of the vampire on film. Similar to the vampires of *Stake Land,* he is obviously not human, but monstrous in his face and actions. See Alain Silver and James Ursini, *The Vampire Film: From Nosferatu to True Blood, Fourth Edition—Updated and Expanded* (Winona, MN: Hal Leonard Corporation, 2011).
  5. The original scripts for *Stake Land* were written to be a series of webisodes. Each one focused on a type of vampire just as *Zombieland* was intended to be a series featuring a new rule with each episode. When the scripts were eventually combined into a movie format the classifications of vampires was lost in the overall organization of the movie. However, the teeth and their importance remain intact through out the film. Only two classifications of vampires are noted outside of the "normal" vampires—berserkers and scamps. The berserkers are the oldest and least human vampires. The scamps are children who are vampires. Brandon Geist, "Exclusive Interview: 'Stake Land' Actor and Co-Writer Nick Damici on the Vampire Apocalypse," *Revolver*, August 5, 2011, http://www.revolvermag.com/news/exclusive-interview-stake-land-co-writer-and-actor-nick-damici-on-the-vampire-apocalypse.html.
  6. Silver and Ursini, *Vampire Film*.
  7. A similar type of vampiric plaque can be seen in the 2007 movie *I Am Legend*, which features monsters whose behavior closely resembles that of the monsters of *Stake Land*.
  8. W. Scott Poole, *Monsters in America: Our Historical Obsession with the Hideous and the Haunting* (Waco: Baylor University Press, 2011), 201–202.
  9. *Ibid.*, 202.
  10. The sacredness of the shopping-mall Santa is evident in the complex web of age-defined taboos that surround them. Adults, children too old to believe, and the actors who play Santa are proscribed from saying or doing anything that could conceivably weaken younger children's belief and thus sully their presumed innocence. Violations typically result in immediate (albeit subtle) signs of disapproval and correction from bystanders.
  11. Durkheim, *Elementary Forms*.
  12. Damici spoke about this focus on the two conflicting sides in his exclusive interview with *Revolver* magazine posted online on August 5, 2011, by Brandon Geist siting it as an intentional marginalizing of the vampires in the film.

BIBLIOGRAPHY

Cohen, Jeffrey Jerome, ed. *Monster Theory: Reading Culture*. Minneapolis: University of Minnesota Press, 1996.
Durkheim, Emile. *The Elementary Forms of the Religious Life*. Trans. Karen E. Fields. 1912. New York: Free Press, 1995.
Geist, Brandon. "Exclusive Interview: 'Stake Land' Actor and Co-Writer Nick Damici on the Vampire Apocalypse." *Revolver*, August 5, 2011. http://www.revolvermag.com /news/exclusive-interview-stake-land-co-writer-and-actor-nick-damici-on-the-vampire-apocalypse.html.
Poole, W. Scott. 2011. *Monsters in America: Our Historical Obsession with the Hideous and the Haunting*. Waco: Baylor University Press
Silver, Alain, and James Ursini. 2011. *The Vampire Film: From Nosferatu to True Blood, Fourth Edition—Updated and Expanded*. Winona, MN: Hal Leonard Corporation.
Stake Land. Dir. Jim Mickle. 2010. Dark Sky Films, 2011. DVD.

PART III

Horrors of Knowledge and Faith

"They're not in charge here"
The Collision of Religion and Science in [Rec] and Quarantine

BART BISHOP

Zombie films have, since George Romero's *Night of the Living Dead* (1968), frequently presented their undead monsters as a biological plague—products of scientific hubris. Two notable recent examples are *[Rec]* (2007), a Spanish found-footage horror film directed by Jaume Balagueró and Paco Plaza, and *Quarantine* (2008), its virtually shot-for-shot American remake, directed by John Erick Dowdle. Both films send similar main characters—a television news reporter and her camera operator—into a crowded apartment building where, unbeknownst to them, a zombie outbreak has recently taken hold. Until their respective final acts, *[Rec]* and *Quarantine* employ nearly identical plots. Both films, moreover, make extensive use of the found-footage conceit to lend their *mise-en-scène* an immersive quality evocative of the YouTube-and-camera-phone age of amateur video. The two films diverge only at the climax of the story, framing the secrets behind the zombie outbreak in utterly different terms.

[Rec] ultimately reveals itself to be a mash-up of the demonic-possession and zombie subgenres of horror. It involves a scientist-priest who, backed by the Church, kidnaps and experiments on a possessed young girl in the hopes of creating a vaccine capable of driving out demons from the bodies of those afflicted by them. The priest's experiments go horribly wrong, and the mutated vaccine escapes into the Barcelona apartment building where he has set up his secret laboratory, turning the residents into zombies. *Quarantine*, on the other hand, is conspicuously devoid of supernatural elements and, indeed, of any sign of organized religion. *Its* zombies are products of a mutated strain of rabies stolen from a government biological-weapons facility and spread through the building by rats. The individual responsible for creating them is not the agent of a mainstream church, but a member of a shadowy doomsday cult determined to bring about the end of the world.

Quarantine thus diverges from *[Rec]* in ways that highlight the cultural differences between Spain and America: the former shaped by the Catholic Church and fascist regimes and the latter by religious pluralism and secularism. *[Rec]* posits the existence both of divinity and of supernatural evil opposed by holy men, while taking aim at patriarchy and the institutions representing divinity on earth. *Quarantine*, by contrast, gives evil a human face rather than a demonic one and suggests that the end is nigh and no one will intervene to stop it. Changing the individual responsible for the zombie plague from a Catholic priest to a cultist dampens the associations of sexual abuse within the Church that are evident in *[Rec]*, but introduces equally clear echoes of American fears about fringe religious sects.

Both films, in exploring the effects of religion through their distinctive cultural lenses, come to the conclusion that man is, ultimately, corrupting the divine. This essay, then, will explore the cultural differences which lay behind the divergence in the two films' plotlines and themes, and which reveal the malleability of the zombie as a horror archetype able to support interpretations both divine and laic.

A Tale of Two Apartment Buildings

[Rec] follows reporter Ángela Vidal (Manuela Velasco) and her cameraman Pablo (Pablo Rosso) on a ride-along with a Barcelona fire company. Responding to a call at a dilapidated apartment building with an overwhelmingly immigrant population, they find an old woman screaming in her home. She bites a policeman, and things escalate quickly as the military arrives and seals off the building. The residents, diverse in backgrounds and ages, are relatable characters—a sharp contrast to the individuals who represent the shadowy government. A health inspector arrives on the scene and explains that the trouble is due to a rabies-like virus spread by a dog. This is the truth, but the health inspector is not aware of how the dog was infected or the supernatural origins of the events. Immediately following this revelation, however, the dog's owner, a young girl named Jennifer (Claudia Silva), bites her mother and flees upstairs. People panic as the zombies multiply, and Ángela and Pablo, along with firefighter Manu (Ferrán Terraza), attempt to escape through a drainpipe in the basement.

They retrieve the keys to access the drainpipe but are unable to make their way downstairs. Manu is overwhelmed in the process, and Ángela and Pablo are chased upstairs and forced into the penthouse apartment. The place is dilapidated, covered in newspaper clippings and religious paraphernalia, and dominated by a painting of the Virgin Mary. There they discover a tape recording explaining that Father Albelda, on orders from the Vatican, isolated the biological cause of demonic possession. It is heavily implied, however, that his methods went beyond their mandate. The ramshackle apartment indicates an unhinged mind, and his experiments are shown to have crossed the line separating the justifiable from the abominable. He kidnapped a young possessed girl to study, as well as other children—seemingly just one boy in *[Rec]*, but revealed to be many in the film's sequel, *[Rec] 2*—to use as test subjects for an anti-possession vaccine he hoped to create, but the vaccine mutated. The result is zombification, although the sequels reveal that the zombies operate as conduits and puppets, of sorts, for the original demon. Ángela and Pablo are attacked by the demon—once a girl, but now a hammer-wielding monster—Pablo is murdered and Ángela is dragged off-screen in a haunting final shot.

[Rec] 2 resolves any religious ambiguity in the first film's climax through a more overt portrayal not only of demonic possession, but also of priests performing religious rites in opposition to evil. These scenes reinforce one of the major themes of the series: the idea that, even in the face of corrupt religious institutions, individuals can gain power through belief in the divine. Plaza confirmed this in an interview: When asked about the

most important tool in a zombie apocalypse, he replied: "Faith. Faith and strong legs."[1] The film opens with a raid on the apartment building by Grupo Especial de Operaciones (GEO), special forces soldiers, seen through the forward-facing cameras mounted on their helmets. Ángela's recovered camera, and the camcorder carried by three children that break into the building, provide pretexts for the film's use of found footage. The soldiers are accompanied by Dr. Owen (Jonathan Mellor) who claims to be from the Ministry of Health, but turns out to be a priest sent to retrieve a blood sample from the possessed girl-turned-monster from the first film, Tristana Medeiros Da Souza. The GEO forces are quickly whittled down by a series of encounters with the infected, now pawns of Medeiros, who speaks through them—male and female alike—with an amplified, distinctively masculine demonic voice. The soldiers encounter first Ángela and later Medeiros, whom they kill. But before they can get a blood sample it is revealed that the demon has transferred itself into Ángela. The now-possessed reporter shoots Rosso—the remaining GEO soldier, played by Pablo Rosso—and tries to force Owen to order an evacuation of the building that will allow her to escape. When Owen refuses, she kills him too, and—expertly imitating his voice—gives the order herself and slips away in the confusion.

Quarantine, the American counterpart of *[Rec]*, opens with the same premise and setting, using found footage to portray reporter Angela Vidal (Jennifer Carpenter) and cameraman Scott Percival (Steve Harris) experiencing a night of terror in a zombie-filled apartment building. The key difference between the films begins with *Quarantine*'s casting of a member of a doomsday cult, rather than a priest, as the former occupant of the penthouse apartment and the root of the unfolding crisis inside the building. In *[Rec]* the instigator of the outbreak is an insider, and one respected within the community, but in *Quarantine* it is an outsider attempting to bring the system down. The penthouse

The power of God is invoked against an infected child, Jennifer (Claudia Silva), as Manu (Ferrán Terraza) restrains her in *[Rec]* (2007).

apartment itself is also drastically different, decorated not with religious iconography, but with glassware and other scientific equipment, as well as hundreds of cages holding rats—the research animals that initially spread the plague to the dog.² A similar tape recording contains only distorted chanting, but newspaper clippings on the walls reveal the tenant as a member of a doomsday cult and the source of the plague as a virus, stolen from a government bio-weapons lab. The man kidnapped a single young boy, who, we infer, is patient zero. The cult member is now the monster, but—unlike Medeiros in *[Rec]*, who possesses a malevolent intelligence—is too mindless to wield even a weapon as simple as a hammer. Here the only portrayal of religion is as a fallacy practiced by the insane—no counterexamples are offered. The world of *Quarantine* is thus presented in purely secular terms, with no answers for the source of evil. *[Rec]*, on the other hand, is sharply critical of holy institutions, but its sequels—even as they sustain the critique—confirm the spiritual power of individual holy men.

Horror in the Spanish Context

Catholicism is the largest religion in Spain, with about 68 percent of Spaniards self-identifying as Catholic.³ For centuries, it has been mainstream, prosperous, and formally entwined with the governmental and cultural power structure. Catholicism in the United States, though the largest single denomination in a religiously pluralist nation, has a history of being coded as poor, immigrant, ethnic, and above all "Other." This begins to explain the different trajectory of Spanish horror. Under Francisco Franco's dictatorship, "hindrance from the Catholic Church and Spanish government in the form of a Board of Censorship, which rigidly controlled or restricted motion picture content," kept Spanish cinema from flourishing for most of the 20th century.⁴ Spain "preferred to sanction tame and lighthearted domestic products that tended to reinforce Francoist hegemony rather than contradict or subvert it," but in the late 1960s that changed.⁵ Although Spanish film traditions "rely heavily on realism, musicals and comedy, to the extent that fantasy genres and thrillers were almost unprecedented for decades," one of the most popular genres during the dying days of Franco's far-right government—from 1967 to 1978—was horror.⁶ Classics like *The Living Dead at Manchester Morgue* (1974) resulted.

After the Franco regime fell, young upstart filmmakers reveled in their newfound freedom, and produced exuberantly brash and campy films. A fertile cinematic ecosystem was established, and within two decades "Spain suddenly emerged as one of the leading horror exporters on the planet. If it was the US in the 1970s and '80s, and Japan in the '90s, 2000 onwards has seen Spain emerge as the scariest country on Earth."⁷ Notable entries in Spain's horror canon include Alejandro Amenabar's *Thesis* (1996); Juan Antonio Bayona's *The Orphanage* (2007); Nacho Vigalondo's *Timecrimes* (2008); Almodovar's *The Skin I Live In* (2011); and of course, *[Rec]*.

[Rec] is a dual effort by co-directors Paco Plaza and Jaume Balagueró. Prior to *[Rec]*, Plaza made *Second Name* (2002) and *Romasanta: The Werewolf Hunt* (2004), while Balagueró's features include *The Nameless* (1999), *Darkness* (2002), and the *Fragile* (2005)—all horror. This specialization in horror films "with high production values and an original outlook" was a "step forward in Spanish fantasy film tradition, which had previously centered on cheaper and less sophisticated product."⁸ Plaza and Balagueró co-directed the first two while Plaza went solo for *[Rec] 3* as did Balagueró for *[Rec] 4*. They, along with

screenwriters Luis A. Berdejo (*Imago Mortis* [2009], *The New Daughter* [2009], and *Painless* [2012]) and Manu Diez (*The Nun* [2005]), maintained control of the series. Thus the filmmakers *in toto* share a dramaturgy, perspective, and aesthetic, mostly built around found footage, with *[Rec]*, a film that "proposes an extreme horror experience for the spectator, appropriate to its inherent peculiarities: the potential the narration acquires by taking place in real time, the realism obtained from the fact that the actors aren't very well known and, in short, the originality used to display elements from the zombie genre."[9] Part of a boom in found-footage horror that began in earnest with *The Blair Witch Project* (1999), *[Rec]* and films like it "spoke to cultural anxieties about the ubiquity of camera and surveillance technologies and amateur videography more generally, and interwove them with horror traditions that were decades old."[10]

Religion and Science Collide

Religion and science collide repeatedly in the *[Rec]* films, but the preternatural revelation in the first movie has little foreshadowing. The imagery and concepts permeating most of *[Rec]*'s 78-minute running time are familiar: the police and military sealing off the building in plastic tarps, the health inspector in hazmat suit, rabies spread by a dog and the time to catalyze depending on the victim's blood type. Real-world images evoke disease, government oppression, and the idea of people as collateral damage mimetically enough to terrify. The film even allows leeway for the infected to be berserk living beings rather than the undead, much like George Romero's *The Crazies* (1973) or Danny Boyle's *28 Days Later* (2002). This naturalistic interpretation of events remains plausible until the last 15 minutes of the film, which reveal that Father Albelda has been studying a young girl possessed by a demon. In hopes of curing possession through a vaccine, he accidentally weaponizes and unleashes it.

This is elaborated on in *[Rec] 2*, as film scholar CarrieLynn Reinhard points out: "[W]hile it was the Vatican trying to fix things by sending in Dr. Owen [in *Rec 2*] to create the antidote, it was also the Church that created the problem by trying to use scientific methods to produce a more modern approach to dealing with demonic possession. So, in a way, both religion and science are to blame for the zombie apocalypse."[11] The first two *[Rec]* films thus turn on a curious combination of criticizing the Church while leaving a backdoor that absolves it of blame. It is, after all, Albelda's obsession that is ultimately the problem. *[Rec] 2* even presents Owen as determined to seek a cure through a blood sample. He is desperate, but realizes that ritualistic rites only delay zombies.

The presentation of Albelda as both priest and medical researcher is not farfetched. The Vatican has supported science for centuries, with Jesuit priests—such as astronomer and mathematician Christopher Clavius, father of the Gregorian calendar—playing leading roles in numerous fields.[12] The Pontifical Academy of Sciences, given its current name and statutes by Pope Pius XI in 1936, bears a mission to "honour pure science wherever it may be found, ensure its freedom, and encourage research for the progress of science."[13] Summing up the relationship between science and scripture, Pope John Paul II in 1996 said: "[W]e will all be able to profit from the fruitfulness of a trustful dialogue between the Church and science."[14]

The filmmakers, however, envision a world in which the Church's involvement with science has gone horribly awry. Albelda's actions are cruel—not just illegal, but immoral—

and many people die as a result. He kidnaps Medeiros, experiments on her without her consent, and when the experiments fail, he seals her up in a secret room to starve to death instead of killing her outright, keeping her half-naked in perpetual darkness. He does the same with the young boy he keeps locked in the penthouse's attic, and with those found in the crawl space in *[Rec] 2*. The boys still resemble children, but are feral and smeared with dirt from head to toe, with little more than tattered pants to cover themselves.

The actions of Owen in *[Rec] 2*, and the interweaving of science and religion that they represent, are significantly more positive than Albelda's. As a test of its legitimacy, Owen holds a crucifix over Medeiros's blood and recites a religious mantra, intoning: "O omnipotent God, see my distress and come to my aid. Jesus, image of the Father, splendor of the eternal light … comfort for the abandoned, you who came into this world so compassionate of me, who went down to the hells, who resurrected amongst the dead, deliver us from our enemies, have compassion for us." This causes the crucifix to combust, although the sample is accidentally dropped, forcing them to seek out another. Owen also keeps an infected individual imprisoned in a room by hanging rosary beads on the door, and coerces information from another with a crucifix reciting: "In the name of God Almighty, who commands you, tell me where you are, under the protection of God. He gives me the power to walk over snakes, and vanquish my enemies. I will not fear the night terrors, nor the arrow that flies by day, nor the plague that stalks the darkness, in the name of the Father, the Son and the Holy Spirit, tell me where you are."

His heart and stature are pure, in opposition to ultimate evil, and the priest in the third movie takes this a step further by freezing crowds of infected victims in place. Albelda is, compared to his peers, corrupted by his decision to rely on science alone, rather than, like Owen, to find a balance between science and faith.

The films do not, however, present the Vatican as independent from Albelda's actions. When the situation in the penthouse-laboratory devolves, a "telegram from Rome" informs Albelda that "the Medeiros girl must die." On the tape recording, he confesses: "They're very nervous in Rome. Carboni called this morning. He ordered me to stop." As Reinhard provocatively suggests: "The tradition and superstition of exorcism gives way to medical science. Experimenting with children? A reflection of the perception of the Catholic Church after the child abuse scandal?"[15] The action here, as she suggests, brings to mind the child abuse scandals that have plagued the Church in the 21st century, with many recounting abuse that had gone on for decades. Revelations that the Church had known of and deliberately covered up the abuse—denying allegations while moving priests to other parishes when abuse recurred—badly tarnished its reputation. The events of *[Rec]* echo these real life events, while raising the moral stakes. The film depicts Medeiros—the experimental subject declared "expendable" by the Church—as a transformed, gaunt beast, but also shows a photograph of her as an innocent child in her confirmation dress. The connotations of priests preying upon the young and innocent is further emphasized in *[Rec] 2* when the police find files on children (presumably current and future experimental subjects) and rail against Owen in outrage.

It is not surprising that *[Rec]* uses the trope—popularized by *The Exorcist* (1973), and subsequently a staple of religiously themed horror films—of an innocent young girl possessed by, and made a puppet of, a powerful demon. Barbara Creed, writing of *The Exorcist* in terms that could apply to the trope in general, argues that "[h]orror emerges from the fact that woman has broken with her proper feminine role—she has 'made a spectacle of herself'—put her unsocialized body on display. And to make matters worse, she has done all of this before the shocked eyes of two male clerics."[16] Meideiros, though a slightly built girl, speaks through those she has infected with a masculine voice, echoing Regan in *The Exorcist*, and assumes masculine power by mimicking Owen over the radio in order to escape. Her transfer of the demon, and the possession, to Ángela is also significant. Whereas the mutated vaccine passes through bodily fluids, Ángela is infected—and thus possessed—"when the original girl basically sent a big worm like thing down her throat," a method that is "[v]ery sexual, very phallic."[17] The demon's snake-like form makes the parallel between possession and sexual assault inescapable, drawing horror from the spectacle of femininity forcibly penetrated, and permanently tainted, by male entities. The phallocentricity of demonic possession—demons are usually coded male and take over young girls—reinforces the impression of powerful male figures preying upon innocent children.

None of the women presented in the *[Rec]* series are capable of defeating the demons or even avoiding possession. The entire situation is framed in misogynistic terms, for "[e]ven as patriarchal rhetoric portrays powerful women as threats, it simultaneously tries to deny them any real power of their own, presenting them as only using or misusing power given to them by external male sources like Manon, Christianity's Devil, or various demons serving that patriarchal devil."[18] Their enemies, Catholic priests, are also only male.

Quarantine, *Secularism and Armageddon*

In *Quarantine*, the urban sprawl of Los Angeles serves the same purpose as that of Barcelona, the low-income apartment building filled with immigrants is unchanged, and the characters who respond to the crisis—firefighters, police officers, and the reporter and cameraman—are all virtually identical. Why, then, did the Dowdles change the ending—the 15 minutes that reveals what is actually behind the strange events in the building—but nothing else?[19] The change from a demonic possession aggravated by scientific hubris to a purely biological outbreak, and the shifting of blame from a Church-sponsored scientist to a member of a doomsday cult, bothered *[Rec]* co-director Balagueró. "I don't understand why they avoided the religious themes," he said, "they lost a very important part of the end of the movie." The Roman Catholic subplot of *[Rec]* is the precise feature that made the film so uniquely suited to Spanish audiences, while not considered as relevant to those in the United States.[20]

This argument is accurate to a point. There are 69.5 million American Catholics, making up 22 percent of the population.[21] These numbers, however, have not traditionally translated into broad-based cultural—let alone political—influence. America's political and cultural elites were, well into the 20th century, dominated by Protestants from northern and western Europe; Catholic immigrants from France, Spain, Mexico, Ireland, Germany, Italy and Poland were met with widespread prejudice and hostility. Only in the early 1960s, with the election of President John F. Kennedy (1960) and the publicity over the reforms imposed by the Second Vatican Council (convened from 1962 to 1965, and popularly known as Vatican II), did Catholicism begin to enter the American cultural mainstream.

A far more prominent influence in American culture—with roots as deep as the

Puritan-led Massachusetts Bay Colony of the 1630s—is an anticipation of Armageddon. Fascination with the end of the world, and close examination of current events for signs that it is at hand, is a *sui generis* American concern that cuts across denominational boundaries, and across the far-deeper divide between secular and religious worldviews. The Vatican II reforms, designed to demystify the mass and render it accessible and meaningful to a larger population, struck many tradition-minded Catholics as a sign of the Church's irreversible decay. On the fringes of the Catholic community, a "small but intense body of literature developed, linking these changes to satanic elements that had penetrated the Vatican."[22] Elsewhere in the American cultural landscape, "the radical mobilization of the sixties—civil rights, Black and Chicano Power, feminism, gay liberation, the antiwar movement, the legal push for secularization" created by an alliance of secular and religious reformers "destabilized the America that millions knew."[23]

Groups on the fringe of the American religious landscape became a convenient focus for anxieties over the breakdown of traditional American culture, the undermining of traditional American authority figures, and the growing rebelliousness of American youth—a role filled, in prior decades, by Catholics and Jews. Demonization of such groups led, as the 1970s gave way to the eighties, to a moral panic over the physical, emotional, and sexual abuse of young people at the hands of Satanists who used them in violent and sexualized rituals. The Satanic Ritual Abuse "crisis" eventually faded, undercut by a lack of evidence, but anxiety over cults—especially those obsessed with the end of the world—continued, fueled by the mass murder-suicide at Jonestown, Guyana (1978) and the ill-fated federal raid on the Branch Davidian compound at Waco, Texas (1993). The years after 9/11 saw Americans more fixated then ever on their nation's potentially imminent end, via nuclear war, global warming, chemical warfare, and of course biological contagion. This "millennial fever," manifested in everything from warnings about the Y2K bug, through the television show *Doomsday Preppers*, to the success of the *Left Behind* series of Christian adventure novels, includes a tendency "to perceive the world as absent intrinsic value, as existing penultimately as the means to an end."[24] This provides millennialists "with a philosophical basis to ignore civil law and engage in violence that some ... find irresistible."[25]

The major change to *Quarantine* with respect to *[Rec]* reflects this American millennialist fascination. The individual responsible for unleashing the virus is driven by ill intentions, not by good intentions taken too far, and any association with Catholicism is removed. These differences are fundamental. Albelda was trying to save humanity and accidentally caused a mutation. But *Quarantine* presents an unnamed individual whose only evident goal is bringing about the end times and whose beliefs, unlike Albelda's in *[Rec]*, are not revealed within the narrative. Both are punished—Albelda's desiccated corpse is found in *[Rec] 2*, and the cult member becomes the emaciated creature seen at the end of *Quarantine*.

Conclusion

Since Romero's *Night of the Living Dead*, zombies have epitomized the fatalism of man bringing about his own doom. There is no divine intervention with the undead, only the reminder that the universe is random and man should not play God. In Spain, however, an old European mentality persists in the face of cultural shifts. Man should

Reporter Angela Vidal (Jennifer Carpenter) is featured as a recurring character in both *[Rec]* (2007) and *Quarantine* (2008). Still from *Quarantine*.

not play God, but the punishment is not random. Outside forces are in play, and though righteous men have power, the existence of a benevolent God creates a binary. Evil corrupts, but only if man allows it. If faith is placed in the wrong things—science and institutions, rather than God—it can be perverted.

A distilled version of those ideas is evident in Jaume Balagueró and Paco Plaza's view of the world in the *[Rec]* series. They have not completely abandoned Catholicism, but see the religion as independent from the modern Church. They have created an allegory for sex scandals that tarnished the institution's representation, and play with the patriarchal nature of the Vatican and depictions of evil as male. Progress lies in the fact that they are not afraid to criticize.

The Dowdle brothers' *Quarantine*, on the other hand, attempts to avoid any political ramifications and inadvertently functions as a pointed commentary on the American collective consciousness. By playing upon similar, albeit stripped down, imagery and ideas, the Dowdles draw parallels between a fanatical cult and the Catholic Church, suggesting that there is little difference except for a divergence of intention. That the cult wants to end the world for unspecified reasons is, however, suitably American. Americans have a morbid obsession with the end times, but without a religious dimension, that obsession takes on cynical and depressing connotations. One can live without faith and appreciate the moment, but living in constant anticipation of oblivion is a futile existence.

The places where the two countries meet and where they diverge is a fascinating study. Both sets of filmmakers are restless and unsettled by the state of things, but where the Dowdles declare that life is pointless because it can be extinguished on a whim, Balagueró and Plaza hold out hope for something greater than themselves. It is telling that while *Quarantine* ends with Angela being dragged off to her death, Balagueró and Plaza, in the *[Rec]* films, return to the material to show that she lives. By positing that evil exists, they also allow for the possibility that there are ways to fight it. Without the presence of evil, the world of *Quarantine* is desolate and hopeless.

Notes

1. Michael J. Lee, "PACO PLAZA on '[REC] 2,'" *RadioFree*, June 2010, accessed May 18, 2016, http://movies.radiofree.com/interviews/rec2_paco_plaza.shtml.
2. In *[Rec] 2* it is mentioned on the tape recording that mosquitoes spread the virus.
3. "BARÓMETRO DE JUNIO 2015 AVANCE DE RESULTADOS," *CIS*, Centro De Investigaciones Sociologicas, June 2015, accessed May 19, 2016, http://datos.cis.es /pdf/Es3101mar_A.pdf.
4. Nicholas Schlegel, *Sex, Sadism, Spain, and Cinema: The Spanish Horror Film* (Lanham, MD: Rowman & Littlefield, 2015), xvii.
5. Ibid.
6. Alberto Mira, *The A to Z of Spanish Cinema* (Metuchen, NJ: Scarecrow Press, 2010), 165.
7. Phi De Semlyen and Helen O'Hara, "The Rise and Rise of Spanish Horror," *Empire Online*, May 19, 2011, accessed May 18, 2016, http://www.empireonline.com/movies/features /rise-rise-spanish-horror/.
8. Mira, *A to Z of Spanish Cinema*, 31–32.
9. "REC by Paco Plaza and Jaume Balagueró: Encouraging Presentation in Sitges," *Sitges Film Festival*, May 10, 2007, accessed May 18, 2016, http://sitgesfilmfestival.com/eng /noticies/?id=1002765.
10. Alexandra Heller-Nicholas, *Found-Footage Horror Films: Fear and the Appearance of Reality* (Jefferson, NC: McFarland, 2014), 87.
11. CarrieLynn Reinhard, "[REC] 2: When Possession Becomes Infectious," *It's Playing, Just with Research*, August 20, 2016, accessed May 18, 2016, https://playingwithresearch.com /2014/08/20/rec2-when-possession-becomes-infectious.
12. Agustin Udías, *Jesuit Contributions to Science: A History* (Heidelberg: Springer, 2015).
13. "Facts at a Glance," *The Pontifical Academy of Sciences*, accessed May 19, 2016, http://www.casinapioiv.va/content/accademia/en/about.html.
14. Doug Linder, "The Vatican's View of Evolution: Pope Paul II and Pope Pius," *Exploring Constitutional Conflicts*, UMKC School of Law, 2004, accessed May 19, 2016, http://law2.umkc.edu/faculty/projects/ftrials/conlaw/vaticanview.html.
15. Reinhard, "[REC] 2: When Possession Becomes Infectious."
16. Creed, *The Monstrous-Feminine: Film, Feminism, Psychoanalysis* (London: Routledge, 1993), 42.
17. Ibid.
18. Godwin, "Love and Lack: Media, Witches, and Normative Gender Roles," in *Media Depictions of Brides, Wives, and Mothers*, ed. Alena Amato Ruggerio, 91–100 (Lanham, MD: Lexington Books, 2012), 95.
19. Dowdle and brother Drew's changes with *Quarantine* are slight and obfuscated. They collaborated on three horror movies together, *The Poughkeepsie Tapes* (2007), *Quarantine* and *As Above, So Below* (2014), all of which have little in common aside from being found-footage. Consequently, there's no consistent concerns or through line across their oeuvre.
20. Heller-Nicholas, *Found-footage Horror Films*, 187.
21. "Celebration Guide/Guía De Celebració: Semana Nacional De Educacion Religiosa Parroquial National Parish Religious Education Week," National Catholic Educational Association, November 1–7, 2015, accessed May 19, 2016, https://www.ncea.org/sites /default/files/documents/_reled_parish_re_wk_celebration_guide_2015.pdf.
22. Bill Ellis, *Raising the Devil: Satanism, New Religions, and the Media* (Lexington: University Press of Kentucky, 2000), 109.
23. Andrew Hartman, *A War for the Soul of America* (Chicago: University of Chicago Press, 2015)
24. Paula D. Nesbitt, *Religion and Social Policy* (Walnut Creek, CA: AltaMira, 2001), 206.
25. *Ibid.*

Bibliography

"BARÓMETRO DE JUNIO 2015 AVANCE DE RESULTADOS." *CIS*. Centro De Investigaciones Sociologicas. June 2015. Accessed May 19, 2016. http://datos.cis.es /pdf/Es3101mar_A.pdf.
"Celebration Guide/Guía De Celebración: Semana Nacional De Educacion Religiosa Parroquial National Parish Religious Education Week." *NCEA*. National Catholic Educational Association. November 1–7, 2015. Accessed May 19, 2016. https://www.ncea.org/sites/default/files/documents/_reled_parish_re_wk_celebration_guide_2015.pdf.
Creed, Barbara. *The Monstrous-Feminine: Film, Feminism, Psychoanalysis*. London: Routledge, 1993.
De Semlyen, Phi, and Helen O'Hara. "The Rise and Rise of Spanish Horror." *Empire Online*, May 19, 2011. Accessed May 18, 2016. http://www.empireonline.com/movies/features/rise-rise-spanish-horror/.
Ellis, Bill. *Raising the Devil: Satanism, New Religions, and the Media*. Lexington: University of Kentucky Press, 2000.

"Facts at a Glance." *The Pontifical Academy of Sciences*. Accessed May 19, 2016. http://www.casinapioiv.va/content/accademia/en/about.html.
Godwin, Victoria L. "Love and Lack: Media, Witches, and Normative Gender Roles." In *Media Depictions of Brides, Wives, and Mothers*, ed. Alena Amato Ruggerio, 91–100. Lanham, MD: Lexington Books, 2012.
Hartman, Andrew. *War for the Soul of America: A History of the Culture Wars*. Chicago: University of Chicago Press, 2015.
Heller-Nicholas, Alexandra. *Found-footage Horror Films: Fear and the Appearance of Reality*. Jefferson, NC: McFarland, 2014.
Lee, Michael J. "PACO PLAZA on '[REC] 2.'" *RadioFree*, June 2010. Accessed May 18, 2016. http://movies.radiofree.com/interviews/rec2_paco_plaza.shtml.
Linder, Doug. "The Vatican's View of Evolution: Pope Paul II and Pope Pius." *Exploring Constitutional Conflicts*. UMKC School of Law, 2004. Accessed May 19, 2016. http://law2.umkc.edu/faculty/projects/ftrials/conlaw/vaticanview.html.
Mira, Alberto. *The A to Z of Spanish Cinema*. Metuchen, NJ: Scarecrow Press, 2010.
Nesbitt, Paula D. *Religion and Social Policy*. Walnut Creek, CA: AltaMira, 2001.
"REC by Paco Plaza and Jaume Balagueró: Encouraging Presentation in Sitges." *Sitges Film Festival*, May 10, 2007. Accessed May 18, 2016. http://sitgesfilmfestival.com/eng /noticies/?id=1002765.
Reinhard, CarrieLynn. "[REC]2: When Possession Becomes Infectious." *It's Playing, Just with Research*, August 20, 2016. Accessed May 18, 2016. https://playingwithresearch.com /2014/08/20/rec2-when-possession-becomes-infectious/.
Schlegel, Nicholas G. *Sex, Sadism, Spain, and Cinema: The Spanish Horror Film*. Lanham, MD: Rowman & Littlefield, 2015.
Udías, Agustin. *Jesuit Contributions to Science: A History*. Heidelberg: Springer, 2015.

Prince of Darkness
The Metaphysics and Quantum Physics of Evil

MATTHEW A. KILLMEIER

While horror and science fiction often overlap in their focus on unknown phenomena, the types of explanations on which their plots rely serve as key points of genre distinction. Horror routinely invokes religious or supernatural forces, and even horror-film monsters that appear to be products of the natural world often have supernatural dimensions. Science fiction, in contrast, deals almost exclusively with materialistic threats, and entities that may appear, at first, to be divine are ultimately revealed to be products of nature after all. Supernatural explanations exist in science fiction, just as naturalistic ones exist in horror, primarily as straw men: presented so that they can be overturned or explained away as familiar genre conventions take over.

John Carpenter's *Prince of Darkness* (1987) breaks this pattern by portraying a physics professor and a multi-disciplinary group of graduate students joining forces with a Roman Catholic priest in a battle against evil. A hybrid of horror and science fiction, the film depicts evil in both religious *and* scientific terms. For most of its narrative, religious and scientific explanations are given equal weight. Physics professor Dr. Howard Birack (Victor Wong), for example, posits that good and evil, God and Satan, may have physical equivalents—particles and anti-particles. Rather than rejecting the idea, the Priest (Donald Pleasance) engages Birack and the graduate students in a cerebral, ratiocinating dialogue involving spiritual and material conceptions of evil. The film fulfills horror conventions by referencing Catholic theology, visual signifiers of evil (dark lighting, shadows, a dilapidated church), and a monster (Satan) that threatens the characters, but simultaneously references scientific theories and natural phenomena—quantum mechanics, string theory, and light particles from a Precambrian supernova—to create a science-fictional atmosphere.

The storyline of *Prince of Darkness* revolves around the idea that evil—including Satan himself—can be understood in material rather than spiritual terms, and analyzed using the principles of quantum physics. This approach enlivens the story, and provides a refreshing infusion of non-mad science into a genre (supernatural horror) where it is rarely seen.[1] The film does more, however, than simply rewrite genre conventions. It also argues—implicitly throughout and explicitly in the climax—that science and religion are not necessarily antithetical. Made and released at a time when American fundamentalist Christians were vigorously promoting educational and public-health initiatives rooted in a literal reading of the Bible and American scientists were just as vigorously opposing them, such an inclusive discourse had clear political undertones.

The script of *Prince of Darkness* alludes, in multiple ways, to the work of British screenwriter Nigel Kneale: the creator of Professor Bernard Quatermass, whose adventures were the subject of three serials aired on the BBC in the 1950s. Carpenter wrote the screenplay under the pseudonym of Martin Quatermass and made one of the principal characters, graduate student Brian Marsh (Jameson Parker), a transferee from Kneale University. *Prince of Darkness* follows the Quatermass serials (and their subsequent film adaptations) by suggesting that, in many respects, religion's capacity to explain reality pales beside that of scientific reason. Satan, in the film, is a material being: a pre-biotic life form that begins to self-organize, influences some of the investigators through emissions of energy, and eventually takes over the body of one in a biological parasite-host relationship. Jesus, likewise, is presented not as a divine being but an extraterrestrial visitor whose followers hid this secret until humankind had become advanced enough to understand it. A similar rationalizing spirit is particularly apparent in *Quatermass and the Pit* (1958–59), in which the ghosts, poltergeists, and other supernatural apparitions that bedevil a London street known as "Hobbs Lane" are linked to an alien spacecraft buried there five million years before.[2] While the Quatermass franchise "rationaliz[ed] supernatural forces in scientific terms," *Prince of Darkness* never really dismisses religious explanations of the supernatural.[3] Instead, both religion and science remain relevant throughout the film, providing different but not contradictory narrative explanations.

Prince of Darkness draws on quantum theory to bolster its complementary treatment of religion and science. Throughout the plot, distinctions between the reality of classical mechanics and that of quantum mechanics drive key scientific explanations. One key difference is that in classical mechanics, matter is composed of particles and light is composed of waves, whereas in quantum mechanics matter is simultaneously both particle-like and wave-like—the pair existing in a state of "quantum superposition." The act of measurement or observation, according to quantum mechanics, collapses the both/and of quantum reality into the either/or dichotomy of classical reality. These distinctions also provide a metaphor for the film's handling of religion and science. *Prince of Darkness* holds that Satan can be both supernatural evil incarnate and a material phenomenon composed of antimatter, but the act of observation (or interpretation) and the observer's (or interpreter's) frame of reference determine which of these realities actually represents Satan. As Birack is a theoretical physicist, and several of the principal characters are his graduate students, the plot of the film provides multiple examples of these quantum principles, which undergird its intertwined understandings of the monster.

Plotting (Meta)Physics

Prince of Darkness begins with the last member of a secretive Catholic order known as the Brotherhood of the Sleep dying, alone, in a shuttered church in downtown Los Angeles. He is discovered by the Priest, who in turn seeks out Professor Birack and asks for his help. For two thousand years, the Priest explains, members of the Order have been the guardians of a dark secret "that can no longer be kept." Hidden in a catacomb beneath the church is a large, cylindrical vessel, locked from the inside, that contains a swirling, glowing green liquid. The Priest contends that the vessel contains Satan himself, long-dormant but now beginning to revivify. The Prince of Darkness's awakening is, the Priest believes, the reason for a cluster of unsettling phenomena he has been observing for the last month. Concluding that he and the Church are ill-equipped to tackle the threat alone, the Priest seeks the aid of Birack and science.

The natural and supernatural are juxtaposed throughout the film. Images of swarming red ants and the sun hanging in the sky just below a crescent moon—portents that evoke the language of religious prophecies—are juxtaposed with scenes of Birack and his students discussing the implications of quantum theory. The camera shows Brian watching a news report on an exploding supernova that has just become visible from Earth, but then cuts to the back of his television set to reveal that red ants are swarming inside it. In one scene, the Priest leads Birack deep into the catacombs—prompting the physicist to observe that the Brotherhood was "living in the 1500s"—and tells him that the strange sensation he feels is "[Satan's] power"; In the next, graduate students Catherine (Lisa Blount) and Walter (Dennis Dun) walk across a modern college campus in the bright sunlight, discussing difficult quantum-mechanics precepts.

These juxtapositions reinforce the film's pattern of presenting alternate explanations—religious and scientific—of a single phenomenon, reflecting quantum theory's challenge to dichotomous ways of thinking. It suggests, on one hand, that the vessel contains a natural, developing life form, and on the other, that it holds an awakening supernatural being. The contradictory information heightens suspense by preventing viewers from forming a clear idea of the vessel's contents.

Birack enlists a group of graduate students to stay at the church for the weekend in order to analyze the vessel, and—using the roomful of sophisticated equipment they bring with them—they amass a wealth of data on both the container and the contents. Susan (Anne Howard), a radiologist, determines that the vessel itself approximately seven million years old, and Brian, a physicist, determines that the life form inside is "growing out of pre-biotic fluid. It's not winding down into disorder. It's self-organizing. It's becoming something." An equally critical piece of information comes from Lisa (Ann Yen)—a student of ancient languages and the group's sole humanist—who translates a complex, multilingual manuscript, a palimpsest kept by the Brotherhood, revealing equations that Catherine, an applied physicist, enters into her computer. The immense age of the vessel, and the presence of differential equations in "a book written 2,000 years ago"—long before the invention of calculus in the mid–17th century—make it clear to the scientists that forces they do not (yet) understand are at work. The text of the book, though written from a religious perspective, points to a similar conclusion. It indicates that the vessel does, in fact, contain Satan; that Satan's father, who imprisoned him in it, was "a god who once walked the Earth before man, but was somehow banished to the dark side"; and that Christ was an extraterrestrial from a humanlike species who came to Earth to warn its inhabitants of the threat that Satan posed. After Christ's death, Lisa explains, his true origins were hidden by his disciples and by the Church, which chose to characterize Satan not as a material being but as the essence of pure evil.

Susan, alone in the room with the vessel while the others are gathered around the book, is watching the green liquid inside swirl and bubble when a stream of it—spewing through the gap between vessel and lid—suddenly strikes her in the mouth. Contact with the liquid brings her under the influence of Satan, a fate that also befalls her fellow students Mullins (Dirk Blocker), Calder (Jessie Ferguson), and Lisa. Two other members of the team try to leave the church, but the homeless people gathered outside—who have been brought under Satanic control by other means—cut them down with improvised weapons. Brian concludes that the green liquid can not only generate and direct bursts of energy, but that it is "conscious." Birack hypothesizes that its ability to act may be limited by its liquid state, and—in a discussion with the Priest that mixes science and theology—concludes that it is the offspring of an even-more-potent entity, an "anti–God," that bears the same relation to God that antimatter does to ordinary matter.

An image in the mysterious palimpsest text in *Prince of Darkness* (1987).

At this point most horror films would, with the presence of the monstrous firmly established and the characters gradually coming to recognize it as a threat, allow supernatural explanations of the events on screen to completely eclipse scientific ones.[4] In *Prince of Darkness*, however, scientific arguments remain in play, even though they become, temporarily, less prominent than those made by religion.

The un-possessed members of the group now begin to experience a shared vision that, the Priest explains, members of the Brotherhood (and anyone else close to the vessel) were also able to see. The dream begins with a dark, grainy video image of the front of the church accompanied by a distorted male voice. "This is not a dream," the voice intones. "We are using your brain's electrical system as a receiver. We are unable to transmit through conscious neuro-interference. You are receiving this broadcast as a dream." The dream sequence—shown on screen multiple times, but fully revealed to audiences only at the end of the film—begins outside the church's courtyard and moves inside it and toward the building, from which emerges a shrouded, backlit figure whose face is hidden. The voiceover continues. "We are transmitting from the year 1999. You are receiving this broadcast in order to alter the events you are seeing. Our technology is known to those with transmitters strong enough to reach your conscious state of awareness. But this is not a dream. You are seeing what is actually occurring for the purpose of causality violation." Causality here refers to the physics' principle that effects are temporally preceded by causes, which in theory could be violated by information being transmitted back in time from the future.

The uncanny nature of the shared dream leads to a vigorous discussion within the group of what the "dream" actually is and how it is being shared with them. As scientists, they are immediately drawn to the "how" question, quickly framing and discarding a range of hypotheses to explain it. Significantly, given the film's catholic approach to science and religion, these tentative explanations include the pseudo-scientific (precognition), the preternatural (premonitions), and the outright supernatural (omens). The group quickly settles, however, on an explanation grounded firmly in physics: that the "dream" is a recorded image of events that have transpired in the future, transmitted to the past using tachyons: theoretical particles that can travel faster than the speed of light and thus violate the principle of causality by triggering events that take place before they are transmitted. The dream, Brian concludes, is a warning from future scientists whose grasp of physics is more advanced than their own, a "sort of remote camera view of the future, so that we can change it." Immediately afterward, as if the unseen future scientists are confirming Brian's theory, a playing card that he has been manipulating between his fingers disappears without a trace. .

As if aware that the scientists have made a critical breakthrough, the liquid entity goes on the offensive. The power fails, and with it, the scientists' instruments, and the members of the group who have come into contact with the liquid begin to openly attack the Priest, Birack, and their fellow scientists. Susan and Lisa, two of those under Satan's control, bring the still-free Kelly—as yet untouched—into contact with the vessel. The remainder of the green liquid pours into her mouth, and she begins to metamorphose, her body becoming a new vessel for Satan: one with the ability to instantly regenerate and, crucially, to move about and directly manipulate physical objects. Finding a small pocket mirror, Kelly-Satan turns it into an interdimensional portal and reaches through it, attempting to bring the anti–God to Earth. The plot does not provide a clear explanation for the mirror-portal, but hints that Birack's anti-matter analogy—that the anti–God is a "mirror image" of God as the particles that make up anti-matter are mirror images of those that comprise ordinary matter—may be literally true, and that the "dark side" to which the anti–God belongs may be a parallel universe made up of anti-matter.

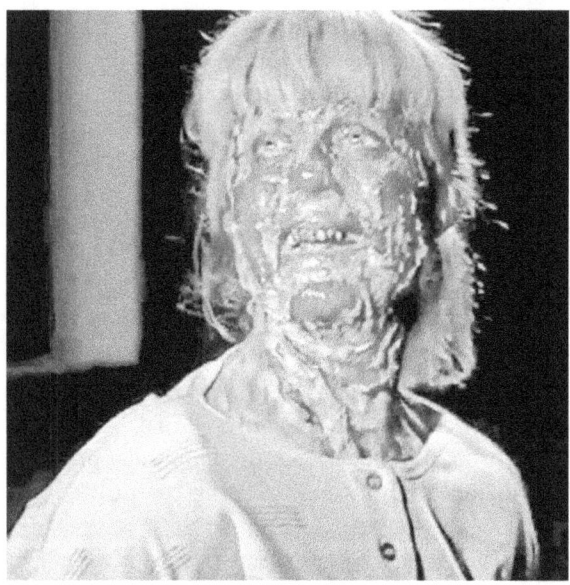

Kelly (Susan Blanchard), now merged with Satan, in *Prince of Darkness* (1987).

When the hand mirror proves too small to serve as a portal for Kelly-Satan's purposes, "she" finds a full-size one and, reaching through it, begins to pull the anti–God (represented by a forearm and hand with deep red skin, and conical black claws) into our world. The Priest hacks at Kelly-Satan with a fire ax, to no avail. She regrows a severed arm in seconds and casually reattaches her severed head. Desperate, Catherine tackles her and they both fall through the mirror-portal, which immediately returns to its solid state. The Priest, invoking the name of Christ, throws his axe at the mirror, shattering it and presumably imprisoning Satan, the anti–God, and Catherine on the dark side.

The survivors celebrate their victory over evil, and disperse, but a final scene suggests that the story may not be over. At home, in a bed he shared with Catherine during their brief affair earlier in the film, Brian experiences the full dream, and sees that the face of the hooded figure in the church is Catherine's. He wakes and, now convinced that she is trapped in the dark (anti-matter) universe, stretches his hand toward his bedroom mirror.

Supernatural, Natural, Both/And

Evil and good, throughout the film, are represented in both religious and scientific terms. The evil force trapped in the containment vessel is "the person of Satan who opposes God"[5] and who is described, in Revelation 12:9, as "the deceiver of the whole world."[6] Lisa translates a passage from the palimpsest that describes how "the Prince of Darkness was himself sealed, that old life, called the Devil and Satan, which deceiveth the whole world." Other portions of the palimpsest quote Revelation 17:5, which describes Satan as "Mystery, Babylon the Great, The Mother of Harlots, and the Abominations of the Earth," as well as the "Whore of Babylon."

Satan acts, throughout the film, in accordance with Catholic theology and horror-film convention. He functions as an unseen, active presence capable of manipulating the world around him, and exerts control over the natural world even before he begins possessing individuals. At several points in the film, the principal characters (the Priest, Birack, and Brian) see a crescent moon hanging just above the sun: proof, the Priest tells Birack, of Satan's power. Ants, maggots, roaches, and worms swarm inexplicably—seemingly controlled by some unseen power. When the group arrives at the church, the area's homeless people also seem to be under some form of invisible control—they stand around looking at the church, as if waiting for a sign. When the Priest arrives, a homeless woman tells him that it is wonderful that he is opening the church again; the camera reveals, however, she is holding a cup full of writhing maggots—suggesting that she, too, is corrupted and under Satan's control. Once Birack and his group enter the church, Satan manifests his ability to target and possess specific individuals. His first conquest, Susan, is sprayed with green liquid in a sacrilegious parody of a priest's anointing of the congregation with holy water. Later, Kelly's friends—now acting as Satan's minions—bring the vessel to her room so that he can take possession of her defenseless, sleeping body, She awakens to find the liquid pouring into her eyes and mouth from above, both literally and metaphorically violating her. The idea of Satan controlling humans aligns with Catholic beliefs about demonic possession, and Kelly—who, after her "pregnancy," acts and communicates as his corporeal representation—comes closest to representing the Catholic conception of possession. Consistent with the film's overall approach, however, Birack and his students offer alternate, scientific explanations of what is happening around them. Birack, searching for an explanation, reaches for biological analogies: "Worker ants, driven to a higher purpose, unknown to the individual; street people, our colleagues, all controlled." When Brian asks if Kelly might be a victim of "demonic possession," Birack acknowledges that this is a possibility, while simultaneously deprecating it as "not what we would expect, though. Never that." He then returns to more familiar ground, in the form of a biological explanation about organism complexity. "He controls simple organisms easily. But maybe he needs something more complex to complete a life cycle, a host in which to live," Birack theorizes, settling on the well-understood parasite-host relationship. Brian even offers a (pseudo-) scientific explanation for Kelly-Satan's ability to move objects by thought: "If it can transmit a signal strong enough, it can move other objects instantaneously across a distance without outside intervention: psychokinesis."

This juxtaposition of, and tension between, physics and metaphysics deepens as the Priest, Birack, and the students discover the true origins of Satan and Jesus. *Prince of Darkness* follows Catholic dogma in linking Satan and evil, but diverges from the Church's teaching that Satan is an angel who was good when he was created but became evil as he rejected God. It presents Satan not as one of God's creations, but as the son of "a god who once walked the earth before man, but was somehow banished to the dark side." Jesus's origin is, likewise, modified in the film. According to the palimpsest, Jesus was "of extraterrestrial ancestry" and came to warn the human race about Satan trapped in the container. Jesus was killed because officials determined he was mad and gaining too much power. His disciples kept Satan's material existence and containment secret until science became advanced enough to back Christ's claims. The Priest deduces that the Church decided "to characterize pure evil as a spiritual force, even within the darkness in the hearts of men. It was more convenient; in that way man remained at the center of things."

The protagonists of *Prince of Darkness*—the Priest, Birack, and the other scientists— are thus obliged to confront a truth previously known only to the Brotherhood of Sleep: that, far from standing at the center of Creation, humans are insignificant parts of a vast, complex universe. The resulting disorientation is profound both for characters on both sides of the science-religion divide, but for different reasons. The Priest, confronted with evidence that evil is material rather than spiritual, is appalled that he (and, for two thousand years, his fellow clergy) have been spreading a lie in the guise of the truth. The deception was, he concludes, a ruthlessly practical choice on the part of the Church. If evil is material rather than spiritual, then ideas such as free will, the autonomous ego, and human agency—central to the Church's moral teaching—would be undermined, and the Church's authority would be brought to the brink of collapse. Birack and his students are less troubled by this de-centering of humanity (it is, to them, a familiar side effect of the work of Copernicus, Darwin, Freud, and other scientists). *Their* disorientation comes from the realization that Satan and Jesus are real, and that "evil" is not an abstract moral concept but a material reality that, as the Priest says, "lives in the smallest parts" of the universe ... "in the atoms ... smaller ... invisible ... he [the anti-God] lives in all of it."

The film reinforces, visually, this shared sense of a familiar world dissolving into something strange and terrifying. It situates people "at the bottom of a cosmic hierarchy," in part through close-up shots of a full moon and an off-kilter sky.[7] The large cast works against audience identification with any one character, and viewers are given no information about, and little opportunity to become emotionally invested in, even the four principals: Birack, the Priest, Brian, and Catherine. A romance develops between the latter pair, and the former are clearly old friends, but both relationships figure so slightly in the plot that few viewers likely experience any affective resonance.[8] This stymieing of emotional identification keeps the focus of the film squarely on cosmic forces, turning humans into insignificant figures buffeted by them. It thus underscores a worldview that modern science matter-of-factly embraces, and Christianity fiercely rejects: that the universe, far from being created for and centered on humans, is indifferent to them and their emotions. People are, *Prince of Darkness* suggests, no more significant than insects— easily falling under Satan's control and "living in a much larger universe than they can possibly suspect."[9] Satan stirs from his long confinement not because of anything humans do (or fail to do), but because a stream of particles emitted hundreds of millions of years ago by a distant supernova finally reaches Earth and interacts with the liquid in the ancient vessel.

Such potentially bleak aspects of the film are tempered, however, by the collaboration between the Priest, Birack, and the scientists in fighting a monster that threatens humanity. Carpenter uses the dialogue that establishes this partnership to dramatize the film's unification of metaphysics and physics. Birack posits that if God, "a universal mind controlling everything," wills the actions of every subatomic particle, then it follows that each particle must have an anti-particle, "its mirror image, its negative side," and that an anti–God must therefore exist, bringing darkness and chaos to the world instead of light and order. Birack's musings suggest an alternate, materialist explanation for evil, but also a guide for understanding the film's treatment of religion and science. Religion, as represented by the Priest, accepts that evil is material, and the tools of science are necessary to understand it; science, as represented by Birack, comes to terms with the presence of ancient, immensely powerful beings that can manipulate the material world at will. Each, in other words, finds a place for their other's ideas within their own worldview.

The film's depiction of an alliance between science and religion also refashions the horror genre's frequent presentation of scientists—and by extension science—as dangerously delusional and monomaniacal. Science and scientists are, in *Prince of Darkness*, integral parts of the group that stops Satan. They help defeat evil, and in no way are they implicated it its rise.[10] Religion alone cannot defeat a revivifying devil, the Priest realizes, and despite all the theories, data, and sophisticated instruments at their disposal, Birack and his grad students also are ill-equipped to battle evil on their own. A budding physicist, rather than the Priest, ultimately thwarts Satan's plan, and it could be argued, following critic Bryan Dietrich, that the film casts science in the role once played by the Church.[11] However, Satan and his father are defeated neither through science nor religion as such, but through the Christ-like self-sacrifice of Catherine, who—as Birack tells Brian at the end of the film—"died for us."

Prince of Darkness *and 1980s Culture Wars*

Prince of Darkness, by treating religion and science as having complementary explanatory power, also provided its audiences with a subtle critique of contemporaneous U.S. culture wars, in which science was often at the heart of debate. Christian fundamentalists had, since the anti-evolution crusades of the 1920s, seen science as a handmaiden of liberal secularism and a threat to their values and beliefs. When they rose to prominence in U.S. politics in the late 1970s, allying themselves with the conservative wing of the resurgent Republican Party to form the "religious right," they acted, aggressively, to limit what they saw as the corrosive effects of science on morality.

The campaign suffered a setback during the 1980s, when courts rejected fundamentalist-sponsored laws requiring that evolution and "creation science" (an interpretation of the history of the Earth, and the history of life, derived from a literal reading of the Bible) be given equal time and attention in public-school science classrooms. In *McLean v. Arkansas* (1983), for example, a U.S. district court ruled that the state of Arkansas's 1981 law mandating the teaching of "creation science" contravened the First Amendment's establishment clause as it attempted to teach religious belief in public schools. This decision was made binding nationally by the U.S. Supreme Court's ruling in *Edwards v. Aguillard* (1987) that overturned a similar 1981 Louisiana law. "Creation science," these rulings indicated, was not science at all but religious doctrine, placing both states' laws in violation of the "establishment clause" of the First Amendment.

Conservative interpretations of Christianity fared better, and science fared worse, in debates over public health. North Carolina senator Jesse Helms, who shared the view of many on the religious right that AIDS was God's punishment for the sin of homosexuality, enacted a 1987 ban on travel or immigration to the U.S. by individuals with HIV. The religious right also challenged the efficacy of condoms in preventing AIDS, and criticized condom distribution programs—which they believed encouraged premarital sex and increased promiscuity—while promoting abstinence-only sex education programs in public schools. A parallel campaign by the religious right led to a federal ban on needle-exchange programs, which they claimed bolstered illegal drug usage. As with the teaching of evolution in public schools, the religious right perceived science-based efforts to address HIV-AIDS as immoral and likely to further the spread of a godless, materialistic culture. In these cases and others since—anthropogenic climate change, stem-cell research, and sexuality (contraception, abortion, in vitro fertilization)—the religious right has regarded science as one of its principal enemies in the culture wars.

By depicting religion as open to and informed by science, and suggesting that the two fields were not contradictory but potentially complementary, *Prince of Darkness* tapped into a different way of thinking. It thus shared common ground with the views of prominent scientists, such as Kenneth R. Miller, a molecular biologist at Brown University, and Stephen Jay Gould, a Harvard paleontologist and evolutionary biologist. Each scientist served as a witness in significant trials on the teaching of "creation science." For Miller, a Catholic, the fundamentalist idea that religion is threatened by science was erroneous because "the question of God is a nonscientific one and therefore is entirely beyond our reach as scientists."[12] Questions of first cause, Miller argued, "properly belong to the realms of philosophy and theology."[13] Like all scientific theories, biological evolution does not include or exclude a creator. Miller saw the push for teaching "creation science" as attempting "to establish a false duality" between a supernatural creator and biological evolution and exhorting students to choose between purposely distorted positions.[14]

An atheist and a popular public intellectual, Gould saw science and religion separate, but complementary, domains of knowledge that he dubbed Non-Overlapping Magisteria (NOMA).[15] Science, Gould argued, attempts to ascertain the facts of the natural world and explain its character and functioning by advancing empirically informed theories. In contrast, religion concerns "the equally important, but utterly different, realm of human purposes, meanings, and values—subjects that the factual domain of science might illuminate, but can never resolve."[16] Gould advanced a principle of "respectful non-interference" between the two fields, based on two claims: "First, that these two domains hold equal worth and necessary status for any complete human life; and second, that they remain logically distinct and fully separate in styles of inquiry, however tightly we must integrate the insights of both magisteria to build the rich and full view of life traditionally designated as wisdom."[17]

Prince of Darkness proceeds from assumptions similar to Gould's. It consistently acts as if science and religion as are of equal worth, and both are necessary for a full, complete view of a problem, particularly one with natural and supernatural facets. The Priest reaches out to Birack for assistance with the vessel and its contents, and Birack agrees to help and enlist the efforts of his students. Indeed, the film suggests that the collaboration has precedent. According to Brian, Birack engaged in a series of BBC-sponsored debates with the Priest, a reaffirmation that religion and science have equal status. *Prince of Darkness* also, however, upholds Gould's claim that religion and science are, for the most part, logically distinct. The Priest relies upon exegesis for deriving knowledge, first learning of the vessel and its contents through the diary of a member of the Brotherhood. He also, at least initially, filters what he learns from Birack and the other scientists through Catholic dogma and Biblical texts. The iconography of the chamber where the vessel is kept—numerous candles provide the chief light source in the basement and crucifixes adorn practically all the wall space—creates strong associations with religion and the supernatural, suggesting the Church's belief in the power of religious signs to keep Satan trapped and dormant. In contrast, Birack and his students are depicted using a variety of instruments to analyze aspects of the vessel and computers to calculate equations from the palimpsest, which conveys science's empirical orientation and commitment to objective analysis.

The film shows that both religion and science use approaches driven by their respective theoretical positions, but are open to new information. This is most clear with the Priest. He holds firm his dogma-derived interpretations that the liquid is Satan and that Satan is the chief evil force in the world, but he becomes persuaded by Birack and his students that Satan also has a natural, material basis. The Priest's commitment to religious dogma regarding Christ's divinity and the Church's concomitant teachings seem to suffer as a result of revelations derived from the palimpsest (although these come courtesy of the translations of a theology student). Many of the graduate students seem skeptical of the Priest and religious explanations, but key narrative developments—the seeming possession of some of their colleagues and especially Kelly's transformation—lead them to accommodate religious explanation, though not to abandon science.

The film does violate NOMA in suggesting that science may be able to prove elements of religious doctrine, an idea that both Gould and Miller find problematic. After Birack and the students decamp at the church, the Priest tries to enlist Birack in helping to persuade the public that Satan is real. "You must prove it scientifically," he tells Birack; "convince the outside world." Later, Lisa summarizes part of what she has translated from the palimpsest about Christ's disciples keeping secret his extraterrestrial ancestry "until man could develop a science sophisticated enough to prove what Christ was saying." Both examples illustrate what Gould decries as syncretism, "the oldest fallacy of all … where the facts of science reinforce and validate the precepts of religion, and where God shows his hand (and mind) in the workings of nature."[18] However, these exceptions alter neither the film's handling of religion and science nor the subtle criticism it offers. *Prince of Darkness* suggests that religion and science are not antagonists, as some culture warriors hold, and it indicates that problems drawn from the two fields' respective domains can be addressed collaboratively.

Conclusion: Ghosts and Shadows

Prince of Darkness strongly implies that common sense is the enemy of understanding, inhibiting belief in Satan *and* the more elegant principles of physics. In both cases, the film suggests, common sense prevents observers from seeing larger truths. Early in the film, Catherine and Walter are introduced through a discussion of Schrödinger's cat, a quantum physics thought experiment in which a cat is placed in an opaque box along with a mechanism that will feed the cat either food or poison. In classical mechanics, if we opened the box and observed its contents the cat would either be dead or alive. Our observation thus confirms a physical reality. Whereas with quantum mechanics, the cat is both dead and alive at the same time until we observe its contents. "The point is,"

Catherine says, "until the cat is observed by someone, he's not in any definite state, either alive or dead. He's in a wave superposition state, both dead and alive at the same time." Walter replies that this makes no sense. Catherine concurs, noting that this is the point of the thought experiment. "Our common sense breaks down on a subatomic level," she says, echoing a point that Birack makes in a lecture on quantum mechanics. "Say good-bye to classical reality," he tells his class, "because our logic collapses on the subatomic level, into ghosts and shadows." Just as the common-sense logic of classical mechanics hinders our understanding of quantum theory, Birack's empiricist science inhibits his ability to understand the swirling green liquid as Satan. "It's your disbelief that powers him," the Priest says, "your stubborn faith in—in common sense—that allows his deception."

The main characters in the film—Catherine, Brian, Birack, and the Priest—all, however, successfully overcome these limitations. Casting off the constraints imposed by the worldviews of their respective fields, they come to recognize that Satan cannot be fully understood in purely religious *or* purely scientific terms—that he is both supernatural *and* natural. Birack and the Priest undergo the most profound transformations, each recognizing that the worldview he has spent a lifetime learning, refining, and defending is, in fact, only one aspect of a more complex picture. Both thus instantiate the seer figure that is a fixture of religious horror: the individual whose transcendent perception and erudition allows them to grasp the larger truths that remain hidden to others. What Birack and the Priest know, that less enlightened scientists and clergy do not, is that there is a reality greater than their respective fields can account for alone, and that it is only through collaboration that they can hope to grasp that reality and contain the evil that dwells there.

Notes

1. Bryan Dietrich, "Prince of Darkness, Prince of Light," *Journal of Popular Film and Television* 19, no. 2 (1991): 91–96.
2. The supernatural elements in *Quatermass and the Pit* run even deeper: An alien symbol consisting of five interlocked circles suggests the occult pentacle, and one character notes that "Hobbs Lane" was originally "Hob's Lane"—a reference to "Old Hob," one of the Devil's many nicknames.
3. Peter Nicholls, "Prince of Darkness," in *The Encyclopedia of Science Fiction*, ed. John Clute and Peter Nicholls (New York: St. Martin's, 1993), 962.
4. Noël Carroll describes these, respectively, as the "onset" and "discovery" phases of a horror narrative; see *The Philosophy of Horror* (New York: Routledge, 1990), 99–100.
5. Vatican, *Compendium of the Catechism of the Catholic Church* (Vatican City: Vatican Publishing House, 2005), http://www.vatican.va/archive/compendium_ccc/documents/archive_2005_compendium-ccc_en.html.
6. U.S. Conference of Catholic Bishops and Vatican Publishing House, *Catechism of the Catholic Church* (Vatican City: Vatican Publishing House, 1997), 685.
7. John Muir, *The Films of John Carpenter* (Jefferson, NC: McFarland, 2000), 141.
8. Colin Odell and Michelle Le Blanc, *John Carpenter* (Harpenden, UK: Pocket Essentials, 2001), 56.
9. Ibid.
10. Dietrich, "Prince of Darkness," 91–92.
11. Ibid.
12. Kenneth R. Miller, "Scientific Creationism versus Evolution: The Mislabeled Debate," in *Science and Creationism*, ed. Ashley Montagu (New York: Oxford University Press, 1984), 59.
13. Kenneth Miller, "Answers to the Standard Creationist Arguments," *Creation/Evolution* VII (Winter 1982): 5.
14. Miller, "Scientific Creationism," 61.
15. Ibid., 5.
16. Stephen Jay Gould, *Rock of Ages: Science and Religion in the Fullness of Life* (New York: Ballantine, 1999), 4.
17. Ibid., 58–59.
18. Ibid., 212.

BIBLIOGRAPHY

Carroll, Noël. *The Philosophy of Horror, or Paradoxes of the Heart*. New York: Routledge, 1990.
Dietrich, Bryan. "Prince of Darkness, Prince of Light: From Faust to Physicist." *Journal of Popular Film and Television* 19, no. 2 (1991): 91–96.
Gould, Stephen Jay. *Rock of Ages: Science and Religion in the Fullness of Life*. New York: Ballantine, 1999.
Miller, Kenneth R. "Scientific Creationism versus Evolution: The Mislabeled Debate." In *Science and Creationism*, ed. Ashley Montagu, 18–63. New York: Oxford University Press, 1984.
Miller, Kenneth R. "Answers to the Standard Creationist Arguments." *Creation/Evolution* VII (Winter 1982): 1–13.
Muir, John K. *The Films of John Carpenter*. Jefferson, NC: McFarland, 2000.
Nicholls, Peter. "Prince of Darkness." In *The Encyclopedia of Science Fiction*ed. John Clute and Peter Nicholls, 961–962. New York: St. Martin's Press, 1993.
Odell, Colin, and Michelle Le Blanc. *John Carpenter*. Harpenden, UK: Pocket Essentials, 2001.
United States Conference of Catholic Bishops and Vatican Publishing House. *Catechism of the Catholic Church* (Second Edition). Vatican City: Vatican Publishing House, 1997.
Vatican. *Compendium of the Catechism of the Catholic Church*. Vatican City: Vatican Publishing House, 2005. http://www.vatican.va/archive/compendium ccc/documents/archive_2005_ compendium-ccc-en.html.

The Folly of Faithlessness in *Dracula Has Risen from the Grave*

MARTIN F. NORDEN

It's not often that an actor criticizes a film in which he or she has just appeared, especially if it's a box-office hit. Such was the case, however, when Christopher Lee went public with his views on *Dracula Has Risen from the Grave* (1968), his third outing as Dracula for Hammer Film Productions Ltd. In an interview published in January 1969— only two months after the film's record-setting premiere in Britain and well ahead of its release in other countries[1]—Lee had little positive to say about the production. He had kind words for director Freddie Francis, but in general the tone of his commentary ranged from lukewarm to condemnatory. The aspect of *Dracula Has Risen* that rankled him the most was a scene late in the film in which a youthful protagonist plunges a wooden stake into Dracula's chest while a priest looks on. Despite the excessive gore that ensues, the action has no lasting effect; the vampire shockingly pulls out the stake and flings it back at the hapless hero. "It was all wrong that Dracula should have been able to remove the stake," Lee grumbled. "Everyone knows a stake through the heart is the very end of a vampire. I objected at the time, but it was overruled."[2]

Though experts in vampire lore would certainly agree with Lee's assessment, audiences reacted to this singular moment in a remarkably different way; they were completely fascinated by it. Even the saturnine Lee, who prided himself on his knowledge of all things Dracula,[3] was forced to admit that "the scene made a tremendous impact on the screen" and that "the audience at the time thought it was stunning."[4] It is a key moment in a film that enjoyed enormous popular and financial success around the world.

This powerful scene and the movie itself are best understood in terms of *Dracula Has Risen from the Grave*'s considerable religious dimensions; in particular, the fellow who drove the stake into Dracula's heart was an avowed atheist and the onlooker a lapsed cleric, and the film makes it clear that their faithlessness accounted for the staking's failure. It's not hard to imagine the series of larger questions that the Hammer filmmakers asked themselves as they developed the film's premise: What if Dracula's adversaries included protagonists who had lost, or never held, spiritual values? Would the traditional Christian objects and rituals observed in Bram Stoker's 1897 novel *Dracula* and earlier Dracula films have any effect? If not, what tools and strategies for combatting consum-

Dracula unplugged: the vampire (Christopher Lee) wields the bloody wooden stake that he pulled out of his own chest just moments before in *Dracula Has Risen from the Grave* (1968).

mate evil would be available to such "faith-free" characters? In the course of answering these questions, the resulting film reveals contentious perspectives on the Roman Catholic Church and the Church of England in both the latter's High and Low doctrinal strands, particularly regarding the value of certain religious rituals and accouterments—crosses, crucifixes, and Communion wafers among the latter—as ingredients in the noble quest to defeat the evil that Dracula represents.

This essay explores the religious themes and motifs of *Dracula Has Risen from the Grave* and their connections to Stoker's novel. Though the film is no masterpiece—indeed, I find its occasional crudeness of construction and uneven continuity to be part of its appeal—I hope to show that it holds a complex set of perspectives on the place of religious symbols, ritual, and faith (or lack thereof) in the struggle against vampiric evil.

Hammer Predecessors

Dracula Has Risen from the Grave was born of economic imperatives, and it is well worth examining the immediate context of its production. The film resulted from a confluence of factors, including Hammer's previous successes, market-driven philosophy, and rush to get the film into production. Various socio-historical factors also came into play, such as church and graveyard desecrations in the UK during the 1960s and, more broadly, the questioning of God's existence and the decline of spiritual values in the decades following World War II.

The main force behind the film was a mild-mannered, affable fellow named Anthony Hinds. A screenwriter and producer known for his creativity while working within budgetary restraints, Hinds had produced one of Hammer's most famous and profitable films to that point: 1958's *Horror of Dracula*, starring Christopher Lee as the title character and Peter Cushing as his chief nemesis, Prof. Van Helsing. Written and directed respectively by Hammer stalwarts Jimmy Sangster and Terence Fisher, *Horror of Dracula* grew into a global phenomenon.[5] Its stupendous—one might even say monstrous—popularity prompted the Hammer forces to consider developing a sequel, perhaps a whole series of sequels if audience demand persisted.

In 1966, the studio created the first of many sequels to feature Lee as the Count: *Dracula Prince of Darkness*, which tells the story of two English couples on holiday in the Carpathians and their deadly encounters with Dracula. Hinds knew going into the production that Peter Cushing would be unavailable to play Van Helsing,[6] so he had screenwriter Jimmy Sangster convert the character into an explicitly religious figure: Father Sandor, a Catholic priest who comes to the aid of the English tourists.[7] *Dracula Prince of Darkness* turned the standard Dracula narrative into an expressly religious battle of good and evil, from the powerful presence of its rifle-toting priest to its titular reference to Dracula as the "Prince of Darkness," a label far more commonly applied to Satan.

An embodiment of Hammer's renowned market-driven approach to filmmaking, *Dracula Prince of Darkness* was designed not only as a follow-up to *Horror of Dracula* but also as a lead-in to an as-yet-undeveloped sequel that would become *Dracula Has Risen from the Grave*. Terence Fisher argued that *Dracula Prince of Darkness* and *Dracula Has Risen* should not be regarded as narrative continuations of *Horror of Dracula*. "I don't think you can call them sequels in a continuity at all," he said. "You've got to approach [each film] out of context, with its own context, only not related to what has gone before."[8] Fisher had a point; except for the sanguinary title figure, each film features a completely different set of characters from the others in the series. Despite Fisher's disclaimer, however, *Dracula Has Risen* does build on a major event at the end of *Dracula Prince of Darkness*, and a brief reconstruction of the latter film's conclusion is therefore in order.

Dracula Prince of Darkness ends with a series of clashes involving Dracula, his minion Klove (Philip Latham), Father Sandor (Andrew Keir), and the surviving British tourists, Diana and Charles Kent (Suzan Farmer, Francis Matthews), as the characters speed toward Castle Dracula. Here is Sangster's own summary: "Dracula escapes with Diana in a wagon driven by Klove. Sandor and Charles intercept the wagon and Charles shoots Klove. The wagon crashes and Dracula's coffin falls from it onto the frozen surface of the castle moat. Charles struggles with Dracula until Sandor recalls that running water is fatal to the undead. He directs his rifle fire at the ice around Dracula's feet. The ice gives way and, as Charles runs to safety, Dracula slips to his doom in the icy water."[9] Dracula thus ends up frozen under the ice in a rivulet that encircles his castle. This fate—a sort of cryogenic suspended animation—is notably different from that which befell Lee's character in *Horror of Dracula*, in which he famously withers into a pile of dust after Van Helsing exposes him to sunlight and holds him at bay with two crossed candlesticks. As Fisher himself readily acknowledged, *Dracula Prince of Darkness* had set the stage for another go-round.[10]

A Tortuous Production Process

Hinds was eager to get a third Dracula/Lee film quickly into production but ran into numerous issues that threatened to derail the project. By the 1960s, Hammer had turned into a veritable movie factory with a highly active and complicated production schedule. Swamped in work as a studio executive, Hinds decided to turn over the film's production reins to Aida Young, a Hammer associate producer. Young, however, had no prior experience producing horror films; in fact, she had never even seen one, a situation that she redressed by sitting through a half dozen such movies in a row once Hinds had given her the assignment. "I'd never been to see a horror film in my life and I staggered out into the sunshine feeling quite sick and terrified," she said after her binge-watching experience. Nevertheless, she approached the project with the professionalism of a seasoned trouper. "When you're making a picture you throw yourself into it—even with Dracula," she said.[11]

Other concerns surfaced. Jimmy Sangster, the studio's go-to screenwriter who had crafted the scripts for more than two dozen films produced between *Horror of Dracula* and *Dracula Prince of Darkness*, was uneasy with the prospect of writing yet another horror film. "I am not and have never been a particular fan of the Gothic horror cinema, even my own. Correction: *especially* my own," he wrote.[12] Sangster had already signaled his ambivalence toward the genre by insisting on a pseudonym, "John Sansom," for the *Dracula Prince of Darkness* credits and, heavily involved in other Hammer projects, begged off of the new one.

Known for his non-confrontational and good-humored executive style, Hinds acceded to Sangster's request.[13] Sensing an opportunity to contain costs, Hinds decided to construct the script himself under his own longstanding *nom de cinéma*, "John Elder." Intriguingly, he and fellow Hammer executive James Carreras had prepared pre-sales materials for *Dracula Has Risen* in August 1967, well before Hinds had actually developed a script or even a narrative summary for it.[14] In their haste to make a deal, Hinds and Carreras pre-sold the film to the studio's distributor, Warner Bros.–Seven Arts, with a promise of Lee in the title role even though the actor had not yet formally agreed to participate. Lee, who had grown disenchanted with Hammer's Dracula franchise (he had no dialogue in *Dracula Prince of Darkness*, which made it difficult for him to channel Stoker's erudite and urbane Count), found himself being roped into the production. As he remembered: "I got a call at home from Jimmy Carreras saying, 'You must do this film, on my knees, I beg you. Do you know how many people you will keep from working at Hammer if you don't agree to do this film?' It really was a form of emotional blackmail."[15] While Carreras cajoled Lee into reprising the Count, Hinds under intense deadline pressure began developing a script that traded on Hammer's Dracula brand but required fresh and timely twists. Aware of Terence Fisher's flair for depicting Manichaean struggles of good and evil, Hinds built on the religious material that he and Sangster had introduced in *Dracula Prince of Darkness*, ultimately creating not one cleric but two who fulfill vastly different functions.

The final complication concerned Fisher himself, the film's presumptive director. Fisher had helmed many a Hammer film up to that point, including *Horror of Dracula* and *Dracula Prince of Darkness*, and was the obvious choice to direct. He was slated to begin filming on March 18, 1968, and continue over a six-week period, but these plans collapsed when he was struck by a car and suffered a broken leg shortly before filming was to begin.[16] Not wishing to delay the pre-sold film, which had already been announced to the trade press in mid–February that year,[17] Hinds and Carreras assigned the directorial duties to Freddie Francis, a journeyman cinematographer-*cum*-director who had made several horror films but whose professional storytelling interests lay elsewhere.[18] Hinds, who was still laboring over the screenplay at the time of Francis's hiring, took advantage of the late substitution and included narrative material that he knew would not have sat well with Fisher, a High Church Anglican who shared Bram Stoker's perspectives on the objective power of religious symbols and rituals.[19] With Francis's recruitment, the key members of the hastily assembled production team were now in place.

The film went before the cameras on April 22 at the company's new facilities at Pinewood Studios and on location at Iver Heath and Buckinghamshire, and filming continued through June 4. Much to producer Aida Young's credit, the film ran only a few thousand pounds over budget and a mere two days over schedule. Delighted, Hinds and Carreras delivered the 92-minute film to Warner Bros.–Seven Arts on October 11, and it debuted on November 7 at London's New Victoria Theatre.[20]

The haste and turmoil that haunted the production process had some bearing on the quality of the film that greeted British audiences in late fall 1968 and the rest of the world the following year. It is often difficult to determine if the ideas expressed in the film resulted from careful planning or hurried decisions. As we shall see, the very first scene in the movie exhibits some of this uncertainty.

Faith, Faithlessness and Desecration

Set in a village nestled in the Carpathians,[21] *Dracula Has Risen from the Grave* presents a religious thematic concern almost immediately; a nameless and rather wormlike Catholic priest (Ewan Hooper) discovers a young woman's corpse stuffed inside his church's mammoth bell. A close-up of the corpse's neck reveals two bite marks oozing blood that looks like it came out of a ketchup bottle (fitting, perhaps, since we later learn that the victim's surname is Heinz). The priest knows immediately who is responsible but cannot bring himself to utter the name. "Dear God, when shall we be free? When shall we be free of his evil?" he whimpers off-screen while the camera lingers on the corpse's wounds and inverted cleavage. Poignant questions, indeed.

This shocking and titillating scene occurs a year before the film's main action, and it supposedly dovetails with the conclusion of *Dracula Prince of Darkness*. However, the scene does not connect with any specific development in the previous film, and it raises more questions than it answers: Why did Dracula target this particular woman? How was he able to attack her inside a church, a consecrated space? How did he manage to stuff her body upside-down inside a giant church bell?

Though the film doesn't answer these questions, this brief scene nevertheless introduces a religious-minded concern: the desecration of a church. Hinds likely took his cue from the notorious "vampire panic" that gripped Britain in the 1960s and centered on Highgate Cemetery, a large graveyard north of London overrun by would-be vampire hunters. Making a compelling case for *Dracula Has Risen*'s connection to the vampire panic, historian Scott Poole detailed the country's widespread fear that churches and graveyards were becoming the sites of satanic rituals and therefore defiled. Desecrated churches, he noted, "had become a central symbol of 1960s Britain's discourse about the growing power of the devil."[22]

Dracula's desecration of the tiny church in *Dracula Has Risen* sets the remainder of the film's narrative into motion. The priest's plaintive questions are addressed a year later by the arrival of Ernst Mueller (Rupert Davies), a monsignor based in the nearby city of

Keinenburg.[23] In his brief voice-over narration as he guides a horse-drawn buggy into town, Ernst refers to the "perpetrator of these obscene evils." He is aware that the church, in his words, "was once vilely desecrated, but the perpetrator of that ghastly deed was destroyed some twelve months ago." After learning that the townspeople have stopped attending services, Ernst alludes to the event that concludes *Dracula Prince of Darkness* by asking them, "Was he not sent to his doom in the waters of your mountains? And was he not therefore destroyed forever?" They tell him they can still feel Dracula's evil; in a development that defies scientific understanding, the shadow of Dracula's mountaintop castle now touches the church and they believe it a continuation of the church's defilement. In response to this information, Ernst decides to undo the desecration by traveling to Dracula's castle to exorcise it. His major tool, strapped to his back, is an ornate four-foot cross taken from the church's altar.

With a cross strapped to his back, Monsignor Ernst Mueller (Rupert Davies) recites the Latin text for an exorcism of Castle Dracula in *Dracula Has Risen from the Grave* (1968).

After a daylong journey through the mountains to Dracula's castle (audience members are left to wonder how a castle that far away can cast its shadow on the town church so precisely), Ernst reaches the castle's gigantic front doors. Believing Dracula a particularly tough customer, the intrepid monsignor conducts an excommunication ceremony, employing traditional bell, book, and candle, before beginning the rite of exorcism. Amid a portentous display of thunder and lightning, Ernst starts the exorcism by reading the service aloud in Latin. His intonation begins: "Exorcizo te, immundissime spiritus, omnis incursio adversarii, omne phantasma, omnis legio, in nomine Domini nostri eradicare, et effugare ab hoc plasmate Dei. Ipse tibi imperat, qui te de supernis caelorum in inferiora terrae demergi praecepit. Ipse tibi imperat, qui mari, ventis et tempestatibus imperavit." However, Ernst may have made a deadly mistake; he inadvertently leaves out Christ's name from the service. (According to standard exorcism texts, "Jesu Christi" should have appeared between "nostri" and "eradicare.") Since exorcisms are performed in Jesus Christ's name, the film implies that the monsignor's omission may have invalidated the rite.

While Ernst conducts the exorcism in the midst of an escalating storm, the priest, who accompanied the monsignor only part way up the mountain and now awaits his return, slips and falls on the icy terrain and hits his head. Blood from his wound trickles down into a crack his fall created in the ice, where Dracula happens to be resting, frozen, in a state of suspended animation.[24] Meanwhile, back at the castle, high winds have snuffed out Ernst's candle and blown it over. Since candles symbolize the light of Christ in such a context, the extinguishing of the flame speaks volumes. Shortly after Ernst attaches the cross to the door, sealing the entrance in effect, we see a tight close-up of

Dracula's twitching lips; the priest's blood has reached the vampire's mouth and brought him back to life. The priest, who perhaps had been summoned to that precise location via Dracula's silent directive, falls under the vampire's complete control moments later.[25]

Puzzled by the priest's disappearance, Ernst travels back to the village alone and tells the townspeople that he plans to return to Keinenburg now that his work is finished. He is sadly mistaken, however; unbeknownst to him, a thoroughly defrosted Dracula has journeyed back to his castle only to discover that it has been rendered uninhabitable, at least by him. "Who has done this thing?" he snarls upon seeing the cross fastened to the door handles. His newly recruited lackey, the priest, meekly says, "Monsignor—it was the monsignor." By fingering his superior, the priest has unwittingly cleared the way for a revenge-driven intensification of conflicts.

Throughout these scenes, it appears as if Ernst will be the film's primary combatant against Dracula. A clash of rival patriarchs—"good father" Ernst and "bad father" Dracula—seems to be brewing, and the film underscores the characters' similarity through their costuming; each wears a flowing black robe that covers them from neck to foot throughout the film. In addition, Ernst's robe is trimmed in red, a visual echo of the flashes of red occasionally visible from the underside of Dracula's cape. As the vampire begins plotting his revenge against the monsignor, the two, visually at least, seem rather twin-like.

However, Hinds and Francis threw a twist into the works with the introduction of Paul (Barry Andrews), a college student who works in a Keinenburg pub as a baker. He is romantically involved with Ernst's niece, Maria (Veronica Carlson), who shares a home with Ernst and her mother Anna (Marion Mathie), Ernst's widowed sister-in-law. When Dracula learns via the priest that Ernst has a niece, he decides to target her as part of his vengeful scheme. In so doing, he inadvertently pulls Paul into his orbit.

Paul is everything that Ernst is not: young, exuberant, athletic, college-educated, and, intriguingly, atheistic. He reveals his lack of faith in the following dinner-table exchange at the monsignor's home:

> ERNST: There are six churches here, you know, Paul.
> PAUL: Yes, sir.
> ERNST: Which one do you attend, by the way?
> MARIA: Paul doesn't come from Keinenburg, Uncle. This isn't his home.
> ERNST: I know, but…
> MARIA: He works very hard in the bakery. He doesn't have much time.
> ERNST: But on Sundays?
> PAUL: I don't go to church, sir.
> ERNST [incredulously]: You don't go to church.
> PAUL: No, sir.
> ERNST [leaning forward]: You're not a Protestant, are you?
> PAUL: No, sir.
> ERNST [sitting back]: Thank Heaven for that!
> PAUL [long pause]: I'm an atheist, sir.
> ERNST: I beg your pardon!
> PAUL: I'm an atheist, sir.
> ERNST: You mean you deny the existence of God?
> PAUL: I don't deny it. I just don't believe it. It's my own opinion, sir.
> ERNST: You know who I am?
> PAUL: Yes, sir.
> ERNST [standing]: And you come here to my house, speaking this blasphemy?

PAUL: You asked for my beliefs, sir, and I've given them. It was an honest answer, sir. You said you liked people to be honest.
ERNST: Don't be impertinent!

In essence, Hinds and Francis took Stoker's Van Helsing character—a multi-degreed Catholic intellectual who understands that Dracula's defeat will require more than science—and split it into two extremes: the exceptionally pious and devout Ernst, who depends heavily on age-old Catholic rituals and has no truck with science; and Paul, a free-spirited, well-educated atheist. We never actually learn Paul's scholarly focus (Anna merely tells Ernst that Paul "is going to be a doctor or professor or something"), but he tells his boss Max (Michael Ripper) that he only wants to learn "what life's about; something of the truth"—presumably, a scientifically derived truth. His student employment as a baker only accentuates his distinction from Ernst; he feeds the body while the monsignor feeds the soul.

Paul's higher education and atheism, which the movie conflates to some extent, can be seen as reflections of the times. As suggested by *Time*'s controversial cover story "Is God Dead?" in April 1966, the decade was marked by an intense questioning of God's existence amid the increasing secularization of society and concomitant rise in scientific inquiry as a means of explaining the natural world. Though *Dracula Has Risen* is set around 1905, Paul is very much a figure of the 1960s (indeed, the actor who played him, Barry Andrews, bore an uncanny resemblance to '60s British rock music icon Roger Daltrey of The Who). However, it is he who bears the brunt of the unpleasant surprise that his staking of Dracula has no effect, his lack of faith and inability to pray constituting the main causes.

A Stokerian Ambiguity

In retrospect, it is not surprising that Anthony Hinds and his Hammer colleagues should play up spiritual concerns as much as they did. They understood the truism that a number of scholars have observed over the years: that Stoker's Dracula narrative is the Christ story turned hideously inside out.[26] Consider some of the novel's more salient aspects: (1) Dracula desires to achieve eternal life by drinking others' blood, an inversion of the sacrament of Communion through which Christians achieve eternal life by drinking Christ's blood. (2) In an alternative befouling of the Communion rite, Dracula slices open his chest and tries to force Mina Harker to drink his own blood. (3) His chief victim Lucy Westenra is "resurrected" and emerges from a tomb as an undead entity who, unlike Christ, doesn't feed lamblike children; she feeds *on* them. (4) R.M. Renfield, the fly-eating wretch who acts as a kind of barometer for Dracula's comings and goings, venerates the Count as a Messiah. He builds his adoration on a promise of thousands of consumable lives that will extend his own indefinitely "if you will fall down and worship me," in the vampire's words.[27]

Hinds and company wasted little time emphasizing the similarities, beginning with a title that specifically evoked, if not parodied, Christ's triumphant emergence from the tomb. The film, which played in many countries during the 1969 Easter season, also featured an advertising campaign that proved problematic for some. At least one film critic—Vincent Canby of the *New York Times*—detected a bit of mockery in one of the movie's advertising taglines. As he wrote: "Now that Easter, 1969, has come and gone it might be noted that one of the movies with which Warner Bros. Seven Arts greeted the season was a horror film called *Dracula Has Risen from the Grave*, which was advertised, 'You just can't keep a good man down.' Apparently nobody found it offensive, which may mean, as I've always suspected, that ad men, like poets, sometimes write only for each other's amusement."[28]

The film itself underscores the Christ-Dracula comparison in a number of its more violent moments. For instance, Paul's staking of the coffin-bound Dracula, though not administered with a hammer (an ironic omission, given the name of the studio), is not so different from the nailing of Christ to the cross, and its ineffectiveness mirrors Christ's ultimate victory over death.

A later example is even more pronounced. Near the film's end, Dracula orders Maria to dispose of the shimmering gold-plated cross that has sealed his castle's doors. "Get that thing out of my sight," he bellows. "Throw it away." She heaves it over the balcony, and it somehow manages to land upright in the rocks below. Paul arrives moments later, and he and Dracula grapple before falling over the railing onto the rugged terrain. Though Paul manages to save himself by grabbing onto a small tree in the rock outcropping, Dracula plunges down the mountainside and ends up impaled on the cross. Weeping tears of blood, he thrashes about on the cross while the wayward priest redeems himself by reciting the Pater Noster over the gruesome proceedings. Dracula is thus crucified, his body eventually dissolving into a bloody puddle. However, extra-textual evidence in the form of the countless subsequent Dracula films—including four more with Christopher Lee at Hammer alone—shows that the Count's death is only temporary. Clearly, "you just can't keep a good man down."

Though these vivid moments reflect perhaps the novel's most obvious influences, the book's representations of faith-based differences have bearing as well. They deserve a closer look, as they reveal subtleties and complexities that carry over to the film.

The novel notably does not include any clerics in the struggle of good and evil; it's Dracula versus a team of well-meaning laypersons. This team, which literary scholar Christopher Craft famously labeled the "Crew of Light,"[29] consists of only one identifiable Catholic: the group's leader, Van Helsing. The others—John Seward, Arthur Holmwood, Quincey Morris—are presumably Protestants. Jonathan Harker, who later joins the "Crew," is unquestionably a Protestant; specifically, he's a member of the Church of England. We may infer from his diary entries that he is a Low Church Anglican: one who views religious icons, objects, and rituals as potentially sinful since they may divert worship away from God and toward themselves. Shortly before Jonathan begins his journey to Castle Dracula, a local woman offers him a crucifix. This gesture perplexes him, as he notes in his diary: "I did not know what to do, for, as an English Churchman, I have been taught to regard such things as in some measure idolatrous."[30] She puts it around his neck, and it proves a most fortuitous act; the crucifix later protects him from Dracula after he accidentally cuts himself shaving. Jonathan is exceptionally grateful and ruminates on the object's power: "Bless that good, good woman who hung the crucifix round my neck! For it is a comfort and a strength to me whenever I touch it. It is odd that a thing which I have been taught to regard with disfavour and as idolatrous should in a time of loneliness and trouble be of help. Is it that there is something in the essence of the thing itself, or that it is a medium, a tangible help, in conveying memories of sympathy and comfort?"[31] It's a key question, and he and the others soon realize that the accouterments distributed by Van Helsing have a power independent of their wielders; following the beliefs of Catholics and High Church Anglicans, the wafers and, by extension, the other holy objects embody the "real presence" of Jesus Christ. Consider, for example, Dr. Seward's reaction to Dracula's sudden arrival: "Instinctively I moved forward with a protective impulse, holding the Crucifix and Wafer in my left hand. I felt a mighty power fly along my arm, and it was without surprise that I saw the monster cower back." Seward also quotes Van Helsing, who speaks to Mina: "The Professor held up his golden crucifix, and said with wonderful calmness, 'Do not fear, my dear. We are here, and whilst this is close to you no foul thing can approach. You are safe for tonight.'"[32]

One of the more delicious aspects of Stoker's novel is what we might call its authorial ambiguity. We are never quite certain of the novelist's perspective on the religious issues presented in his book. Was Stoker, a member of the Church of Ireland, mocking Catholics and/or Protestants? Sympathizing with them? Proselytizing on their behalf? Is his book saying that Jonathan Harker sees or should see the value of sacred objects and realize Low Church Anglicans' folly on this point? We don't know.

Dracula Has Risen features a similar type of ambiguity. Freddie Francis was known for injecting humor into his films,[33] and, armed with that knowledge, we are tempted to ask a series of questions: Does the film mock certain aspects of Christianity? Of Stoker's general Dracula narrative? Is the film a satiric response to the novel and subsequent *Dracula* spinoffs that emphasize objects and rituals and the characters' newfound awareness of their power? The infamous staking scene could be seen as a slam against the Catholic and High Anglican Churches' emphasis on symbols and rituals, yet Paul crosses himself at the end—a gesture common to both churches. Again, we don't know.

Whether by accident or design or a potent combination thereof, *Dracula Has Risen* is a multivalent text particularly in its regard for the Catholic Church; it supports it on some levels but attacks it on others. On one hand, it celebrates such things as devout faith, charity, and the primacy of the family and, at least in a few scenes, suggests that holy objects and rituals do have objective power arising from Christ's defeat of sin and death. A key example is Dracula's inability to enter his castle because of Ernst's cross, but there are others. For instance, the priest spies a small bejeweled cross around the neck of a sleeping Maria but is unable to grasp it; a force from the cross, represented by a cross-shaped light projected onto the priest's agonized face, pushes him back. Another example occurs during one of Dracula's invasions of Maria's bedroom. Before he can assault her, Ernst appears and flashes a small crucifix. In a moment that could have been lifted from Stoker's novel, Dracula growls, holds his hands in front of his face, and flees out the window.

On the other hand, the film underscores Catholic intolerance (e.g., Ernst's exaggerated happiness when he learns that Paul isn't a Protestant; the rigidity of his faith; his unwillingness to engage Paul in dialogue once he learns of the latter's atheism, though they do become allies at the end) and holds up the priest as a weak-willed, sickly looking, alcoholic toady who is completely dominated by Dracula for most of the film. In addition, the staking scene counters Catholic views by indicating a complete absence of Christ's presence. It implies that the film's spiritual battle is not so much a conflict of Christ versus evil as it is a conflict of *Christians* versus evil—a key distinction. In other words, Christians have to pick up where Christ leaves off in the war against evil, and they do so through their faith. As the staking scene shows, people with no faith battle evil at their peril; a reliance on objects and rituals won't help. Such a perspective likely resonated with 1960s audience members uncertain about the roles of God and faith in contemporary society.

It is possible that *Dracula Has Risen*'s muddled theological perspectives arose from Hammer's desire to have the film speak to people of all the faiths noted in this essay. Though Anglican churchgoers presumably made up the majority of its British audience members, Hammer certainly had no desire to alienate its domestic and international Catholic customers. As Christopher Lee noted, the Hammer Dracula films enjoyed high popularity in heavily Catholic countries: "[An] aspect of these films which draws audiences to them everywhere is that the Dracula type of film is basically a morality play, with an admixture of pantomime, fairy story and melodrama. The characters are straightforward and strictly defined: this is black, this is white; this is good, this is bad. When evil meets good it must inevitably fail; it must always lose in the end. This is one reason why the church doesn't object to these films, and why they are so popular in Ireland, Spain and Italy."[34] Despite its unusual twists on the Dracula narrative—in particular, its motley Crew of Light consisting of an atheistic college student, an extremely malleable priest who comes under Dracula's control, and a portly monsignor who's a bit long in the tooth to be clashing with vampires—*Dracula Has Risen* celebrates a highly predictable triumph of good over evil and ultimately reaffirms Christian values. It encapsulates these messages at the very end, when Paul, the erstwhile atheist, engages in the simple act of crossing himself following the vampire's demise.

Paul's conversion, symbolized by his *signum crucis*, is reminiscent of another Paul who saw the light, literally, and converted: Paul the Apostle, who under the name of Saul had persecuted Christ's early followers but later became a key figure in the spread of Christianity and believed in faith-based salvation. The details of Paul the Apostle's story don't quite fit the movie's Paul; the latter hasn't persecuted anyone and, at least at first, seems mainly interested in flirting with barmaids and hoisting a few pints with his friends. Yet each figure, pointedly well-educated, converts to Christianity after a life-changing experience. The newly religious Paul is the only surviving member of the film's Crew of Light (the priest had mortally wounded Ernst in a rooftop struggle, and the priest himself expires simultaneously with Dracula's crucifixion), and the movie loosely implies that the young man will represent a new generation of religious leaders in the mold of Paul the Apostle.

Yet even this interpretation, admittedly tenuous, is fraught with uncertainty. Consider this question: Did Paul's conversion to Christianity occur immediately before Dracula perishes, or after? If it came before, the moment would perhaps reflect a Low Anglican perspective: Paul's newfound faith has obliterated the vampire. If it happened after, it would reflect more of a Catholic/High Anglican view: the presence of Christ, as channeled through the four-foot cross, destroys Dracula with Paul serving mainly as an onlooker. Taking a charitable view, we might say that the filmmakers' ambiguity on this point and many others only adds to the richness of their highly conflicted film.

Concluding Thoughts

At the end of his admirable book on the British horror film, *Hammer and Beyond*, Peter Hutchings makes a rather curious and ostensibly contradictory plea: let's not praise such films too highly and risk elevating their stature. As he wrote:

> We must constantly be aware of British horror's disreputability, for this quality comprises an integral part of the genre's working. It is a fundamental condition of British horror's existence that no one

"really" takes it seriously; therein lies dispensation for its transgressions, its often very lucid uncoverings and explorations of structures and assumptions that otherwise would have remained hidden.... Rendering these films worthy and respectable would be doing them a disservice. More, it would be like forcing them into the light and then watching helplessly as they crumble into dust.[35]

We would do well to remember Hutchings' admonition, and it is entirely possible that *Dracula Has Risen*'s embodiment of colliding religious themes and motifs resulted partially from the rather haphazard production schedule observed earlier: a schedule that involved a pre-sold film with no story, a novice producer, a hastily written script, an unsigned star, and a last-minute directorial substitution. These are obviously not ideal conditions under which to create any film, let alone one with so weighty a topic as a spiritual battle. And yet, and at the risk of running afoul of Hutchings' eloquent warning, I argue that *Dracula Has Risen from the Grave* succeeds in spite of itself and its checkered production history. Though the film closely follows the Hammer tradition of offering what appears to be a simplistic struggle of good and evil, I hope this essay has shown that *Dracula Has Risen* rises above that level by offering an intriguing amalgam of theological perspectives and inviting a range of interpretations in no way limited to the ones offered here.

Notes

1. *Kinematograph Weekly*, a British trade journal, reported in its November 30, 1968, issue that "all records were broken by *Dracula Has Risen from the Grave* on the first day of its ABC [Associated British Cinemas] release. The film set a new circuit record by taking more money at the box-office on a Sunday than ever before." Quoted in Wayne Kinsey, *Hammer Films: The Bray Studios Years* (London: Reynolds & Hearn, 2002), 353. See also Howard Maxford, *Hammer, House of Horror: Behind the Screams* (Woodstock, NY: Overlook Press, 1996), 101. Knowing that the filmmakers were experimenting with concepts that would subvert the traditional Christ narrative, I find it interesting that the film should set a record for a Sunday, a major day of the week for Christians.
2. Lee quoted in Tim Stout, "Dracula Has Risen from the Grave," *Supernatural: Horror Filming* (January 13, 1969), 18.
3. Lee's introduction to an illustrated edition of the Bram Stoker novel, timed to coincide with the release of *Dracula Prince of Darkness* in 1966, is a fine example of his prodigious knowledge of Dracula lore. See Christopher Lee, "Dracula," in *Dracula*, adapted by Otto Binder and Craig Tennis, illustrated by Alden McWilliams (New York: Ballantine, 1966), 5–8.
4. Lee quoted in Robert W. Pohle and Douglas C. Hart, *The Films of Christopher Lee* (Metuchen, NJ: Scarecrow Press, 1983), 130; Lee quoted in Tom Johnson and Mark A. Miller, *The Christopher Lee Filmography: All Theatrical Releases, 1948–2003* (Jefferson, NC: McFarland, 2004), 186. Lee originally uttered the second line in a 1971 interview with Gary Parfitt.
5. As Lee proudly recalled in 1966, the film, simply titled *Dracula* for British audiences, "swept the world. The talents of production designer Bernard Robinson, cameraman Jack Asher, and director Terence Fisher, combined with a well-chosen cast, which performed with absolute conviction and total sincerity, resulted in one of the most successful British films ever made." See Lee, p. 7.
6. Cushing does make a brief appearance as Van Helsing at the beginning of the film via archival footage taken from the conclusion of *Horror of Dracula*.
7. Denis Meikle with Christopher Koetting, *A History of Horrors: The Rise and Fall of the House of Hammer* (Metuchen, NJ: Scarecrow Press, 1996), 188; Jimmy Sangster, *Inside Hammer* (London: Reynolds & Hearn, 2001), 111.
8. Fisher quoted in Gary R. Parfitt, "The Fruitation of Terence Fisher," *Little Shoppe of Horrors*, no. 3 (1974), pp. 53–54.
9. Sangster, 113.
10. Parfitt, 54.
11. Young quoted in "The Problem of Finding the Lady—or Ladies," *Times* (London), 26 August 1968.
12. Sangster, 52.
13. Sangster characterized Hinds as "an extremely nice man and very funny" and "non-aggressive and non-confrontational which made him a joy to work for." See Sangster, 12.
14. Marcus Hearn and Alan Barnes, *The Hammer Story: The Authorised History of Hammer Films*, rev. ed. (London: Titan Books, 2007), 122.

15. *Ibid.*; Lee quoted in Tom Johnson and Deborah Del Vecchio, *Hammer Films: An Exhaustive Filmography* (Jefferson, NC: McFarland, 1996), 302.
16. Johnson and Del Vecchio, 298.
17. Hearn and Barnes, *Hammer Story*, 122.
18. As Francis himself noted, he was far less interested in the film's horrific aspects than he was in developing its romantic subplot. Much to his chagrin, however, Hinds and the other Hammer powers-that-were edited out much of the love-story material. See Freddie Francis with Tony Dalton, *Freddie Francis: The Straight Story from* Moby Dick *to* Glory, *a Memoir* (Metuchen, NJ: Scarecrow Press, 2013), 159.
19. Fisher revealed a sense of his Anglican High Church perspectives during an interview with Gary Parfitt. While discussing the legendary conclusion of *Horror of Dracula*, in which Peter Cushing as Van Helsing destroys Dracula with two crossed candlesticks, Fisher touted "the inevitable triumph of good over evil" that occurred when "Peter forces him down or rather, the sign of the cross does." Fisher's slight correction at the end makes it clear that, in his view, the job was accomplished by the symbol, not the person. Fisher quoted in Gary R. Parfitt, "The Fruitation of Terence Fisher," *Little Shoppe of Horrors*, no. 3 (1974): 54.
20. Hearn and Barnes, *Hammer Story*, 89, 123.
21. The town is identified as Carlsbad in *Dracula Prince of Darkness* but the name is not actually mentioned in *Dracula Has Risen*.
22. W. Scott Poole, "The Vampire That Haunts Highgate: Theological Evil, Hammer Horror, and the Highgate Vampire Panic in Britain, 1963–1974," in *The Undead and Theology*, ed. Kim Paffenroth and John W. Morehead (Eugene, OR: Pickwick Publications, 2012), 65.
23. In *Dracula Prince of Darkness*, the city is called "Kleinberg." However, it is listed as "Keinenburg" in the authorized history of Hammer films and pronounced that way by the characters. This new title suggests that Hinds may have been plying a bit of in-joke humor. The name translates as "no castle," and indeed no actual castles or castle-like interior sets were used in the film's production. Though Dracula's castle is visible a number of times in the distance, the image is a matte painting created by Hammer artisan Peter Melrose. See Hearn and Barnes, 122.
24. It isn't clear how Dracula ended up so far away from his castle, since *Dracula Prince of Darkness* shows him falling into icy water right by its entrance. A strong undertow, no doubt.
25. Though this may be an example of slipshod filmmaking that relies far too heavily on coincidence, it is possible that Dracula had silently and telepathically summoned the weak-willed priest to that very spot. I offer this as a possibility since a similar moment occurs much later in the film when the vampire, ensconced in his coffin, gives a directive to the priest. Though Dracula is apparently unconscious, we actually hear his disembodied voice utter a two-word command—"Destroy her"—to the priest.
26. For example, see Mark A. Miller, *Christopher Lee and Peter Cushing and Horror Cinema* (Jefferson, NC: McFarland, 1995), 74; D. Bruno Starrs, "Keeping the Faith: Catholicism in *Dracula* and Its Adaptations," *Journal of Dracula Studies* 1 (2004), 1.
27. Bram Stoker, *Dracula* (London: ElecBook Classics, 2000), 338.
28. Vincent Canby, "'Columbus'—A Happy Discovery," *New York Times*, 13 April 1969, D1.
29. Christopher Craft, "'Kiss Me with Those Red Lips': Gender and Inversion in Bram Stoker's *Dracula*," *Representations*, no. 8 (Autumn 1984), 109.
30. Stoker, *Dracula*, 18.
31. *Ibid.*, 45.
32. *Ibid.*, 370, 343.
33. See Wheeler Winston Dixon, *The Films of Freddie Francis*, Filmmakers No. 24 (Metuchen, NJ: Scarecrow Press, 1991), 115.
34. Lee quoted in *The House of Horror: The Complete Story of Hammer Films*, ed. Allen Eyles, Robert Adkinson, and Nicholas Fry (London: Lorrimer Publishing, 1973), 17.
35. Peter Hutchings, *Hammer and Beyond: The British Horror Film* (Manchester: Manchester University Press, 1993), 187.

BIBLIOGRAPHY

Canby, Vincent. "'Columbus'—A Happy Discovery." *New York Times*, April 13, 1969, D1.
Craft, Christopher. "'Kiss Me with Those Red Lips': Gender and Inversion in Bram Stoker's *Dracula*." *Representations*, no. 8 (Autumn 1984): 107–133.
Eyles, Allen, Robert Adkinson, and Nicholas Fry, eds. *The House of Horror: The Complete Story of Hammer Films*. London: Lorrimer Publishing, 1973.
Francis, Freddie, with Tony Dalton. *Freddie Francis: The Straight Story from* Moby Dick *to* Glory, *a Memoir*. Metuchen, NJ: Scarecrow Press, 2013.
Hearn, Marcus, and Alan Barnes. *The Hammer Story: The Authorised History of Hammer Films*, rev. ed. London: Titan Books, 2007.
Hutchings, Peter. *Hammer and Beyond: The British Horror Film*. Manchester: Manchester University Press, 1993.

Johnson, Tom, and Mark A. Miller. *The Christopher Lee Filmography: All Theatrical Releases, 1948–2003*. Jefferson, NC: McFarland, 2004.
Kinsey, Wayne. *Hammer Films: The Bray Studios Years*. London: Reynolds & Hearn, 2002.
Lee, Christopher. "Dracula." In *Dracula*, adapted by Otto Binder and Craig Tennis, illustrated by Alden McWilliams, 5–8. New York: Ballantine, 1966.
Maxford, Howard. *Hammer, House of Horror: Behind the Screams*. Woodstock, NY: Overlook Press, 1996.
Meikle, Denis, with Christopher Koetting. *A History of Horrors: The Rise and Fall of the House of Hammer*. Metuchen, NJ: Scarecrow Press, 1996.
Miller, Mark A. *Christopher Lee and Peter Cushing and Horror Cinema*. Jefferson, NC: McFarland, 1995.
Parfitt, Gary R. "The Fruitation of Terence Fisher." *Little Shoppe of Horrors*, no. 3 (1974): 49–62.
Pohle, Robert W., and Douglas C. Hart. *The Films of Christopher Lee*. Metuchen, NJ: Scarecrow Press, 1983.
Poole, W. Scott. "The Vampire That Haunts Highgate: Theological Evil, Hammer Horror, and the Highgate Vampire Panic in Britain, 1963–1974." In *The Undead and Theology*, ed. Kim Paffenroth and John W. Morehead, 54–76. Eugene, OR: Pickwick Publications, 2012.
"The Problem of Finding the Lady—or Ladies." *Times* (London), August 26, 1968.
Sangster, Jimmy. *Inside Hammer*. London: Reynolds & Hearn, 2001.
Starrs, D. Bruno. "Keeping the Faith: Catholicism in *Dracula* and Its Adaptations." *Journal of Dracula Studies* 1 (2004). http://eprints.qut.edu.au/5244/1/5244_1.pdf.
Stoker, Bram. *Dracula*. London: ElecBook Classics, 2000.
Stout, Tim. "Dracula Has Risen from the Grave." *Supernatural: Horror Filming* 1 (January 13, 1969): 16–21.

Unquenchable *Thirst*
Morality, Theology and Vampires in Chan-wook Park's Horror Romance

MICHAEL C. REIFF

Dammern: German: Verb:
1. To Grow Light/To Dawn
2. To Grow Dark/To Fall

It seems like vampires aren't as thirsty as they used to be. A recent spate of vampire films and television series have played with genre conventions, formal elements and character types, but one clear trend connects many of them: vampires aren't sucking as much blood as they used to. Much has been made of Stephenie Meyer's supernatural romance *Twilight* (2008): A vampire and human fall in love, and their repressed yearnings for blood and intimacy drive the teen film's narrative tension (and sexual metaphors). The more recent, mockumentary-style *What We Do in the Shadows* (2014) depicts a group of vampires—some relatively young, some ancient—living together in an apartment. Despite fighting over who has to do the dishes next, they agree on one thing: they won't suck the blood of Stu, a regular human who's been hanging around. Why not? Because he's a nice guy. Both vampire texts use the motif of rejecting a need as fodder for genre expansion, either to develop a different type of romantic tension, or to play up goofy supernatural camaraderie.

Chan-wook Park's 2009 film *Thirst*—another genre-busting vampire narrative—incorporates a torrid love affair and a vampire resisting his supernatural urges, but it also has other things on its mind. Centered around a Korean Catholic priest who becomes a vampire through a medical experiment gone awry, *Thirst* includes—along with Park's usual highly stylized compositions and violence—a much more thorough wrestling with the moral, theological and genre implications of human-to-vampire conversion. The film explores a new ethical and existential code of vampiric conduct that emerges out of the supernatural, as well as religious, conversion of Father Sang-hyun: one centered on the tempering of both vampiric and human urges, for both theological and secular reasons. *Thirst* provocatively showcases the seemingly inescapable and primordial urges burbling within humanity itself as it explores the root causes of human and supernatural mayhem alike.

Thirst can be viewed as an archetypal post-modern vampiric text, particularly in its presentation of Father Sang-hyun, a figure who combines the divine with the supernatural. The film breaks with literary and cinematic tradition in its presentation of this character's progression from priest to vampire. As a vampiric priest, Sang-hyun exemplifies elements of Catholic characters that have been ignored or submerged in more conventional literature, particularly his linkage to supernatural mysticism. Additionally, the priest's wrestling with, and creation of, ethical codes that address issues beyond the strictly religious, and instead delve into the supernatural, expand the purview of earlier vampire texts.

In wrestling with his human and un-human urges, Sang-hyun forges an ethics of vampirism in response to his crisis of faith and his vampiric conversion. Juxtaposing the actions and ethics of Father Sang-hyun with those of his lover Tae-ju, this essay will explore the unique, hybridized ethical code that *Thirst* presents, along with Park's suggestions that human nature—not vampiric, or other supernatural, tendencies—is actually at the root of the tragic events the film presents, and that a theologically or morally sacrificial act may be the only way to quell humanity's darkest compulsions, whether or not they are vampirically enhanced.

A Crisis of Faith and Vampirism

Park himself has been a bit fuzzy about the true generic structure of *Thirst*,[1] at various times describing it a supernatural romance, a horror comedy, or another one of his revenge thrillers. All these descriptions actually do apply to the film, giving it a complex genre profile as well as a fairly labyrinthine plot. In broad strokes, however, *Thirst* is concerned with a Korean priest experiencing a crisis of faith. Feeling disconnected and in doubt about the efficacy of his pastoral works, he volunteers for a dangerous operation that might lead to a cure for a virulent disease. Sang-hyun contracts the disease and seems to die, but a last-minute transfusion of blood mysteriously saves his life—at the cost of turning him into a vampire.

This traumatic transformation changes Sang-hyun's outlook on life in a number of ways. He may "live" again, but the disease still lurks within his system, and he can only keep its debilitating symptoms at bay by consuming human blood. His seemingly miraculous resurrection makes him a prophetic figure within the community, and parishioners flock to him, but he seems to shun this wave of spiritual admiration. His quasi-celebrity also piques the interest of an erstwhile cousin, who invites him to take part in weekly mahjong games. There he meets his cousin's maltreated wife, Tae-ju, and the two characters begin an illicit relationship, finding liberation in each other. Sang-hyun's religiously repressed sexual urges are unleashed by Tae-ju, and her monotonously repressive home routine is shattered by Sang-hyun's attentions.

The second half of *Thirst* begins to resemble Chan-wook Park's earlier revenge thrillers, such as *Oldboy* (2003) and *Lady Vengeance* (2005), as Sang-hyun demonstrates his love for Tae-ju by killing her unfeeling and abusive husband. Sang-hyun eventually realizes that he has been tricked by Tae-ju—the signs of abuse marring her body turn out to be self-inflicted—and attempts to thwart her vicious scheme by killing her. At the last minute, however, he relents and, instead of killing her, transforms her into a vampire.

Sang-hyun has, up to this point, largely resisted using and spreading his newfound powers, but Tae-ju embraces them, becoming a gleeful vampiric monster who preys upon her neighbors. Though Sang-hyun has forged an ethical code of restraint and mercy to go with his new vampiric form, Tae-ju continually brings out his worst human instincts—vengeful rage, fear, and lust. This leads Sang-hyun to call into question the basic value of his continual wrestling with the ethics of vampiric life—what good is tempering his vampiric nature, if his human nature can be so easily manipulated? Toward the end of the film, Sang-hyun has been able address his moral qualms by becoming a supernatural and spiritual giver of peace as he continues administering last rites to dying patients, as well as assisting in the suicides of those who wish for it, relying only on their blood (and whatever else he can steal from blood banks) for sustenance. However, in the final scene of the film, he realizes the full destructive scope of what he has created in Tae-ju, a supernaturally enhanced embodiment of human nature's worst elements. Sang-hyun traps her on a seaside cliff as the sun rises, ending both of their lives, as well as the supernatural/human threat they pose to the rest of humanity.

In this final sequence, Sang-hyun extends his newly formed theological-supernatural ethical code of physical and existential restraint to its limit. With his sacrifice at the end of the film, the viewer is confronted with an outcome that Sang-hyun seems to have wished for from the outset of his journey. While Sang-hyun battles his human and unhuman urges throughout *Thirst* by interweaving his darker desires with equal parts restraint and action. His final act of self-destruction simultaneously ends his existence and benefits humanity—his flock—on a much grander scale.

Sang-hyun and Tae-ju are, in surprising ways, two sides of the same vampiric coin. Outwardly, Sang-hyun may be the most theologically and cinematically subversive creation in the film, but the character's ethos is conservative by nature, and the narrative arc tracks his struggles to contain his vampiric urges. Only when his natural human tendencies slip out does he become destructive. Contrarily, Tae-ju, the most vicious and violent of the two, and yet also the most in tune with her human urges, is more akin to the classical Gothic monster. While Tae-ju may seem to be the most disruptive force within the film, her vampiric identity is actually far more traditional, in the mold

Post-transformation, Father Sang-hyun (Song Kang-ho) continues administering last rites in *Thirst* (2009), and fights off the temptation in front of him—a bloody, suffering human, Professor Ku (Hwa-ryong Lee), as Nurse (Hee-jin Choi) stands by.

of Bram Stoker's *Dracula* or the neo-Gothic vampires popularized by Anne Rice's novels.

Through the contrary characterizations of Sang-hyun and Tae-ju, Park presents a bifurcation of vampiric nature in *Thirst*, and in doing so creates a window into the vampire's theological nature. On one hand, as Anne Rice notes in her "Essay on Early Works," the vampire can act as "a metaphor for human consciousness or moral awareness," and can be an expression "of grief for a lost religious heritage" and a "hungering for transcendence."[2] On the other hand, as Julia Kristeva points out in her book *Powers of Horror*, the vampire is "a living projection of human death," bringing with it "the threat and fear of identity-effacement."[3] Narratively, Park balances these dual qualities of the vampire, with Sang-hyun exemplifying Rice's aspirational conception and Tae-ju embodying Kristeva's existential effacement of humanity. These contrasting elements play a key role in the explicit ethos Sang-hyun contemplates and strives for in the film, and in the implicit sacrificial morality he embodies in the final scene.

The complex brew of elements that Park stirs up in *Thirst*—from the figure of a vampiric Catholic priest to the centuries-old literary vampire motifs filtered through and towards the disruption of cultural (and cinematic) norms—creates a heady film. While clearly a product of its own era, *Thirst* is rooted in long-standing literary traditions related to the vampire as a subversive character, the integration of vampires into Catholic texts, and portrayals of Catholics in literature and films.

The Disruptive Vampire Through Time

Father Sang-hyun's characterization as a personal and institutional disruptor of natural orders is reflective of how vampires have, for centuries, been viewed and used in literary texts involving religious as well as secular characters. J'annine Jobling notes in her book *Fantastic Spiritualties* that the vampire, with its elements of "transgressive desire and alienation ... interrogates conceptions of what is means to be human,"[4] while Niall Scott argues in *Monsters and the Monstrous* that monsters, such as vampires, help us "reflect and critique human existence," and that vampire narratives "point towards an identity model based on existential choice rather than essentialism ... one which grounds choice in bodily and social particularity."[5] Vampires, especially in their current form, are confronted with issues of choice—how to fulfill their needs, what groups to integrate with, what happens to them after a dramatic change—and Park makes these issues, tied to the vampire's violent and ghoulish nature, central to Father Sang-hyun's core identity. Sang-hyun's initial crisis of faith in both the utility of his good works for the Church, and his ability to contain his sexual urges, forces him to grapple with the deeper implications of choice, transgressive actions, and alienation from groups and self once his vampiric identity is born.

Vampirism enables Sang-hyun and Tae-ju to explore alternative lifestyles beyond what is conventional either in the Church or in secular society. William Day notes in *Vampire Legends in Contemporary American Culture* that by "transcending death, time and space, unbound by the laws of God, nature or society," vampirism can offer "freedom, and the gratification of all desires, ultimate affirmation of the individual."[6] Crucial to Day's observation is the fact that the vampire is simultaneously undead and conscious—a supernatural creature "unbound" by theological or sociological constructs. Sang-hyun's vampirism is a morally hazardous burden he must control, but also an opportunity to reassess his place within traditional society and the Church. Additionally, Tae-ju's role as a submissive housewife and shopkeeper, an identity she chafes against, is at first "transcended" and "unbounded" when she becomes romantically involved with a vampire; that traditional role becomes even more eradicated when she converts to vampirism.

William Day also notes that literary vampirism allows for what he calls "transcendent individuality," which fulfills "aspirations of psychological and spiritual freedom."[7] This, too, reflects the experience of Sang-hyun and Tae-ju, who "transcend" their limiting situations in divergent ways, with the priest finding the drive within himself to craft a new and useful ethical path, and the repressed housewife embracing a supernaturally-empowered hegemony over her neighbors and family.[8] Tae-ju takes Day's conception of the vampire to the limit, but Sang-hyun, who experiences the same spiritual freedom, feels compelled to rectify the damage he has done by putting an end to Tae-ju's brief reign of bloodshed.

Park complicates the matter, however, by presenting a paradoxical convergence between the supposedly evil vampiric nature and supposedly good human nature. While Sang-hyun is the original and most "fully-lived" of the vampires in *Thirst*, he is far more restrained than Tae-ju, and is only led astray by human nature. Indeed, for much of the film Tae-ju's *human* depravity and viciousness are the true threat to those around her, and her vampiric powers, appearing late in the film, merely amplify them.

Historically, the disruptive and dialectic nature of the vampire that Park emphasizes in *Thirst* have run through vampire literature from the Gothic to the Victorian. Isabella Van Elferen notes in her article "Music That Sucks and Bloody Liturgy" the transgressive nature of the vampire in Gothic narratives, specifically their function as a vehicle for critiquing contemporaneous views on religion, sexuality and class in the 18th century.[9] Additionally, Alberto Mira points out in "The Dark Heart of the Movida" that 19th-century Victorian vampire narratives "feature moralistic storylines ... with monsters represented as a threat to normality that has to be exterminated."[10] These historic narrative elements—moralistic messages and subversive cultural critiques—undergird and shape *Thirst*'s contemporary narrative. Sang-hyun's elimination of the monstrous Tae-ju at the

Tae-ju (Kim Ok-bin) as a vampire in *Thirst* (2009): gleefully embracing violence and destruction, and willing to kill even Sang-hyeon.

end of the film has a Victorian quality, but so does his suppression of his "monstrous" urges early in the film, and his self-destruction at the end. The juxtaposition of the vampiric with the Catholic in *Thirst* creates, concurrently, a Gothic dialectical struggle within Sang-hyun. A similarly Gothic confrontation with cultural and traditional norms is also found, however, in Tae-ju's status, early in the film, as a victim of traditional family strictures imposed by her mother-in-law and husband.[11] Those limits are then broken and transcended through her personal and sexual relationship with Sang-hyun, and—in characteristic Gothic fashion—through her later vampiric transformation.

The 1970s *Gaillo* films—a subgenre of shocking, subversive works, often with supernatural elements—form a bridge between the Gothic/Victorian literature of vampires and 21st-century Korean cinema. As Shelley F. O'Brien notes in her consideration of the iconoclastic "Killer Priest" motif in *Gaillo* cinema, the 1970s films of directors like Lucio Fulci and Antonio Bido examined "the ir/rational and super/natural borderlands where opposites converge … [and] evil resides in good."[12] Contrary to conventional vampire narratives, the disturbing dualities found in the Giallo films are most apparent in *Thirst* when Father Sang-hyun kills Tae-ju's husband out of personal rage and not vampiric bloodlust. Indeed, when Sang-hyun engineers Tae-ju's death (as well as his own), he does so out of human guilt rather than vampiric self-preservation. The *Gaillo* films in general, and *Thirst* in particular, use their dark characters to raise questions about the world they inhabit. Park confronts the viewer not only with the inner contradictions of his two principal characters, but also the contradictions of the Church Sang-hyun works for and the social norms that trap Tae-ju in a destructive home life while fomenting her violent and vindictive urges.

Vampirism and Catholicism

Among the array of ghouls that haunt literature, none is better positioned to simultaneously confront and illuminate Christian, and specifically Catholic, belief than the vampire. This aspect of the vampire, exemplified in Father Sang-hyun in *Thirst*, gives the work theological and philosophical heft, significant for both the genre and the representation of the religion on screen. James Twitchell notes in his book *Dreadful Pleasures* that "aside from the devil, the vampire is the most popular malefactor in Christianity,"[13] and as Christopher Moreman has observed of texts like *I Am Legend*, the presence of vampires in contrast to Catholicism is especially stark when considering the concept of the final resurrection—the idea that only Christ can bring back the dead.[14] Catholicism and vampires have, from Bram Stoker onward, been tailor-made to act as antagonists and foils for one another. If *Thirst* were merely the tale of a human priest battling back a shop-keeping succubus vampire, the film would fit neatly within the traditional fold of films featuring Catholic priests and vampires. *Thirst*, of course, does not, but upon closer inspection neither do many Catholic texts.

Catholicism, as Isabella Van Elferen notes, has acquired over time "an uncanny, Gothic dimension in vampire fiction, as its supernatural dimensions … aligned closely with vampiric ghostliness and transgression."[15] The Catholic faithful, for example, believe that those who consume a communion wafer and wine during a Mass are, through a process known as transubstantiation, literally ingesting the body and blood of Jesus Christ. Though clearly mystical and theological in nature, the ritual—when viewed from the outside—can take on an inescapably vampirical quality.[16] Indeed, while a literal representation of this mystical concept can be viewed through Father Sang-hyun's vampirism in *Thirst*, Park provides subtler visual evocations of this metaphor as well throughout the film, as through the glimpses of the crimson-red wine Sang-hyun ponders in a communion chalice during church services.

Additionally, Catholic belief in the daily blending of the real and the supernatural is fertile ground for a character like Father Sang-hyun to thrive upon. As Regina Hansen notes in her introduction to *Roman Catholicism in Fantastic Films*, "Catholics, at least in theory, believe in the reality of everyday marvelous occurrences and powers, and … enhance people's experience of the marvelous through use of showmanship and spectacle."[17] Belief in the active and commonplace supernatural, as well as an eagerness to spectacularize and visualize the unquantifiable, is clearly reflected in the ghastly supernatural side of Father Sang-hyun, as well as the mundane interactions he has with parishioners and his mahjong club, for instance. Taken a step further, Hansen notes that the 20th-century novels of Hugh Walpole and Ann Radcliffe, as well as the "Gothicized representations of Catholicism and Catholics as unnatural and uncanny threats" found in "overtly anti–Catholic American 'nativist' tracts," helped to develop an overall cultural perception of Catholicism as "mysticism," "superstition" and "transgression" in the 1930s.[18] Park's combination of a mystical holy man and a transgressive unholy threat in *Thirst* is not, therefore, simply a by-the-numbers exercise in provocation, but part for a long, rich, and complex historical and literary lineage. This alignment of the holy with the supernatural is enmeshed within *Thirst*, and is the foundation for its subversive dialectic on how one can fashion a new ethics through the dueling crises of faith and vampirism. Park's film is therefore not outright disruptive, but instead acts within a more subversive trend that meshes Catholic and vampiric literary elements and traditions, as previous literary texts have done in more circumspect ways.

Beyond its literary and theological background, however, *Thirst* showcases Park, true to form, melding cinematic and narrative elements in surprising and unconventional ways, combining the seemingly un-synthesizable. *Thirst* mixes genres and blurs the traditional supernatural lines between predator and prey, a conflict further explored in the narrative itself, both in the collision of Father Sang-hyun and Tae-ju's vampiric worldviews, in Sang-hyun's attempts to fashion a morality and ethics from seemingly and opposite urges and compulsions: the human and supernatural, "living" urges and "undead" ones. Father Sang-hyun's identity as a Catholic priest, however, gives him, as described above, the perfect foundation for acting as a vampiric protagonist, and not merely a genre aberration. Indeed, because of how *Thirst* combines genres, and because it further complicates elements of both the vampire and the Catholic faith, the intra-text discussion between characters on theological and ethical grounds helps *Thirst* transcend its predecessors in becoming a fully post-modern text.

A Postmodern Thirst for Change

Jobling argues that the modern vampire—which acts far more consciously, and reflects human tendencies far better than other contemporary ghouls—presents oppositional dichotomies that allow for a more thorough wrestling with modern issues of identity and culture. Jobling notes that "vampiric bodies are liminal, betwixt and between two terms of oppositions by which human culture is organized: dead/not-dead; human/not-human," and contends that to engage with the post-modern vampires is "to collapse these oppositions ... disintegrate the means by which cultures make sense of the world."[19] The collapse is consistent with what Patricia Pender has seen as an overall postmodern trend of the "archaic 'either or'" transitioning into the "anarchic 'neither/nor.'"[20] The postmodern vampire of *Thirst*, therefore, need not be a bloodthirsty, uncontrollable beast, but rather, can be a truer, more complicated null-vision of human experience—a negative-space reflection of our humanity. Father Sang-hyun embodies this stance both in his Catholic/vampire personal identity and in his larger religious crisis and ethical mission. His placement within the evolving postmodern tradition helps give *Thirst* its complicated texture and illuminates its core message: while vampirism presents a dangerous and subversive problem, human nature remains the true existential threat to the individual and society.

From the outset, Sang-hyun's liminal or "neither/nor" nature is at the core of his narrative journey and his vampiric transformation. Having early on wrestled with the utility of his pastoral works he undergoes the operation that turns him into a vampire. Sang-hyun emerges as Jobling's "human/not human" and "dead/not-dead" figure by dint of his vampiric nature. He certainly appears human to the mahjong players who welcome him into their home, and to Tae-ju who brings him into her heart. Yet his supernatural abilities of flight and rapid healing belie this. Sang-hyun is also, as Pender notes, "neither/nor" as he is clearly no long affiliated officially with the church, and yet continues to administer merciful acts, at times under a religious guise. Early on in his transformation, Sang-hyun cries out "I'm no longer a priest or a friar! Forget the rules! Forget the Vatican!" However, after that tumultuous moment and throughout the remainder of the film, he still presides over the dead and dying, and is seen by other Catholics as a holy man by dint of his "resurrection," his dress, and his theologically-inflected good works. He is simultaneously a divine healer and someone who continues to reject the institutions and trappings of organized divinity. He is, both visually and through actions, a man who deals with life and death, but also one who embodies the undead urges of vampirism.

Sang-hyun's contradictory identity is further underscored as he wrestles with Tae-ju after her transformation from human to vampire, and is exposed to her own philosophy of vampiric superiority. Though Tae-ju's perception of vampiric dominance over humans[21] would alleviate the moral and physical burden of Sang-hyun's vampiric urges and moral pangs,[22] he still rejects her ethos. However, even in this metaphysical debate, Sang-hyun doesn't argue on strictly religious grounds, but on individually personal ones. Sang-hyun may not speak primarily as a man of God, but he comports himself in accord with a moral commitment to respecting life, even at the cost of his own pain and suffering. Sang-hyun refuses to allow vampirism, or even Tae-ju's vampiric hegemonic views, to alleviate his suffering or bring a new equilibrium to his life, instead opting for a harder vampiric ethical code that tempers the worst of both sides of his new nature.

A further contradiction in Sang-hyun's mindset is that, while his initial restlessness was born out of a lack of external achievement and stewardship, the foundation of his vampiric ethical system is broadly akin to a doctor's Hippocratic oath—first, do no harm. Upon transformation, Sang-hyun instantly sees the need to curtail his new, inherently murderous nature; there is no initial spate of uncontrolled bloodlust in the film. Understanding that his condition has tremendous physical (hyper-sensitivity to light) and moral limitations, Sang-hyun only takes blood from patients who wish to end their lives, in the hope that they may live on in him,[23] and refuses to give his own blood to his mentor Father Noh, who wishes to become a vampire himself in order to reacquire his sight. Sang-hyun has the ability to radically transform life, but doesn't—he merely soothes the pain of those in dire need, while maintaining his own vampiric/human equilibrium. The vampiric essence allows for him to spread his monstrous quality; he rejects this urge with Father Noh, opting for lonely theological, ethical and supernatural exile. However, a final contradiction in his ethical code emerges, though subtly, through his interactions with the dying and suffering. While Sang-hyun may reject his new vampiric urges that compel him to destroy life, the peace he brings to suffering patients—even as they willingly give up their blood to him—is an effective echo of the destructive nature he restrains. This altruistic destruction of life neatly foreshadows the final scene of the film, in which he eliminates the threat of Tae-ju's power and twisted morality.

Indeed, it is not simply Tae-ju's threatening vampiric nature that Sang-hyun confronts; it is what her human nature does to him. When morally and physically wrestling with Tae-ju, Sang-hyun's vampiric ethical code twists and then breaks, and it is not because his human side is overtaken by vampiric needs, but the opposite. When he gives into Tae-ju's human desire for revenge against her husband (and, by extension, her domineering mother-in-law), he unleashes a series of events that push him towards a more nihilistic view of his role in the world. That ethical shift pushes him deeper into his identity as a postmodern vampire, raising questions about the existential nature of the soul and the evolving theological and practical role of the sacrificial act.

The Soul of a Vampire

Though Father Sang-hyun never directly addresses the soul as a universal construct in *Thirst*, his identity as priest, and his evolving personal crisis—from simply being dissatisfied with his pastoral works to wrestling with and containing his new and personal existential hungers—are the driving force of the first half of the film. This fits neatly into evolving ideas about the literary vampire, particularly Michelle Callandar's theory that the vampiric soul is not so much non-existent as it is a personal element which must be re-found after conversion to vampirism, bestowing upon the vampire a sense of "exquisite consciousness" of the weight of a soul, and its importance.[24] Indeed, with this evolution of the vampiric soul in mind, Father Sang-Hyun's ability to transform his condition into an avenue for transcendent action—taking the blood of suffering patients and giving them peace—evokes Longbon's conception of engaging in "action on behalf of others." This is a radically different take on the vampiric soul from that offered by Stoker, but of course, it should be—*Thirst* is a radical vampire text. With a priest at the center of *Thirst*, the question of the soul is not only central to the narrative, but also to the modern conception and evolving state of the vampire as a moral agent—a thematically central role that, once again, raises the issue of vampire ethics.

The existence of potentially altruistic vampiric souls in texts like *Thirst*—one acquired through "exquisite consciousness" in action—places human nature, with its destructive impulses, in sharper contrast to that of the vampire. Sang-hyun's act of vengeance against Tae-ju's husband, his rejection of the Vatican over the selfish demands of his fellow priest Father Noh, and his pre-vampiric sexual urges, all establish his human nature as a disruptive and destructive force. His vampiric nature and identity acts as a mediating force, focusing his energies away from some of those emotions (the destructive) and giving him outlets for others (the sexual). His human urges are presented as the sole reasons for the mistakes and mayhem that take place toward the end of the film, from killing Tae-ju's husband and Father Noh to instigating Tae-ju's transformation out of guilt and shame. The stark contrast is a fascinating subversion of the normal vampire scenario, but one in keeping with Chan-wook Park's oeuvre-wide motifs on human nature, as well as the subversive nature of the contemporary vampire.

The last scene of the film, in which Sang-hyun sacrifices himself to eliminate the scourge of Tae-ju, comes across as humanistic—an urge towards martyrdom to cleanse guilt—and anti-vampiric, at least in the classic, Gothic sense. Why would a vampire destroy himself if he was merely a monster bent on nothing more than the consumption of blood and the creation of more vampires? Jarrod Longbons contends in "Vampires Are People, Too" that "the real difference between the human and the vampire is ... their ability to have a conscience, feel guilt, and act through self-sacrifice,"[25] and Sang-hyun and Tae-ju, in their dichotomous human/vampire forms, prove this. As noted above, Father Sang-hyun's initial code of personal vampiric control seems to have created an equilibrium between his vampiric and ethical yearnings. But his human impulses towards violence, and Tae-ju's human yearning for revenge, point toward what Sang-hyun is truly eradicating at the end of the film: human nature's darkest elements amplified by supernatural means, not supernatural urges overtaking human nature's better angels. Park's inclusion of this idea completes the film's subversion and expansion of what the vampiric nature or soul truly signifies in the postmodern era. For Park, human nature remains the primordial cause of violence, namely man and woman's fashioning of conscious and deliberate mythologies that lead to bloodshed. Compared to the dark and easily twisted human soul, the vampiric nature is simple—an urge or hunger that the vampire can repress, and even point toward a better purpose, and in doing so, as Callander notes, acquire a righteous and coveted vampiric soul. The vengeful narratives Tae-ju creates, and Sang-hyun succumbs to, are seemingly irredeemable, and even override Sang-hyun's fledgling control of his new thirsts. It is therefore Sang-hyun's final self-sacrificial act that firmly positions the priest within both the Catholic tradition and the postmodern vampiric mode, while aligning the film with the themes of redemption and destruction—through either vengeful or righteous acts—that recur throughout Chan-wook Park's body of work.

The Vampire as Paraclete and Protector

Anthropologist and theorist Rene Girard describes a "Paraclete" as a spiritual advisor in life, and especially in death. In practical terms a Paraclete is someone who intercedes—in law, life, or wherever it may be needed. The theological Paraclete can also be seen as a self-sacrificial entity for good, as in the passion narrative of Jesus Christ.[26] When Christ is crucified in the Gospels, Girard notes, "Jesus crosses the abyss which separates us from the Father. He himself becomes our Paraclete, i.e., our defender."[27] This dual sacrifice/protector role is key to the view that, through time, Paracletes inform and protect not only through their actions (sacrifice) but through their inherent messages (what they stood for, what they fought against.)[28]

The idea of the Paraclete provides the crucial context for Father Sang-hyun's final sacrificial act. In destroying himself and Tae-ju, he is not simply removing a threat. Sang-hyun contemplates, discusses, or anticipates his own suicide multiple times throughout the film. Over the course of these scenes, his thought process evolves from an early dialogue with a nun, in which he views suicide as stealing from God, to a later incident in which he attempts suicide in order to remove the threat of his vampiric nature from the world. It is clear, however, that by the end of the film Sang-hyun has come to grips with the broader implications of vampirism. His newly developed ethics of vampirism may be sound, but neither Tae-ju nor the petulant Father Noh pay it heed. Deeply aware of the true nature of those around him and the dangerous implications of their possible future actions, Sang-hyun takes it upon himself to become, like Christ, a self-sacrificing Paraclete for humanity. Where he once gave physical and spiritual comfort to those who wished for it by using his vampiric powers for good, he ends the film by eliminating threats to humanity (Tae-ju, the literally blood-thirsty Father Noh, and his own flawed and rage-filled self) at the cost of his own life.

Matthew Kratter argues in "Twilight of the Vampires" that in vampire texts "it appears that the hidden has been brought to light by the Paraclete only to be plunged back into darkness of glorified violence by stubborn humanity; the twilight of the vampires may be just one more dawn in the long history of sacrifice."[29] The "stubborn humanity" in *Thirst* is not an external threat, but the internal and monstrous narratives and emotions that overtake Sang-hyun's ethical code and drive Tae-ju's vengeful spirit. These dark human impulses are what make Sang-hyun's vampiric sacrifice all the more holistic. Sang-hyun embodies both contradictory and concomitant elements—vampire and human, holy man and supernatural aberration, creator of ethical codes and destroyer of ethos. He is both the Paraclete and its destroyer, the abyss that humanity must cross and the one that will cross the abyss for humanity.

Conclusion

Thirst shocks and awes with its medley of violence, beauty and philosophy. It also lays bare paradoxes deeply rooted in the tangled history of vampirism and Catholicism in literature. That Father Sang-hyun is both a holy man and a vampire is not the only, or even the most interesting, contradiction in the film. We see, for a fleeting moment, Sang-hyun symbolically acting out Christ's giving of blood as he holds a chalice of wine for a congregation; his true conversion and leading of a "flock" of course comes when he converts, and then must destroy, the vampiric Tae-ju.

Van Elferen notes that while Catholics have long been "described as superstitious, irrational or transcendent, in Gothic vampire fiction [they] also offer a weapon against occult irrationality and transgression."[30] From the outset of *Thirst*, however, it is the Catholic priest Sang-hyun who recognizes elements of the "irrational" within his faith, along with the inherent irrationality in his own human nature. To Matthew Kratter, the vampire is, traditionally, "a terrifying sacred figure, a monstrous Other who threatens to destroy," but one that also possesses "the ability to benefit the community."[31] This tension between threat and benefit is at the core of Sang-hyun's quest, and of the ethical code he creates but cannot maintain.

Beneath these deep, complex theological matters, however, lies a simple foundation. Agapiestic love of his fellow humans—"Christian love"—is truly at the core of Sang-hyun's character, from his initial volunteering for the operation that inadvertently makes him a vampire, to his final sacrifice. It is this that is his greatest weapon against vampirism and his own inner demons. Like the evolving vampire—ethical, moral, even Catholic— it is *dammern* cinema: a work that evokes both dawning light and descending darkness within the soul of an individual man. If, however, humans are the monsters in Park's fable, and monsters are the saviors, *Thirst* raises a troubling question for our literal and demystified times: Who can save us from our own twilight? Who can bring us to our own dawning day?

Notes

1. Andrew O'Hehir, "It's the Priest-Vampire-Ghost Story of Summer!" Salon.com, July 31, 2009, http://www.salon.com/2009/07/31/thirst/: 1.
2. Anne Rice, "Essay on Earlier Works," *Anne's Bookshelf*, August 15, 2007, http://www.annerice.com/Bookshelf-EarlierWorks.html: 1.
3. Julia Kristeva, *Powers of Horror: An Essay On Abjection*, trans. Leon S. Roudiez (New York: Columbia University Press, 1982), 4.
4. J'annine Jobling, *Fantastic Spiritualties: Monsters, Heroes and the Contemporary Religious Imagination* (London: Bloomsbury/T&T Clark, 2010), 199.
5. Niall Scott, *Monsters and the Monstrous: Myths and Metaphors of Enduring Evil* (Boston: Rodopi, 2007), 1.
6. William Patrick Day, *Vampire Legends in Contemporary American Culture: What Becomes A Legend Most* (Lexington: University Press of Kentucky, 2002), 5.
7. Ibid.
8. While Father Sang-hyun tempers his vampiric urges to aide others, as noted above, Tae-ju uses her vampiric abilities to not only seek retribution against her mother-in-law, but callously hunt motorists for blood. Her justification for her actions, as enumerated later in this essay, postulate a sense of supernatural superiority; humans are like animals to her, and should be treated thusly.
9. Isabella Van Elferen, "Music That Sucks and Bloody Liturgy: Catholicism in Vampire Movies," in *Roman Catholicism in Fantastic Films: Essays on Belief, Ritual and Imagery*, ed. Regina Hansen, 97–113 (Jefferson, NC: McFarland, 2011), 98.
10. Alberto Mira, "The Dark Heart of the Movida: Vampire Fantasies in Ivan Zulueta's *Arrebato*," *Arizona Journal of Hispanic Cultural Studies* 13 (2009): 157.
11. Early in the film, Tae-ju is seen as sexually repressed by her husband, and economically and socially repressed by her mother, as she is forced to work in the clothing store below their apartment every day, serve but never play at the mahjong games, and in general remain subservient to men and elders. She achieves freedom through not only her vampiric powers, but also through her initial relationship with a Catholic priest, including doing "good works" at a hospital. Therefore, setting aside for a moment the sexual and supernatural nature of her relationship with Sang-hyun, Chan-wook Park provides an initial juxtaposition of religious ethics and purity that is leveraged against her non-religious and traditional structures and rules—one dogma liberates a victim from another.
12. Shelley O'Brien, "Killer Priests: The Last Taboo?" in *Roman Catholicism in Fantastic Films*, ed. Regina Hansen, 256–267 (Jefferson, NC: McFarland, 2011), 257.
13. James B. Twitchell, *Dreadful Pleasures: The Anatomy of Modern Horror* (New York: Oxford University Press, 1987),106.
14. Christopher Moreman, "Let This Hell Be Our Heaven: Richard Matheson's Spirituality and Its Hollywood Distortions," *Journal of Religion and Popular Culture* 24, no. 1 (2012): 131.
15. Van Elferen, "Music That Sucks and Bloody Liturgy," 97.
16. Ibid., 99.
17. Regina Hansen, "Introduction," in *Roman Catholicism in Fantastic Films: Essays on Belief, Ritual and Imagery*, 2–16 (Jefferson, NC: McFarland: 2011), 5.
18. Ibid., 6.
19. Jobling, *Fantastic Spiritualties*, 171.
20. Patricia Pender, "I'm Buffy and You're History: The Postmodern Politics of Buffy," in *Fighting the Forces: What's at Stake in Buffy the Vampire Slayer*, ed. Rhonda V. Wilcox and David Lavery, 35–44 (Lanham, MD: Rowman & Littlefield, 2002), 39.
21. Tae-ju expresses this sense of superiority through numerous gleeful expressions, guttural sounds, and actions as a vampire, though perhaps sums it up best verbally when she laughingly says in the same dialogue exchange, "I'm not ashamed! … We're human-eating beasts!"
22. In a climatic dialogue between Sang-Hyun and Tae-ju over the proper behavior of vampires, Father

Sang-hyun asks, "you know how hard I tried not to kill people? You can't even begin to imagine. A blood thirsty beast is growing inside me! But I tiptoed around afraid to hurt anyone."

23. Earlier in a film, while giving her blood and life to Sang-hyun, a woman says, "Doing it this way, feels like I'll live on inside you…." Later on in the film, Sang-hyun explains that this act is him "helping people who want to commit suicide." He notes that "they face death more peacefully, if I help them."

24. Michelle Callander, "Bram Stoker's *Buffy*: Traditional Gothic and Contemporary Culture," *Slayage: The Online International Journal of Buffy Studies* 1, no. 3 (2004), http://www.slayage.tv/essays/slayage3/callander.html: 1

25. Jarrod Longbons, "Vampires are People, Too: Personalism in the Buffyverse," in *The Undead and Theology*, ed. Kim Paffenroth and John W. Morehead, 34–53 (Eugene, OR: Pickwick Publications, 2012), 38.

26. Rene Girard, "History and the Paraclete," *The Ecumenical Review* 35, no. 1 (1983): 6.

27. Ibid., 11.

28. Girard also postulates in "History and the Paraclete" that the scapegoating or martyrdom of a persecuted individual can make the victim a retrospective Paraclete, an individual who, upon reflection, can indicate where a society has gone wrong. While this can be seen in a historical reading of Jesus of Nazareth versus the Roman Empire, it has less weight in our current discussion with *Thirst*, though the film does critique, on the margins, practices in the Catholic Church and within contemporary domestic Korean life through Sang-hyun's experiences.

29. Matthew Kratter, "Twilight of the Vampires: History and Myth of the Undead," *Contagion: Journal of Violence, Mimesis, and Culture* 5 (1998): 42.

30. Van Elferen, "Music That Sucks and Bloody Liturgy," 101.

31. Kratter, "Twilight of the Vampires," 32.

Bibliography

Callander, Michelle. "Bram Stoker's *Buffy*: Traditional Gothic and Contemporary Culture." *Slayage: The Online International Journal of Buffy Studies* 1, no. 3 (2004). http://www.slayage.tv/essays/slayage3/callander.html.

Day, William Patrick. *Vampire Legends in Contemporary American Culture: What Becomes a Legend Most*. Lexington: University of Kentucky Press, 2002.

Girard, Rene. "History and the Paraclete." *The Ecumenical Review* 35, no. 1 (1983): 3–16.

Hansen, Regina. "Introduction." In *Roman Catholicism in Fantastic Films: Essays on Belief, Ritual and Imagery*, ed. Regina Hansen, 2–16. Jefferson, NC: McFarland, 2011.

Jobling, J'annine. *Fantastic Spiritualties: Monsters, Heroes and the Contemporary Religious Imagination*. London: Bloomsbury/T&T Clark, 2010.

Kratter, Matthew. "Twilight of the Vampires: History and Myth of the Undead." *Contagion: Journal of Violence, Mimesis, and Culture* 5 (1998): 30–45.

Kristeva, Julia. *Powers of Horror: An Essay on Abjection*. Trans. Leon S. Roudiez. New York: Columbia University Press, 1982.

Longbons, Jarrod. "Vampires Are People, Too: Personalism in the Buffyverse." In *The Undead and Theology*, ed. Kim Paffenroth and John W. Morehead, 34–53. Eugene, OR: Pickwick Publications, 2012.

Mira, Alberto. "The Dark Heart of the Movida: Vampire Fantasies in Ivan Zulueta's *Arrebato*." *Arizona Journal of Hispanic Cultural Studies* 13 (2009): 155–169.

Moreman, Christopher M. "Let This Hell Be Our Heaven: Richard Matheson's Spirituality and Its Hollywood Distortions." *The Journal of Religion and Popular Culture* 24, no. 1 (2012): 130–147.

O'Brien, Shelley. "Killer Priests: The Last Taboo?" In *Roman Catholicism in Fantastic Films: Essays on Belief, Ritual and Imagery*, ed. Regina Hansen, 256–267. Jefferson, NC: McFarland, 2011.

O'Hehir, Andrew. "It's the Priest-Vampire-Ghost Love Story of Summer!" Salon.com, July 31, 2009, http://www.salon.com/2009/07/31/thirst/.

Pender, Patricia. "I'm Buffy and You're History: The Postmodern Politics of Buffy." In *Fighting the Forces: What's at Stake in Buffy the Vampire Slayer*, ed. Rhonda V. Wilcox and David Lavery, 35–44. Lanham, MD: Rowman & Littlefield, 2002.

Rice, Anne. "Essay on Earlier Works." *Anne's Bookshelf*, August 15, 2007. http://www.annerice.com/Bookshelf-EarlierWorks.html.

Scott, Niall. *Monsters and the Monstrous: Myths and Metaphors of Enduring Evil*. Boston: Rodopi, 2007.

Thirst. Dir. Chan-wook Park. Universal Home Video, 2009. DVD.

Twitchell, James B. *Dreadful Pleasures: The Anatomy of Modern Horror*. New York: Oxford University Press, 198.

Van Elferen, Isabella. "Music That Sucks and Bloody Liturgy: Catholicism in Vampire Movies." In *Roman Catholicism in Fantastic Films: Essays on Belief, Ritual and Imagery*, ed. Regina Hansen, 97–113. Jefferson, NC: McFarland, 2011.

Of Heresy and Horror
Stigmata

CYNTHIA J. MILLER

"Split a piece of wood, and I am there. Lift up the stone, and you will find me."[1] This short verse, scrawled on a napkin, holds the key to the otherworldly horrors of Rupert Wainwright's 1999 supernatural horror film, *Stigmata*. As the narrative unfolds, the verse marks the intersection of a dead priest, a statue weeping blood, a young atheist, the Vatican, and an ancient scroll of the Gospel According to Thomas.

Denounced by the Catholic Church as heresy, the Gospel of Thomas is a key text of the Gnostic Gospels, and thought to be the closest existing rendition of the words of Christ. Its suggestion that relationships with God are individual and knowledge-based threatens the authority of the Church and has been the cause of global controversy for over half a century. In *Stigmata*, however, the words of Thomas refuse to be suppressed. When a young hairdresser receives a dead priest's rosary as a "souvenir" gift from her unwitting mother, she begins to manifest stigmata—the wounds experienced by Christ during his crucifixion—and her body becomes the site of rapidly escalating war between supernatural forces of good and evil, as well as between the Vatican and the truth.

Moral poles are reversed as the body and soul of rebellious unbeliever Frankie Page become the instrument of divine expression—one that Vatican emissaries seek to silence by any means necessary—defended only by a scholar-priest who is a man of science as well as a man of God. This essay, then, examines the tension among truth, knowledge, and doctrine in the film, as the divine struggles for expression in the mundane, against evil in both demonic and earthly form.

The Kingdom of God

In a remote corner of Brazil, a parish priest, cloistered in his sanctuary, translates an ancient text: "Jesus said the kingdom of GOD is within you—NOT in buildings of wood and stone...." Clutching his rosary, he presses it to his brow and closes his eyes in prayer.

As the next scene opens, throngs of faithful, bearing offerings and icons, make pilgrimage down a dusty road into the courtyard of the old stone church. Those who can no longer walk are carried; raising their arms to the skies, they pray, weep, and give thanks for the miracles they are about to witness. An outsider, dressed in black, moves among them, taking in the scene. As he enters the church and makes his way through the crowd of worshippers, a young deacon approaches him, asking: "Are you the investigator? Thank God you've come."

These initial scenes set the stage for a divine mystery—and divine horror—as the investigator, Father Andrew Kiernan (Gabriel Byrne) is increasingly confronted with events that he cannot explain. Dark and brooding, Kiernan is a man of great integrity, but holds little faith in manifestations of the Almighty on Earth. His God is a distant figure, one that does not routinely reveal Himself in the world, or bestow His gifts lightly. The priest has been sent by the Vatican to disprove claims of a miracle—a statue of the *Virgen de Guadalupe* weeping blood—ever since the parish priest (and translator of the sacred text above), Father Alamieda (Jack Donner), died. As Kiernan gazes at the weeping Madonna, a flock of doves startles and takes flight from the sanctuary. Countless candles burning in tribute extinguish and then reignite, signaling that there are, indeed, supernatural forces at work here. What begins as a holy spectacle in this small, isolated village, however, quickly becomes a complex battle between the forces of darkness and light, on a scale that threatens the future of humanity, as careless human acts open a complex narrative about faith, reverence, and the role of the sacred in the contemporary world.

Defiling the holy site, a young boy steals the rosary that was once pressed to Alamieda's brow from his open casket and sells it as a tourist trinket to a woman who neither knows nor cares about its significance—who thinks it simply "pretty." A street vendor's warning, "You're stealing from the dead," goes unheeded. The rosary passes to its new owner, the woman's daughter Frankie Paige (Patricia Arquette), and the setting shifts to her home in Pittsburgh, where

The Madonna weeping blood in the sanctuary at Belo Quinto draws throngs of the faithful in early scenes of *Stigmata* (1999).

once again, bizarre occurrences come to the attention of the Vatican, and Kiernan is summoned to investigate. He will see no connection between these manifestations in the U.S. and the earlier events in Belo Quinto, Brazil until he discovers the journey of Father Alamieda's rosary, and the story of the sacred secrets taken by the priest to his grave.

The cause for Kiernan's summoning is the appearance of the stigmata—bleeding wounds on the wrists, ankles, and head, where Christ was pierced during his crucifixion—and other bizarre metaphysical manifestations on Frankie, an ordinary, working-class non-believer. She has been examined by doctors, quizzed by psychiatrists, and yet, the agonizing manifestations resist diagnosis and treatment, until there is no explanation left but the supernatural. The wounds, which Kiernan ultimately realizes have been brought on by her possession of Alamieda's rosary, continue, and in fact, worsen. Just as, we later learn, they did with Father Almeida. She begins to suffer signs that more closely resemble demonic possession than inhabitance by the Holy Spirit: losing control of her body, experiencing hallucinations, reciting verse in an ancient tongue, and displaying powers of telekinesis. As Frankie's condition advances, Kiernan becomes a believer, but the rebirth of his faith in the unseen places him squarely in the midst of multiple battles—one to save the young woman's life before the final sacred wound appears; another to prevent her life from being ended by Vatican emissaries led by Cardinal Daniel Houseman (Jonathan Pryce), who are intent on eradicating any evidence of such a miracle; and finally, a battle for the truth. It is revealed that the sacred manuscript translated by Alamieda—and now supernaturally made known to Frankie—was, in fact, the suppressed Gospel According to Thomas. The text, attributed to Jesus himself, negates the authority of the Church—the "buildings of wood and stone"—a power that the Vatican is willing to use extreme measures to maintain. Frankie, Kiernan, and all who stand in the way are, for the Church hierarchy, acceptable losses: Divine horror, evoked by ecclesiastical conspiracy.

Kiernan learns the true story of the text, and of Alamieda's clandestine work to retrieve its message, when he is approached by the late priest's confidante, Marion Petrocelli (Rade Serbedzija). Petrocelli deems the sacred scroll "maybe the most significant Christian relic ever found," written in the first century and discovered near the caves where the Dead Sea Scrolls were found. He relates the story of their work, how the Vatican ordered them to stop their translation, and then excommunicated them when they refused. Kiernan does not understand.

> PETROCELLI: Look around you, Father, what do you see?
> KIERNAN: I see a church.
> PETROCELLI: It's a building. The true Church of Jesus Christ is so much more. Not buildings made of wood and stone. I love Jesus. I don't need an institution between him and me. You see? Just God and man. No priests, no churches. The first words in Jesus' gospel are "The kingdom of God is inside you, and all around you. Not in buildings of wood and stone. Split a piece of wood, and I am there; lift up the stone …
> KIERNAN: … and you will find me."

The threads of each of the film's mysteries quickly merge, as Kiernan realizes that it is the spirit of Alamieda that has inhabited Frankie, and it is she whom Houseman and the Vatican emissaries must eliminate in order to silence his voice. He rushes to intervene, and narrowly prevents the Cardinal from choking the life from Frankie in a desperate attempt to silence her. Alamieda's spirit sets the room ablaze, only allowing Kiernan to pass through the flames unharmed after the priest offers himself as Alamieda's messenger. Frankie intones the revelatory verse: "Jesus said 'The kingdom of God is inside you, and all around you …'" and as Kiernan beseeches Almeida to release her, the young woman screams as she suffers the tortures of the crucifixion. Kiernan blesses the dead man's soul, and as Frankie falls unconscious, a white dove rises through the flames. The fire recedes, and then vanishes.

The crisis past, the scene shifts back to where the story started: Belo Quinto, Brazil. Fr. Kiernan enters the church sanctuary, and instinctively retrieves the sacred scroll from its hiding place. As he runs his fingers over the text, the voices of Alamieda and Frankie recite the verse in chorus: "The kingdom of God is inside you, and all around you. Not in buildings of wood and stone … " Text fills the final scenes, attesting:

> IN 1945, A SCROLL WAS DISCOVERED IN
> NAG HAMADI, WHICH IS DESCRIBED AS

> "THE SECRET SAYINGS OF THE LIVING JESUS."
> THIS SCROLL, THE GOSPEL OF ST. THOMAS,
> HAS BEEN CLAIMED BY SCHOLARS
> AROUND THE WORLD TO BE THE CLOSEST
> RECORD WE HAVE OF THE WORDS OF
> THE HISTORICAL JESUS.
> THE VATICAN REFUSES TO RECOGNIZE
> THIS GOSPEL AND HAS DESCRIBED IT
> AS HERESY.

The Exploitation of Thomas

This final bit of text is carefully crafted to address an aspect of audiences' response to the film that would have been familiar to St. Thomas[2]: doubt that anything in this fantastic tale of the supernatural had any bearing on reality, that the Church might be involved in a longstanding conspiracy to preserve its power, and that Christ might have believed that that human relationship with the Divine required no authoritative mediation, no tithes, no rituals—just love. With these last screens, the film plants the seeds of authenticity, suggesting that, perhaps, what viewers have just witnessed is not only possible, but real. It is the cinematic version of the carnival sideshow banner claiming that the Snake Girl is "ALIVE!" and not a fabrication: "Based on a true story" ... "Based on actual events" ... "What you are about it see is true." In doing so, *Stigmata* joins tales of divine horror such as *The Exorcist* (1973), *Possessed* (2000), and *The Exorcism of Emily Rose* (2005),[3] along with an extensive tradition in the horror genre as a whole, of films that draw their potency, in part, from the suggestion that their narratives have (or could have) happened.

In the case of *Stigmata*, this claim hinges on the controversy surrounding the "lost" or Gnostic gospels. Derived from the Greek *gnosis*, translated as "knowledge," these gospels lay claim to an intimate knowledge and insight of the Divine. At its core, *gnosis* involves knowing oneself, and at its deepest level, knowing God. The Gnostic teacher Monoimus admonished: "Abandon the search for God and the creation and other matters of a similar sort. Look for him by taking yourself as the starting point. Learn who it is within you who makes everything his own and says, 'My God, my mind, my thought, my soul, my body.' […] If you carefully investigate these matters you will find him in yourself."[4] The Gnostic gospels thus advocate a knowledge of the Divine through the self—unmediated by doctrine or creed; freed of icons and archetypes; loosed, as the film's unseen spirit suggests, from "buildings of wood and stone."

In December 1945, Muhammad 'Ali al-Samman and his brothers unearthed a red earthenware jar near the town of Naj 'Hammadi at the Jabal al-Tarif, a mountain riddled with caves. The jar contained 13 papyrus books, bound in leather. While various tales of the discovery—and the fates of the books—have been circulated, the most widely accepted indicates that many of the manuscripts were sold on the black market in Cairo, and were ultimately either bought or confiscated by the Egyptian government and placed in the Coptic Museum.

A significant portion of one, however, containing five texts, was smuggled out of Egypt and, offered for sale. Purchased by the Jung Foundation in Zurich, and translated by religious historian Gilles Quispel, the manuscript was identified as a new scriptural text that claimed, "These are the secret sayings which the living Jesus spoke, and which Didymos Judas Thomas wrote down."[5] This Gospel According to Thomas made the familiar teachings of Christ unfamiliar, containing New Testament verses in different contexts, which, as Elaine Pagels observes, suggested other layers of meaning,[6] as well as new passages, such as "Jesus said, 'If you bring forth what is within you, what you bring forth will save you. If you do not bring forth what is within you, what you do not bring forth will destroy you.'"[7] The Gnostic Gospels, which, in their entirety, include secret gospels, poems, myths and mysticism, and philosophical treatises on the nature and origin of the universe—52 texts in all—were ultimately deemed to be Coptic translations of even more ancient manuscripts, though the exact dating of these originals is the subject of disagreement. While some argue that to be considered "heretical," they must have been written after the gospels of the New Testament (c. 60–110), others hold that some portions may predate the standard gospels—possibly as early as the second half of the first century.[8]

The collection's criticism of many traditional beliefs, such as the need for and authority of a hierarchical administrative body (the Church), as is highlighted in *Stigmata*, as well as the virgin birth and the bodily resurrection, were denounced as heresy by orthodox Christians in the middle of the second century,[9] despite their inclusion of traditional scriptural passages and use of Christian terminology. Bishop Irenaeus, head of the church in Lyons, promised "to show how absurd and inconsistent with the truth are their statements.... I do this so that ... you may urge all those with whom you are connected to avoid such an abyss of madness and of blasphemy against Christ."[10] Similarly, the Roman Hippolytus, wrote his own refutation, in order to "expose and refute the wicked blasphemy of the heretics."[11] Once Christianity became an officially approved religion, writing, owning, or promoting books denounced as heresy became a criminal offense, and most were destroyed. Only their burial saved the Gnostic gospels.

The unearthing of these "secret" gospels has, for centuries, fanned the flames of speculation about the true nature of Jesus, the authority and doctrine of the Church, and of course, the nature of the boundary between the human and the Divine, leading theologian Rudolf Bultmann, one of the leading figures in 20th-century biblical studies, to suggest that the mythic (or perhaps, the supernatural), is merely "a breakthrough of the sacred into history."[12] Attempts to demythologize Christian teachings and the life of Christ have, in turn, created their own mythic archetypes. *Stigmata*—like later cinematic divine conspiracy narratives, such as *The DaVinci Code* (2006)—seizes on this dynamic interplay to reveal the conflict between Church and Truth, and releases the Gospel According to Thomas into the world. In so doing, the film suggests that the true horror in this tale of miracles and possession originates with neither God nor Satan, but with those who would represent the supernatural and claim their authority on Earth. Institutions, even those claiming to be the most holy, invite corruption, while the unmediated relationship between God and the individual—even in times of struggle—is only ever pure.

Possession: The New Reality

Yet, it is supernatural horror, rather than earthly evil, on which *Stigmata*'s narrative depends. The presence of either divine or malevolent forces on Earth, remains the subject of one of horror cinema's most enduring subgenres. In their extensive examination of exorcism cinema, Christopher Olson and CarrieLynn Reinhard map trends in this collection of films, noting the ways in which possession and exorcism speak to both individual and sociocultural anxieties, through issues of body horror, destruction of family and community, and of course, fear that manifestations of evil, such as demons and devils, actually exist.[13] Olson and Reinhard, along with scholars such as Carol Clover, Kevin Wetmore, Richard Woods, Alexandra Heller-Nicholas, and others, consider this body of exorcism films primarily as allegories for tensions present in their own historical moments, yet all share significant commonalities.

Overarching themes emerge that address patriarchy, misogyny, intolerance, and marginalization, as difference and transgression are marked as possession, silenced by authoritative voices, and banished through exorcism. Heller-Nicholas argues that all of these films share an element of "moral spectacle" that leads to a standardized depiction of the Manichean battle between good and evil, wherein malevolent forces possess a virtuous individual and cause them to act in ways that threaten both themselves and the larger society.[14] Good typically takes the form of a spiritual figure, who possesses specialized knowledge of evil and its eradication, and must confront and drive out the evil.

Clearly, even without the devil—or any form of supernatural evil—*Stigmata* (at least loosely) follows this traditional template for exorcism cinema. Frankie, an atheist and hardly virtuous, is nonetheless victimized by a supernatural entity. Rather than a demonic force, her gruesome possession is by the essence of a pious, though very angry priest who saw the truth and was excommunicated for it—but the visual result is the same: her tortured body levitates and writhes, her screams suggest intolerable agonies, wounds

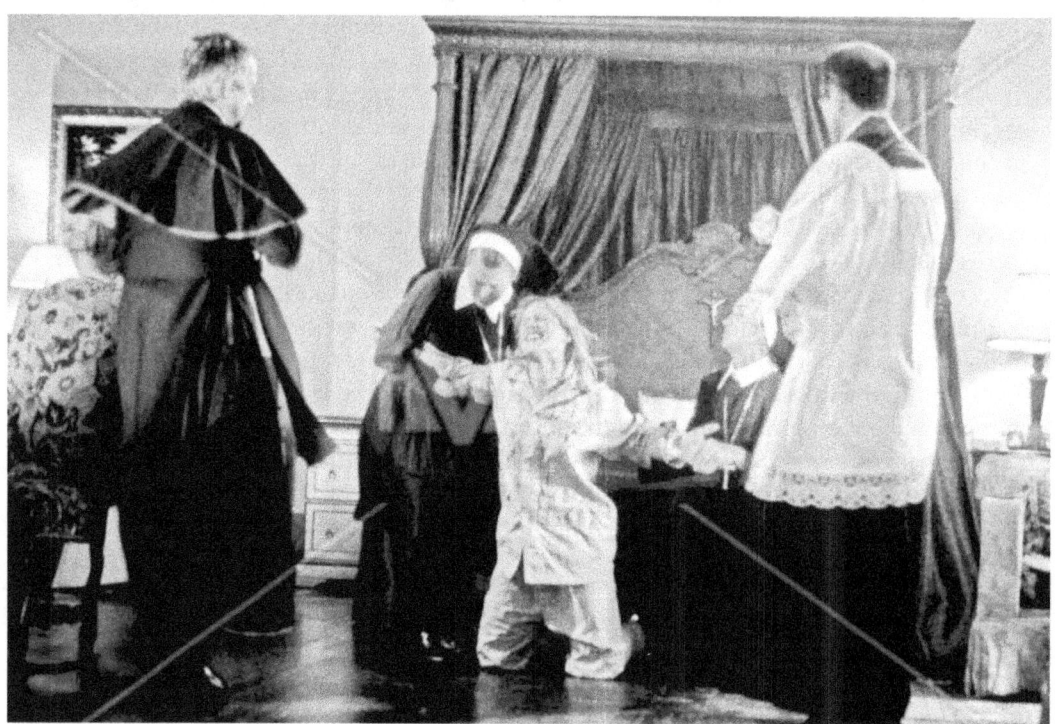

Cardinal Houseman (Jonathan Pryce) attempts to perform an exorcism on Frankie (Patricia Arquette) to insulate his power from the Gospel According to Thomas in *Stigmata* (1999).

spontaneously appear as if she has been whipped, and the soul that looks at the world through her eyes is clearly not her own.

This is the model of supernatural victimization that was established by *The Exorcist*, a film that marked a watershed in the subgenre, and captured the collective imagination in ways that the handful of exorcism films that predated it had failed to do.[15] *Stigmata*, released just over 25 years later, was clearly produced in its predecessor's image. But what made the path-breaking film so successful? Looking, with the scholars above, at the film's historical moment, within and outside the motion picture industry, we see a culture in the midst of a significant moral, economic, and social shift. Beginning with *The Exorcist*, exorcism cinema mirrored that change, in ways that carried forward through the 1980s and '90s and exploded post–9/11: that of a shift to "real stories" of possession and exorcism, precisely at a time when the subgenre was waning.[16]

In 1979, President Jimmy Carter expressed deep concern for the existential well-being of his fellow Americans, boldly asserting that "in a nation that was proud of hard work, strong families, close-knit communities, and our faith in God, too many of us now tend to worship self-indulgence and consumption. Human identity is no longer defined by what one does, but by what one owns. But we've discovered that owning things and consuming things does not satisfy our longing for meaning. We've learned that piling up material goods cannot fill the emptiness of lives which have no confidence or purpose."[17] Journalist Tom Wolfe similarly pointed to the era's dangerous "presentism," which he perceived as a lack of social responsibility and self-contextualization,[18] a perspective that historian Christopher Lasch expanded into cultural critique in *The Culture of Narcissism*, his description of an era brimming over with superficiality and the inability to create an authentic sense of self.[19] All of this paints a picture of a culture in moral crisis, and it is from this context—loss of faith in the Divine, self-indulgence, lack of meaning, emptiness—that exorcism cinema's "reality shift" began.[20]

Did this existential emptiness cause tales testifying to the real presence of the Divine and the horrific to resonate with audiences in ways that they had not in the past? Perhaps. Nearing the end of the 20th century, *Stigmata* was released into a socio-cultural milieu that faced its own challenges, some similar, some different. The Catholic Church faced global fallout from sex abuse scandals and cover-ups, and impeachment proceedings were carried out against then-President Bill Clinton. Audiences were thus well positioned to believe the worst of both church and state. Throughout this period, third-wave feminism was changing perceptions of women's roles and sexuality, creating subtle shifts in portrayals of female victimization, as well. For some scholars, such as Olson and Reinhard, this shift is particularly notable in considerations of Frankie's role. The film introduces her character through a montage of images that juxtapose her lustful and indulgent lifestyle with holy iconography, yet in her final scenes near the film's end, freed of Alamieda's possession, she appears in a flowing white gown that echoes the monastic garb of a nearby statue of St. Francis of Assisi. They observe that "while the film establishes Frankie as a sexually rebellious woman who refuses to conform to patriarchal ideals of feminine behavior, her possession nevertheless positions her as the only person capable of speaking the truth that could potentially change the world."[21] Thus, Frankie's possession, in the end, functions as a form of redemption, saving both her and Christianity. It (at least temporarily) grants her a voice through which she conveys Christ's message to the world, and rectifies the tainted nature of the Church, even as its emissaries seek to silence her. Through that temporary transformation, she is permanently changed. As

Olson and Reinhard note, hers is not the story of the Virgin Mary, but that of Mary Magdalene; not the saint, but the whore that has been redeemed.[22]

Getting It Wrong

Critic Roger Ebert deemed *Stigmata* to be "possibly the funniest movie ever made about Catholicism—from a theological point of view," observing that the film "confuses the phenomenon of stigmata with satanic possession, thinks stigmata can be transmitted by relics, and portrays the Vatican as a conspiracy against miracles."[23] In short, when it comes to the nuts and bolts of Catholicism, for Ebert, *Stigmata* "gets it wrong." A wayward atheist becomes afflicted with the wounds of Christ—a phenomenon that the Church regards as a gift from God, bestowed on only the most pious—which are passed from Father Alamieda to her, as apparently is his spirit, through his rosary. Once inhabited by the spirit of the dead priest, Frankie levitates, speaks in ancient Aramaic, has telekinetic abilities, and possesses Alamieda's intimate knowledge of the text of the secret gospels, not only quoting them, but also transcribing a segment in its entirety on her apartment wall. Until the final scenes, in fact, her experience much more closely mirrors the demonic possession of *The Exorcist* than any form of Divine transformation chronicled in scripture. When Frankie (in Alamieda's menacing, otherworldly voice) berates Cardinal Houseman in the film's climactic exorcism scene, viewers are far more prepared for elements of the template established by its predecessor than for the events that take place. But there are no spinning heads, no projectile vomiting, and no gloating force of evil; there is only the righteous anger of a dead man of God, and the haunting replay of the crucifixion in agonizing montage. Thus, as audiences and critics complained, the film actually fails to get its subgenre conformation right, as well.

What the film does get right, however, is its exploitation of audiences' fear and fascination surrounding the Divine and the possibility of supernatural manifestations in everyday life, as well as its representation of religious suppression of contentious voices and a (perhaps particularly American) mistrust of the Catholic Church. The constellation of events of the film—with the Gospel According to Thomas at their core—speak directly to these sentiments as they culminate in uncovering a suppressed "truth." In doing so, the film relies less on "accuracy," and more on "evocation," a strategy that is both its greatest strength and its greatest weakness.

As John O'Connor, Peter Rollins, and other scholars considering the role of film in our understanding of "the real" have pointed out, one of the first steps in developing a constructive approach to considering a given film is to move beyond questions of verisimilitude and consider carefully the impact that the narrative has created—the overall message it has constructed for audiences—as an interpretation designed to convey meaning and carry emotional impact. The details, in short, are subordinate to the "big picture"—the *gestalt* that is being conveyed.[24] Thus, while Ebert's criticisms are valid, they may not tell the whole story, which is one that interrogates faith and belief, both in the supernatural and in the Catholic Church.

Douglas Cowan argues that "[r]egardless of differences in belief, doctrine, or ritual, the thread that binds religions together is the relatively simple conviction that *this is not all there is.*"[25] Across the spectrum of religion and spirituality, belief in the unseen persists, manifested in acts as simple as prayers, and as complex as perceptions, Cowan notes, of daily battles "against the spiritual forces of evil."[26] All suggest that, to varying degrees, we *want* to believe. In fact, the highest endorsement that the Catholic Church bestows on an alleged act of the Divine, is to deem it "worthy of belief."[27] Catholics (and Christians more generally) are, by definition, people who have to believe in at least two miracles of the supernatural on Earth, according to Michael O'Neill: that of Christ's incarnation and his resurrection.[28]

The stigmata have formed a major category of miraculous occurrences since the days following Christ's crucifixion. In his letter to the Galatians, the apostle Paul states, as evidence of his divine authority: "Henceforth let no man trouble me; for I bear on my body the marks of Jesus."[29] Famous religious figures such as St. Francis of Assisi, Sister Anne Catherine Emmerich, and St. Padre Pio del Petrelcina have all been cited as having received the stigmata, along with accompanying gifts of vision, bilocation, and other supernatural phenomena not so far removed from *Stigmata*'s fictional portrayals. According to O'Neill, 35 claims of stigmata have been made to the Vatican in the 20th century, and of these, three have been officially approved.[30] Claims of these supernatural manifestations continue to be advanced, and while most will never receive official recognition, they continue to draw throngs of onlookers, as devotees and skeptics alike press close to witness and determine for themselves if the sacred has indeed broken through into history. The dramatic (and horrific) impact of *Stigmata*, then, is partially located in its evocation of the dozens—hundreds overall—of claims to sacred authenticity, most of which have gone unacknowledged or been denied by the Vatican.

In its role as gatekeeper of the Divine, the Catholic Church is also the subject of faith and belief. While claiming a role as the reputed highest moral voice in the world, it has also been deemed the most ambitious and the most secretive. Its leaders have claimed authority over presidents and kings, and exemption from governance by any nation-state, while its hierarchy has been the focus of charges of scandal, conspiracy, and corruption—from the finances of the Holy See, to Mafia affiliations and Fascist alliances, to pedophilia and other sex scandals.[31] Such accusations, and the resultant findings, have affirmed the fears of outsiders and shaken the faithful. In the predominantly Protestant-dominated U.S., concerns about Vatican power, and its abuse, have been particularly acute, growing rather than receding with time. Those concerns become the driving force of *Stigmata*'s narrative, with the Gospel According to Thomas—declared heretical and suppressed in real life—as their focal point. Alamieda and Petrocelli are ordered to cease their translations of the texts, and continue in secret, fearing for the fate of the truth if the documents are lost to them. The film's narrative strategy suggests that, since the Vatican did, in fact, suppress the Gnostic gospels and exclude their contrary rhetoric that spoke truth to power, its "suppression" of all those who might bring that truth to light is also possible—even to the murder of an unwilling young messenger, halfway around the world.

Conclusion

Supernatural horror films like *Stigmata* are frequently viewed as simulations that expose the uncertainties in our existential worlds and encourage us to speculate about other possible, unseen realities. They allow us to imagine—free of material (or spiritual) consequences—the collision of such realities with our own, and so to undergo what Isabel

Pinedo has termed "the bounded experience of fear."[32] However, in setting up the Church as the true (earthly) source of evil, *Stigmata* turns traditional supernatural horror in general, and the exorcism subgenre in particular, on its ear, casting a troubled young woman as complex forces of "right." In this, she is championed by a man of both God and science—a "miracle-buster"—a priest who is valued for, of all things, his doubt, and who finds belief through her. The Church's hierarchy, represented by the obsessively corrupt Cardinal Houseman, are cast as stale icons of social, political, economic, and spiritual power intent on denying and eradicating new knowledge and ostracizing those who would pursue it, in an effort to preserve their own status and structures of belief.

The film thus avoids what Cowan and Bromley have referred to as the "good, moral, and decent fallacy"—the misconception that religion is always a force for good—and so, portrays the lived complexities and contradictions of the Church in the world.[33] Religion, as Jonathan Smith offers, "is not nice; it has been responsible for more death and suffering than any other human activity."[34] Yet, as the film illustrates, it is not religion that is at issue here, in the film, or in the sociocultural context from which it arises, but the claims to absolute power, authority, and truth made by its emissaries. This is where the film locates the true horrors of evil: in corruption and the suppression of difference, and in the insistence that relationships with the Divine must be mediated, directed, and controlled by a self-interested institution. The Truth—here represented by the Gospel According to Thomas and all those become its agents—rebels. Father Alamieda, its voice from beyond the grave, thus creates a tortured messenger in Frankie, using her body as an instrument to challenge the word of the Church with the Word of God: heresy confronting heresy on behalf of humankind.

Notes

1. The Gospel of St. Thomas, verse 77.
2. St. Thomas is historically remembered as "Doubting Thomas" for his refusal to believe that Jesus had been resurrected until he could see and touch the wounds He received on the cross. The phrase "doubting Thomas" has come to describe an individual who is skeptical and requires proof.
3. Both supposedly based on real life stories of possession and exorcism.
4. Hippolytus, *Refutationis Omnium Haeresium* I 8, 15, 1–2.
5. Tau Malachi, *The Gnostic Gospel of St. Thomas: Meditations on the Mystical Teachings* (Woodbury, MN: Llewellyn Publications, 2004), 1.
6. Elaine Pagels, *The Gnostic Gospels* (New York: Vintage, 1979), xv.
7. "Gospel of Thomas" 32:10–11, quoted in *The Nag Hammadi Library*, ed. James M. Robinson (New York: Harper & Row 1977), 118.
8. Helmut Koester, "Introduction to the Gospel of Thomas" *The Nag Hammadi Library*, ed. James M. Robinson (New York: Harper & Row, 1977), 117.
9. Pagels, *Gnostic Gospels*, xviii.
10. *Ibid.*
11. *Ibid.*
12. Cited in J.F. Bierlein, *Parallel Myths*, 320. See also Mircea Eliade, *Myth and Reality*, trans. Willard R. Trask (1963. New York: Harper & Row, 1975), 5–6.
13. Christopher J. Olson and Carrielynn D. Reinhard, *Possessed Women, Haunted States: Cultural Tensions in Exorcism Cinema* (Lanham, MD: Lexington Books, 2017), 8.
14. Quoted in *Ibid.*, 10.
15. *Ibid.*, 185. The authors note seven such films. Of these, only two were produced in the U.S.: Ken Russell's *The Devils* (1971) and Waris Hussein's *The Possession of Joel Delaney* (1972).
16. *Ibid.*, 18. It is also important to note that of the 127 exorcism films produced since 1937, 82 were released after 9/11.
17. Daniel Horowitz, *Jimmy Carter and the Energy Crisis of the 1970s* (Boston: Bedford/St. Martin's, 2004), 113.
18. Tom Wolfe, "The 'Me' Decade and the Third Great Awakening," *New York*, August 23, 1976.
19. Natasha Zaretsky, *No Direction Home: The American Family and the Fear of National Decline* (Chapel Hill: University of North Carolina Press, 2007), 209.

20. It is of interest here that while the subgenre produced few films during the 1980s, possession was the ascendant narrative trope in American comics at the time.
21. Olson and Reinhard, *Possessed Women*, 119.
22. *Ibid.*, 119–120.
23. Roger Ebert, "Stigmata," January 1, 1999, http://www.rogerebert.com /reviews/stigmata-1999.
24. See John E. O'Connor, *Image as Artifact: The Historical Analysis of Film and Television* (Malabar, FL: Robert E. Krieger, 1990); Peter C. Rollins, ed., *Hollywood as Historian: American Film in a Cultural Context* (Lexington: University Press of Kentucky, 1983); and Robert Brent Toplin, *History by Hollywood* (Urbana: University of Illinois Press, 1996). These discussions are focused on the presentation of history, but may be fruitfully applied in this context, as well.
25. Douglas E. Cowan, *Sacred Terror: Religion and Horror on the Silver Screen* (Waco: Baylor University Press, 2008), 63.
26. *Ibid.*, 64.
27. Mary Rezac, "A Crash Course in Catholic Miracles," *Catholic News Association*, May 9, 2016, https://cruxnow.com/church /2016/05/09/a-crash-course-in-catholic-miracles/
28. Michael O'Neill, *Exploring the Miraculous* (Huntington, IN: Our Sunday Visitor, 2015).
29. Galatians 6:17.
30. Here, O'Neill draws on the work of Michael Freze SFO, in *Voices, Visions, and Apparitions* (Huntington, IN: Our Sunday Visitor, 1993), http://miraclehunter.com/stigmata /1900–2000.html. Both O'Neill and Freze note that over 300 claims of stigmata have been made since the first recorded.
31. See, for example, Brenda Ralph Lewis, *The Dark History of the Popes: Vice, Murder, and Corruption in the Vatican* (Metro Books, 2009); Helen Ellerbe *The Dark Side of Christian History* (Morningstar and Lark, 1995).
32. Isabel Pinedo, *Recreational Terror: Women and the Pleasures of Horror Film Viewing* (Albany: State University of New York Press, 1997).
33. Douglas E. Cowan and David G. Bromley, *Cults and New Religions: A Brief History* (Oxford: Blackwell, 2008), 10–11.
34. Jonathan Smith, *Imagining Religion: From Babylon to Jonestown* (Chicago: University of Chicago Press, 1982), 110.

Bibliography

Bierlein, J.F. *Parallel Myths*. New York: Ballantine Wellspring, 1994.
Cowan, Douglas E. *Sacred Terror: Religion and Horror on the Silver Screen*. Waco: Baylor University Press, 2008.
Cowan, Douglas E., and David G. Bromley. *Cults and New Religions: A Brief History*. Oxford: Blackwell, 2008.
Ebert, Roger. "Stigmata." January 1, 1999. http://www.rogerebert.com/reviews/stigmata-1999.
Eliade, Mircea. *Myth and Reality*. Trans. Willard R. Trask. 1963. New York: Harper & Row, 1975.
Ellerbe, Helen. *The Dark Side of Christian History*. Orlando: Morningstar and Lark, 1995.
Freze, Michael SFO. *Voices, Visions, and Apparitions*. Huntington, IN: Our Sunday Visitor, 1993. http://miraclehunter.com/stigmata/1900–2000.html
Heller-Nicholas, Alexandra. "'The Power of Christ Compels You': Moral Spectacle and The Exorcist Universe." *Roman Catholicism in Fantastic Film: Essays on Belief, Spectacle, Ritual and Imagery*, ed. Regina Hansen, 65–80. Jefferson, NC: McFarland, 2011.
Hippolytus, *Refutationis Omnium Haeresium*. I 8,15, 1–2.
Horowitz, Daniel. *Jimmy Carter and the Energy Crisis of the 1970s*. Boston: Bedford/St. Martin's, 2004.
Koester, Helmut. "Introduction to the Gospel of Thomas." *The Nag Hammadi Library*, ed. James M. Robinson, 117–126. New York: Harper & Row, 1977.
Lewis, Brenda Ralph. *The Dark History of the Popes: Vice, Murder, and Corruption in the Vatican*. New York: Metro Books, 2009
Malachi, Tau *The Gnostic Gospel of St. Thomas: Meditations on the Mystical Teachings*. Woodbury, MN: Llewellyn Publications, 2004.
O'Connor, John E. *Image as Artifact: The Historical Analysis of Film and Television*. Malabar, FL: Robert E. Krieger, 1990.
Olson, Christopher J. and Carrielynn D. Reinhard. *Possessed Women, Haunted States: Cultural Tensions in Exorcism Cinema*. Lanham, MD: Lexington Books, 2017.
O'Neill, Michael. *Exploring the Miraculous*. Huntington, IN: Our Sunday Visitor, 2015.
Pagels, Elaine. *The Gnostic Gospels*. New York: Vintage, 1979.
Pinedo, Isabel. *Recreational Terror: Women and the Pleasures of Horror Film Viewing*. Albany: State University of New York Press, 1997.
Rezac, Mary. "A Crash Course in Catholic Miracles." *Catholic News Association*, May 9, 2016. https://cruxnow.com/church/2016/05/09/a-crash-course-in-catholic-miracles/.
Robinson, James M., ed. *The Nag Hammadi Library*. New York: Harper & Row, 1977.

Rollins, Peter C., ed. *Hollywood as Historian: American Film in a Cultural Context*. Lexington: University of Kentucky Press, 1983.
Smith, Jonathan. *Imagining Religion: From Babylon to Jonestown*. Chicago: University of Chicago Press, 1982.
Toplin, Robert Brent. *History by Hollywood*. Urbana: University of Illinois Press, 1996.
Wolfe, Tom. "The 'Me' Decade and the Third Great Awakening," *New York*, August 23, 1976. http://nymag.com/news/features/45938/.
Zaretsky, Natasha. *No Direction Home: The American Family and the Fear of National Decline*. Chapel Hill: University of North Carolina Press, 2007.

The Power of Film Compels You!
Transgressing Taboos and the War on Demonic Possession in The Exorcist

STEVE WEBLEY

> "I feel that there's certainly a hell of a lot there that people understand but that has not been mined. It has a lot to say to future generations."—William Friedkin[1]

On Boxing Day 1973, *The Exorcist* opened at 26 selected venues. Adapted by William Peter Blatty from his best-selling novel, and directed by William Friedkin—whose grittily realistic *The French Connection* (1971) had been lauded by critics—the film was awaited with eagerness and trepidation. It immediately captured the popular imagination and had a profound and lasting impact on cinematic horror. No one associated with the film had anticipated the chaos that would result at every premiere, nor did they foresee that the film would gross $232 million in the U.S. alone, a figure (over $900 million by today's standards) that easily bested contemporary box office hits.[2] Moviegoers fainted, vomited, and left theaters traumatized; some reported symptoms of PTSD that required therapy, while others sought out local clergy for prayers of protection. Theater owners hired security guards for crowd control as audience numbers swelled, and Blatty and Friedkin purchased thousands of cups of coffee to be handed out to those who stood in line for hours just to buy a ticket.[3]

Boasting an army of Jesuit advisors, the film attracted both praise and vehement criticism for its religious content, which depicted a 12-year-old girl's pubescent body as a profane battleground, with priests warring against the demonic forces that possessed her. *The Exorcist*'s portrayal of evil oscillated between a Manichean struggle against a "radical" evil and the characters' own subjective ethical conflicts and beliefs—a different sort of evil, which Hannah Arendt had provocatively labeled "banal."[4] Conservative voices frequently condemned the film, despite its seeming validation of their belief in both the reality of evil and the sanctity of Christian ideals. Wilson Bryan Key claimed that the film contained dangerous subliminal content, television evangelist Billy Graham deemed the very celluloid on which it was imprinted evil, and the fundamentalist Hal Lindsey declared that the film had set the stage for a future of Satanic attacks on the American public.[5]

Even in today's age of high-tech gore, *The Exorcist* is able to terrify, and frequently tops lists of the scariest films ever made. It still screens in theaters for commemorations of its release, as well as at Halloween, and has had several releases on DVD and Blu-ray. The film remains director Friedkin's most popular work, and its defining tropes continue to be appropriated for use in lesser sequels, homages, and outright imitations.

On one level, the power of the film can be attributed to Blatty and Friedkin's use of realism. The source novel was based on an actual account of the possession and exorcism of a young American boy in 1949. Blatty had studied the case closely as a student, had access to the priests involved, and had originally planned to write a non-fiction account of the ordeal. The author's choice of Pazuzu—an Assyrian deity of import to the creation of Christianity—to symbolize the Devil also gave the narrative a deep and rich real-world history. Our contemporary notions of theological, ethical, and philosophical dualism, as well as of the ongoing battles between entities of good and evil, can trace their origins to the creation of the Assyrian demon gods.[6] Pazuzu is represented in the film as he was worshipped by the Assyrians: in therianthropic form—a mixture of animal and human elements. This imagery taps into primordial conceptions of dualism, desire, taboo anxiety, transgression, and the creation of myths as deep structural devices for maintaining social bonds in the face of the change.[7] Such visual representations date back to cave art and the animistic belief systems that offered humankind an early and complete understanding of the cosmos and our place within it.[8]

In content, form, and function, then, *The Exorcist* tested the limits and desires of modernity, and exploded with the very real anxiety faced by a society in the process of "becoming"—transitioning into the postmodern condition. Utilizing Freud's notions of transgression and the uncanny, this essay explores the deep, lingering effects of *The Exorcist* on the American psyche, and offers suggestions about why it still has a profound impact on popular culture.

Tides of Chaos

In his seminal study of *The Exorcist*, critic Mark Kermode considers the timing of the film's release key to understanding its impact and legacy.[9] By the early 1970s, the U.S. was in social turmoil. The popular hedonism and optimism of the 1960s' counterculture generation had come to an abrupt end. Unrest was always looming, and the boundaries of home, work, family, and community were stressed by mounting ideological tensions and rapidly expanding consumerism. A military that had recently dropped food parcels to the crowds at Woodstock was now shooting at students who might well have been among that earlier throng. Hippies, once characterized by their embrace of love and peace, were now pilloried as potential cultists in the wake of the Manson murders; free festivals were being scrutinized after the death of Meredith Hunter at Altamont; and President Richard Nixon was under increasing pressure in response to his legal and ethical indiscretions and disconcerting reportage from Vietnam.[10]

The film's release also resonated with religious concerns of the day. The previous year, Pope Paul VI released an official proclamation voicing serious concerns about demonic forces in a world undergoing challenges to symbolic authority:

> Evil is not merely a lack of something, but an effective agent, a living spiritual being, perverted and perverting. A terrible reality.... So we know that this dark and disturbing spirit really exists and that he still acts with treacherous cunning; he is the secret enemy that sows errors and misfortunes in

human history. The question of the Devil, and the influence he can exert on individual persons as well as communities ... is a very important chapter of Catholic doctrine which is given little attention today, though it should be studied again.[11]

Despite this troubled context, Kermode is at a loss to fully explain *The Exorcist*'s capacity to shock, or to fully articulate why the film somehow evolves with each viewing.[12] While it clearly had the ability to shock and offend moviegoers, the film was not a low-budget exploitation flick or cult movie explicitly developed as a transgressive piece of filmmaking.[13] It used subtle, well-honed portrayals of believable characters to construct the story of a credible postmodern urban family decimated by an ancient and uncompromising evil.[14] For the first time, mainstream moviegoers were witness to the desecration of the last vestiges of the American Dream: home, family, church, and even child.[15] Viewers sat transfixed as a middle-class white girl spouted infernal obscenities, urinated in front of distinguished house guests, projectile-vomited on the local clergy, abused her mother, masturbated with a crucifix, and generally transgressed all of the norms of the day.[16]

Given the complexities at work behind the scenes of the production—between a deeply Catholic writer-producer who had concrete ideas about the movie's overt values, an intense and independent-minded Jewish director, and the publicity department of Warner Bros.—it is unsurprising that the film resonated with the public's sense of unease. Blatty was a conservative making the case for the real presence of supernatural evil in the modern world,[17] and the publicity department of Warner Bros. was quick to exploit the film's basis in reality.[18] Friedkin furthered this verisimilitude through the publication of carefully blended rumors and outright lies about illnesses, injuries, and accidents involving the cast and crew—events suggesting that some form of evil was at work in the studio.[19]

The social and religious transgressions depicted in the film, however, had a credible, realistic quality that made them disturbing even without the presence of supernatural evil behind them. Children who "acted out" in a rebellious but undecipherable manner, the breakdown of the traditional patriarchal familial unit, and the lack of respect for religious and patriotic traditions all concerned society at large and mobilized ideological debate. Moreover, the film appeared to offer ideologically acceptable solutions to those in the thrall of moral turpitude. It portrayed a clear-cut war between good and evil in which priests, policemen, good parents, and devout sons fought a holy battle to release a white middle-class American child from the clutches of an ancient Middle-Eastern devil—a war that was ultimately won by an adherence to conservative values, and an act of self-sacrifice.

Ancient Evil, Modern World

The Exorcist's successful grounding of the supernatural in a contemporary setting was, in part, due to radical revision of the screenplay. Director Friedkin rejected Blatty's first draft, which clung to genre conventions, demanding a return to the nuances of the novel and often working straight from its pages.[20] The result was an unruly screenplay that disturbed the modernist norms of the horror genre as it treated the topic of possession as seriously as a malignant illness, and portrayed the Devil as a serious character in a respectable drama.[21]

The resulting script focuses on Regan MacNeil (Linda Blair), the 12-year-old daughter of a noted actress, who begins to exhibit bizarre, inexplicable behaviors. Her mother, Chris (Ellen Burstyn)—a well-known film actress living in Georgetown while working on a new production—suspects that mental disorder is responsible, but the physicians and psychiatrists she consults are unable to identify, let alone cure, Regan's problem despite her undergoing a battery of invasive medical examinations. As a last resort, they suggest the possibility of an exorcism, presenting it not as an antidote to a genuine demonic possession but as a way to "cure" Regan of what they suspect is a psychosomatic disorder.

One night, however, while Chris is away from their Georgetown home, her friend and director Burke Dennings (Jack McGowran) falls to his death from a second-story window while babysitting Regan. The director's history of alcoholism suggests an accident, but Lieutenant Kinderman (Lee J. Cobb), the kindly but forceful detective investigating the death, suspects that Regan may somehow be involved. Later that night Chris hears a disturbance in Regan's room and enters to find her daughter masturbating with a crucifix while a deep, seemingly male voice commands her to "Do it!" Chris tries to intervene, but Regan fights her with superhuman strength, her head rotating in a circle atop her neck as an unseen force slams furniture across the room.

Terrified, Chris turns to Father Damien Karras (Jason Miller), a local Jesuit priest with a doctorate in psychiatry who had been present on the set of the film on which she was working. Karras is a deeply conflicted man: doubting his faith, questioning his vocation, and wracked by guilt over his inability to provide financially for his elderly mother in New York. A rationalist at heart, he is skeptical when Chris asks him to arrange for an exorcism, but after investigating the case more deeply and witnessing Regan's uncanny behavior firsthand. When Chris confides in him that she believes Regan killed Dennings, Karras concludes that the girl's soul is indeed at risk, and persuades his equally skeptical superiors to approve an exorcism. Father Merrin (Max von Sydow), who has already mystically foreseen the coming battle, arrives in Georgetown and is placed in charge, with Karras designated to assist.

Together Merrin and Karras confront the Devil and invoke the Power of Christ, but Karras' weakened faith causes him to waver and Merrin orders him from the room. Facing the Devil alone, Merrin succumbs to the strain and suffers a fatal heart attack. Karras re-enters the room and, unable to revive the older man, confronts the Devil on his own. An ex-boxer, he physically assaults Regan, demanding the Devil enter his own body instead. The Devil obliges, but Karras—in a an act of self-sacrifice made possible by a last, desperate assertion of free will—throws himself from the bedroom window before the Devil can compel him to harm Regan. His friend Father Dyer (William O'Malley) happens upon him and, realizing that Karras is dying, administers the last rites. Regan, freed from the demon, has no memory of her ordeal, but Chris, having seen the Devil face-to-face, now believes in God. They return to their home in California, leaving Dyer and Lt. Kinderman to investigate Karras's death.[22]

The evil that Merrin and Karras confront is not only ancient, but familiar—one that Merrin had encountered before. The film begins with a dream-like sequence of events in Mosul, Iraq, on the outskirts of which the ancient Assyrian city of Nineveh once stood. The film opens to discordant screeching as the title tiles give way to the burning dawn sun. Amidst the Arabic call to prayer and the dysrhythmic hammering of anvils and picks, audiences are introduced to Father Merrin the exorcist, Pazuzu the demon, and a

Merrin (Max von Sydow) and the therianthropic Pazuzu "face off" again across the abyss of time and space in *The Exorcist* (1973).

mise en scène that establishes audio and visual motifs that will recur throughout the film.[23] These screeching and syncopated cues are those heard again at the end of the film, in the exorcism scenes—an *après coup* that gives these early scenes a prophetic resonance. As the action follows Father Merrin to and from an archaeological dig, the sights and sounds of Mosul form a montage of discordant allusions to the notion that future horrors derive from the past. The priest struggles lugubriously, as if against the tide of sleep, perceiving the evil eye of a half-blind blacksmith, a prefiguring of the demonic gaze to come.[24] When he arrives at the dig site, there is tension in the air, and he moves through the ruins to a vantage point at the top of a mound. He finds himself engaged in a "high-noon"-like standoff with an ominously glaring statue of Pazuzu.[25] Later, as the exorcism unfolds, we are sure that the demon remembers him.

A St. Joseph medal is uncovered amongst the ruins, along with the head of a Pazuzu figurine. The medal is an amulet from another time, not meant to be there. It functions to create what Chesterton called "eerie realism,"[26] and serves as an example of Friedkin's genius for uncanny narrative layering and subverting modernist convention. The Christian medal creates an unknowable resonance throughout the rest of the film, a focal point of the dialectic of past-present-future within the narrative arc. It is present during a dream sequence in which Karras relives the death of his mother, is mysteriously ripped from the priest's neck at the instance of his possession and self-sacrifice, and appears once again in the final scene of the film: passed, symbolically, from Chris to Fr. Dyer, who will carry on the battle against evil. Each appearance of the amulet accelerates the narrative and heightens the cinematic assault on viewers' already vexed senses, but in the final scenes, it offers no formal narrative closure or meaning.

It's postmodernity that compels you! Merrin (Max von Sydow) and Karras (Jason Miller) invoke the Power of Christ as they exorcise Regan in *The Exorcist* (1973). The scene included the cutting-in of actual audio recording from an exorcism.

Evoking Darkness

As Merrin stares at Pazuzu's statue, the film cuts to a more familiar scene of urban life in Georgetown, and Friedkin utilizes the contrast between light and dark to create a binary emphasis between good and evil, past and present. The brightest scenes, almost surreal, occur at the opening in Iraq and during a later dream sequence. Georgetown, in contrast, is grey and subdued. New methods of panning and camera tracking, together with Rembrandt-esque lighting techniques, throw the viewer off balance, giving the documentary-style footage a compelling otherness and sense of raw minimalism that sets the stage for the elemental confrontation between innocence and corruption that will take place there. Light and dark, silence and sound, are constantly contrasted and combined with cuts to trouble the viewers' normal connotations of comfort and light. Intercutting enables Friedkin to upset quieter scenes dealing with important characterization with sudden cacophonous explosions of dysrhythmic sound and shocking imagery.

The film's special effects were part of Hollywood's golden age of puppetry, model-making, and practical effects, giving the horrific imagery onscreen a sense of solidity and realism. The voice of Devil, provided by radio veteran Mercedes McCambridge, was enhanced by an admixture of raw eggs, alcohol, and cigarettes, rather than electronic manipulation, and audio recordings from a real exorcism were spliced into the soundscape of the film's exorcism scenes.[27] Nothing was wasted as Friedkin used experimental exposures from the cutting room floor to shortcut demonic images at unexpected times. Any hint of social normalcy, family stability, or psychic wellbeing is juxtaposed with a contrasting scene or interjected by the uncanny. Likewise, moments of reflection, touching interactions, and moments of characterization on behalf of subtle performances are either intercut with or followed by harrowingly dramatic episodes. Caught between the rational and irrational, the viewer has nowhere to turn for answers, or even comfort.

And the psychic onslaught does not stop there. The normal cadence of the modern working lifestyle is itself summoned and then seemingly exorcised away. The narrative within the narrative—that is, the film that Chris is working on within the film—appears at the start, and then simply fades from view. Before it does, however, it firmly and explicitly calls viewers' attention to the youth-centered social and political upheavals of the era, making them available—indeed, irresistible—as a context within which to read the supernatural events to come. In the film-within-a-film, Chris plays the role of an academic struggling to convince rebellious students that attacking and tearing down their own institution would be a senseless act. On the set, with Karras observing from the margins, we see Chris (in character), explain to the angry young people that only change from within the system is valid, that those who are silent have rights too, and that even youthful rebellion and calls for change should adhere to established principles. The scene ends, and the illusion of the film-within-a-film dissipates, but the themes it introduced remain, shaping the rest of the film and becoming, for Chris, intensely personal and horrifyingly real. The uncontrollable youth she confronts will be not fictional student radicals, but her own daughter; the world threatened by unreasoning rage will be not a distant college campus mentioned in newspaper headlines, but her own home.

From the moment of that transition, there is no more respite; the film is a lesson in the traumatic nature of "becoming." Transgressions of normal bodily, worldly, psychic, societal, and cinematic boundaries are relentlessly evoked. Every intercut between Chris and Karras punctuates their sense of normalcy with a sense of dread and doubt about what they are becoming. Beginning with everyday concerns, Chris fears becoming just a "normal" actor while Karras fears an existence as a faithless psychiatrist. Each intercut revels in an escalating sense of weakness and self-doubt that finally borders on hysteria. This transgressive sense is magnified by the film's use of quotidian locations such as subways, hospitals, suburban streets, and bedrooms, which take on an uncanny corrupted character and can no longer be navigated without significance. When Father Karras, in a brief dream sequence, sees his (now dead) mother emerge from a New York City subway station and call to him from the top step before descending again, the snippet of a scene evokes a torrent of associations. His dream-face betrays renewed guilt over her lonely death, his frustration at his inability to comfort her as she died, and anxiety over passage into an afterlife in which he no longer fully believes. The sense of unnerving, uncontrollable change is uncomfortably palpable.

This unnerving sense, however, is both understated and carefully choreographed. The strongest influence on Friedkin's style at this period of his career was the work of the Italian filmmaker Michelangelo Antonioni, who redefined the idea of psychological drama, and disturbed established narrative ideas of storytelling. His films advanced the idea that we could not find the answers to the conundrums of the human condition, and that attempting to do so only led to further indecipherable riddles.[28]

Demons of the Human Soul

Psychoanalysis has traditionally offered a means to solving those riddles. Erupting into popular consciousness at the same moment as cinema, it developed, over subsequent decades, a close relationship with the horror genre.[29] It was viewed by filmmakers as a progressive way of understanding the world—what we desire, what terrifies us, and why, in some cases, those are one in the same. Freud's topology of superego-ego-id, set in motion by what he described as unconscious desires and the human fascination with that which we find uncanny, became a model for writers and directors. Like cinema, psychoanalysis became a defining pillar of modernity and remained hugely influential until the counterculture generation of the 1960s condemned it as elitist.[30] However, its saturation of western culture was so complete that its influence was impossible to escape, and it became part of the very medium of storytelling.[31]

Psychoanalysis is designed to disturb the demons of the human soul, to evoke what haunts us from the past and tortures our daily lives.[32] As such, it has structural influences on the medium of film that run much deeper than the psychology of character writing, and extend to the human condition as a whole. Film has, as psychoanalytical perspectives have become more mainstream, portrayed the human condition as one of fragility and uncertainty; we certainly are not what we think we are, and neither, perhaps, is our world.

Thus, film has increasingly portrayed vulnerable human subjects, irrevocably split between conscious and unconscious thought; the individual sought continuity, but was forced into a perturbed process of becoming. Story itself is about the dynamic conflict of becoming something one could not fully understand. The subject of film was now a subject of a terrible void, a void filled with socialized forms of human instincts that Freud called the "drives," a void into which we stuff the objects of desire. This was a notion of the human subject hard to accept—fetishistically disavowing it was part of the modernist condition.

It also follows that the most vibrant stories we tell ourselves have been an attempt to unpack the meanings inherent in Freud's discovery, and the resonance between that process and the storytelling convention of the horror genre is reflected in their long, intimate relationship. Freud himself warned that to grasp the lessons of psychoanalysis one had to be prepared to upend, reverse, and then relearn everything that rationalism had taught about reality. The overriding concern of psychoanalysis is to disturb the continuity of past-present-future, to evoke in the present the demons from the past that we unconsciously know haunt our futures, so as to exorcise them. Horror stories, though designed to entertain rather than enlighten, use similar techniques: turning reassuringly familiar settings alien and threatening; revealing dark secrets lurking behind never-opened doors; and placing characters at the mercy of powerful forces they barely comprehend, let alone control. Horror literalizes the demons of our individual or shared pasts—the ones that, Freud explains, appear when we tell ourselves stories that make background assumptions about desires, fantasies, and gaps in our knowledge, or the motivations that structure the ordering of reality.[33]

Freud's uncanny, which he used to signify the return of long repressed thoughts, fears, and desires, lies at the core of the horror genre. In the gothic tradition it came to represent some "thing" long buried that returns with a rebellious force that transgressed moral, patriarchal, and even scientific tradition—something monstrous, something uncanny. However, for Freud, the uncanny was a problematic concept that coalesced with taboos and the desire for transgression. Freud's uncanny involves the German concept of *heimlich*—homely, cozy, intimate, secure—and is thus suggested to infer its opposite, *unheimlich*. Implied within *heimlich* is also the concept of something that is hidden away, concealed from the outside world, secretive. By extension, what is hidden may also be threatening, fearful, occult, dismal, ghastly—and uncanny.[34] The term *unheimlich* describes, then, the point of negation.[35] What is homely and restful can, in a sublime instant, negate any barriers between subject and other, mind and body, spirit and matter, psychic and real; ultimately creating a profound moment of transgression, leading to reactions of both anxiety and excitement, fear and fascination. It is no coincidence that the horror stories we find most terrifying typically unfold not in dark forests or brooding gothic castles, but in quiet suburban neighborhoods or (as in *The Exorcist*) the bedrooms of young girls on their way to becoming women.

Freud obsessed over the uncanny as it signified a central "knot" of universal human experience, a dimension that haunts humanity, particularly at times of societal change and insecurity.[36] The real horror of the uncanny is when one can no longer see where one's desires are leading, or what it is one is becoming—or as Freud observed: "I think that the feeling of something uncanny is directly attached … to the idea of being robbed of one's eyes…."[37]

Dissolving Boundaries

While Kermode argues that the film represents clear-cut tensions at the boundaries between the progressive and the regressive, the divine and the demonic, and the hidden and the apparent, there is more at work than has previously been accounted for in *The Exorcist*. What was unleashed in the film was a powerful concoction of form, characterization, and symbolic content that seemingly bubbled forth to undermine social, temporal, and cinematic, modernist conventions. These elements had a powerful impact on poorly prepared sophomoric audiences of the 1970s, and their power can still be felt in our contemporary desensitized times.

Our earliest primordial depictions of the boundaries of human existence are of the demons that stalk humanity in the liminal world of dreams; a space of "terrible freedom" that bears witness to our inner fears and longings.[38] To dream and waken is a daily process of transgression and becoming. To fall asleep, we transgress the boundaries of subjective reality and are at our most vulnerable; awakening is also a complex process of becoming, as we pull our conscious reality back together. We access a primal, animistic stage in our dreams, where the objective rules of reality and identity no longer function. It is through animism that animal and human combined to create the mythic Therianthropes, such as the demon Pazuzu, whose form and function date back to a time predating organized religion. These Therianthropes were neither diabolic nor sacred, but symbolized a daemonic *potential*—the potential for change, whether for good or ill.[39] Animism also advanced belief in the soul's ability to travel between animate and inanimate objects, piercing the membrane between life and death, and suggesting that there was no ultimate boundary of the human body and identity. It was the function of early myth, like those surrounding Pazuzu, to regulate these permeable boundaries between the spirit realm and the integrity of the physical body, allowing enough fantasy to creep through in order for individuals and communities to cope with the realities of change and progress.

Although animism was gradually surpassed by theology, and later science, it was human's only complete world system that fully accounted for the nature of reality. Both theistic and scientific world systems left mankind with an impenetrable doubt regarding the future and what we are to become, and traces of the Therianthropes remained in both art and scripture across generations as debased demonic forms of evil. Freud argued that these became encoded in the very foundations of our modern laws and systems of knowledge, and account for part of the anxiety we experience when face with transgressions or the uncanny.[40]

Emulating Antonioni's techniques, Friedkin similarly utilized dreamlike layering of motifs to disturb the boundaries of the audiences' understandings of reality and the supernatural. The result was a film that broke free from its own constraints as a work of fiction to become myth, revitalizing mainstream horror by producing a narrative within a narrative that had deeply disturbing unconscious resonance for a society on the cusp of the postmodern condition.

What Does the Devil Want?

We are left with the question "What does *The Exorcist* really want from us?" In the recut version of the film Father Merrin, when asked by Karras what it is the Devil wants, responds that it wants us to despair, to see ourselves as animal and ugly. The attack is not upon Regan but on society at large—the Devil has bigger things in mind. Made at the cusp of postmodernity, *The Exorcist* forces us to recognize that hegemonic power depends on, rather than shrinking from, transgression, which sustains it as the cause of desire. The 1960s were a period when the call to pervert tradition, to be free of shame and guilt, was the watchword of a new generation. By the 1970s, however, their politicized rallying cry had been appropriated and commodified by very the power structure against which it had been directed. Its purpose lost, it became a meaningless form of acting out: an experience to be consumed rather than a philosophy to be lived, the uneasy object of a desire rather than its cause. What was left was a loss of identity, and a perception of falsity—that the call to transgression was sustaining, rather than challenging the status quo.[41]

Transgression creates tension between the individual's desire to violate taboos, on one hand, and society's need to punish transgressors lest they bring about society's downfall, on the other. One way of controlling the sites of transgression was to situate them narratively, allow them spaces and places to become ritual, to allow them to tell stories and become myths. As such, transgression becomes one of the earliest socio-cultural narratives to mythologize death, rebirth, and becoming.

Psychoanalysts have argued that the uncanny is a fundamental aspect of modernity, and that what we call postmodernism is merely a new consciousness regarding its function[42]—a new awareness of modernity's construction of desire, the workings of guilt and shame, and the hegemonic appropriation of sites of transgression. To be shameless and guilt free is the province of radical evil, it is also interestingly and increasingly an embodiment of the postmodern condition.[43]

In adapting Antonioni's form, Friedkin eclipsed the apogee of modernity—an age that was on the cusp of becoming something other, characterized by a frustrated, but ever-present optimism. Antonioni's style and form agitated notions of becoming, heralding the possibilities of an increasingly secularized future charged with desire, in which old traditions and values were gradually supplanted by technology and pleasure, while asking at what spiritual cost?[44] Friedkin mirrors this form in the constant prefiguring of both narrative scenes and intercutting, and in his quick-cutting of demonic faces, all of which he uses to develop the uneasy sense that evil is already present in Georgetown; that like Regan's condition, and all the characters' feelings of discontent, it has always been creeping unnoticed and unquestioned from the unconscious.[45]

Ultimately, *The Exorcist* is an exemplar of a new generation of narratives that questioned the psychosocial anxieties of threatened societal boundaries. Friedkin created a narrative that in form, function, and content piques our fears over what we are becoming and our anxiety over a loss of continuity in our normal everyday lives. In this context, the film was a work of new-age "boundary fiction" that brought ancient religious fears and contemporary social anxiety together within the genre of theological horror. Playing out on the psychic battleground of good and evil, the film takes us to a liminal space that is as old as humanity: a site where our oldest notions of truth are rendered vulnerable to transgression. It is, therefore, best understood not simply as a triumphant appropriation of religious imagery and ideas in the service of horror, or as a work of self-conscious and thus postmodern transgressive art, but as an argument that the anxieties wracking American society in the late '60s and early '70s—fears that bold transgressions of cultural norms signalled the impending dissolution of civilization—are in fact as old as civilization itself.

Notes

1. Daniel Olson, "Editor's Preface," in *Studies in the Horror Film: The Exorcist*, ed. David Olson, 11–13 (Westview, CO: Centipede Press, 2011).

2. See Jordan Raup, "The Cultural Impact of The Exorcist," *The Film Stage*, August 22, 2014, accessed August 2, 2016, https://thefilmstage.com/news/the-cultural-impact-of-the-exorcist/ and Philip French, "The Exorcist Review—Philip French on William Friedkin's Stark, Demonic Horror," *The Guardian*, January 11, 2015, accessed August 10, 2016, https://www.theguardian.com/film/2015/jan/11/the-exorcist-william-friedkin--dvd-blu-ray-philip-french-classic.

3. Recently a short 1974 documentary tracing the initial impact of the film has been released on video hosting sites. Most interesting are the interviews with audience members who had to leave the screening unable to cope with the psychic onslaught of the film. See "The Exorcist: The Cultral Impact," 1974, YouTube.com, accessed April 22, 2016, https://www.youtube.com/watch?v=6OtrZoqN-xo. See also Raup, "Cultural Impact," and Nick Cull, "*The Exorcist*," *The Guardian*, May 2000, accessed August 2, 2016, http://www.historytoday.com/nick-cull/exorcist.

4. Hannah Arendt expounded, in *The Origins of Totalitarianism* (1951) on Kant's philosophy of radical evil, and in had in earlier post-war debates labelled Nazi atrocities as a diabolical evil. In *Eichmann in Jerusalem* (1963) she focused on the banality of evil citing as an example Eichmann's actions in administering and bureaucratizing the Holocaust. Henry Zvi Lothane, "The Lie of the Banality of Evil: Hanah Arendt's Fatal Flaw," in *Ethics of Evil: Psychoanalytic Investigations*, ed. Ronald C. Naso and Jason Mills (London: Karnac, 2016), 233.

5. Quoted in Marc Kermode, *The Exorcist: Revised 2nd Edition* (London: BFI, 2003), 45. See also David Bartholomew, "The Exorcist: The Book, the Movie, the Phenomenon," *Cinefantastique* (Winter 1974), 10; Wilson Bryan Key, *Media Sexploitation: The Hidden Implants in America's Mass Media* (Englewood Cliffs: Prentice Hall Trade, 1976). The film was also restricted if not officially banned in the UK between 1986 and 1999 due to Warner Bros. concerns that a home video/DVD re-release would be officially banned under the Video Recordings Act of 1984. The original UK theatrical release was always legal.

6. Stephen Langdon, "Babylonian and Hebrew Demonology with Reference to the Sopposed Borrowing of Persian Dualism in Judaism and Christianity," *Journal of the Royal Asiatic Society of Great Britain and Ireland* 1 (January 1934), 45–56.

7. Therianthropes and their creation have an interesting role to play in the transgressive arts movements. They were a mainstay of the surrealist movement, with Picaso's Minotaur perhaps the most famous, and are in part accountable for the movements longevity—with Minotaure journal being the figurative publication of the movement that demonstrated its collective interests in its close attention to the study of myths and the creation of myths. See Anthony Julius, *Transgressions: The Offences of Art* (London: Thames & Hudson, 2002), 140–145 and Chris Jenks, *Transgression* (London: Routledge, 2003), 135–160.

8. Werner Herzog's film *Cave of Forgotten Dreams* (2010) is an intoxicating examination of the oldest known piece of therianthropic cave art, which dates to c. 40,000 BC.

9. See Kermode, *The Exorcist*.

10. *Ibid.*, 8.
11. *Ibid.*, 8–9. See also Bartholomew, "*The Exorcist*" (1974), 9; and David Bartholomew, "The Exorcist," in *The Exorcist: Studies in the Horror Film*, ed. Danial Olson, 15–34 (Westview, CO: Centipede Press, 2011).
12. Kermode states he has seen the film over 200 hundred times and every time, inexplicably and uncannily, it seems different. Mark Kermode, "Kermode and Mayo's Film Review," *YouTube,* November 2, 2010, https://www.youtube.com/watch?v=xcUXtEeVy-Y, accessed April 21, 2016. His thoughts are further developed in "The Fear of God," his documentary on *The Exorcist,* included as an extra on the 1998 "25th Anniversary Edition" DVD of the film. See also Stuart Samuels' documentary *Midnight Movies* (2005) and Andrew Monument's *Nightmares in Red, White and Blue: The Evolution of the American Horror Film* (2009).
13. See *Midnight Movies* and *Nightmares in Red, White, and Blue.*
14. Kermode, *The Exorcist,* 8–9.
15. *Ibid.*
16. *Ibid.*
17. Cull, "*The Exorcist.*"
18. For the detailed account of the actual case see Thomas Allen, *Possessed* (London: Corgi, 1994).
19. William Peter Blatty, *William Peter Blatty on* The Exorcist *from Novel to Film* (New York: Bantam, 1974). See also the "Fear of God" featurette on the *Exorcist: 25th Anniversary Edition* DVD.
20. Friedkin, quoted on the Exorcist: 25th Anniversary Edition DVD.
21. Dejan Ognjanovic, "The Exorcist," in *101 Horror Movies You Must See Before You Die*, ed. Steve Jay Schneider, 201–203 (London: Cassell Illustrated, 2009).
22. *Ibid.*
23. Kermode, *The Exorcist,* 23–25.
24. *Ibid.*
25. *Ibid.*, 25.
26. The concept of eerie realism is of a "thing" that uncannily appears before us but represents in rebus form something hidden in our internal psychic lives that we wish to remain unaware of. That there is something ghastly and terrible secreted inside each of us the even we "ourself" do not clearly understand. See Jela Krečič and Slavoj Žižek, "Ugly, Creepy, Disgusting, and Other: Modes of Abjection," *Critical Inquiry* 43 (Autumn 2016).
27. Friedkin, quoted on the *Exorcist: 25th Anniversary Edition* DVD.
28. Jason Ankeny, *Michelangelo Antonioni,* accessed November 16, 2016, http://www.allmovie.com/artist/michelangelo-antonioni-p79780.
29. Slavoj Žižek, *Looking Awry: An Introduction to Jacques Lacan Through Popular Culture* (Cambridge: MIT Press, 1991); *Everything You Always Wanted to Know About Lacan but Were Afraid to Ask Hitchcock* (London: Verso, 1997); *How to Read Lacan* (London: W.W. Norton, 2006); *The Pervert's Guide to Cinema: parts 1, 2 & 3,* dir. Sophie Fiennes, perf. Slavoj Žižek, 2006.
30. Catherine Liu, "Psychoanalysis, Popular and Unpopular," in *A Concise Companion to Psychoanalysis, Literature, and Culture*, ed. Laura Marcus and Ankhi Mukherjee, 216–232 (London: Wiley-Blackwell, 2014).
31. Stephen Frosh, *Hauntings: Psychoanalyis and Ghostly Transmissions* (Basingstoke: Palgrave Macmillan, 2013), 3.
32. *Ibid.*, 2–3.
33. *Ibid.*, 3–6.
34. Mladen Dollar, "I Shall Be with You on Your Wedding-Night": Lacan and the Uncanny," *Rendering the Real* 58 (Autumn 1991): 5–23.
35. A properly Freudian way to consider the uncanny is actually as a negation of a negation—in and of itself a downwards spiral of negativity. This is an essential Hegelian reading of dialectical negation, where each negation carries an inscribed trace on the underside of its meaning of the prior negation.
36. Freud's repeated returns to the uncanny however, did little to actually solidify a working theory of how these unique and co-dependent phenomena function as a human constellation of psychic affects, or how they coalesce in clinical praxis.
37. Sigmund Freud, *The Uncanny*, ed. James Strachey (1919; London: Hogarth Press, 1955).
38. Ralph Waldo Emerson, "Demonolgy," *The North American Review* 124 (1877): 179–190, accessed March 13, 2014, http://www.jstor.org/stable/25110019.
39. In ancient Greek mythology for example the term Daemonic referred to therianthropic creatures and lesser gods that signified change, transgression, or even opportunity, and as such could be benevolent or even wholly indifferent to the plight of humanity and the human condition.
40. Sigmund Freud, *Totem and Taboo: Resemblances Between the Psychic Lives of Savages and Neurotics* (London: George Routledge & Sons, 1919).
41. Krečič and Žižek, "Ugly, Creepy, Disgusting, and Other," 67–69.
42. Dollar, "'I Shall Be with You on Your Wedding Night," 23.
43. Jenks, *Transgression,* 79–80.
44. Stephen Holden, "Antonioni's Nothingness and Beauty," *New York Times,* June 4, 2006, accessed November 2, 2016.

45. For Friedkin's own commentary on Antonioni's influence on his style and form and its use to create the sense of Regan's creeping unconscious see Friedkin, the *Exorcist: 25th Anniversary Edition* DVD.

BIBLIOGRAPHY

Allen, Thomas. *Possessed*. London: Corgi, 1994.
Ankeny, Jason. *Michelangelo Antonioni*. Accessed November 16, 2016. http://www.allmovie.com/artist/michelangelo-antonioni-p79780.
Bartholomew, David. "The Exorcist: The Book, the Movie, the Phenomonon." *Cinefantastique* (Winter 1974): 8–13.
Bartholomew, David. "The Exorcist." In *Studies in the Horror Film: The Exorcist*, ed Danel Olson, 15–34. Westview, CO: Centipede Press, 2011.
Blatty, William Peter. *William Peter Blatty on The Exorcist from Novel to Film*. New York: Bantam, 1974.
Cull, Nick. *The Exorcist*. 200. Accessed August 2, 2016. http://www.historytoday.com/nick-cull/exorcist.
Dollar, Mladen. 1991. "'I Shall Be with You on Your Wedding-Night': Lacan and the Uncanny." *Rendering the Real* 58 (Autumn): 5–23.
Emerson, Ralph Waldo. "Demonolgy." *The North American Review* 124 (1877): 179–190. Accessed March 13, 2014. http://www.jstor.org/stable/25110019.
The Exorcist: 25th Anniversary Edition. 1973. Dir. William Friedkin. Warner Home Video, 1998. DVD.
"The Exorcist: The Cultral Impact." YouTube.com. Accessed April 22, 2016. https://www.youtube.com/watch?v=6OtrZoqN-xo.
Foucault, Michel. *Madness & Civilization*. Translated R. Howard. New York: Vintage, 1988.
French, Philip. "*The Exorcist* Review—Philip French on William Friedkin's Stark, Demonic Horror." *The Guardian*, January 11, 2015. Accessed August 10, 2016. https://www.theguardian.com/film/2015/jan/11/the-exorcist-william-friedkin-dvd-blu-ray-philip-french-classic.
Freud, Sigmund. *The Uncanny*. 1919. London: Hogarth Press, 1955.
_____. *Totem and Taboo: Resemblances Between the Psychic Lives of Savages and Neurotics*. London: George Routledge & Sons, 1919.
Frosh, Stephen. *Hauntings: Psychoanalyis and Ghostly Transmissions*. Basingstoke: Palgrave Macmillan, 2013.
Holden, Stephen. "Antonioni's Nothingness and Beauty." *New York Times*, June 4, 2006. Accessed November 2, 2016. http://www.nytimes.com/2006/06/04/movies/04hold.html.
Jenks, Chris. *Transgression*. London: Routledge, 2003.
Julius, Anthony. *Transgressions: The Offences of Art*. London: Thames & Hudson, 2002.
Kermode, Mark. "Kermode and Mayo's Film Review." YouTube.com, November 2, 2010. Accessed April 21, 2016. https://www.youtube.com/watch?v=xcUXtEeVy-Y.
_____. *The Exorcist: Revised 2nd Edition*. London: BFI, 2003.
Key, Wilson Bryan. *Media Sexploitation: The Hidden Implants in America's Mass Media*. Englewood Cliffs: Prentice Hall Trade, 1976.
Krečič, Jela, and Slavoj Žižek. "Ugly, Creepy, Disgusting, and Other: Modes of Abjection." *Critical Inquiry* 43 (Autumn 2016).
Langdon, Stephen. "Babylonian and Hebrew Demonology with Reference to the Sopposed Borrowing of Persian Dualism in Judaism and Christianity." *Journal of the Royal Asiatic Society of Great Britain and Ireland* 1 (January 1934): 45–56.
Liu, Catherine. "Psychoanalysis, Popular and Unpopular." In *A Concise Companion to Psychoanalysis, Literature, and Culture*, ed. Laura Marcus and Ankhi Mukherjee, 216–232. London: Wiley-Blackwell, 2014.
Lothane, Henry Zvi. "The Lie of the Banality of Evil: Hanah Arendt's Fatal Flaw." In *Ethics of Evil: Psychoanalytic Investigations*, ed. Ronald C. Naso and Jason Mills, 233–264. London: Karnac, 2016.
Nightmares in Red, White and Blue: The Evolution of the American Horror Film. Dir. Andrew Monument. Lionsgate, 2009. DVD.
Ognjanovic, Dejan. "The Exorcist." In *101 Horror Movies You Must See Before You Die*, ed. Steve Jay Schneider, 201–203. London: Cassell Illustrated, 2009.
Olson, Daniel. "Editors Preface." In *Studies in the Horror Film: The Exorcist*, ed. David Olson, 11–13. Lakeview, CO: Centipede Press, 2011.
Raup, Jordan. *The Cultural Impact of The Exorcist*, August 22, 2014. Accessed August 2, 2016. https://thefilmstage.com/news/the-cultural-impact-of-the-exorcist/.
Midnight Movies: From the Margin to the Mainstream. Dir. Stuart Samuels. Meridian, CO: Starz/Encore, 2005. DVD.
Žižek, Slavoj. *Everything You Always Wanted to Know About Lacan but Were Afraid to Ask Hitchcock*. London: Verso, 1997.
_____. *How to Read Lacan*. London: W.W. Norton, 2006.
_____. *Less Than Nothing: Hegel and the Shadow of Dialectical Materialism*. London: Verso, 2012.

_____. *Looking Awry: An Introduction to Jacques Lacan Through Popular Culture.* Cambridge: MIT Press, 1991.
_____. *The Most Sublime Hysteric: Hegel with Lacan.* Trans. Thomas Scott-Railton. Cambridge: Polity, 2014.
_____. *The Pervert's Guide to Cinema: parts 1, 2 & 3.* Dir. Sophie Fiennes. Prod. Sophie Fiennes. Perf. Slavoj Žižek. 2006.

About the Contributors

Catherine **Becker** is a Ph.D. student in English and the teaching of English at Idaho State University in Pocatello. Her areas of expertise are American literature, early British literature, and writing and rhetoric. Her research focuses on rhetorical ecologies in early American print culture and on online writing pedagogy.

Eleanor **Beal** is an associate lecturer in English literature and film at Manchester Metropolitan University. She is the author of *Postsecular Gothic* (forthcoming). Her research interests include the politics of countercultural spiritualities and the spectacle of religion and the female body in Gothic and horror texts.

Bart **Bishop** teaches online composition classes at Cincinnati State Technical and Community College. He has written on theater, pop culture, food, literature and movies for the *Spartanburg Herald-Journal*, *CityBeat*, *Cincinnati Magazine*, and *LitReactor*. His interests include feminist criticism, gender/queer studies and critical race theory.

Rhonda R. **Dass** is an associate professor at Minnesota State University, Mankato, in the anthropology department. Her research focuses on cultural examinations of issues that highlight areas of conflict and collaboration. Her teaching covers a broad range of cultural topics from American indigenous studies, anthropology, and museum studies.

Brad L. **Duren** is a professor of history and chair of the Department of Behavioral and Social Sciences at Oklahoma Panhandle State University. His research focuses on the intersection of historical inquiry and popular culture studies, particularly film, television, and music. He is a member of the national Popular Culture/American Culture and Southwest Popular Culture Associations.

Mark **Henderson** teaches at Tuskegee University. His research interests include the American Gothic, American modernism, surveillance studies and film horror, film noir, science fiction, dystopia, and disaster. He has published works on the significance of fire and diabolism in Richard Wright's *Native Son* and (forthcoming) dark nature as metaphor in the works of Edgar Allan Poe.

Matthew A. **Killmeier** is an associate professor of communication and theatre at Auburn University at Montgomery. His research interests include U.S. radio and film history. His publications have focused on radio drama adaptations of film *The Adventures of Mark Twain* (1944) and the radio drama anthologies *Dark Fantasy* (1941–42) and *The Witch's Tale* (1931–1938).

Sue **Matheson** is an associate professor of English literature at the University College of the North in Manitoba, Canada. She teaches American film and popular culture, Canadian literature, and children's literature. She the editor of *A Fistful of Icons* (McFarland 2017) and the author of *The Westerns and War Films of John Ford* (2016).

About the Contributors

Cynthia J. **Miller** is a cultural anthropologist specializing in popular culture and visual media. Her writing has appeared in numerous journals and collections and she has edited several essay collections. The editor for Rowman & Littlefield's *Film and History* book series, she serves on the editorial advisory boards for *The Journal of Popular Television* and Bloomsbury's *Guide to Contemporary Directors* series.

Martin F. **Norden** is a professor of communication at the University of Massachusetts Amherst, where he teaches film and is the faculty supervisor for the Bachelor's Degree with Individual Concentration Program. He has more than 100 publications and has presented his research at dozens of professional conferences. He consulted on the documentaries *CinemAbility* and *Be Natural: The Untold Story of Alice Guy-Blaché*.

Fernando Gabriel **Pagnoni Berns** is a professor at the Universidad de Buenos Aires (UBA)–Facultad de Filosofía y Letras (Argentina). He teaches seminars on international horror film and has published numerous essays in edited collections on various popular culture topics.

Daniel Otto Jack **Petersen** is a Ph.D. student at the University of Glasgow. His research focuses on an "ecomonstrous" reading of the fiction of Cormac McCarthy and R.A. Lafferty. His research areas include monster studies, ecocriticism, ecotheology, speculative realism, and object-oriented ontology.

Thomas **Prasch** is a professor and chair of history at Washburn University. His publications include essays on Roman Polanski's *The Fearless Vampire Killers*, Richard Lester's *Bed Sitting Room*, and Alfred Russel Wallace's fusion of Spiritualism and evolutionary thought.

Michael C. **Reiff** is a CollegeNow instructor through Tompkins Community College at Ithaca High School, where he also teaches film studies and advanced placement courses. He also teaches the Auburn Film Seminar through Cayuga Community College.

Lúcio **Reis-Filho** is a historian, author, and Ph.D. student in film and media studies at University Anhembi Morumbi | Laureate International Universities (São Paulo, Brazil). He specializes in the relations between cinema, history and literature and has written essays on zombies in contemporary Brazilian and Latin American films for journals such as the *SFRA Review* and in horror-themed edited collections.

A. Bowdoin **Van Riper** is a historian who specializes in depictions of science and technology in popular culture. He is the author or editor of a wide range of volumes, ranging from science to science fiction to horror. His collection *Learning from Mickey, Donald and Walt* was published by McFarland in 2011.

James J. **Ward** is a professor of history at Cedar Crest College, teaching modern European history, urban history, art history, and film and history. His articles and reviews have appeared in *The Journal of Contemporary History*, *The Journal of Interdisciplinary History*, *Central European History*, *The Historical Journal of Film, Radio and Television*, *The Journal of Popular Culture*, and *Film & History*.

Steve **Webley** is a lecturer and researcher in game design, war studies, and psychoanalysis in the School of Computing and Digital Technologies at Staffordshire University. His teaching specializes in military games design and development, interactive narrative design, and psychoanalytic game and film criticism.

Kevin J. **Wetmore**, Jr., is the author or editor of more than a dozen books on a range of topics as well as the author of dozens of articles and essays on everything from *Star Trek* to *Godzilla*, zombie cinema, werewolves, Greek tragedy in horror movies and postcolonial approaches to exorcism films. He is also a fiction writer.

Index

abjection 71–72, 236n26
abuse, child 84–85, 86n9, 164, 168–170, 219, 221
agnosticism 30; *see also* atheism
aliens 105, 109, 110, 111n13, 175, 184n2
allegory 2, 218
amorality 90, 93, 97, 113–115, 117–119, 122
amulets 69, 126, 229
animism 233–234
Antichrist 5, 7, 36, 53–55, 57–61, 64–69
anxiety 22, 26n57, 56, 67–68, 72, 79, 98, 170, 226, 231, 233–235
apocalypse 5, 7, 27, 53–55, 57, 60, 84, 127, 141, 149, 151–154, 160, 165, 167; *see also* End of Days
Apostles 34, 36, 151, 196, 221
Aquinas, Thomas 129–130
Arendt, Hannah 226, 235n4
atheism 5, 125, 135 182, 186, 192–193, 195–196, 213, 218, 220; *see also* agnosticism
authenticity 18–20, 216–217, 219, 221

Balagueró, Jaume 163, 166, 169, 171
Barker, Clive 113–114, 117
Beal, Eleanor 7, 78–86, 239
Beal, Timothy 30
Beast of the Apocalypse 127
Becker, Catherine 8, 140–149, 239
the Bible 18–19, 54, 59, 61, 84 107, 119, 142–143, 145, 175, 181
Bishop, Bart 8, 163–173, 239
Black, Andy 113
blasphemy 6, 192, 217
Blatty, William Peter 225–227
body horror 116–117, 218
boundaries 117, 140, 154, 231; denominational 170; good/evil 7, 14, 114, 119; horrific/divine 116; natural/supernatural 2, 84, 117, 146; sacred/profane 150–152; social 16, 226, 235; of subjective reality 233–234
Boyer, Paul 16
Bradley, Doug 8, 117–119, 121
Briggs, Robin 42
Bultmann, Rudolf 217

Callandar, Michelle 208
Calvinism 20, 22, 77, 81–85
Canby, Vincent 193
Carpenter, John 174–175, 180
Carter, Jimmy 55, 62n2, 219
catechism 19, 21, 37, 128
Catholic Church 174–175, 220–221, 226–227; Gnostic gospels suppressed by 9, 213; as patriarchy 35, 169; portrayed as agent of evil 5, 59, 143–145, 168–169; portrayed in *Dracula* mythos 190, 193–196; sexual abuse scandals 169, 219; suppression of dissent within 42–43; (attacks on, division in); teachings about science 182–183; *see also* Vatican
Catholicism 56–57, 109, 182, 193, 201, 205–207, 209–211; doctrines 1, 3, 8, 31–38, 60, 62n5, 127–131, 134, 141, 143, 145, 174–175, 179; influence on filmmakers 8, 125–126, 135, 137n43, 227; portrayed as oppressive 102, 104–106, 110; in Scotland 77–79; in Spain 166, 170–171; symbolism 7, 65, 69–70, 121, 131, 147
Cavanaugh, William 102
Cenobites 114–121, 123–124
censorship 10n17, 42, 166
chaos 41, 80 104, 108, 114, 118, 121, 123–124, 127, 130, 142, 156, 181, 225
Chesterton, G.K. 229
Children of the Corn (1988) 4
choice 7, 9, 29, 35–36, 70, 81, 91, 128–129, 148, 159, 180, 203
chosen people 77, 94, 95
Christ 2–3, 9, 41–43, 46, 86, 118, 176, 178, 183, 191, 213, 215, 228; as agent of salvation 32, 83, 129, 148–149, 205, 209, 215–216; characters' resemblance to 35–36, 38, 83–84, 120, 121, 181, 210; power of, invoked 228, 230; second coming 5, 57, 60, 144; symbolism of, inverted 193–196, 197n1, 219; witnesses for 6, 29, 33–36; *see also* Crucifixion, stigmata
Christianity 6, 79, 93, 129, 136n15,

137n50, 186, 195–196, 217–219, 226; ancient 196, 205; early modern 6, 43–45; medieval 29–33, 35, 41, 43, 45–46, 144; modern 38, 55–56, 69, 93, 107, 180–181; *see also* Calvinism; Catholicism; Evangelicalism; Fundamentalism; Methodism; Presbyterianism; Puritanism
cinematography 55, 66–69, 71, 79, 83, 85, 97, 176, 178–179, 189, 230
clergy 8, 15, 41, 56, 131, 180 184, 225, 227; ministers 57, 60; monks 46–48, 117–118; nuns 43, 48, 158–159, 210; priests 6, 8, 9, 29–30, 33–34, 40, 42, 54, 56, 59–60, 117, 119, 121, 145, 156, 163–169, 174–185, 186, 188, 190–196, 198n25, 200–212, 213–215, 218, 220, 222, 225–229
Clover, Carol 218
Cohen, Larry 7, 101–104, 109, 111n11
"A Confession of Unfaith" (1922) 122
conspiracy 215–217, 220–221
Constantine (2005) 8, 140–149
conventions 84, 94, 233; genre 80, 116, 174, 200, 227
corpses 43, 114, 170, 190
cosmicism 121–122
counterculture 56, 102, 107–109, 111, 226, 232
courts 13–17, 29–33, 35–37, 44–45, 54, 114–115, 121, 220, 222
Cowan, Douglas E. 2, 10, 30, 36, 54, 114–115, 121, 220, 222
Craft, Christopher 194
"creation science" 181–182
Creed, Barbara 168
criticism/critique 82, 95, 107, 131, 166, 181, 183, 203–204, 212n28, 217, 219–220, 235
cross 5, 40, 42, 121, 128–130, 154, 156, 159; weapon against vampires 191–192, 194–196, 198n19
crucifix 34, 121, 129, 131, 166, 181, 152, 168, 194, 227–228
the Crucifixion 5, 9, 79, 83, 129, 144, 213, 215, 220–221
Cthulu mythos 113, 116, 119, 122
Cult of Domesticity 65–66, 73

241

cults 3, 8, 64, 163, 165–166, 170–171; *see also* religion
culture wars 9, 73, 181–183

Darby, John Nelson 58–59, 61, 62*n*2
Dass, Rhonda 8, 150–169, 239
Davies, Rob 67
Del Toro, Guilliermo 8, 125–139
demonization 17, 170
demons 1–9, 40–41, 64, 69, 104, 213, 218; Balthazar 141–143, 145–147; Cenobites as 119–123; conflict with 89–98, 140–147; Ogdru Jahad 127, 130; Pazuzu 6, 226, 228–230, 233; possession by 29–34, 35, 37–38, 39*n*23, 45, 48, 163–169, 179, 215, 220, 225–237; redemption of 125–139; soldier 144–145, 147
Demos, John 16
Derleth, August 113–114, 116, 120, 122
Derrida, Jacques 144, 149*n*1
desecration 187, 190–191
desire 20, 37, 53, 56, 81, 84, 133, 159, 193, 202; for understanding 23, 61, 105; transgressive 30, 202–203, 208, 228, 232–234
The Devil 1–4; as agent of justice 7; as corrupting influence 2, 16, 19, 23; *see also* Lucifer; Satan
The Devil's Advocate (1997) 4, 40
The Devils (1971) 6, 40–44
dialectic, subversive 204–206
the divine 1–9, 61, 115–116, 151–152, 164; absence of, in modern life 101, 103, 130, 150, 170; boundaries of blurred 119, 174–175, 201, 207, 217, 233; experienced through torment 33, 116; manifestations of 29–31, 35–36, 38, 85, 90, 90–96, 104–106, 109–110, 134, 154, 213–216; mediated by Catholic church 218–220
doctrine 1, 3, 8–9, 41, 46, 94, 97–98, 102, 126, 181, 183, 213, 216–217, 220; Calvinist 80, 84; Catholic 60, 128, 130, 134, 227; Methodist 36; Puritan 21–22, 26*n*52, 53; secular 90, 95
dogma 30, 35–36, 56, 106, 108–110, 126, 128, 179, 183, 211
Donner, Richard 53, 59
doubt 22, 36–37, 105, 201, 216, 222, 228, 231, 233
Dowdle, John and Erick 163, 169, 171–172
Dracula 9, 153, 186–199, 203
Dracula Has Risen from the Grave (1968) 186–199
Dracula Prince of Darkness (1966) 188
dualism 120, 182, 205, 226
Dunsany, Lord 131–132, 135
Duren, Brad L. 6, 53–64, 239
Durkheim, Emile 151, 153, 156

Ebert, Roger 71, 89, 220
eco-horror 8, 125–139
ecstasy 43, 107, 114, 116, 129
Edwards, Jonathan 97
"eerie realism" 229, 236*n*26
Eggers, Robert 6, 13–14, 17–20, 23, 23*n*1, 24*n*17, 24*n*19–20, 25*n*39, 25*n*42
elder gods 113, 117, 120, 127; *see also* Cthulu mythos
elemental 132–133
Eliade, Mircea 69, 73
End of Days (1999) 5
End of Days (End Times) 3, 5, 57; *see also* the Apocalypse; the Great Tribulation; Premillenial Dispensationalism; the Rapture
enlightenment 57, 107–108, 110, 117, 123
Enoch, Book of 143; *see also* Bible
ethics 7, 9, 107, 110, 134, 201–202, 206, 208, 210–211
eucatastrophe 8, 125–126, 130–131, 133–134, 137
Euthyphro Dilemma 7, 103
Evangelicalism 6, 53–55, 61–63, 90, 98, 107, 125, 154
evangelism 35, 125
evil 1–4, 6–9, 84–85, 94, 96–97, 127, 190, 228–229; conflict with good 20, 53, 56, 60, 69, 102, 104, 110, 114–115, 120, 140, 142, 145–148, 152, 171–172, 188–189, 194–197, 198*n*19, 213, 218, 226, 229–230; embodiment of 29; nature of 163–164, 166, 168, 171, 175–176, 179–181, 183–184, 204–205, 220–222, 234–235; omnipresence of 14, 77, 80; radical 225; supernatural 30, 34, 37, 41, 48, 57, 108, 117–119, 122, 155, 186–187, 227
existential crisis 2–3, 56, 101, 200–203, 207–208, 219
exorcism 6, 29–39, 43, 141, 168, 191, 217–220, 222, 225–231; films, themes 218–219
Exorcism of Emily Rose (2005) 6, 29–39
The Exorcist (1973) 4, 6, 9, 29, 31, 39*n*23, 40, 53, 60, 64, 89, 120, 126, 169, 216, 219, 220, 225–238

faith, loss of 5, 9; in God 45, 122, 125–126, 135, 150, 186–199, 201, 203, 219–220, 228, 231; in secular institutions 55–56, 219
Fallen (1998) 4
family 13–28, 29, 33, 35, 65, 73, 82, 86, 95–96, 108, 133, 138*n*69, 195, 205, 218, 226–227, 230
fantasy 1, 81, 84, 108, 135, 137*n*42, 166, 233
Faust 4, 73, 98, 113
fear 1–3, 117, 121, 151–153, 168, 195, 202–203, 222, 231–233, 235; of fringe religious sects 164; of god(s) 1, 7, 9, 38, 90, 220; as motivation 47; in Scottish culture 76–79, 81–82, 84; of secular threats 16, 45, 101, 107, 155; of supernatural evil 1, 29–30, 190, 218; of witches 14, 48
feminism 16–17, 24*n*17, 65, 105, 170, 239
Fiedler, Leslie 98
Final Girl 84–86, 120
forgiveness 30, 37, 158
found-footage film 8, 163–167
Frailty 7, 89–100
Fraker, William 67
Francis, Freddie 186, 189–190, 192–193, 195, 198*n*18
Franco, Francisco 166
free will 90, 108, 129, 144, 180, 228
Freud, Sigmund 145, 180, 226, 232–234, 236*n*35–36
Friedkin, William 53, 225–227, 229–231, 234–237
Frum, David 56
fundamentalism 53, 56–58, 60, 81, 174, 181–182, 225

Gabriel (angel) 141–142, 147–148
Gaillo films 205
Gair, Christopher 101
Garrett, Clarke 16
gateway 4, 115–116, 120, 127–128, 145, 147, 178
gender roles 16, 25*n*29, 84, 108
Genesis, Book of 69, 94, 119, 140, 142–143, 146; *see also* Bible
Geneva Bible 18–19
Girard, Rene 209
gnosis (knowledge) 216
God (nature of) 4–5, 6–9, 14, 21–22, 29–31, 34, 38, 56–58, 60–61, 77, 80–85, 89–100, 101–112, 119–121, 125–139, 140–149, 168, 170–171, 174, 176–181, 183, 214, 215–217
God-fearing 81–82, 84
God Told Me To 7, 101–112
Goethe 113
Gospels 3, 13, 18, 143, 209; Gnostic 213, 216–217, 221; "secret" 220
the Gothic 67, 76, 79, 121, 134, 137*n*43, 137*n*45, 189, 232–233; American 90, 97–98; female 65, 84; Scottish 81; in vampire fiction 202–206, 209–210
Gould, Stephen Jay 182–183
grace 1, 5, 8, 14, 19–20, 22, 69, 82, 84, 85, 126, 130, 134
Graham, Billy 59, 225
Great Tribulation 57–58, 61–62

Hammer Films 9, 164, 166, 186–189, 193–194, 196–198
Hansen, Regina 206
heaven 1–3, 7, 35, 40, 57, 60–61, 69, 86, 108, 118, 140–145, 148, 192
Heidegger, Martin 131, 134
heimlich/unheimlich 232–233
hell 2–4, 6–8, 14, 40, 60, 77, 86, 113–124, 140–149
Hellblazer (1988–2003 graphic novel series) 141
The Hellbound Heart (1986 novella) 113, 117

Index 243

Hellbound: Hellraiser II (1988) 115, 118, 120
Hellboy (2004) 8, 125–131, 135
Hellboy II: The Golden Army (2008) 8, 126, 130–135
Heller-Nicholas, Alexandra 218
Hellraiser (1987) 4, 113–115, 117, 120, 122
Hellraiser: Bloodline (1996) 115, 121–122
Hellraiser franchise 7–8, 113–124
Hellraiser III: Hell on Earth 115, 119, 121
Henderson, Mark 7, 89–99, 239
heresy 9, 45–48, 50n26, 215–217, 220–221
hierarchy 65, 215, 221–222; cosmic 144, 148–149, 180
hierophany 7, 65, 69–70, 72, 117
Hinds, Anthony 187–190, 192–193, 197n13
Horror of Dracula (1958) 188–189, 197n6, 198n19
hubris 80, 118, 163, 169
Huguenots 41
Hutchings, Peter 72, 196–197
hybridization 201; of beings 133–134, 153; of genres 116, 125, 174

individualism 15, 84, 96, 102, 128, 201
indoctrination 156
Inferno 121, 143
Inquisition 46–47, 50
intellectualism 30, 33, 36, 182
intolerance 14, 46, 48, 81, 195, 218
Ireland 58, 77–79, 169, 195–196
Ives, Eric 72

Jesuits 39n23, 167, 225, 228
Jesus *see* Christ
Jewett, Robert 97
Jobling, J'annine 203, 206–27
Jonestown 170
Jorstad, Erling 107
Joshi, S.T. 128, 130
justice 7, 36–37, 56, 76–78, 80–84, 94, 101, 107, 128

Kane, Paul 113, 119–120
Karlsen, Carol F. 16
Kermode, Mark 49n13, 226–227, 233, 236n12
Key, Bryan 225
Kierkegaard, Søren 90
Killmeier, Matthew A. 9, 174–185, 239
Kneale, Nigel 175
Korea 9, 200–201, 205, 212n28
Kratter, Matthew 210
Kristeva, Julia 72, 203

labyrinths 7, 71–72, 114, 120
Lament Configuration 114–116, 119–120
landscapes 132, 142; American 6, 95–97; European 43, 79, 84
Lasch, Christopher 219

The Late, Great Planet Earth 6, 57–58
Latham, William 114
law 203; civil 4, 7, 13, 30–31, 82–84, 86, 97, 103, 106, 110, 170, 181, 234; natural 135, 144
Lawrence, Francis 8
Lawrence, John Shelton 97
Lee, Christopher
Legion (2010) 5
Let Us Prey (2014) 7, 76–86
Levack, Brian 33–34, 42
Lima, Robert 70
liminality 140, 147–148, 206–207, 233, 235
Lindsey, Hal 6, 57–59, 61
Longbons, Jarrod 209
love, divine 129
Lovecraft, H.P. 7, 113–114, 116–122, 128, 130–131, 135
Lowenstein, Adam 107
Lucifer 2, 34, 40, 86, 108; *see also* Satan

Macfarlane, Alan 15–16
Manifest Destiny 90, 95
manifestation, supernatural 1, 3, 15, 31.34–36, 70, 84, 213–222
Marcus, Sharon 65
martyrdom 30, 32, 34–36, 209, 212n28
Mary *see* Virgin Mary
Mather, Cotton 19, 25n41, 25n42
Matheson, Sue 7, 64–75, 239
McElhaney, Joe 66–67
McWilliam, David 119
mercy 30, 36–37, 159, 202
metaphysics 9, 56, 122, 174–185, 207, 214
Methodism 30, 36–37, 107
Michaelsen, Robert 22
Mickle, Jim 150
Mignola, Mike 126, 128, 135
millennial fever 170; *see also* Premillennial Dispensationalism
Miller, Cynthia J. 1–10, 213–224, 240
Miller, Kenneth R. 182–183
Milton, John 40, 108, 143–144, 147
Mira, Alberto 204
miracles 3, 30–31, 38, 135, 210, 214–217, 222
mise-en-scène 66, 68–69
monks *see* clergy
monsters 7–9, 29, 41, 72, 94, 118, 125–126, 128, 130, 133–134, 136n5, 137n42, 137n45, 142, 152–153, 155, 160n7, 163–166, 174–175, 180, 195, 202–204, 209, 211; monstrophilia 125; monstrosity 45, 72, 94, 125; the monstrous 2, 6, 30, 40–41, 45, 71, 78, 80, 83, 90–91, 94–95, 116, 118, 126, 133–134, 160n4, 188, 203–205, 208, 210, 232
Monsters in America 152
morality 93, 103–110, 115, 157, 181, 196, 200, 203, 206, 208; moral purity 16, 65–66, 69, 97, 118, 120,

157, 159, 211n11; moral spectacle 218
Moreman, Christopher 205
motherhood/pregnancy 65–73, 131, 137n65, 179; birth 3, 5, 54, 65–72, 78, 133, 137n65, 145, 147, 217, 234
Muir, John Kenneth 61, 119,
multiculturalism 107, 109
Munger, Robert 59, 61
murder 2, 7, 41, 46–47, 54, 82, 89–98, 101, 103, 105–107, 110, 119, 122, 130, 154, 164, 170, 221, 226
mystics 33, 40; *see also* saints

Naj 'Hammadi 216
Name of the Rose (1986) 6, 40, 45–48, 50nn25–26, 28
nature, human 2, 129, 201–202, 204, 207–210
Nelson, Victoria 135, 147n43
New England 6, 13–14, 16–18, 53
New French Extremity 76
New York City 64, 66–67, 70, 102–103, 133, 228, 231
New York Times 193
Nietzsche, Friedrich 90, 93–94, 97
Nissenbaum, Stephen 16
Norden, Martin F. 9, 186–199, 240
nuns *see* clergy
objects, holy 3, 9, 125, 144, 151–152, 156, 186, 194–195

O'Brien Shelley F. 205
the occult 64, 80–82, 126, 210, 233
O'Connor, Cardinal John 3
Olson, Christopher 217–220
The Omen (1976) 4, 6, 40, 53–64, 89, 101, 11n6, 120
O'Neill, Michael 221
ontology 128; participatory 134; sacramental 126, 134
opposition, binary 8, 69, 118, 140–149, 171, 230
Orsi, Robert A. 3
other/otherness 3, 76, 78, 107–108, 152, 166, 210
Otto, Rudolf 1

Pagels, Elaine 217
Pagnoni Berns, Fernando Gabriel 7, 101–112, 240
palimpsest 176–177, 179–180, 183
pandemic 150
Paraclete 209–210, 212n28
Paradise Lost 5, 40, 108, 143–144, 146–147
Park, Chan-Wook 9, 200–212
patriarchy 218
Paul (the Apostle) 34–35, 59, 196, 221
Pender, Patricia 207
Perkins, Judith 32
Petersen, Daniel Otto Jack 8, 125–139, 240
Peterson, Jeanne 65
Pinhead 8, 115–124
plague 8, 42, 44, 150, 154, 163–164, 166, 168

244 Index

Plaza, Paco 163–164, 166, 171
Polanski, Roman 7, 17, 53, 64–73
police/law-enforcement 4, 7, 46, 54, 76–77, 80–85, 95, 104, 106, 110, 141, 164, 167–169, 227
Poole, Scott 152–153, 190
Pope Paul VI 1, 226
possession 2–3, 6, 9, 14, 16, 19–20, 23, 25nn41–42, 29–37, 40, 42, 45, 48, 129, 163–164, 167, 169, 179, 215–220, 225–235
postmodernism 3, 206–209, 226–227, 230, 234, 242
potential, daemonic 233
Prasch, Thomas 6, 13–28, 240
predestination 6, 14, 22, 26, 77, 80, 82
pregnancy 65–72, 131, 137n65, 179
Premillennial Dispensationalism 6, 53–62
Presbyterianism 77, 79, 81–82
priests *see* clergy
Prince of Darkness (1987) 8–9, 174–185
production 41, 44, 59, 77, 102, 166, 186–190, 197, 227–228; cinematography 13, 18, 65–69, 71, 79, 83, 85, 97, 109, 190; lighting 174, 230; minimalism 230; experimental exposures 230; realism 166–167, 226, 230; soundtracks 40, 78, 102
profane 7, 151, 155–157, 225
prophecy 6, 54–61
psychoanalysis 231–232; *see also* Freud, Sigmund
punishment 6, 30, 36–37, 40–41, 43, 45–46, 48, 60, 85, 120, 123, 171, 182
purification 30, 42, 151
Puritanism 13–26, 45, 48, 53, 98, 170
purity 16, 65–66, 69, 97, 118, 120, 153, 157, 159, 211n11

Quarantine (2008) 8, 163–172

rabies 163–164, 167
rape 4, 7, 43, 45, 64, 69–70, 72, 109, 158
the Rapture 57–58, 61–62, 90, 93, 95
The Rapture (1991) 90, 96
Ratzinger, Cardinal Joseph 129–130
realism 128, 166–167, 226, 229–230, 240
reason 6, 38, 46, 94, 102, 104, 175
rebellion 40–41, 85, 108, 148, 231
[Rec] (2007) 8, 163–173
[Rec] 2 (2009) 167–168, 170
redemption 31, 77, 85, 97, 133, 141, 149, 157, 209, 219
Reformation 14, 18, 22
Reiff, Michael C. 9, 200–212, 240
Reinhard, CarrieLynn 167–168, 217–220
Reis-Filho, Lúcio 7, 113–124, 240
relics 5, 125, 144–147, 149, 220, 225; *see also* palimpsest, sacred objects, Spear of Destiny
religions *see* Calvinism; Catholicism; cults; Evangelicalism; Fundamentalism; Methodism; Presbyterianism; Puritanism; religions, arcane; religions, fringe
religions, arcane 113, 122
religions, fringe 107–108, 164, 170
resurrection 36, 98, 115, 193, 210, 205, 207, 217, 221
retribution 45, 82, 211n8
Revelation, Book of 57–61, 140, 144–145, 179; *see also* the Bible
Rice, Anne 203
ritual 3, 9, 36, 42, 44, 49n18, 60, 64, 68–69, 156, 170, 187, 205, 220, 234
Romero, George 163, 167, 170
rosary 128–130, 213–214, 220
Rosemary's Baby (1968) 2, 4–5, 7, 17, 59, 64–75, 89
Russell, Ken 41–43, 48n5, 48n6, 49n15

sacrament 3, 37, 126, 134, 193
the sacred 1–3, 8, 30, 37, 57, 69, 71, 102, 129, 131, 150–160, 195, 210, 214–215, 217, 221, 233; *see also* sacred objects
sacred objects 151–152, 156, 195; *see also* amulets; crucifix; cross; Lament Configuration; relics; rosary; Spear of Destiny
sacrifice 37, 40, 64, 80, 84, 94, 98, 101, 103, 119, 121, 142, 148; self- 5, 31, 35–36, 67, 91, 155, 181, 202, 209, 227–229
sadomasochism 43, 113, 118
saints 3, 31–37, 126, 220; *see also* mystics; Virgin Mary
Salem witch trials 16–17, 19, 24n14, 24n15, 24n20, 24n21
salvation 1, 20–22, 29, 32, 34–35, 38, 41, 60, 77, 82, 130, 142–143, 153, 157, 196
Satan 2–8, 17, 23, 24n20, 29–30, 35, 40–41, 46, 54, 59, 64, 68–70, 76–78, 85–86, 108–100, 118, 120, 140–149, 170, 174–184, 188, 190, 217, 220, 225; *see also* Lucifer
Satanic ritual abuse 170
savior 5, 35, 56, 133, 157, 211
science 3, 18, 37, 72, 86, 141, 167–168, 200, 228 3, 8–9, 26n52, 33, 36–37, 56, 82, 86, 163, 168–171, 175–177, 180–184, 193, 213, 233; medicine 3, 18, 37, 72, 86, 141, 167–168, 200, 228; physics 9, 174–183
science fiction 116, 119, 174
Scotland 7, 76–84
Scott, Niall 203
scriptures 1–3, 53, 57, 59–61, 145, 167, 220, 234; *see also* the Bible; Genesis, Book of; Gospels; Revelation, Book of
secular humanism 128
secularization 170, 193
Seltzer, David 59–60
The Sentinel (1977) 4–5, 101
The Seventh Sign (1988) 5
sexuality 16, 20, 73, 182, 204, 219
sin 2, 6, 19–21, 35, 40, 108, 118, 141, 157, 182, 195
"Sinners in the Hands of an Angry God" (sermon) 97
Slotkin, Richard 95
Smith, Jonathan 222
soul 2–3, 5, 8, 21–22, 29–30, 33, 46, 48, 70–73, 77, 82, 98, 102, 113–115, 120, 128–129, 140, 142–143, 146–148, 193, 208–211, 213–216, 219, 228, 231–233; vampiric 208–209
Spain 47, 163, 166, 169–170, 196
Spear of Destiny 144–145, 147
spectacle 34–35, 67, 83, 169, 214, 218
spirituality 33–34, 56, 108, 118, 126, 220
splatterpunk 118
Stake Land (2010) 8, 150–159
Stevens, R. Paul 22
stigmata 3, 31, 35, 121, 213–222
Stigmata (1999) 9, 213–222
symbols *see* miracles; relics; sacraments; sacred objects; stigmata

taboo 9, 72, 151–152, 160n10, 225–235
technology 3, 102–103, 177, 234
temptation 2, 19, 34, 86, 202
Thavis, John 38
theology 6, 9, 14, 19–20, 29–38, 43, 105, 128, 134, 141, 174, 177, 179, 182, 200, 233
theosis 8, 125–126, 128, 134
therianthropes 226, 229, 235n7, 235n8, 236n39
Thirst (2009) 9, 200–212
Thomas, Keith 15–16, 22, 42
Tolkien, J.R.R. 8, 126, 131, 134–135
torture 3, 6, 29–30, 36, 41–49, 76–77, 79, 89, 92, 116, 119, 134, 215, 218, 222, 232
transcendence 93, 102, 116
transformation 5, 33, 86, 118–119, 122, 132–133, 152, 183–184, 201–202, 205, 207, 209, 219–220
transgression 36, 41, 116, 197, 205–206, 210, 218, 226–227, 231–235
transubstantiation 3, 205
trials (tests) 2, 6, 15–17, 19, 29–37, 44, 141, 168
Turner, Frederick Jackson 95–96
Twitchell, James 205

uncanny 78–79, 84, 117, 145, 177, 193, 205–206, 226–234
universe, alternate 113–122, 135, 143–144, 178–180

Valerius, Karen 65
values, Christian 20, 33, 36, 79,

102, 118, 152–153, 156–159, 181–182, 186–187, 196, 227, 234
"vampire panic" 190
vampires 8–9, 150–160, 186–187, 190, 192–193, 196, 200–211
Van Elferen, Isabella 204–205, 210
Vatican 107, 164, 167–171, 207–208, 213–216, 220–221; *see also* Catholic church
verisimilitude 220, 227
Versluis, Arthur 41
victimization, female 6, 84, 169, 218–219
Vinci, Tony 132
Virgin Mary 3, 29–33, 35, 37, 66, 69, 105, 159, 164, 220
von Balthasar, Hans Urs 134

Wainwright, Rupert 213
Walsh, David 66
Ward, James J. 6, 40–52, 240
Warner Bros. 189–190, 194, 227, 235n5
Weaver-Zercher, David 110
Weber, Max 22, 26n52 26n57
Weber, Samuel 22
Webley, Steve 9, 235–238, 240
weird fiction 113, 121
Wentz, Richard E. 102
West, American 98
Wetmore, Kevin 6, 29–39, 131, 133, 135, 218, 240
The Wicker Man (1973) 80
Williams, David 134
Winstead, Antoinette 108

The Witch (2014) 6, 13–28
witches 13–28, 43–48, 64, 70, 73, 120
Witchfinder General (1968) 6, 40–49
Wolfe, Tom 219
Woods, Richard 218
worldview 114, 130, 131, 133, 135, 136n15, 156, 159, 170, 180–181, 184; Christian 19, 119, 121, 142–145; scientific 30, 36

Yarri, Donna 31

zombies 8, 152–153, 163–167, 170

www.ingramcontent.com/pod-product-compliance
Lightning Source LLC
Chambersburg PA
CBHW081550300426
44116CB00015B/2821